AF478003

PRINTS OF A NEW KIND

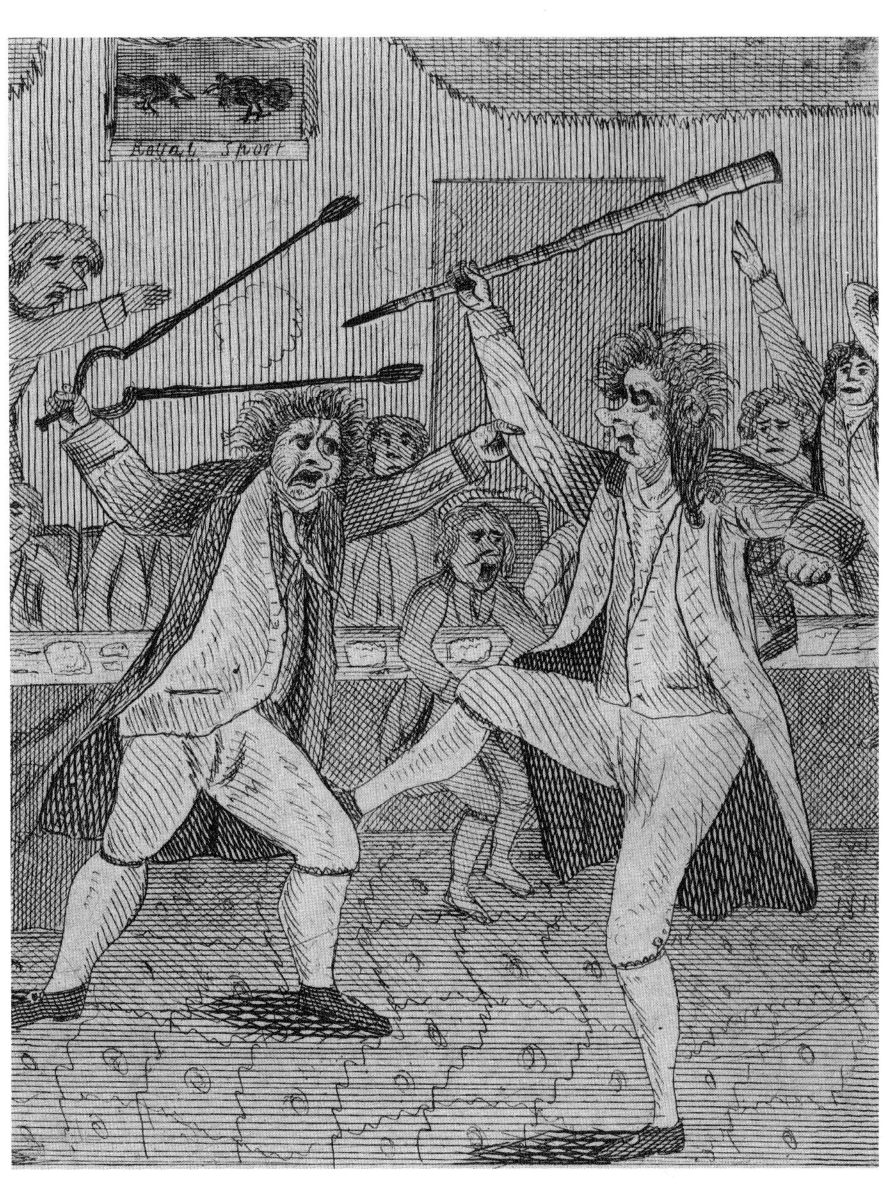
Royal Sport

Prints *of a* New Kind

POLITICAL CARICATURE
IN THE UNITED STATES, 1789–1828

Allison M. Stagg

THE PENNSYLVANIA STATE UNIVERSITY PRESS
University Park, Pennsylvania

Published with the support of the Gerda Henkel Foundation, Düsseldorf.

This publication has been supported by the American Historical Print Collectors Society through the Wendy Shadwell and Ewell L. Newman Funds.

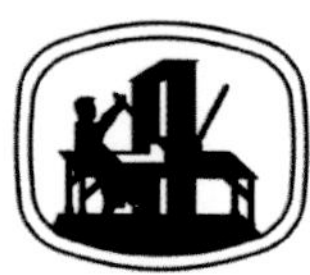

Publication of this book has been aided by a grant from the Wyeth Foundation for American Art Publication Fund of CAA.

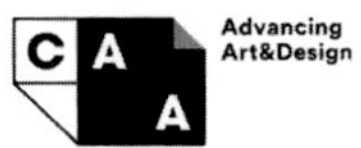

Library of Congress Cataloging-in-Publication Data

Names: Stagg, Allison M ., author.
Title: Prints of a new kind : political caricature in the United States, 1789–1828 / Allison M. Stagg.
Description: University Park, Pennsylvania : The Pennsylvania State University Press, [2023] | Includes bibliographical references and index. | Summary: "Explores the creation and circulation of political caricatures in early US history. Includes a catalog of caricature prints published between 1789 and 1828"—Provided by publisher.
Identifiers: LCCN 2022045716 | ISBN 9780271093321 (cloth)
Subjects: LCSH: Caricatures and cartoons—Political aspects—United States—History—18th century. | Caricatures and cartoons—Political aspects—United States—History—19th century. | Prints, American—18th century. | Prints, American—19th century. | United States—Politics and government—18th century—Caricatures and cartoons. | United States—Politics and government—19th century—Caricatures and cartoons.
Classification: LCC NC1423 .S73 2023 | DDC 769.973—dc23/eng/20221104
LC record available at https://lccn.loc.gov/2022045716

The Pennsylvania State University Press is a member of the Association of University Presses.

It is the policy of The Pennsylvania State University Press to use acid-free paper. Publications on uncoated stock satisfy the minimum requirements of American National Standard for Information Sciences—Permanence of Paper for Printed Library Material, ANSI Z39.48–1992.

Additional credits: frontispiece, detail from anonymous, *Congressional Pugilists*, February 1798 (fig. 27); page vi, detail from James Akin, *Philadelphia Taste Displayed. Or, Bon-Ton Below Stairs*, n.d. (fig. 123).

For

M. and M.

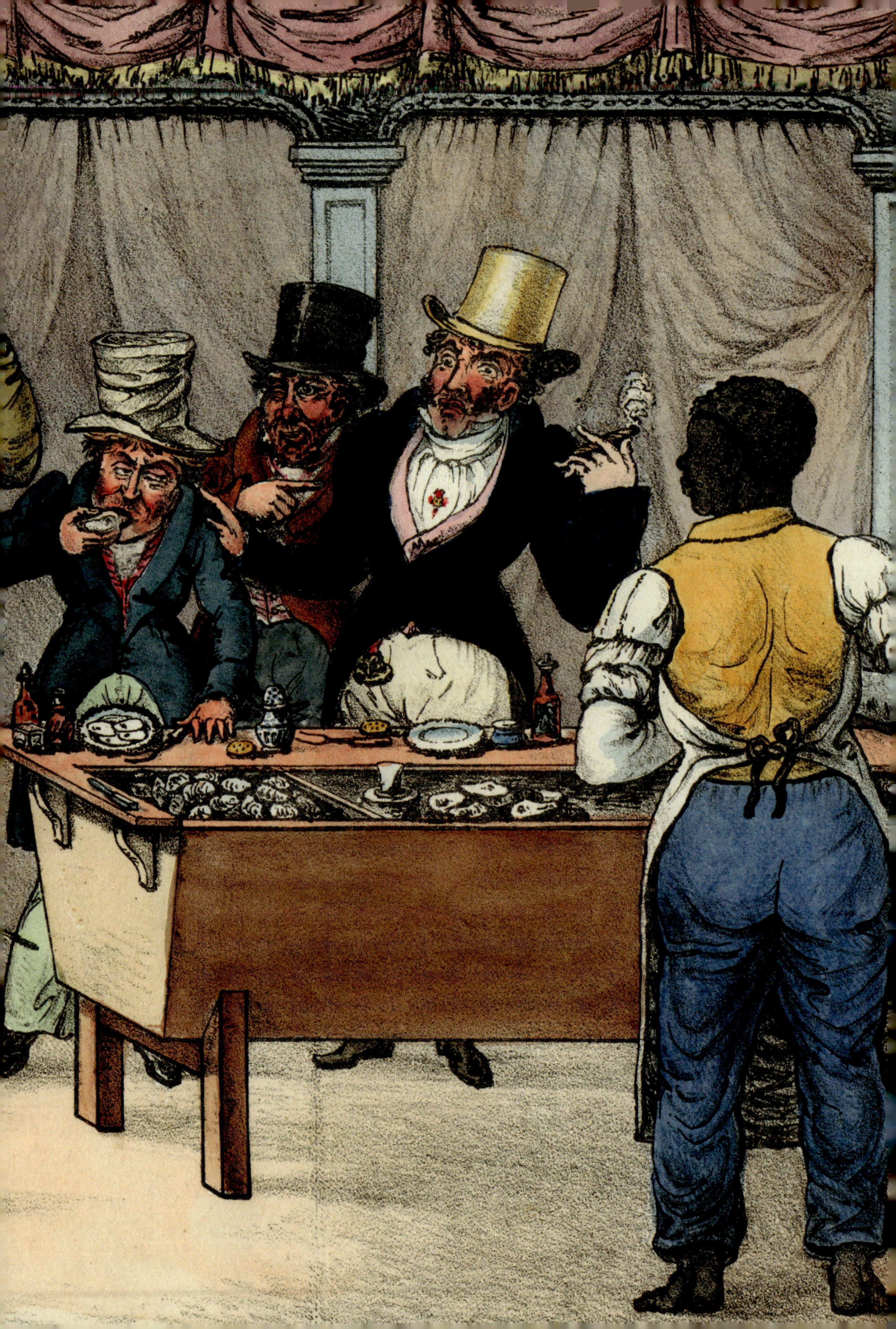

Contents

x

Acknowledgments

So many people played a role in this book that the best place to start is with my master's supervisor David Bindman, Professor Emeritus of Art History at University College London. David was the first person to listen to me talk about caricature in the United States. He recognized that there was a gap in the scholarship and encouraged me to pursue it. My doctoral examiners, Diana Donald and Stephen Conway, were equally enthusiastic about my research, and their comments propelled me forward. I am especially grateful to Diana for her invaluable knowledge on caricature and her continued interest in my research. William Vaughn, Professor of Art History at Birkbeck College, University of London, was a source of wisdom in the early stages of this project. Helen Weston, Tom Gretton, Diane Dethlof, and Tamar Garb in the History of Art Department, and Emma Chambers, Andrea Fredericksen, and Subhadra Das at the UCL Art Collections were equally supportive.

I have lived most of my adult life outside the United States, far from where these historical objects live on in museums, libraries, and archives. I am fortunate that when I started this project there were already a number of digitized collections online, but as most of us will acknowledge, there is no better feeling than to work in a reading room with others, looking closely at an object that is only known to be in that museum or collection. Without the generosity of external funding and fellowships I would not have been able to travel to see in person the caricatures, newspapers, diaries, invoices, letters, and other remarkable pieces of ephemeral objects. It is with heartfelt gratitude that I acknowledge the following institutions in the United States for awarding me grants to work in their collections: the New-York Historical Society, the International Center for Thomas Jefferson Studies at Monticello, the New York Public Library, the American Antiquarian Society, the American Philosophical Society, the Library Company of Philadelphia, the Lewis Walpole Library at Yale University, the Gilder Lehrman Institute of American History, the Smithsonian American Art Museum and the National Portrait Gallery, the Metropolitan Museum of Art, and the Huntington Library, Art Museum, and Botanical Gardens. European institutions have been equally generous in providing travel funding and the support necessary to complete the manuscript: the German Historical Institute, the Marie Skłodowska-Curie Actions COFUND Programme of the European Commission at the Technische Universität Berlin, the Eccles Centre for American Studies at the British Library, and the Gerda Henkel Stiftung.

These fellowships and grants provided opportunities to meet curators, archivists, historians, collectors, librarians, conservators and educators, all of whom enriched this project with their knowledge, generosity, conversations, and interest, especially: Nic Butler, Frances Carey, Ashley Catalado, Jessica David, Paul Erickson, Andrew Edmunds, Becky Geller, Babette Gehnrich, George Goldner, Lauren Hewes, Susan Kriete, Kate Lemay, Clayton Lewis, Elenor Ling, Constance McPhee, David Mihaly, Martin Myrone, Sheila O'Connell, Jackie Penny, Erika Piola, Wendy Wick Reaves, Elisabeth Reich, Cindy Roman, Sharon Spieldenner, Rachel Stephens, Simon Turner, Gisela Vetter-Liebenow, Susan Walker, Sarah Weatherwax, Nan Wolverton, and Helena Wright. My thanks to colleagues and friends who consistently cheered me on: Wendy Blanton, Emily Burns, Pilar Diez del Corral, JeanAnn Dabb, Catherine Elliott, Eleanor Harvey, Galina Mardilovich, Anna O. Marley, Amy Radnor, Carol Ward, and John Wolfe.

Researching and writing this book while based in Germany has often been a solitary task, but I have been fortunate to have held a number of academic positions with supportive colleagues. Thanks to Oliver Scheiding at the Obama Institute for Transnational American Studies at the Johannes Gutenberg Universität in Mainz for being my first contact in Germany and providing me with the opportunity to broaden my ideas around caricature by sharing it with German students in the American Studies department, and to Frank Obendland for our many conversations over coffee at the Baron. In 2016, I was named the Terra Foundation for American Art Visiting Professor at the John F. Kennedy Institute, Freie Universität in Berlin. That academic year was enormously productive. I taught several courses on American caricature while also completing research toward this book. My thanks to Winifred Fluck, Frank Kelleter, Martin Lüthe, and the wonderful Regina Wenzel for their comradery and encouragment. Diego Candil, the former European director of the Terra Foundation, has been a great champion of my research.

At a crucial and early stage of research, this project was awarded funding from the Gerda Henkel Stiftung in Germany, allowing for me to visit collections of caricatures in German museums and institutions, expanding on my knowledge of transnational imagery and humor. They also awarded funding toward the publishing of this book, and for this I am so very grateful. In this, Jana Frey was especially helpful. Generous publishing support has also been awarded from the American Historical Print Collectors Society, an important group of collectors, scholars, curators, and enthusiasts who have embraced me and my research, and the College Art Association.

Nancy Siegel, Christopher Stagg, Georgia (Gigi) Barnhill, Mazie Harris, and Caroline Sloat all read chapters and challenged me to think about American caricature in new ways. They also forced me to confront my incorrect use of the past tense and present tense, among other issues! My prose is better because of them; however, all mistakes found here are mine alone. I must single out Caroline for pushing me to the finish line; her daily emails with constructive comments made all the difference. Gigi is the mentor that every early career scholar should have and that every mentor should aspire to be. When in 2009 I received funding to attend a Center for Historic American Visual Culture summer course at the American Antiquarian Society, I had no idea how that experience would change my life. There I met Gigi, then curator of graphic art, who introduced me to the society's impressive and rare collection of caricatures. Over the years, she has been my biggest supporter and one of my dearest friends.

xvii

In March 2020, our world was turned upside down by a global pandemic and government-enforced lockdowns. At Penn State University Press, my heartfelt thanks go to Kathryn Yahner, Maddie Caso, Laura Reed-Morrisson, and Nick Taylor, who ably ushered this book to completion and were generous with deadlines and patient with delays. I am indebted beyond words to the assistance from curators, archivists, librarians, interns, education staff, photographers, reproduction staff, and volunteers that answered my emails and phone calls from Germany, when I was unable to visit in person, and went above and beyond. The caricatures discussed in this book are often difficult to understand, and in pursuing research there were moments of frustration, followed by a realization that what I couldn't locate, what I didn't know, others would. It is my deepest hope that the caricatures referenced here in the text and those in the appendix will serve other art historians and historians in their quest to understand their own material. I extend my gratitude to past scholars who built the foundation of scholarship on which I was able to further pursue this topic, notably William Murrell, Clarence Brigham, Robert Vail, Frank Weitenkampf, Maureen O'Brien Quimby, and Lorraine Welling Lanmon. I must single out the eminent print historian and curator Wendy Shadwell, as she and I share a common connection: we were both students at Mary Washington College, albeit decades apart.

This book is dedicated with love to my husband, Martin Knöll, and to our daughter, Millicent, and in memory of my parents, Denise Manning Stagg and Dard Francis Stagg.

Introduction

I must begin with an apology to the subject matter discussed within this book. In the fall of 2004, I began a one-year master's degree in art history at University College London, enrolled in the subject course "British Caricature and Visual Satire." Truth be told, I was not the most enthusiastic student. I had come to London to study nineteenth-century British paintings, not British caricature, but that course had been canceled at the last minute. Having had a relatively traditional undergraduate art history experience at Mary Washington College in Fredericksburg, Virginia, the subject of caricature was a mystery to me. So, I was quick to judge when I briefly flipped through a book on the subject. To leave the program meant delaying my studies and moving back home to New York. It is only a year, I thought at the time. I grudgingly stuck with it. However, within a few class sessions the subject of caricature had me hooked. Taught by David Bindman, the course focused on the output of satirical imagery in London by caricaturists of the long nineteenth century. The greats of British caricature were discussed in class: James Gillray, Thomas Rowlandson, Richard Newton, and Isaac Cruikshank, among others. The course often met at the print study room in the British Museum, where our small student group huddled around colorful caricatures propped up on wooden stands. Designed and published with immediacy to lampoon sensational events and people, exaggerating and embellishing physical attributes and situations, the caricature told varied stories of the time, the people, the market for art, gender, and politics. I soon found the prints and their layered histories intoxicating.

As the course continued, an important question loomed for me: Was there an American equivalent? Living an ocean away from my home in the United States, I looked initially at the culture and politics of America's founding in the 1780s and 1790s. Reading David McCullough's biography of John Adams, America's second president, I was struck by the derogatory way in which Adams's enemies referred to him in newspapers and pamphlets.[1] "Rotund" and "balding" are descriptors that should have been perfect bait for a caricaturist. Surely, there must be an abundance of caricature prints devoted to the rotund and bald Adams. Initially my searches did not find any caricatures of Adams, nor of Washington; but as my research continued, I found that caricatures were made during this period of the two leaders (including *The Times; a Political Portrait* [fig. 14]). However, the prints published in the United States at this time were nowhere near the numbers of caricatures made in London. Where were the hundreds of caricatures depicting American politicians and commenting on the problems of the day in the 1790s?

One challenge was the lack of existing scholarship on American caricature. There was not an American companion to the foundational text on late Georgian satirical prints by Diana Donald. When published in 1998, Donald's *The Age of Caricature: Satirical Prints in the Reign of George III* was the first major study to analyze British caricature and connect the historical, social, and political context in which caricatures were made. Donald's important scholarship has since inspired a great number of studies, including this book, but also, for example, Mark Hallett's *The Spectacle of Difference: Graphic Satire in the Age of Hogarth*, Amelia Rauser's *Caricature Unmasked: Irony, Authenticity, and Individualism in Eighteenth-Century Prints*, and Vic Gatrell's *City of Laughter: Sex and Satire in Eighteenth-Century England*.[2] Additionally, the many caricatures published in London between 1780 and 1830 were treated differently from those also published at the same time in America. British caricatures were published in higher numbers but an incredible number were also saved, allowing many of these prints to be available today. Searches for specific prints by an artist such as Gillray can usually be found in British and European museum collections online. So thorough is the research that often lengthy descriptions can be found alongside beautifully digitized high-resolution images. The interest in British caricature from this period has prompted special exhibitions, such as *The Art of Satire: London in Caricature* (2006) held at the Museum of London, *High Spirits: The Comic Art of Thomas Rowlandson* (2013) organized by the Royal Collection Trust, and *Bonaparte and the British: Prints and Propaganda in the Age of Napoleon* (2015) at the British Museum. In British museums, historical caricatures can be found alongside paintings and sculpture in permanent collection displays. Consciously or not, this has built awareness in the British public to the satirical prints made two centuries ago. One has only to look at modern British newspapers to see how influential these historical images are for cartoonists of today. Examples of this are plentiful and can be found regularly in British newspapers, with many cartoonists referring directly back to the historical caricature or artist that inspired the modern image. James Gillray is of particular interest to many contemporary cartoonists, with his name often referred to somewhere within the modern print. One sees this, for example, in the cartoon *Britannia Rules the Second Waves* (fig. 1) by the British artist Ben Jennings and published in the December 22, 2020, edition of *The Guardian* newspaper. Jennings's visual commentary on contemporary events, here Brexit and the coronavirus, was directly inspired by Gillray's April 1793 caricature *Britannia between Scylla & Charybdis* (fig. 2). If the audience for Jennings's cartoon was not immediately reminded of Gillray and the tradition of caricature in England, Jennings provided in the upper right-hand corner the following prompt: "Ben Jennings After Gillray." There is great asymmetry when comparing modern cartoons made in the United States, which rarely draw on historical imagery.

In the twentieth century, there were several significant champions for American caricature prints, on which research for this book has relied. In 1933, William Murrell was the first to write on caricature known at that time, in his two-volume *A History of American Graphic Humor*, the first volume of which covers caricature prints between 1746 and 1865.[3] Of particular importance, even more than the book's commentary, are the reproductions of caricatures discussed between its covers. At a time before museums began to routinely digitize a great number of their collections, Murrell provided visual examples of the prints discussed. Despite this, Murrell's index is incomplete, with instances of omitted citations and incorrect location information. His scholarship, though vital for the images, did not provide critical analysis or an engagement with American history or art of the period. Frank Weitenkampf addressed some of these oversights. Weitenkampf's interest in caricature dates to at least 1887, when he published an essay titled "Some American Caricaturists," followed by a chapter on the subject in his *American Graphic Art*.[4] He was appointed the New York Public Library's first curator of prints in 1921. He served in that position until his retirement in 1942, when he focused almost exclusively on researching eighteenth- and nineteenth-century caricature prints published in the United States, resulting in two important publications: *A Century of Political Cartoons: Caricature in the United States from 1800 to 1900* (1944) and *Political Caricature in the United States in Separately Published Cartoons* (1952). Weitenkampf also completed an unpublished manuscript, "The Social History of the United States in Caricature," all the while writing frequently to curators and museum directors regarding caricatures in their collections.[5] His correspondence with Clarence Brigham, director of the American Antiquarian Society in Worcester, Massachusetts between 1930 and 1959, and Robert W. G. Vail, director of the New-York Historical Society between 1940 and 1960, reveals their mutual knowledge and shared enthusiasm for early American caricature.

In preparing *A Century of Political Cartoons*, Weitenkampf recognized that the subject required an authoritative and well-respected figure in American history. He sought

4

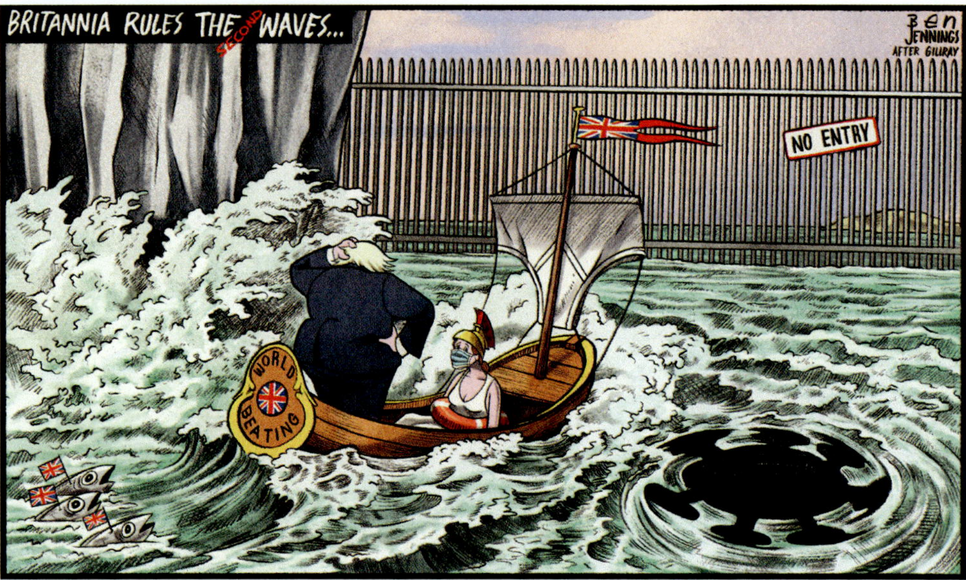

Figure 1 | Ben Jennings, *Britannia Rules the Second Waves*, cartoon published in
The Guardian, December 23, 2020. Courtesy of Ben Jennings.

out Allan Nevins, the renowned scholar of American history, to be his coauthor, but
this was very much Weitenkampf's project: he had chosen the one hundred prints to
be included in the book and written much of accompanying text. The work earned
praise, with one contemporary review noting that "this is one of the most useful books
to the student of American history that has been published in a long time."[6] Weitenkampf's museum colleagues were equally positive. Brigham wrote his congratulations
to Weitenkampf with the hope that he would complete a catalogue on American caricature: "I was much delighted with your *Century of Political Cartoons*. It is a fine book,
evidencing much research and a thorough knowledge of political history of the century,
and containing an interesting selection of illustrations. It shows what can be done on a
larger scale if one made the volume more comprehensive. . . . I hope that some day . . .
you and I can combine on a bibliography of political cartoons—or perhaps better, I can
turn my material over to you."[7] In the ensuing years, Weitenkampf visited museums and
collections along the East Coast, amassing files on caricature made in the United States
between 1778 and 1898 for his catalogue, which was first published in 1952 in the *New
York Public Library Bulletin*; in 1953 it was published as a separate volume. This is a critical body of primary research and was greatly influenced by the catalogues of the collection of caricature in the British Museum collection. Modern scholarship on British

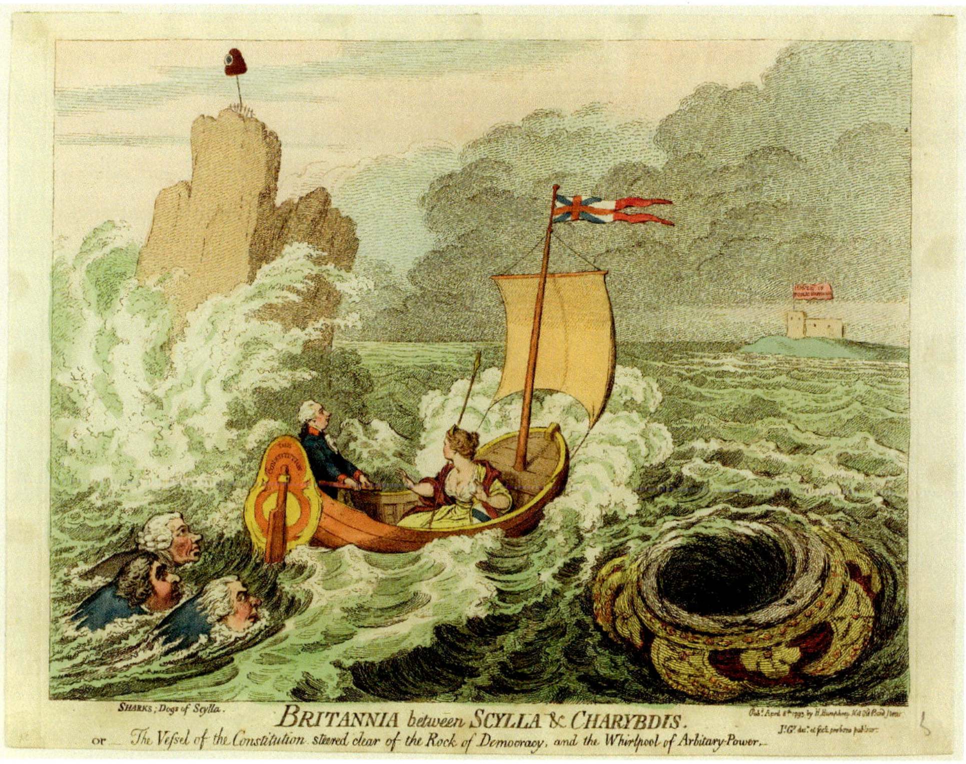

Figure 2 | James Gillray, *Britannia Between Scylla & Charybdis*, April 8, 1793. Etching in dark brown, with hand-coloring, on cream wove paper, plate 303 × 364 mm, sheet 311 × 393 mm. Gift of Thomas F. Furness in memory of William McCallin McKee, 1928.1529, Art Institute of Chicago.

caricature is greatly indebted to the *Catalogue of Political and Personal Satires in the British Museum*, compiled between 1870 and 1954, firstly by Frederic George Stephens in the late nineteenth century and from the 1930s through the 1950s by M. Dorothy George. George's six volumes (5–10) catalogued caricature prints held in the British Museum collection that were made between 1771 and 1827 and, crucially, provided indexes of names and subjects for quick searches. Like M. Dorothy George's catalogue, Weitenkampf also included an index for searches related to subjects. Brigham hypothesized that the catalogue would be "consulted frequently,"[8] and he was correct: since its publication in the 1950s, Weitenkampf's catalogue has remained the only such publication on caricature prints published in the United States up to 1898 in American museum collections. Visiting archives, libraries, and print rooms on the East Coast of the United States to work with the caricature prints, I found I wasn't alone in marking up my copy of Weitenkampf.

Despite its utility, his list has not been amended or corrected until now; the appendix of this book contains an updated catalogue with newly discovered caricatures, contemporary references to caricatures not yet known to have survived, and corrections to the Weitenkampf catalogue, including factual attributions of dates, titles, and artists.

From their correspondence, it is evident that Vail and Weitenkampf believed the most complete collection of caricature prints was not at either of their institutions in New York City but in Worcester, Massachusetts. Brigham was also aware of this, writing, "The Antiquarian Society collection for the eighteenth and nineteenth centuries is one of the most comprehensive to be found in any library. It has been gathered from many sources during the last thirty years."[9] In the second half of the twentieth century, his successors would continue to foster that reputation. Marcus McCorison (director, 1967–92) supported collecting in this area and encouraged Georgia B. Barnhill, whom he appointed curator of graphic arts, to develop contacts with fellow curators, collectors, and scholars and to become active in the American Historical Print Collectors Society founded in 1975. Barnhill followed Weitenkampf's model of championing further research into American caricature.[10] The list of scholars in the twentieth century who worked to promote scholarship on caricature includes Wendy Shadwell, print curator at the New-York Historical Society from the 1970s until 2002, and an eminent scholar in American prints. The initials "W.S." are frequently found in the departmental archives alongside additions of caricature to the collection and in the print department's copy of Weitenkampf. She had a particular interest in ephemera, especially nineteenth-century trade cards and catalogues, and as an author she was instrumental in bringing early American printmaking to the view of a wide audience with *American Printmaking: The First 150 Years* (1969) and the two-volume *Catalogue of American Portraits in the New-York Historical Society* (1974), both valuable references for historians and collectors.

It is difficult to ignore that caricature prints have been reproduced as illustrations in histories of the early national period, but with little integration or awareness as to how these prints were made, seen, and circulated. In the 1999 introduction to "The Catalogue of American Engravings: A Manual for Users," Georgia Barnhill observed that "when images are read as text, they provide a different perspective, but an important one, as scholars seek to understand the past. Publishers of textbooks have been steady users of reproductions of American prints and illustrations, but even in the past twenty-five years, few have recognized the importance of relating the images reproduced to this historical discussion."[11] Barnhill was echoing the words of Louis Masur, who addressed the need for historians to be more vigilant in using images within texts, particularly as many do not choose the images themselves: "Authors do not situate the images in their historical context or locate those images within the history of visual production and reproduction;

they do not discuss the images within the narrative.... Nor do the authors interpret these images or suggest how to read them as texts within multiple meanings that speak not only to the past but to the present."[12] When Barnhill and Masur wrote their essays, locating caricature was more difficult and time intensive than it is now, as institutions are digitizing their impressions. Because caricatures are becoming accessible online, it is more important than ever to correct the erroneous artist attributions and dates of publication and to uncover a better understanding of why these prints were made and who saw them. That is the intention of this book, although it is important to note here that this history of American caricatures published between 1789 and 1828 is not complete: as more newspapers are digitized, as more caricatures are discovered hidden away in books or in uncatalogued collections, further information can be applied to the ambiguities that do still remain.

The overall focus of this book is on the separately published caricatures engraved on copper plates, ending with a brief discussion of the lithographed caricatures that became popular at the end of the 1820s. This book's main objective is to study caricature engravings made in America between 1789 and 1828 as a collective body of images and to explore, for the first time, the myriad ways domestic caricature evolved during this thirty-nine-year period. Caricatures made after 1830 were more frequently lithographed, and their number overwhelms the small number made between the late 1780s and late 1820s. These later lithographed caricatures have been better preserved, with surviving impressions more readily available in institutional archives. The following chapters explore who made caricature prints in the new republic through 1828 and why and to what degree such prints are to be considered alongside other forms of art of the period. Some of the caricatures explored in this book were naively and hastily conceived, while others reveal a learned skill. This book argues, as has been demonstrated in recent studies on British caricature, that concentrated and focused study of these objects and the artists who created them offers new insights into crucial historical developments. The absence of a comprehensive study on the history and artistic merits of early American political caricatures contrasts sharply with the recent publications on late eighteenth- and early nineteenth-century English caricature and culture.

Through an examination of contemporary documents, the first chapter will consider the market in the United States for political caricatures in the 1790s and first two decades of the 1800s, with a focus on the myriad of ways caricatures were received in cities along the East Coast. Chapters 2, 3, and 4 are centered on the lives of two caricaturists crucial to the early years of the republic: James Akin and William Charles. Chapter 5 considers the 1820s, a decade of transition in printing methods as well as a passing from the first generation of caricaturists to the next generation working in lithography.

A Note on the Terms "Cartoon" and "Caricature"

Within the text, I have used the term "caricature." In recent scholarship, these prints are often referred to as "cartoons"; however, contemporary viewers of these satirical prints and indeed the artists themselves referred to these prints as "caricatures." Contemporary newspaper advertisements and opinion pieces, descriptions found in diaries, and letters refer to these images as "caricature." I have followed this example.

CHAPTER 1

Caricature in the United States, 1789–1820

Separately published caricature prints made in America before 1800 were most often printed anonymously, with the identities of those responsible largely unknown today.[1] Of the twenty-four caricatures published between 1789 and 1800, only three were signed.[2] After 1800, James Akin and William Charles published caricatures; however, many of these prints continued to be published without such signatures. These anonymously made prints cannot yet be linked to other artists, engravers, or publishers active in this period. The varied styles, techniques, and designs of the caricature prints lack similarity to one another, rendering it difficult to assign artist attributions or to connect one anonymous print to another. As such, the identities of the anonymous caricaturists and what can be understood about those that worked in caricature, such as their social status, professional training, and potential relationships to patrons and publishers, is left to broad interpretation based on surviving contemporary source material in newspaper advertisements and personal letters.

In examining surviving archival material, what emerges is an impression of the culture and the audience for visual satire in the 1790s and in the early 1800s. Advertisements found in American newspapers provide details of the venues where caricatures could be seen and purchased. These advertisements, in addition to information extracted from letters, reveal that imported and domestic caricatures could be seen on the walls of coffeehouses, taverns, and barbershops. Caricatures were available for purchase in barbershops as well as the established consumer venues of newspaper offices, bookstores, and print stores. Colleagues, friends, and family members shared caricature prints in letters.

The subject matter of American caricatures was primarily political. It can be assumed that some individuals engaged in caricature feared for their professional livelihoods, as there are so many anonymous caricatures from this period. Working in close proximity to publishers, newspaper editors, and other engravers meant that most of these individuals did not have the luxury of being completely anonymous. References in late eighteenth- and early nineteenth-century newspapers indicate an interest in revealing the identities, such as this notice from Paris: "Some caricature prints, derogatory to the Constitution and the Nation, having been stuck upon the walls of the coffee-house, the people assembled round it, and desired to know whose productions they were."[3] In another example from a New York newspaper, a citizen asked his fellow New Yorkers to assist him in discovering the identity of the individual responsible for a recent caricature in circulation: "some person has taken the liberty of publishing a Caricature," and the signer "thus publicly solicits that he may be favored with the name of the person who designed and published the print."[4] One 1793 newspaper account reported on the publication of a caricature of George Washington and stated clearly that the artists (referred to here as the "authors") were not known. In this notice, "a representation of the President [George Washington], &c. with a coffin and guillotine, was stuck up in Philadelphia, & one thrown into the Post Office; but they were soon destroyed. The authors of them have not been discovered."[5] Advertisements for the 1793 caricature *A Peep into the Antifederal Club* were published widely in newspapers in Philadelphia, New York, and Boston and omitted the name of the artist: "This Day is Published, And may be had of the Printers and Book-sellers, A PRINT, entitled, A PEEP INTO THE ANTIFEDERAL CLUB."[6] The artist responsible for such ephemera was inconsequential.

While at present there is not enough information available to make firm attributions of many of the anonymous caricatures to specific artists, it is possible to make a distinction between the amateur that designed visual satire to exploit a topical event and the professional artist who had training in engravings and fine arts. Most of the caricatures that can be dated to the 1790s and early 1800s show limited technical skill, although at least five caricatures were signed by three engravers: Amos Doolittle, Alexander Anderson, and Elkanah Tisdale. The two most important caricaturists that emerged during this period were Akin and Charles, both of whom designed and published a considerable number of prints, signed them, and adhered to relatively consistent subjects and formats that were often based on British models of caricature. Akin and Charles, in particular, built the foundation for an early American caricature tradition.

This chapter broadly considers the consumer market for caricature published in America between the late 1780s to the late 1810s. It focuses on the interest for British social and political graphic prints by looking at contemporary source material. Additional sections address the audience for political caricature and the historical context in which to consider both British and North American satirical prints. This chapter is arranged chronologically; several of the caricatures included here are considered in detail by addressing their relationship to significant historical events, newspaper references, and influences from British source material as well as specific iconographical subject matter. Further, the social and professional networks of the mostly unidentified caricaturists active in New York and Philadelphia during the 1790s and into the early 1800s are established within this chapter, in order to consider the published caricatures by Akin and Charles in the following chapters. New York and Philadelphia have been selected as case studies because they provided environments that were encouraging for the production and consumption of political caricatures.[7]

Henry William Bunbury and His Social Satires in the United States

As before and during the American Revolution, in the 1790s imported British caricatures continued to be available in the United States.[8] Newspapers in cities along the East Coast frequently published advertisements announcing the arrival of imported goods from London. In addition to items such as furniture, domestic wares, prints, and paintings, imported collections of "curious" caricatures were announced for sale.[9] In New York City, Thomas Durm, the owner of a book and stationery store, advertised in 1796 the arrival of "a Collection of Caricatures. To show the very age and body of the time; its form and pressure." Addressing "Admirers of Genius," the bookseller J. M. Paff provided a lengthy description of "the greatest collection of the most curious Carricatures [*sic*] and Drawings, &c.," that were "to be seen everyday from 8 o'clock in the morning until 10 at night. Price of admittance for grown persons, Two Shillings, Children half price."[10] Paff continued to sell and exhibit imported British caricatures at his shop at least until 1799.[11] The New York City booksellers Monson and James Hayt announced, "A late importation of the most superb PRINTS that have been offered in this city, in gold, burnished and enamelled frames—Together with four Port Folios of unframed prints, and a number of very humorous Caricatures."[12] In Charleston, James Scot announced that he had "a beautiful Assortment of London COPPER-PLATE PRINTS" that included caricatures, "many of them beautifully colored."[13] Such advertisements reveal the sustained interest in both published caricatures and the professional relationships that endured between British and American proprietors.

There are surprisingly few references in American newspapers from this period to any of the popular British caricaturists in London, although it is likely that caricature prints

12

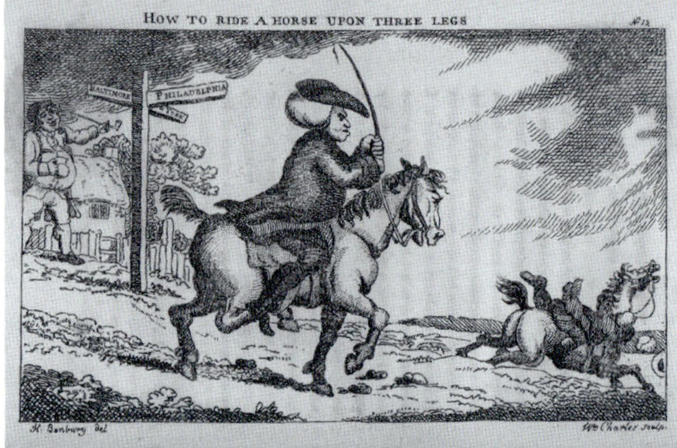

Figure 3 (*left*) | William Charles, after Henry Bunbury, *How to Ride a Horse upon Three Legs*, 1813. The Library Company of Philadelphia.

Figure 4 (*below*) | Henry Bunbury, *The Country Club*, June 26, 1788. Stipple engraving with etching, sheet 34.6 × 46 cm. Lewis Walpole Library. Courtesy of The Lewis Walpole Library, Yale University.

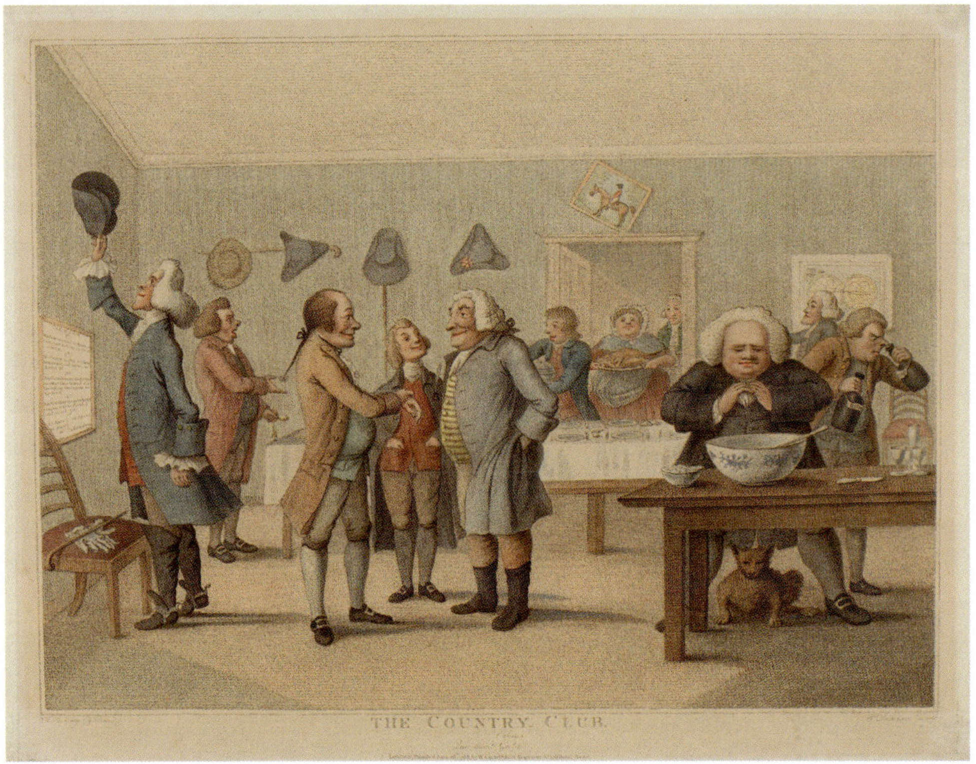

by Thomas Rowlandson, James Gillray, Isaac Cruikshank, and others were included in the imported collections of caricature advertised for sale.[14] American newspaper advertisements reveal, however, that caricatures by Henry William Bunbury (1750–1811) were regularly imported from England. Bunbury was considered to be one of England's most successful "gentleman amateur" artists, active in London during the latter half of the

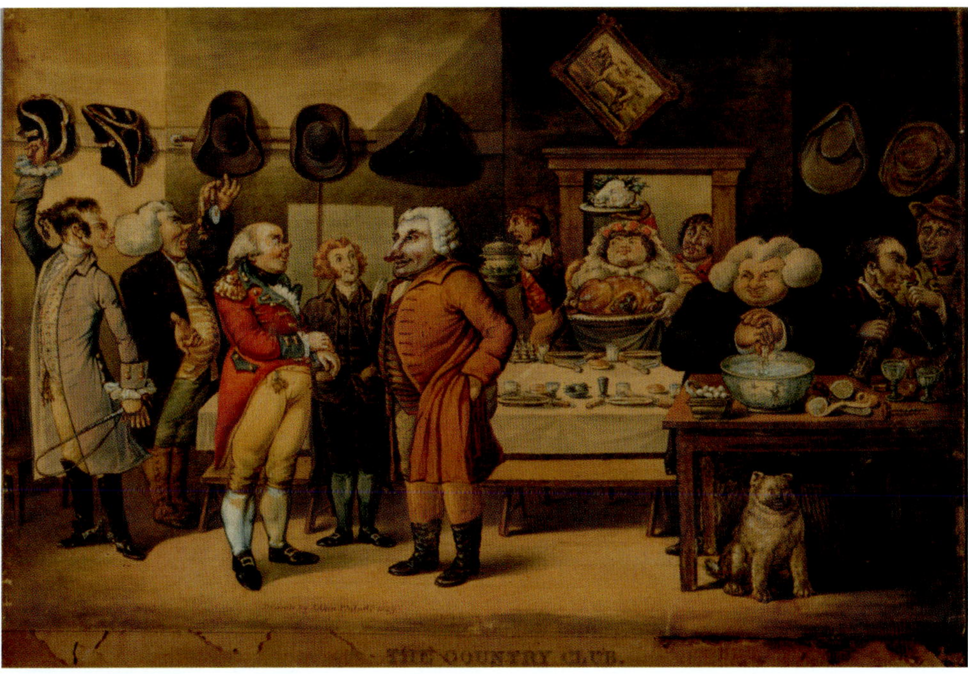

Figure 5 | James Akin, *The Country Club*, 1839. Watercolor. The Library Company of Philadelphia.

eighteenth century.[15] In the early 1770s, he collaborated with the popular print seller Matthew Darly (ca. 1720–1778?) but later changed his professional allegiance to the shop of James Bretherton (ca. 1730–1806). Admirers of Bunbury's caricatures included the Royal Academy president Joshua Reynolds—Bunbury exhibited there—and King George III.[16] Bunbury's satirical prints depicted lighthearted social situations that differed from the often acidic political caricatures of London. Subject matter was generally understood, making them easy to display for any audience: these prints were framed and hung on parlor walls, or bound in books for entertainment. They were not meant to be divisive; rather, they were laughable and imaginative scenes of everyday life. This brand of humor was easily marketable in England and found a ready audience in America during the 1780s and early 1790s. Bunbury's prints have a timeless quality appealing to many: both Akin and Charles were inspired by them. In 1813, Charles copied plates from Bunbury's 1796 publication *An Academy for Grown Horsemen*, published under the name "Geoffrey Gambado, Esq." (fig. 3), and in 1839 Akin copied Bunbury's *The Country Club* (figs. 4 and 5) fifty years after it was first published in London.

As early as 1782, references to imported prints by Bunbury can be found in American newspapers, predating 1787 when the British historian John Riely wrote that he had reached the pinnacle of his success.[17] "Bunbury's Caricaturas, a great variety and many of them new published," could be purchased at Thomas Barrow's shop at 58 Broad Street in New York in 1782.[18] Bunbury prints were also available to purchase in Philadelphia by bookseller Thomas Seddon, who advertised the sale in 1788 of a large collection from London of prints, landscapes, and caricatures by "eminent artists" that included works by Henry Bunbury.[19] Thomas Stephens's wholesale and retail store in Philadelphia sold "Books, Stationary [*sic*], Music, Prints, Oil Painting, Drawing Books, and Fancy Articles," and "curious caricatures" that had lately been received.[20] In 1796, the Philadelphia auctioneer Edward Pole announced that an auction was to be held that offered among various art objects "a collection of HUMOROUS CARICATURE PICTURES, the best ever offered for public sale. They are executed by Bunbury, and other eminent artists [and] engravings may be viewed previous to the sale."[21] In South Carolina, a Charleston newspaper advertisement invoked Bunbury to describe the general style of caricatures on offer: "CARICATURE ENGRAVINGS, after the manner of Bunbury."[22] As seen in these examples, booksellers and print shop proprietors usually included Bunbury's name within a descriptive list of recently imported items. Some notices highlighted his prominence by referring to him as an "eminent Artist," while others included his name alongside established members of the Royal Academy in London such as Angelica Kauffman and Francesco Bartolozzi.[23]

The introduction of Bunbury caricatures in America during the 1780s can partially explain why there were so few caricatures published in the United States during this period that are not politically driven: Bunbury caricatures likely filled that void. Although it is not known if the Bunbury caricatures were popular with American viewers, the frequency with which Bunbury's name appeared in advertisements through the 1790s provides that Bunbury and his prints were relatively well-known by an American audience. If American print and booksellers were receiving imported caricatures depicting humorous social scenes that were selling reasonably well, a market for domestic caricaturists to depict such subject matter was not of interest.

References to British and French Caricatures in American Newspapers, 1790–1810

Newspapers provided information to an American audience on caricature published in Europe, most often reprinting foreign news articles from London and Paris and occasionally from cities such as Rome and Madrid.[24] Some of the notices alluded to the variety and output of caricature in circulation in European cities. This can be seen especially in the 1790s when there was considerable mention in foreign news reports of caricatures made in reaction to events from the French Revolution. "Caricature prints begin to be as common in France, as they are in England," stated one newspaper from London in 1789, reprinted two months later in a Rhode Island paper.[25] An account describing new caricatures in Paris was printed in London in 1790 and reprinted in New York the following year: "A boldness of general satire now prevails in Paris; nor is it deemed political to endeavour to suppress it, however strong an inclination there may be, for such a measure. Caricature prints of elevated characters, are continually hawked about, and bought with avidity."[26] These rarely provided specific titles or artists names. One such notice from Paris was republished in numerous newspapers along the East Coast, including Philadelphia and New York, in addition to Albany, Providence, Hartford, and Norfolk. This particular notice reported that "a caricature print has been published here representing the tyranny or sway of Robespierre. This plate represents the French people on the square of the revolution without heads, and the executioner, who alone remains, is in the act of guillotining himself."[27] Although a title was not provided in the newspaper notice, the description corresponds to the French caricature *Le Bourreau se guillotine lui-même* (The executioner guillotines himself) published in 1794 at the end of Maximilien Robespierre's reign.[28] Another description of a satirical print circulating in Paris was republished in a Philadelphia newspaper and referred to a depiction of King Louis XVI: "Caricatures. Abound in *France*—of the political, there is one, wherein the King is represented in an iron cage—from a small door of which he is permitted by his patriotic guards, to reach out his hand to sign the Constitution."[29] After writing his *Reflections on the Revolution in France* in November 1790, the British politician Edmund Burke was the subject of numerous caricatures.[30] A caricature of Burke in circulation in Paris was reported first in a London newspaper, and its description was reprinted in a Philadelphia newspaper two months later: "A caricature of masterly design and adequate execution has just appeared in Paris, representing the Right Honourable Mr. Burke as the Guy Faux [Fawkes] of the National Assembly. So unpopular is this Gentleman amongst the French Republicans, that his effigy, labelled with the above caricature, was carried triumphantly about the streets by these children of Liberty, a l'Angloise, on the 5th of November."[31]

In addition to King Louis XVI and Edmund Burke, there were other European figures mentioned in the American press as being the subject of caricature prints. An example can be found in a "A very singular caricature" published in 1791 of Louis Joseph, the prince of Condé, "in the act of passing the Rhine, with the Bishop of Spire. He is followed by soldiers mounted upon asses. . . . The humour is heightened by the ludicrous contrast between the diminutive size of the Commander in Chief, and the extreme length of the Marshall's staff, which he holds in his hand. The public derision of these characters shows how little the Parisians apprehend any attempt at a Counter Revolution."[32] Napoleon Bonaparte's small stature provided an excellent opportunity for European caricaturists and would later be copied in America in the early 1800s. A notice published in 1804 commented on a caricature of Bonaparte, "A caricature print is privately handed

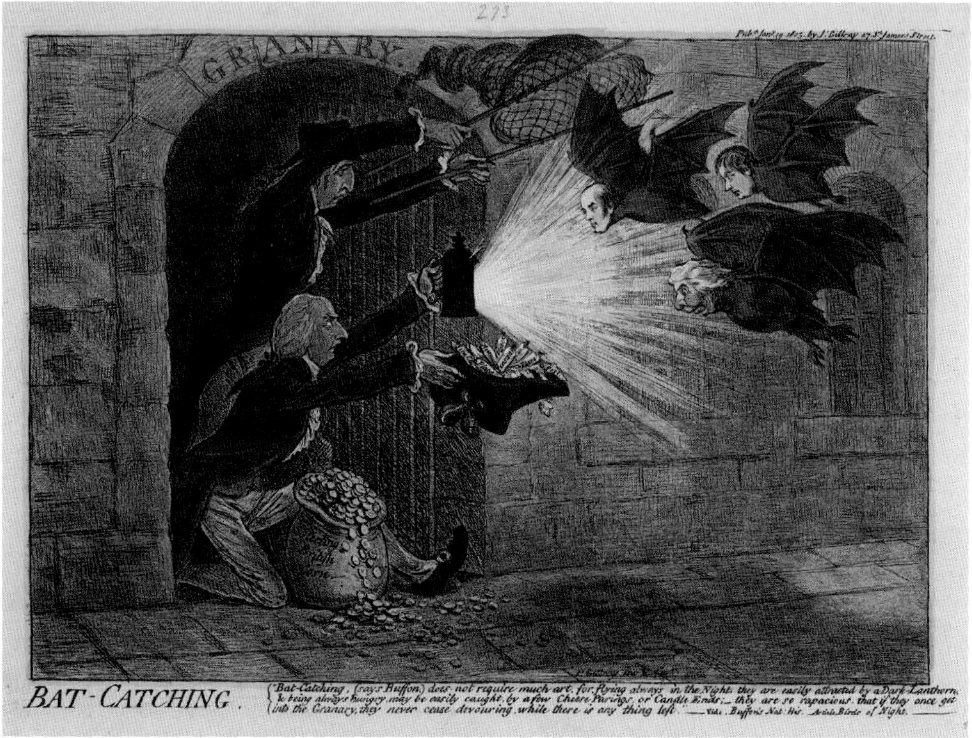

Figure 6 | James Gillray, *Bat-Catching*, January 19, 1803. Etching and aquatint on wove paper, hand-colored, plate mark 25.4 × 35.5 cm, sheet 28 × 38 cm. Courtesy of The Lewis Walpole Library, Yale University.

about, but not sold, in which Bonaparte is represented on his Throne, surrounded by his brothers, with the bloody corpse of the Duke D'Enghien at his feet, over which is written *'princes of blood.'*"[33] Such descriptive reports may have provided inspiration for caricaturists working in the United States.

London was the primary source for information on caricatures, with American newspapers reprinting lengthy and vivid descriptions of prints in circulation in the British capital. The names of artists, engravers, and publishers were often not mentioned in the reports, although at least two of the caricatures described in the following notices were published by James Gillray and Thomas Rowlandson. A description of *Bat-Catching* (fig. 6) by Gillray was first published in London on January 19, 1803, and was reprinted in American newspapers in June 1803.[34] A shorter notice for the caricature *Theatrical Leap Frog* (fig. 7), published in London on November 30, 1804, by Rudolph Ackermann and designed by Rowlandson, was printed the following February in a New York newspaper: "A caricature has been published called *Leap Frog*, in which Young Roscius is represented

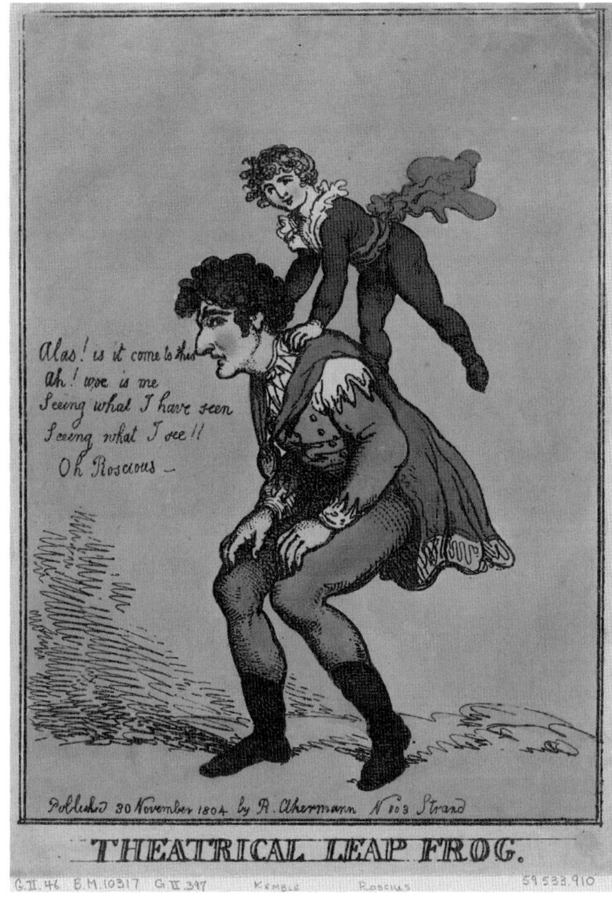

Figure 7 | Thomas Rowlandson, *Theatrical Leap Frog*, November 30, 1804. Hand-colored etching, sheet 12 13/16 × 8 7/8 in. (32.5 × 22.5 cm). The Elisha Whittelsey Collection, The Elisha Whittelsey Fund, 1959. The Metropolitan Museum of Art, New York.

jumping over the back of John Kemble."[35] Caricatures in circulation in European cities outside of London and Paris, such as Rome and Madrid, were also described in American newspapers. One report, published in the *New-Hampshire Spy* on August 21, 1787, provided an account of a caricature on offer in Rome of the Pope and Saint Peter. The artist is not mentioned, but the notice claims that this is because it was not known at that time: "Search is making after the etcher of the caricature, but in vain."[36] Another report of a caricature available in Spain included the following description: "A Caricature has lately been circulated at Madrid, in which the King is treated with unexampled freedom. The verbal admonition to the Monarch is curious.—France is brought to Bed—Spain is in Labor—Charles the Fourth take care of yourself."[37] Although it is not suggested that any of these caricatures were sent to America, the descriptions of and references to European caricatures in circulation found in newspapers demonstrates a growing awareness in the United States of the availability of caricature abroad.

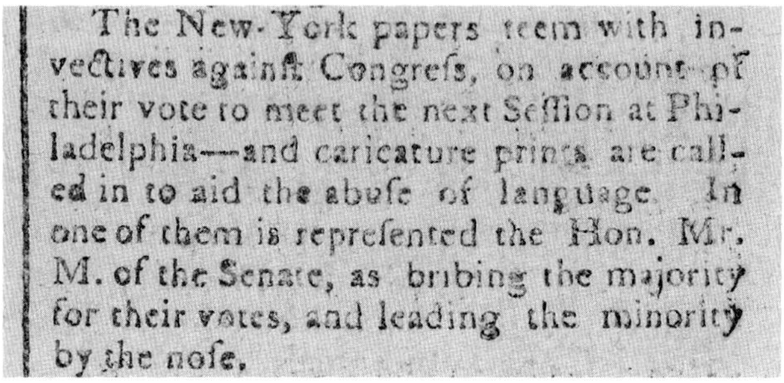

The New-York papers teem with invectives against Congress, on account of their vote to meet the next Session at Philadelphia—and caricature prints are called in to aid the abuse of language. In one of them is represented the Hon. Mr. M. of the Senate, as bribing the majority for their votes, and leading the minority by the nose.

Figure 8 | *New-Hampshire Recorder, and the Weekly Advertiser* (Keene), August 26, 1790. Courtesy American Antiquarian Society.

The First Caricatures Published in America After 1790

By the early 1790s, alongside information on caricatures issued in Europe, American newspapers began to promote the small number of caricatures published in New York and Philadelphia. Some of these advertisements contained lengthy descriptions and even opinions on the emerging market for domestically published caricature prints. The first newspaper accounts referenced the political caricatures published during the summer of 1790, one year after George Washington's inauguration in April 1789. The debates on the location of the capital evocated strong reactions in the press in 1790, 1804, and 1808, prompting the publication of caricatures depicting members of Congress and politicians. In 1790, the new location of America's capital was an important issue to the citizens of New York, who expressed frustration at losing this prominent status. One politician described the situation in a letter to his wife: "For some time the citizens [in New York] have been in violent agitation on account of the proposed removal of Congress from this place to Philadelphia. The event has become probable from a coalition between the Pennsylvanians and the southern members."[38] Newspapers remarked on the publication of caricatures, stating that "the New-York papers teem with invectives against Congress, on account of the vote to meet the next Session at Philadelphia—and caricature prints are called in to aid the abuse of language" (fig. 8).[39]

At least four caricatures were published in reaction to the proposed move of the capital city from New York to Philadelphia, with three of them known: *What think ye of C_o_n_ss now / View of C_o_n_ss on the road to Philadelphia* (fig. 9), *Con-g-ess Embark'd on board the Ship Constitution of America bound to Conogocheque by way of Philadelphia* (fig. 10), and an untitled, hand-colored caricature depicting Robert Morris moving the capital (fig. 11). A fourth caricature was described in private letters, but impressions of it have not been located.[40] These caricature prints, published in New York City in the summer of 1790, had a common feature: the Pennsylvania politician Robert Morris. He was a key supporter of the capital's removal from New York and was blamed as the lone

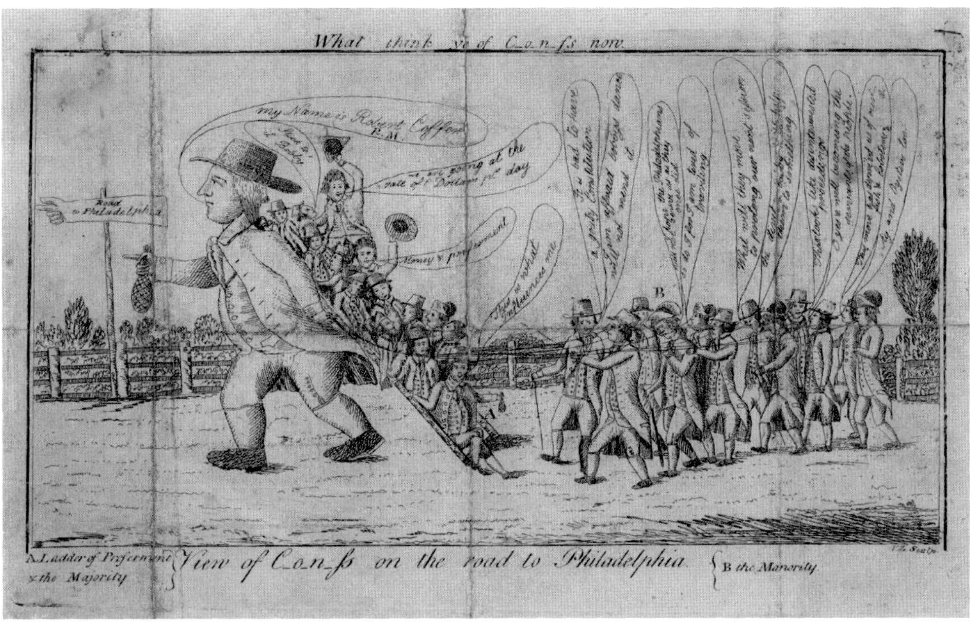

Figure 9 | Y.Z., *What think ye of C_o_n_ss now / View of C_o_n_ss on the road to Philadelphia*, n.d. [1790]. Cartoon and Caricature File, PR 010, 1790-3, image number 44865. Collection of the New-York Historical Society.

culprit. In the three surviving caricatures and in the description of the fourth, Morris is depicted as stealing the capital city away from New York in a variety of ways and moving it to Philadelphia. The target of these anonymous caricaturists' vitriol would have been clear, whether he was carrying Federal Hall on his shoulders or pulling members of Congress by their noses to Philadelphia. The artists responsible for designing and publishing these satirical prints in New York are not yet identified, and because the techniques and designs are varied it is likely they are each the work of separate individuals.[41] Only one of the caricatures, *What think ye of C_o_n_ss now / View of C_o_n_ss on the road to Philadelphia*, is signed with initials, "Y.Z." These initials have not been connected to an artist active in New York, nor have they been located on other prints from this period.

Contemporary newspapers along the East Coast published numerous reports on these caricature prints. A succinct description of the caricature *What think ye of C_o_n_ss now / View of C_o_n_ss on the road* observed that "in one of them is represented the Hon. Mr. [Robert] M[orris] of the Senate as bribing the majority for their votes, and leading the minority by the nose."[42] Contemporary references for this particular caricature are numerous and also include personal responses found in letters written by those that were in attendance for the second session of Congress in New York in

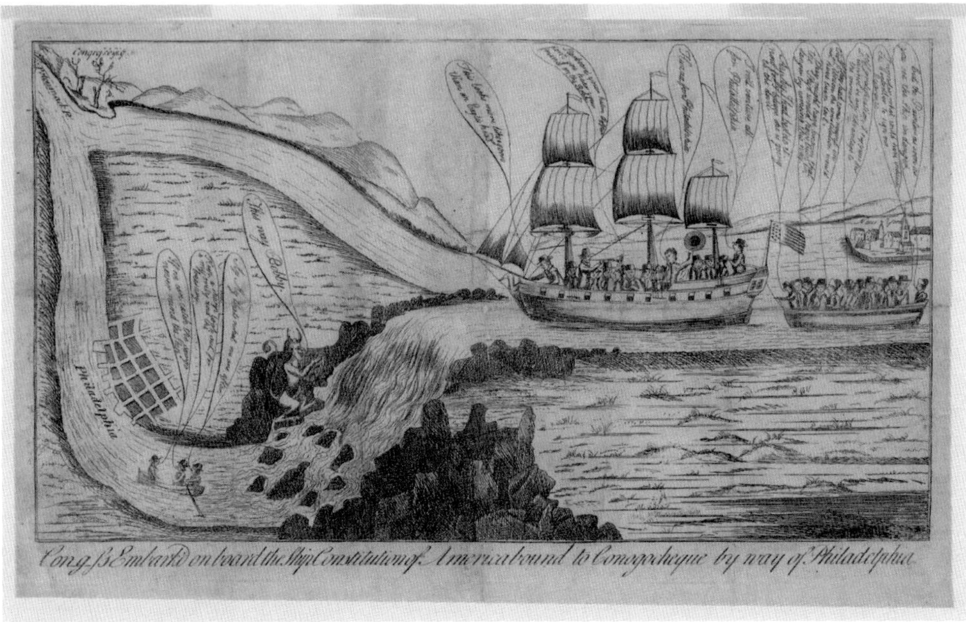

Figure 10 | Anonymous, *Con-g-ess Embark'd on board the Ship Constitution of America bound to Conogocheque by way of Philadelphia*, n.d. [1790]. Prints & Photographs Division, Library of Congress, LC-DIG-ppmsca-19165.

the summer of 1790. In letters sent home to their families and friends, political figures related the news of this caricature in circulation. The New York politician DeWitt Clinton, who would later be the subject of several caricatures, described this caricature in his personal letters to family members: "The Prints contain angry pieces & several caricatures have been circulated ridiculing the principal advocates for the removal. . . . There is one in which Morris is carrying a ladder of promotion on his back to Philadelphia filled with the majority & dragging the minority after him. One of the former holds a purse of gold in his hand and says 'This is what influences me' intimating that some of the members were bribed."[43] In the same letter, Clinton confirmed that he had seen another, the now-lost fourth caricature print, which also depicted Morris. A lengthy description of this caricature can be found in a separate letter, written from the Massachusetts representative Theodore Sedgwick to his wife, Pamela:

> There is a caricature print designed and is said to be executing, which is to present Mr. Morris with the federal building on his shoulders, in one of his pockets Mr. Jay and in the other General Knox. In his right hand is Mr. Jefferson, instead of a walking staff, in his fob Col. Hamilton & at the chain Madison hanging as

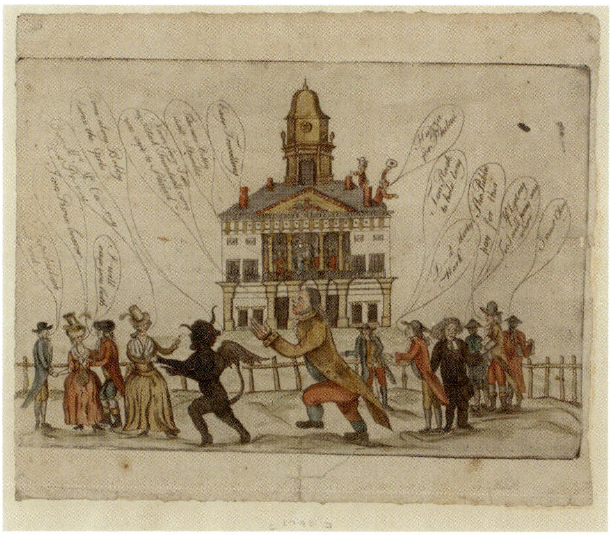

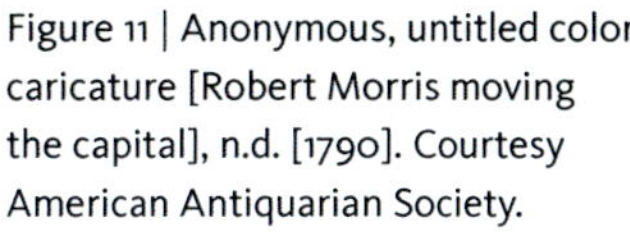

Figure 11 | Anonymous, untitled color caricature [Robert Morris moving the capital], n.d. [1790]. Courtesy American Antiquarian Society.

a bauble. The Senators it should seem caused by the motion of the building are looking out the windows and perceiving the cause they exclaim, "where are you going to carry us Robert?" He answers by a label "wherever I please."—In the back ground are represented members of the house of Representatives, with myself in front. These words are put into my mouth "Stop Robert you rascal and take my assumption with you." To which he answers, "I'll be da—nd if I do."[44]

Sedgwick's vivid description of the caricature reveals that the design was similar to the untitled, hand-colored impression at the American Antiquarian Society that also depicts Morris with Federal Hall on his shoulders. With the availability of imported British caricatures in the United States in the 1780s and the 1790s, especially in New York, it is possible that a source for these caricatures can be found in *A Transfer of East India Stock* (fig. 12), in which the British politician Charles Fox can be seen carrying a building (India House) on his shoulders. If this caricature were indeed published, it would have been a fascinating image of the Founding Fathers that included representations of Alexander Hamilton, Henry Knox, James Madison, Thomas Jefferson, and John Jay.

Politicians living in New York during the summer of 1790 noted the emergence of this new kind of satirical imagery and sent impressions home to family members. Many of the surviving impressions provide evidence as to how they were circulated, with creases where the paper had been folded to fit within a letter. In August, Henry Wynkoop, a representative from Pennsylvania, sent a letter home to his family in which he included several caricatures that were "sold about on the streets, expressive of the Spleen

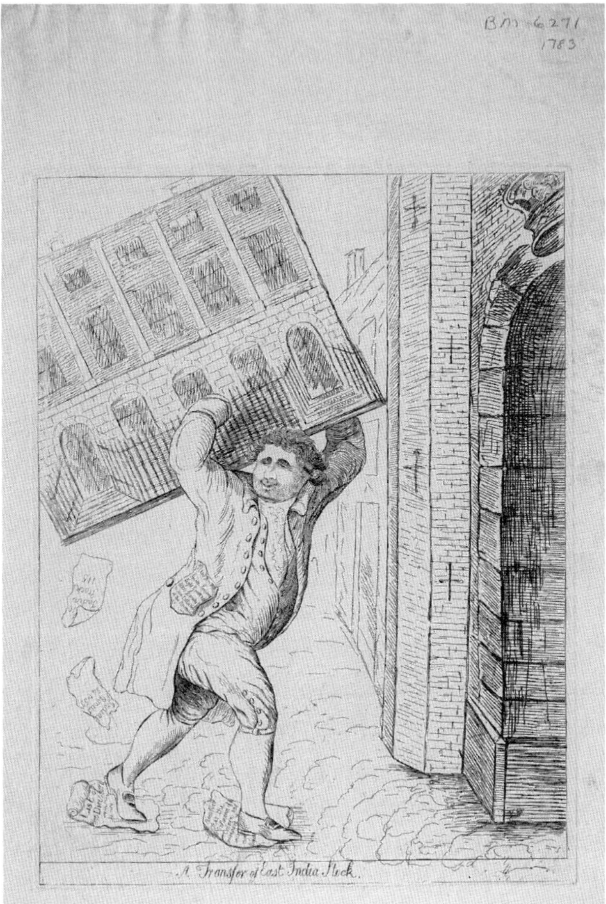

Figure 12 | James Sayers, *A Transfer of East India Stock*, November 25, 1783. Courtesy American Antiquarian Society.

of the citizens on account of the Removal of the Congress." Unfortunately Wynkoop does not give the titles of the caricatures that he sent home, but he directed his family to note the wording within the speech bubbles, writing that "the Rabble here are very free in bawling out some one or other of the dirty expressions you will see in the Labels, when they perceive a Pennsylvania Delegate passing in the Streets."[45] Thomas Jefferson also saw and purchased caricatures during this period, although the dating of one of his letters to early May means that they may not have been the Robert Morris caricatures. Jefferson was in New York with other members of the government as George Washington's secretary of state when he purchased at least one caricature on April 22.[46] Several days later Jefferson wrote to his daughter Mary (Maria), "I send you some prints of a new kind for your amusement. I send several to enable you to be generous to your friends."[47] Unfortunately, Jefferson did not provide the titles or the name of the shop where he purchased the caricatures in his account book, nor does he include this information in his letter to his daughter.[48] The contemporary descriptions in newspapers and the references in letters by politicians such as DeWitt Clinton, Theodore Sedgwick, Henry Wynkoop, and Thomas Jefferson offer insight into the appeal of such satirical imagery and how individuals, particularly those involved in politics, reacted to them.

The caricature prints depicting the removal of the capital from the 1790s were influential to engravers two decades later. With Washington, DC, as the permanent location of the capital, some politicians fought to relocate the capital once more. For example, in 1804 a senator from Maryland, Robert Wright, introduced to Congress a bill that supported a move to Baltimore and inspired at least one caricature on the episode. Although its location is not known, descriptions of the print were published in various newspapers along the East Coast and have survived, including this account: "Senator Wright.—This luminous legislative genius . . . the Bill he lately introduced in the senate to remove the seat of the National Government from the City of Washington to Baltimore, and his speech on that occasion, takes the lead of anything we have seen from him. . . . —We have understood that in consequence of this Bill, some wag drew a caricature of Senator Wright with the Capitol on his back, marching off to Baltimore, and posted it up at the door of the Senate Chamber."[49] The following day further details of the caricature and the nationality of the engraver were provided: "An Irishman advanced and pasted up on the door [of the Senate] a caricature of Mr. Senator Wright from Maryland, carrying off the capitol on his back, with a label issuing from his mouth containing the words 'I can't move it,' alluding to Mr. Wright's motion then pending before the Senate to remove the seat of government to Baltimore."[50] The description of the Maryland senator with the Capitol Building on his back reveals that the design would have been similar to the print of Robert Morris with Federal Hall on his shoulders from 1790, but also to a British source, *A Transfer of East India Stock* (fig. 12).

Wright's attempt to move the capital to Baltimore was unsuccessful, but in February 1808 there was interest in returning the capital to Philadelphia when Senator James Sloan of New Jersey put forth a resolution proposing the "REMOVAL of the Seat of Government." It was reported that "Mr. Sloan, after some prefatory remarks, offered the following resolution: RESOLVED, that it is expedient, and the public good requires, that the Seat of Government should be removed to the City of Philadelphia."[51] In reaction to Sloan's declaration, "some carricatures [sic] are said to be prepared for those who advocate a removal."[52] At least one impression of the caricature *A Trip to Philadelphia; or a hard strain upon the reins of Goverment* [sic] has survived, in which Senator Sloan can be seen in his attempt to move the capital from Washington back to Philadelphia (fig. 13). At some point in its history, this impression was mounted on wood to preserve the paper. On the reverse, written on the wood, is a faded handwritten list that identifies the eight men represented, including the politicians Sloan and Wright. Below

24

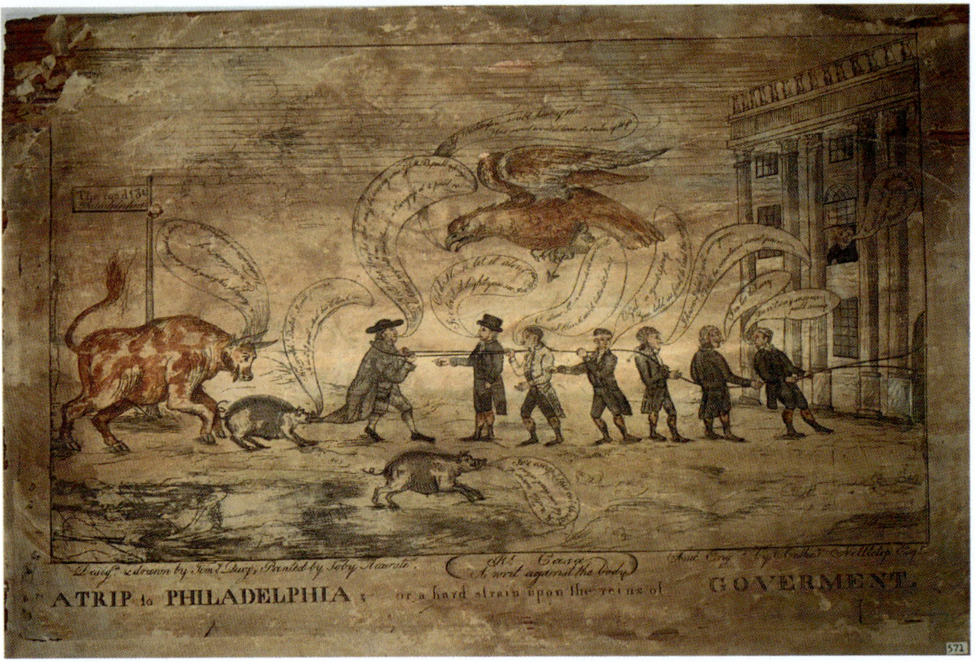

Figure 13 | Designed and drawn by "Timothy Quiz," printed by "Toby Accurate," and engraved by "Anthony Nettletop," *A Trip to Philadelphia; or a hard strain upon the reins of Goverment* [*sic*], n.d. [January or February 1808]. Alexandria-Washington Lodge No. 22, A.F. & A.M. Alexandria, Virginia.

the image are pseudonyms for the individuals involved in the publication of the caricature; it was designed and engraved by "Timothy Quiz," printed by "Toby Accurate," and engraved by "Anthony Nettletop." This is the only association to these aliases, and references to them in contemporary source materials have not yet been located.

Caricatures of George Washington, 1780–1793

George Washington, the first president of the United States, has long been elevated to iconic status.[53] However, in the 1790s he was the subject of at least two caricatures, although no impressions are known to have survived.[54] The first reference to the caricature *The Entry* was described in a letter dated April 7, 1789, from General John Armstrong Jr. to Major General Horatio Gates.[55] Armstrong's letter focused on the days leading up to Washington's inauguration, noting that "all the world here and elsewhere are busy collecting flow[e]rs & sweets of every kind to amuse and delight him [Washington] in his approach and at his arrival." Armstrong indicated that there were some who were less than thrilled with Washington's presidential ascension: "Yet in the midst of this admiration there are Sceptics who doubt its propriety and wits who amuse themselves [with] its extravagance. The first will grumble, and the last will laugh, and the [President] should be prepard [*sic*] to meet the attacks of both with firmness and good Nature." Armstrong's evidence is that a caricature was published that depicted "the Gen. mounted on an Ass & in the arms of his Mulatto Man Billy—Humphreys leading the Jack and Chaunting [*sic*] Hosannas & Birth day odes. The following Couplet makes the motto of this device. 'The Glorious Time has come to Pass When David shall conduct an *Ass*.'"[56] Armstrong's letter to Gates also included his opinion that "wit spares nothing—neither Washington nor God—and that the former like the latter will have something to suffer, and much to forgive." At the end of the nineteenth century, the historian Benson Lossing also published the description of the caricature, but with an additional detail: "On the day after Washington's arrival a caricature appeared—silly enough but charged with bitter feeling. . . . Devil appeared prominent, and from his mouth issued the words: 'The glorious time has come to pass, When David shall conduct an ass.'"[57] Because the first description by Armstrong did not mention the "prominent" devil, Lossing either saw the caricature or embellished the details.[58] A prolific writer of letters, Lossing might have received additional information on the print from one of his contemporaries or friends. No evidence has been found to suggest that Washington saw or knew of *The Entry*.

This was not the case for the caricature titled *The Funeral of George Washington & James Wilson, king and judge &c.* published in the summer of 1793. An impression was shown to Washington in a cabinet meeting and prompted an impassioned response by the president, as recorded by Thomas Jefferson:

> Knox in a foolish incoherent sort of a speech introduced the Pasquinade lately printed, called the funeral of George W—n and James W—n, king and judge &c. where the President was placed on a Guillotin [*sic*]. The Presid[en]t. was much inflamed, got into one of those passions when he cannot command himself. Run on much on the personal abuse which had been bestowed on him. Defied any man on earth to produce one single act of his since he had been in the government which was not done on the purest motives. That he had never repented but once the having slipped the moment of resigning his office, and that was every moment since. That *by god* he had rather be in his grave than in his present situation. That he had rather be on his farm than to be made *emperor of the world* and yet that they were charging him with wanting to be king.[59]

Washington's outburst continued with an attack on Philip Freneau, the editor of the *National Gazette* and a critic of the president, who had taken the liberty of sending him copies of his paper every day. Contrary to recent publications that describe Washington's response to the caricature, Freneau was not the artist responsible for the caricature print, nor was it published in his newspaper, and the identity of the caricaturist responsible was not known at the time.[60] Contemporary newspapers reported that "the authors [artists] of them have not been discovered."[61] Impressions of this caricature were known beyond the cabinet meeting. The vice president's son, Thomas Boylston Adams, reported on the distribution of the caricature to his mother Abigail, writing to her, "Handbills have been distributed representing the President and Judge Willson [*sic*] with their heads under the Guillotine, and proclaiming their death to the Citizens of Philadelphia."[62] Two days after the cabinet meeting, Jefferson sent several impressions of a caricature to his young daughter Martha Jefferson Randolph, with the instruction to share them with friends. The timing of Jefferson's letter to the cabinet meeting strongly suggests that he had personally acquired several copies of the Washington caricature, which were then forwarded to Martha in Virginia.[63] Further to this, during August and September, newspapers from North Carolina to Massachusetts reprinted "an extract of a letter from a gentleman in New-York" dated August 14, 1793, in which a few lines describe the caricature: "A representation of the President, &c. with a coffin and guillotine, was stuck up in Philadelphia, & one thrown into the Post Office."[64] Even if the public outside of Philadelphia did not have the opportunity to see the caricature, through newspaper accounts they would have understood that this was an image critical of the president. As late as December 1793 and January 1794, newspapers continued to mention the caricature, stating, "We have heard of printed caricatures circulating through *Philadelphia*, representing the President of the Union, and a Judge of the Supreme court, with the guillotine suspended over their heads."[65]

Although Washington served two four-year terms as president, ending in 1797, this is the last reference to him in caricature during his time as a public servant. *The Times; a Political Portrait* (fig. 14) had long been thought to depict George Washington during his presidency; however, newspaper advertisements can date its publication to the summer of 1798 when it was made in reaction to the Alien and the Sedition Acts.[66] Although the incorrect date of 1795 given by Weitenkampf has since been corrected to 1798, the long-standing belief that Washington was the main subject continues.[67] With the newspaper advertisements detailing the motivation for its publication in the summer months of 1798, it can be read as a visual comment on the John Adams administration and likely depicts Adams in the chariot, not Washington. The very few caricatures that include depictions of Washington after his death in 1799 are often focused on a comparison narrative in relation to the presidency of Thomas Jefferson. In these early nineteenth-century examples, Washington is no longer the subject of malicious treatment, with a guillotine suspended over his head, but is elevated to a standard that Jefferson could not uphold.[68]

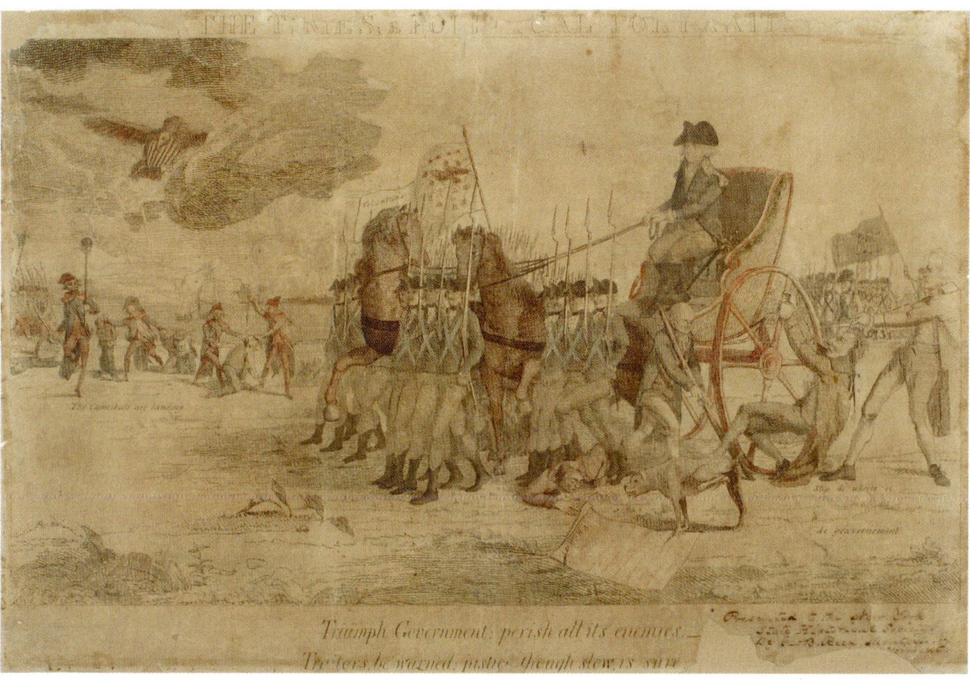

Figure 14 | Anonymous, *The Times; a Political Portrait*, n.d. [July 1798]. Hand-colored engraving, 1795. PR 010, Cartoon and Caricature File, 1795-1. New-York Historical Society, image number 2737. Collection of the New-York Historical Society.

Philadelphia and Early American Caricature Prints

For the modern viewer, there is great complexity in the subject matter found in the American caricature prints from this period. The insider puns and jokes depicted are often limited to the knowledge from the time in which they were made, although some of the figures and events portrayed in caricature even eluded contemporary viewers, and further explanations were requested. An example of this can be seen in an 1809 inquiry related to "a New Caricature—We observe, in a late Baltimore Federal Republican, a neat little cut, representing a Monkey, with a huge sword, chapeau and feather, holding in his paw a rod over the back of a poor terrapin, who has 'courageously retired within his shell in a very dignified manner.'—We wonder if anybody can tell us what this all means."[69] Contemporary newspapers can provide previously unknown information on caricatures, but there are limits to what can be uncovered.

Even when a caricature can be linked to descriptions found in newspapers and letters, it may still prove difficult to unravel the meaning, particularly when the subject of the

28

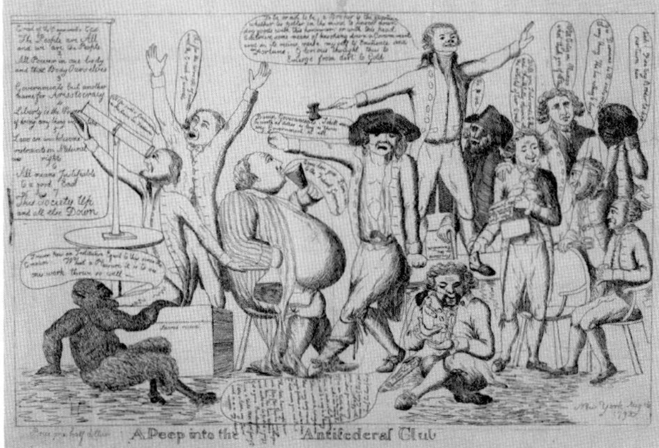

Figure 15 | Anonymous, *A Peep into the Antifederal Club*, August 16, 1793. Courtesy American Antiquarian Society.

print is focused on local politics that has been marginalized in recent studies of American history. *A Peep into the Antifederal Club* (fig. 15) published in August 1793, is one example. The caricature depicts thirteen figures positioned primarily in a row, with little attention to delineating space save for some chairs and a table. While the text found in the speech bubbles might have assisted the contemporary audience, to a modern eye the crowded scene of figures and words is confusing. Conflicting scholarship on this caricature has led to different interpretations of the characters represented, and few historians agree on the identities of those depicted. A problematic figure for scholars has been the individual placed above the group, with his arms raised and a gavel in his right hand, with the most likely candidates being Thomas Jefferson and Aaron Burr. Noble Cunningham, a prominent Thomas Jefferson scholar, did not include this caricature in his discussion of political satires of Jefferson, stating in a footnote that he thought the figure could "easily be Aaron Burr."[70] The assertion that Jefferson is the main character is debatable, especially since this caricature is considered an example of the first political visual satire of Jefferson and is used as an illustration in modern historical scholarship on the period.[71] Murrell did not attempt to distinguish this character or the identities of any of the other figures within the scene. Although devoting a full page to a reproduction, Murrell's short paragraph was dismissive: "This large engraving is most freely drawn, and is not evidently the work of a talented artist with a true satirical gift. He was not satisfied to ridicule, he was out to savagely deride, and anyone who studies the print must admit that the artist certainly made a very thorough job of it."[72] Attributions to other figures have been made, such as Dr. David Rittenhouse, who is seen to the left side of the image alongside his telescope, although it is difficult to confirm these without contemporary sources directly referring to them.[73]

What is certain is that there is general consensus among scholars that this caricature was published in New York and depicts a Philadelphia democratic club. Many such democratic clubs were founded in the early 1790s in Philadelphia, the nation's capital at the time. Americans were consumed by events in Paris, beginning with the storming of the Bastille on July 14, 1789, ten weeks after Washington's inauguration. Initially this news was greeted with approval, with American citizens believing that their own revolutionary ideals had spread to France. The popular support continued through 1792, although many Americans were soon horrified by the bloodier phase of the revolution and the reports of many being sentenced to death by guillotine. In January 1793, Louis XVI, the French king who had aided the American cause in 1778, was executed, and several months later his wife, Marie Antoinette, met the same fate. This period, known as the Reign of Terror, caused many in the United States to question their position on the French Revolution, although this was not the case for all. The British publisher William Cobbett lamented that the news of the French king's death was met with gleeful reaction in Philadelphia: "Never was the memory of any man so cruelly insulted as that of this mild and humane monarch. He was guillotined in effigy, in the capital of the Union, twenty or thirty times every day, during one whole winter and part of the summer. Men, women, and children flocked to the tragical exhibition."[74] When France declared war on Great Britain in February 1793, American support was divided. Members of the Federalist Party, the political party of Washington and Adams, were steadfast in their belief that the French Revolution was uncontrollable and publicly sided with Great Britain; conversely, members of the Republican Party supported Jefferson and James Madison, who favored the French in the belief that George III was suppressing French liberties, as had happened in the American colonies in the 1760s and 1770s. During this period, democratic societies were founded in the United States in support of France, so that at the height of the French Revolution there were more than twenty-seven societies throughout the cities of the East Coast. The Philadelphia democratic society was logically one of the more popular clubs, as it was located in the capital and included many prominent members of government, including Citizen Edmond-Charles Genêt, recently arrived from Paris. Other influential members included a wide assortment of international political leaders from France, Scotland, and Ireland.[75]

The caricature contains a date and the name of a city on the lower right-hand side of the plate: "New York Aug 16 1793." This line is problematic when considered alongside advertisements for the print. Although many of the caricatures published during this time were advertised in newspapers, it is rare to be able to track circulation from city to city. However, notice of the availability of *A Peep into the Antifederal Club* appeared in newspapers in three major cities: Philadelphia, New York, and Boston, in that order. The caricature was first advertised in Philadelphia on August 19 and continued through early September (fig. 16).[76] By the middle of September, advertisements ceased in Philadelphia. From the end of September until early November, advertisements were published

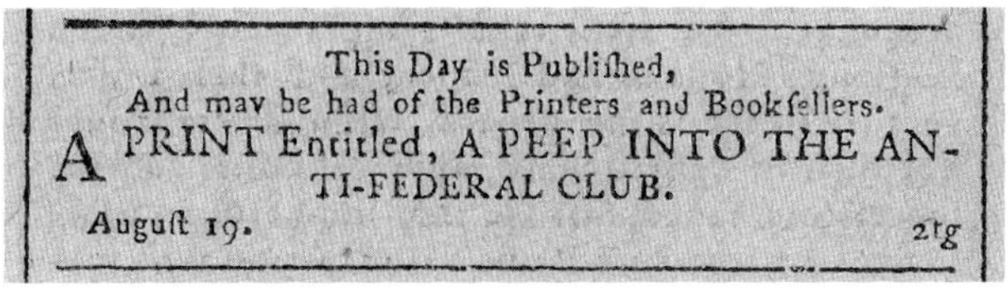

Figure 16 | *General Advertiser* (Philadelphia), August 22, 1793. Courtesy American Antiquarian Society.

Figure 17 | *Columbian Centinel* (Boston), November 2, 1793. Courtesy American Antiquarian Society.

in New York newspapers.[77] By November, the advertisements had moved north, where they were published in Boston.[78]

Because the first newspaper advertisements for this caricature can be found in Philadelphia and not in New York, it is possible that the print was made and published there by an unknown artist. In Philadelphia, Andrew Brown's *Federal Gazette* was the first newspaper to advertise the sale of the print three days after the date on the caricature. Advertisements have not yet been discovered in any New York newspaper prior to September. The question as to why "New York" was placed on the caricature if that was not the place of publication is not easily answered. One possibility is that the caricature mocked a democratic club in New York, meaning that further investigation into the history and rise of democratic clubs in New York is required. At the time of the caricature's publication, at least one newspaper advertisement thought the print represented a New York club, stating in Boston's *Columbian Centinel* that "a Few CARICATURE PRINTS, of a 'PEEP INTO THE ANTIFEDERAL CLUB,' at New-York, are for Sale, at this Office" (fig. 17). This advertisement implies that the information on the print, generally believed to be a publication line, is in fact the location of a democratic club in New York. The problem with this assertion is that the figures represented are largely thought by scholars to be individuals based in Philadelphia and associated with Philadelphia's democratic society. What can be understood is that the subject matter found in some of these earliest caricature prints continues to confound even with information from newspapers and personal letters.

William Cobbett and the Price of Caricatures in Philadelphia in the Late 1790s

The price that caricatures were sold for was not often included on the physical impressions of the prints. An inscription on *A Peep into the Antifederal Club* states that it was

Figure 18 | *Washington Federalist*, December 15, 1808. Courtesy American Antiquarian Society.

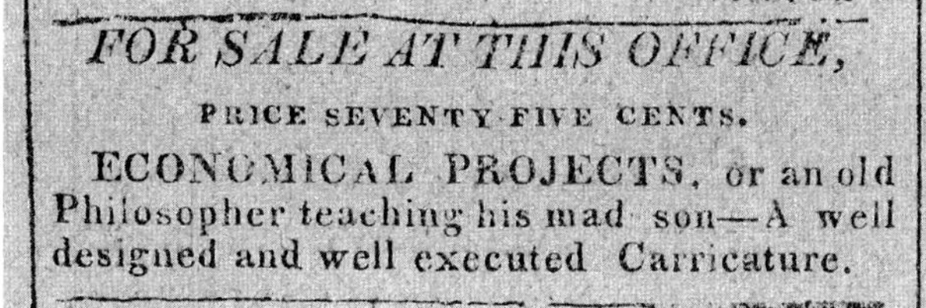

available to purchase for "one half dollar," while the 1807 caricature *All in my eye!* (see fig. 57) contains the price of "25 Cents" handwritten in ink on the top right-hand corner of the print. Newspaper advertisements occasionally provide the price; one example can be found for the colored print *Economical Projects, or an old Philosopher teaching his mad son* (see fig. 61) stating that it could be purchased for "Seventy-five cents" (fig. 18).[79] During the War of 1812, William Charles and his partner Samuel Kennedy sold caricature prints for fifty cents. The surviving account book of William Cobbett, a British radical and publisher who was active as a bookseller in Philadelphia between 1796 and 1800, is an important resource for understanding the market value for caricature prints in the United States.[80] Among the books and pamphlets listed in the account book, Cobbett also sold impressions of four caricature prints: a British caricature by James Gillray titled *New Morality;—or—The Promis'd Installment of the High-Priest of the Theophilanthropes, with The Homage of the Leviathan and his Suite* and at least three American-made caricature prints, *Porcupine, A Print* (previously known as *See Porcupine, in Colours just Portray'd*),[81] *Cinque-tetes, or the Paris Monster*, and *The Times; a Political Portrait*. Cobbett sold two impressions of the Gillray caricature for $1.25 in 1798. The price of impressions of the three American-made caricatures were roughly one-fifth that of the Gillray caricature, between twenty-five and thirty-one cents. Although not located in the account book, Cobbett advertised in December 1798 that he also had for sale "A POLITICAL CARICATURE OF Talleyrand and the Directory."[82] It is likely that this was the British caricature *Property Protected, a la Francoise* by Charles Williams and published by Samuel Fores on June 1, 1798 (fig. 19).

Cobbett's inclination toward the Federalist Party was revealed in his newspaper *Porcupine's Gazette*. Late in August 1796 he was the subject of a caricature, *Porcupine, A Print* (fig. 20), published by a rival bookseller in Philadelphia, Médéric Louis Élie Moreau de Saint-Méry.[83] The caricature depicts Cobbett as a porcupine, cleverly taken from the name of his newspaper. Below the image is the verse, for which previously the first few words had been assigned as the title of the caricature, "See Porcupine, in Colours just Portray'd, Urg'd by old Nick, to drive his dirty trade, Veil'd in darkness, acts the assassins part, And triumphs much to stab you in the heart."

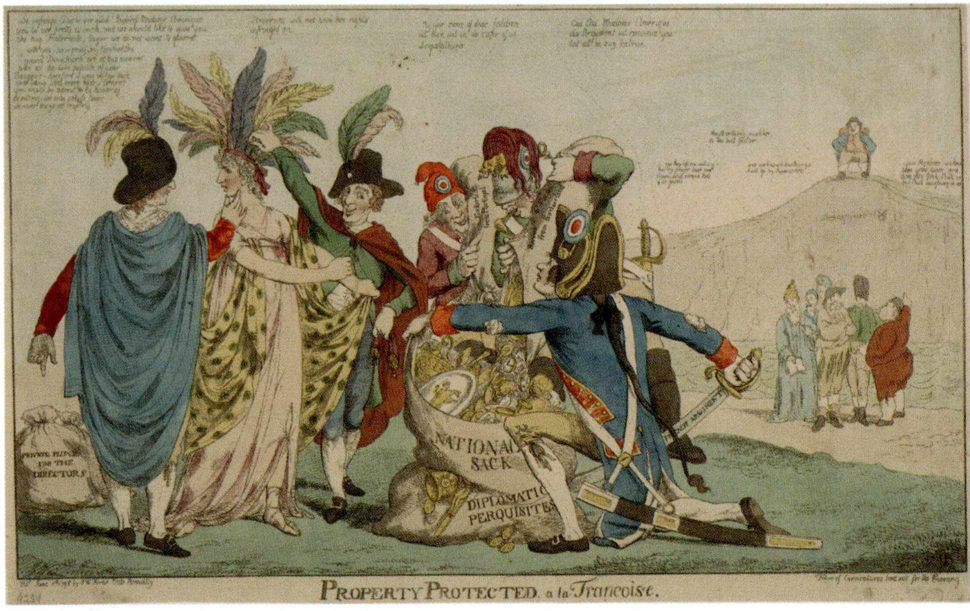

Figure 19 | Anonymous [Charles Williams], *Property Protected, a la Francoise*, June 1, 1798. Prints & Photographs Division, Library of Congress, LC-DIG-ppmsca-31156.

Cobbett provided commentary on the caricature, spanning several pages; an excerpt reveals his account of the subject matter:

> This is a caricature, in which I am represented as urged on to write by my old master King George (under the form of a crowned lion), who, of course, comes accompanied with the devil. The *Jay*, with the treaty in his beak, is mounted on the lion's back, though, by the by, it has ever been said, by the democrats, that the lion rode the *Jay*. His Satanic Majesty holds me out a bag of money, as an encouragement to destroy the idol, liberty, to which he points. The American Eagle is represented as drooping his wings in consequence to my hostility, and America herself, on the same account, weeps over the bust of [Benjamin] Franklin. . . . As to myself, I am the hero of the piece.[84]

According to advertisements for *Porcupine, A Print* published during the first week of September 1796 in the Philadelphia newspapers the *Gazette of the United States* and *Claypoole's American Daily Advertiser*, the caricature could "be had at Moreau de St Mery's book-store, No. 84, Corner of Front and Walnut Streets, and at the principal Booksellers of this city."[85] While the publisher of the caricature was revealed, the question of who

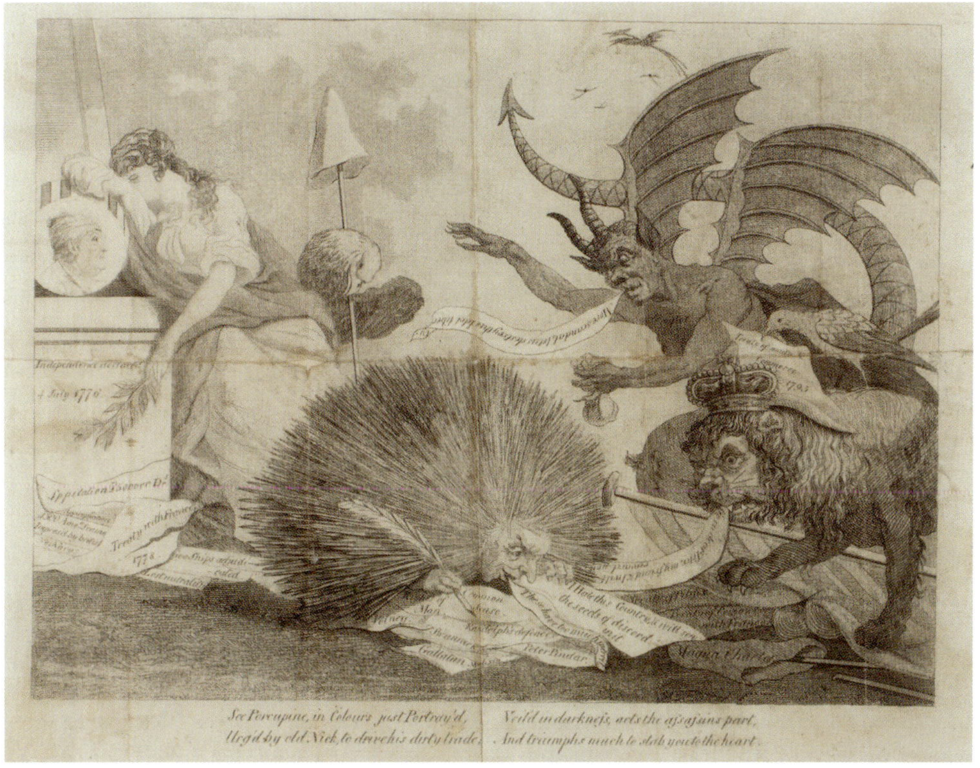

Figure 20 | Anonymous, *Porcupine, a Print*, n.d. [August 1796]. Courtesy American Antiquarian Society.

designed and engraved the piece remains unclear: perhaps it was created entirely by Saint-Méry, acting as artist, engraver, and publisher. It is however more likely that additional individuals were involved in the creation of the print, with Saint-Méry hiring an as yet unidentified artist.

Although the caricature was an attack on Cobbett, his account book reveals that he sold at least ten impressions of the print, despite not advertising its availability for sale through his newspaper, *Porcupine's Gazette*. The three other caricatures that Cobbett sold were advertised in his paper. *Cinque-tetes, or the Paris Monster* (fig. 21) was published in reaction to news of the XYZ Affair. References in Cobbett's account book refer to it as "the Paris Monster" and reveal that fellow Philadelphia bookseller and publisher Benjamin Davies purchased ninety of the ninety-nine impressions sold by Cobbett. In May 1798, Davies advertised the caricature for sale at his and "other booksellers in Philadelphia" with the following description: "A Faithful and Striking Likeness of Cinque-Tetes, or the Horrible Paris Monster, Engaged in a serious dialogue with the *American*

34

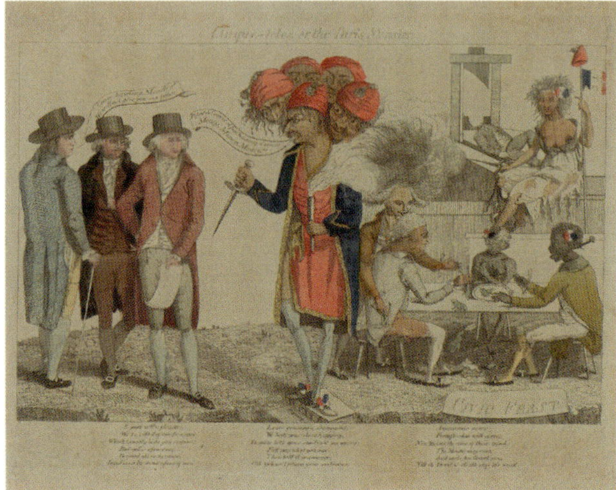

Figure 21 | Anonymous, *Cinque-tetes, or the Paris Monster*, n.d. [May 1798]. priASPC 0020, American Social/ Political Caricatures Collection, The Huntington Library, San Marino, California.

Ministers, on the subject of the French Finances Exhibiting also a curious representation of a *Civique Fete,* celebrated in honor of the *Goddess Liberty* and her amiable hand-maid Madamoiselle [*sic*] *La Guillotine.*"[86] Soon after, impressions of the caricature were advertised for sale as far north as Albany, New York, and as far south as Alexandria, Virginia. A humorous description of the caricature was published in the *Albany Centinel* and reprinted in newspapers in New England:

> The *lovers of fun* may be gratified with a view of a laughable caricature, at Sharp's shop, in State Street. The caricature represents the French Directory, (what it really is) as a hideous monster with five heads—a dagger in one hand—under its feet is *"Equality"*—a label points from its mouth containing the words *"money! money! money!"* addressed to the American Envoys: a label proceeds from the mouth of one of the American Envoys containing the following:—*"Cease, bawling monster, cease, we will not give you six pence!"*—A figure, with distorted features, represents *French liberty*—one hand grasps a pole, on the top of which is a red cap, and the other hand is furnished with a dagger: beside this figure is a representation of the guillotine, and the headless body of a man. A *civic feast* is represented, at which the Devil presides, and frogs are the fare.[87]

There is not a reference in Cobbett's account book to selling any of the caricature impressions to Sharp's shop in Albany or indeed to a shop in Alexandria, Virginia, although in addition to Davies, Archibald Drummond of New York City purchased six impressions of the caricature from Cobbett. By August, impressions could also be purchased at Price's

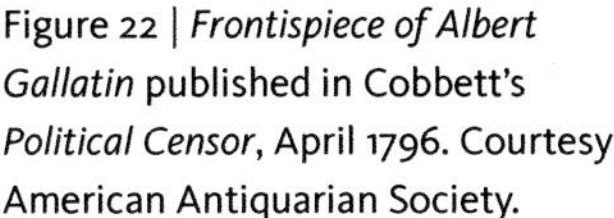

Figure 22 | *Frontispiece of Albert Gallatin* published in Cobbett's *Political Censor*, April 1796. Courtesy American Antiquarian Society.

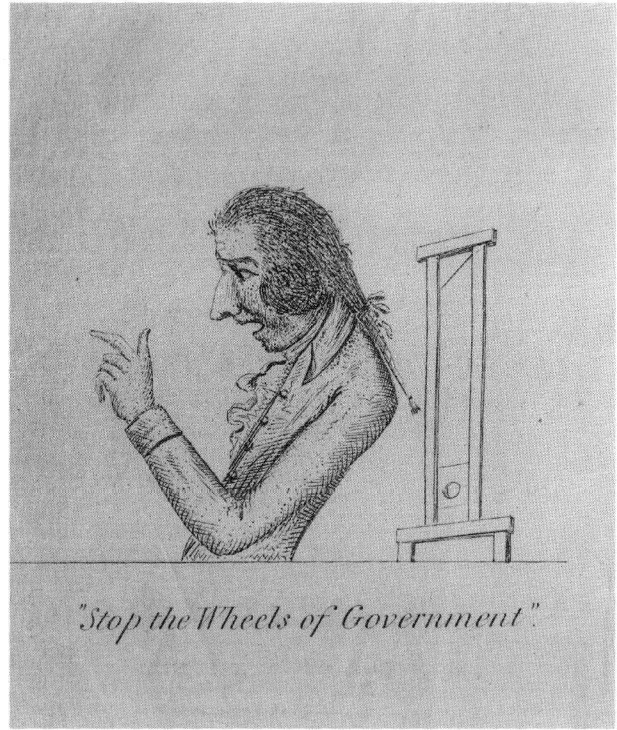

Book Store in Alexandria: "Lately published and for sale . . . Cinques Tetes; *or the Paris Monster. A Caricature.*"[88] Despite a run of at least ninety impressions, only one caricature survives today; perhaps other print runs for caricature prints from this period were just as high.

As with *Cinque-tetes, or the Paris Monster, The Times; a Political Portrait* (see fig. 14) was advertised exclusively in Cobbett's newspaper with the claim that it was "just published for the author" and was sold at Benjamin Davies's bookstore.[89] Included in the notice was a description of the caricature: "Intended as a seasonable hint to all those who have taken more pains to 'Stop the Wheels of Government,' than to check the insults and ravages of a foreign enemy; and who, of course are more terrified by the idea of an alien or a sedition bill, than they would be at the sight of an army of 20,000 French cut-throats."[90] Further evidence that Cobbett may have been involved in some of the elements of its design and execution is that one of the characters depicted in *The Times; a Political Portrait* was Albert Gallatin. This representation, as well as the words placed below Gallatin's impression in the caricature, were taken directly from the *Frontispiece of Albert Gallatin* published in Cobbett's *Political Censor* from April 1796 (fig. 22), in which Gallatin was represented above the words "Stop the Wheels of Government." The unknown engraver

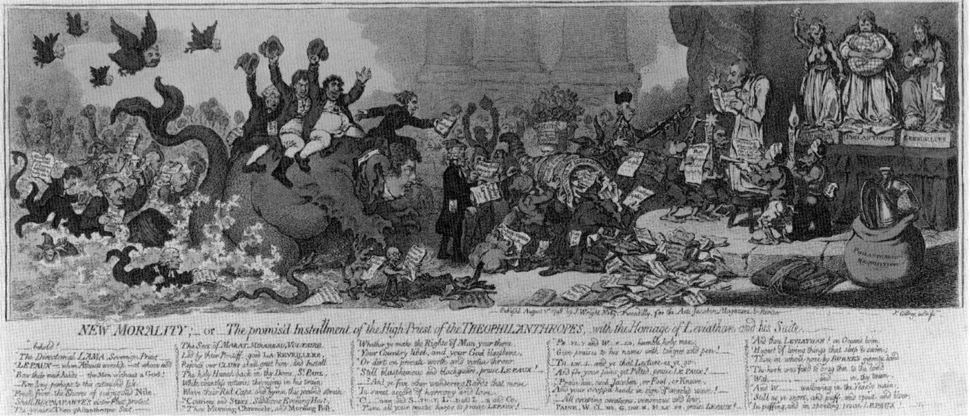

Figure 23 | James Gillray, *New Morality;—or—The Promis'd Installment of the High-Priest of the Theophilanthropes, with The Homage of the Leviathan and his Suite*, August 1, 1798, hand-colored etching. Yale Center for British Art, Paul Mellon Collection, B1981.25.1001.

of this image of Gallatin may have been hired by Cobbett for other engraving projects, perhaps including this caricature.

In 1799, Cobbett advertised that he had for sale "a few copies of a political Caricature" in which "upwards of one hundred and fifty characters are introduced, the countenances all admirably preserved and the dresses and postures most excellently adapted. The whole is beautifully coloured."[91] This was Gillray's *New Morality;—or—The Promis'd Installment of the High-Priest of the Theophilanthropes, with The Homage of the Leviathan and his Suite* (fig. 23) published in London in August 1798; Cobbett sold at least two impressions of it for $1.25 each, the price advertised in the newspaper notice.[92]

Copyright and Suppression in the United States

Copyright was not formally introduced in the United States until the first decade of the 1800s and was not actively enforced until the middle of the nineteenth century. This was vastly different from England, where copyright had been in effect since the early 1730s, at the prompting of William Hogarth. Referred to as "Hogarth's Law," the Engravers Act of 1735 protected the producers of engravings, so long as they were of an original design.[93] In the United States, the first federal copyright law was passed in 1790; however, initially it did not protect artists, publishers, or authors. The law was later amended in 1802 to read: "[An act of the Congress of the United States] for the Encouragement of Learning, by securing the copies of Maps, Charts and Books, to the Authors and Proprietors of such times therein mentioned; and extending the benefits thereof to the Arts of Designing, Engraving and Etching Historical and other Prints." The revised copyright law stipulated that artists were to sign their works with the following model: "Entered, according to act of congress, the x day of x 18 x [here insert the date when the same was deposited in the office] by x of the State of x [here insert the author's or proprietor's name and the State in which he resides]."[94] When these procedures were applied, the law specified that original work would be protected under the copyright law. James Akin and Amos Doolittle sometimes complied and included the inscription on their plates. Some impressions were deposited for copyright, and examples by Akin and William Charles can be found in the collection of American caricature prints at the Library of Congress in Washington, DC.

Despite these measures, there was very little oversight, and it is surprising that there wasn't more copying of such imagery. Newspapers occasionally refer to libels, but not with any frequency until the 1830s. One newspaper reported, with regard to caricatures made of Andrew Jackson that were publicly displayed, "the District Attorney has received instructions to commence suits against the individuals concerned in getting up the late caricatures."[95] These lawsuits were either brought forward with no consequence to the caricaturists or dismissed entirely. With little government intervention, caricatures continued to contain representations of important political figures and events as subject matter throughout the end of 1820s and most of the 1830s.

It does not appear that Congress effectively suppressed caricatures or the artists responsible for them. For example, a sensational encounter in February 1798 between two politicians in Congressional Hall in Philadelphia was the subject of at least four caricatures: *Ve—t Politeness* (fig. 24), *Cudgeling as by late Act in Congress, USA* (Peabody Essex Museum, fig. 25), *Cudgeling. as by late Act in Congress, U.S.A.* (Connecticut Historical Society, fig. 26), and *Congressional Pugilists* (fig. 27). In this grouping are at least two examples of copying. *Cudgeling as by late Act in Congress, U.S.A.* was copied with the same design and format, but with vastly different handling. Both are signed: the Peabody Essex Museum impression contains initials and a last name that are barely legible, with the first initial "C." clear while the middle initial and last name are not known, and the Connecticut Historical Society impression was signed by "J.A."[96] *Congressional Pugilists* was not an original design but was copied from the print *Samsonic Lodge*, drawn by Samuel Collings and etched by Inigo Barlow, included in the February 1790 London journal *Attic Miscellany; or, characteristic mirror of men and things, including the correspondent's museum* (fig. 28).[97] The original print must have been known to the caricaturist who adapted the general scene for a stateside subject. In particular, the figure in the middle of the British print, holding a feather pen and leaning to one side with legs almost crossed, was copied in the American caricature.

38

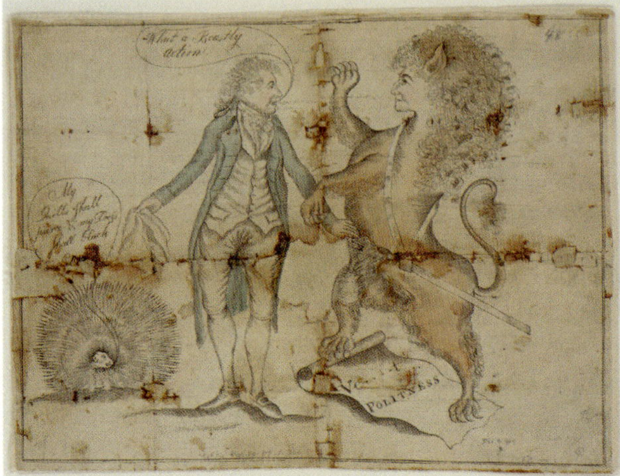

Figure 24 | Anonymous, *Ve—t Politeness*, n.d. [1798]. Arts Department, Boston Public Library.

These caricatures were published in 1798, after the Sedition Act was signed into law by President John Adams. The law punished anyone who published writings against the United States government and primarily focused on newspaper editors publishing pamphlets. For the most part, caricatures continued to be published in the late 1790s and early 1800s without any known retribution from the government. The unknown artist responsible for *The Times; a Political Portrait* (see fig. 14) approved of the act: the caricature depicts President Adams in his chariot, trampling over the opposing Republican newspaper editor Benjamin Franklin Bache. However, one impression of *Congressional Pugilists* bore a rare handwritten comment that mentions the suppression of prints: "This cartoon was purchased by Gad Talcott of Hebron [Connecticut] who hid it for several years. Congress considered all such pictures a libel and by special act, suppressed them."[98]

Local Politics: New York City Caricature in the Early 1800s

When the federal government left New York for Philadelphia, the small number of individuals working in caricature followed the politics and headed south. This was not the case when the government left Philadelphia for its permanent location in Washington, DC, a still-unfinished capital city. There is no evidence to suggest that artists engaged in caricature attempted to settle in the new capital. Rather, the output of caricature in the first decade of the nineteenth century came from New York, a bustling metropolis comparable to cosmopolitan London.[99] Providing a flourishing network for artists and engravers, New York also boasted the American Academy of Fine Arts, founded in 1802 and modeled after the Louvre in Paris.

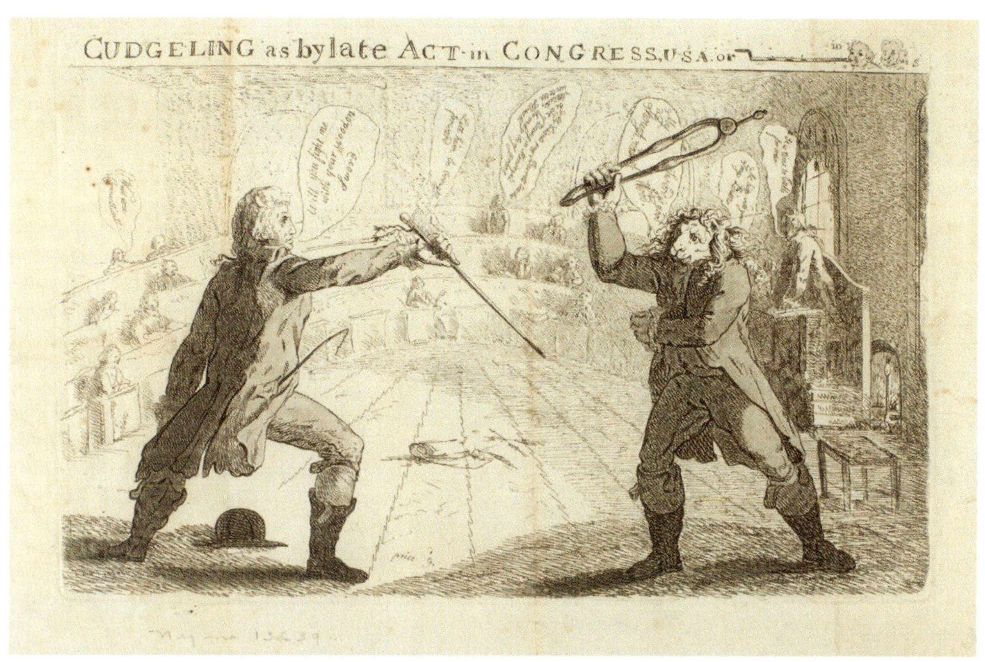

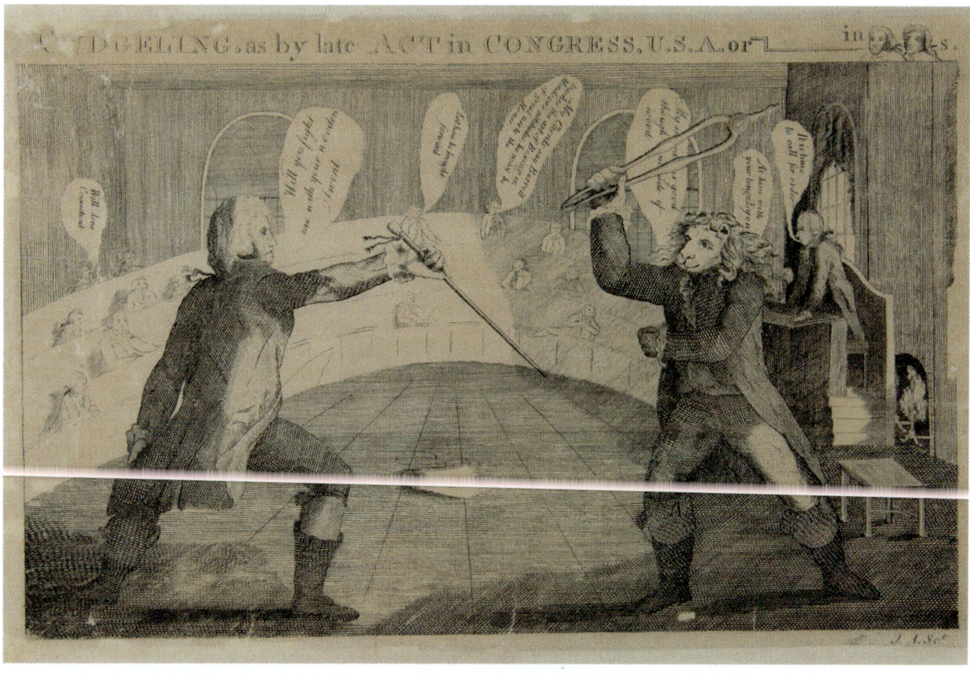

Figure 25 (*top*) | C. [illegible initial and last name], *Cudgeling as by late Act in Congress, USA*, 1798. Peabody Essex Museum. Courtesy of Phillips Library, Peabody Essex Museum, Rowley, MA.

Figure 26 (*bottom*) | J. A., *Cudgeling. as by late Act of Congress, U.S.A.*, n.d. [1798]. The Connecticut Historical Society.

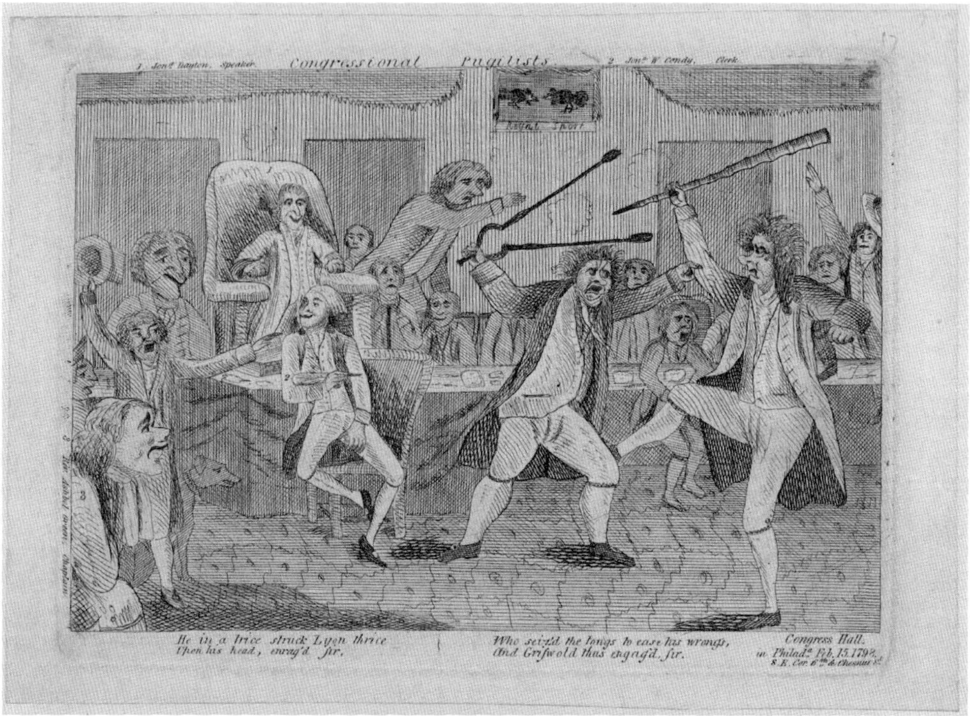

Figure 27 | Anonymous, *Congressional Pugilists*, February 1798. Etching, third state of three (later restrike?), 6 9/16 × 8 3/4 in. (16.6 × 22.3 cm), sheet 7 3/8 × 9 15/16 in. (18.7 × 25.3 cm). Gift of Albert Ten Eyck Gardner, 1950. The Metropolitan Museum of Art, New York.

In New York, caricaturists did not need to look far for inspiration for potential subject matter, as local politics provided enough entertaining material. In July 1802, a duel between New York politicians DeWitt Clinton and John Swartwout provided an ideal subject for a caricature print. Duels were relatively common in this period, but because the activity was illegal in New York City, it was necessary for the combatants to cross the Hudson River to New Jersey.[100] The Clinton and Swartwout duel took place in Weehawken, New Jersey, where the more famous duel between Aaron Burr and Alexander Hamilton would occur in 1804. Burr was not depicted in the caricature of the Clinton-Swartwout duel, but he played an important role. Swartwout, a keen supporter and friend of Burr, had accused Clinton of trying to destroy Burr's political reputation, citing evidence in newspapers and pamphlets. When neither would apologize, a duel was set. As was customary, both individuals were aided by seconds, Richard Riker for Clinton and Colonel William Stephens Smith for Swartwout.[101] The duel was marked by an exchange of five rounds, with Clinton's bullets hitting Swartwout in the fourth and fifth

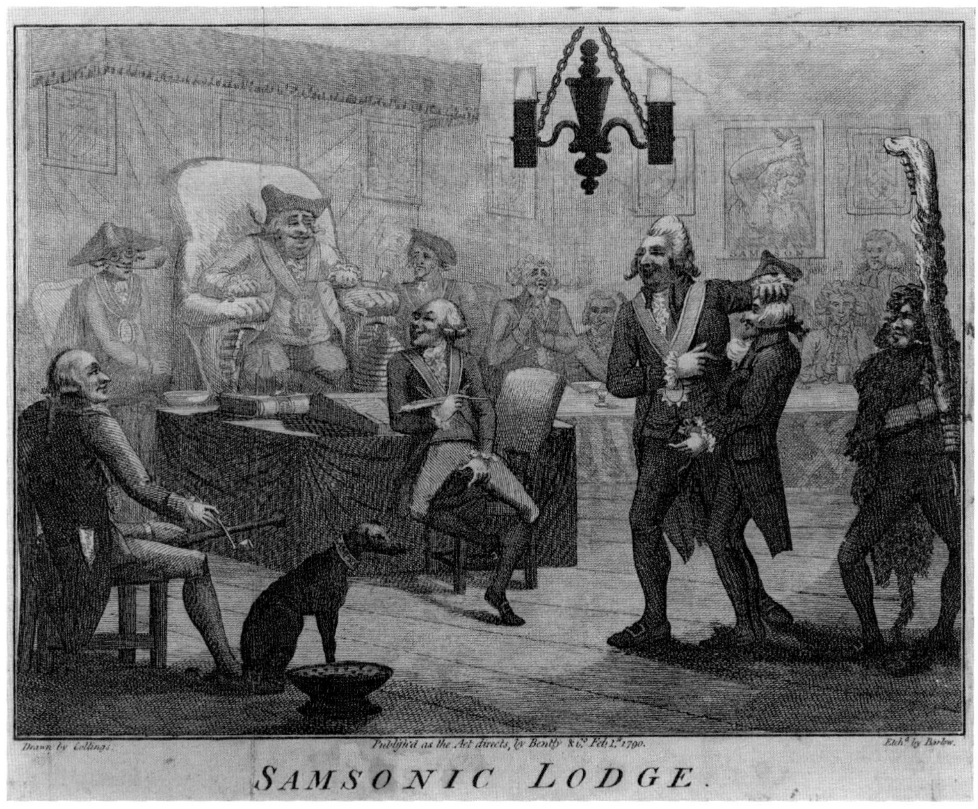

Figure 28 | Drawn by Samuel Collings, etched by Inigo Barlow, *Samsonic Lodge*,
plate from *Attic Miscellany; or, characteristic mirror of men and things, including the
correspondent's museum* 1, no. 3 (February 1790): 161. Etching on laid paper, sheet 19 ×
23 cm. Courtesy of The Lewis Walpole Library, Yale University.

rounds. Soon afterward, *A genuine View of the parties in an Affair of Honor, after the fifth
shot, at Hobuken [sic], 31st July 1802* (fig. 29) was published without a signature.[102] As this
caricature was in support of Swartwout, it is possible that caricaturists active in New
York found patronage with newspaper publishers, political parties, or both. British caricaturists, such as Gillray, Rowlandson, and James Sayers were frequently hired by political parties to create an image critical of the opposition, although this did not deter them
from printing damaging caricatures of both sides. In the United States, only limited evidence suggests such patronage by political parties.[103]

The 1804 New York governor's race was also the subject for caricature by an unidentified caricaturist. In the months before the election, newspapers reported on its sensational aspects, describing it as "a nasty and petty campaign."[104] Supporters of the
candidates were vicious and vengeful, engaged in a paper war in which newspapers and

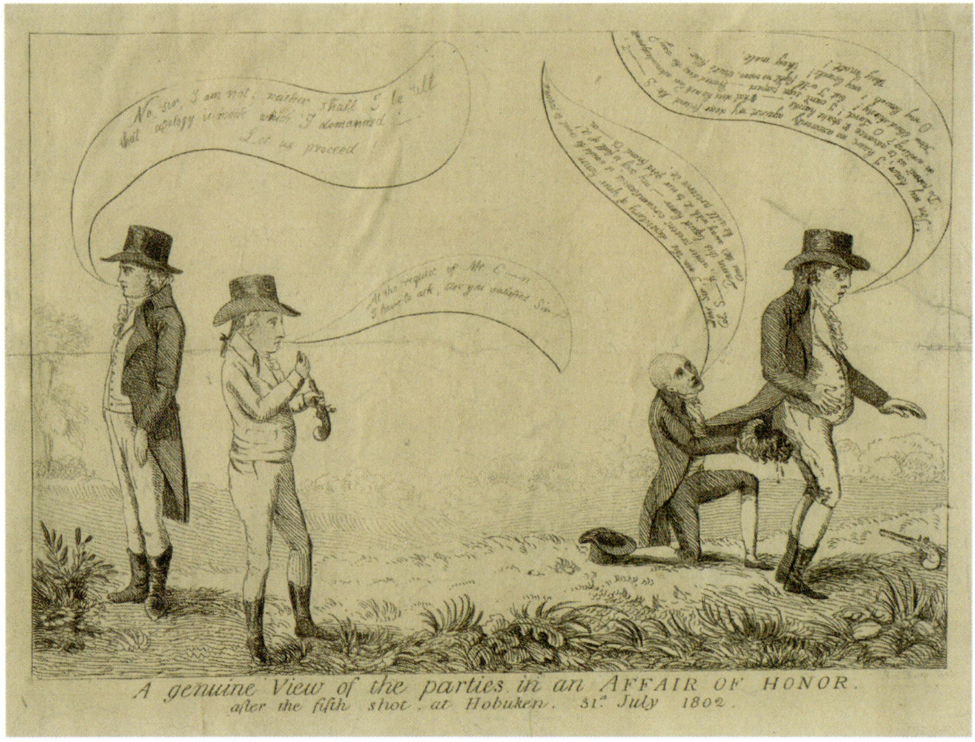

A genuine View of the parties in an AFFAIR OF HONOR. after the fifth shot, at Hobuken. 31ᵗ July 1802.

Figure 29 | Anonymous, *A genuine View of the parties in an Affair of Honor, after the fifth shot, at Hobuken [sic], 31st July 1802*, 1802. Cartoon and Caricature File, PR 010, 1802-1, FF18, New-York Historical Society, image number 43339. Collection of the New-York Historical Society.

pamphlets were utilized for maximum impact. The election pitted Aaron Burr, not yet (in)famous for the duel that would take the life of Hamilton, against Morgan Lewis, who had been appointed by the two most politically influential New York Jeffersonian-Republican families, the Clintons and the Livingstons. *Family-Ambition*, the only caricature that survives from this election campaign (fig. 30), depicts the struggle of key members of the Clinton and Livingston families for the New York gubernatorial office.[105] No signature or date can be found on the only surviving impression, although newspaper advertisements indicate that it was published in April 1804. A letter from "a gentleman in New-York" was reprinted in newspapers and offers an accurate description of the image:

> I have just seen the print of a Carricature [*sic*] called "Family-Ambition," which is now circulating in this city. The design appears to be better conceived than

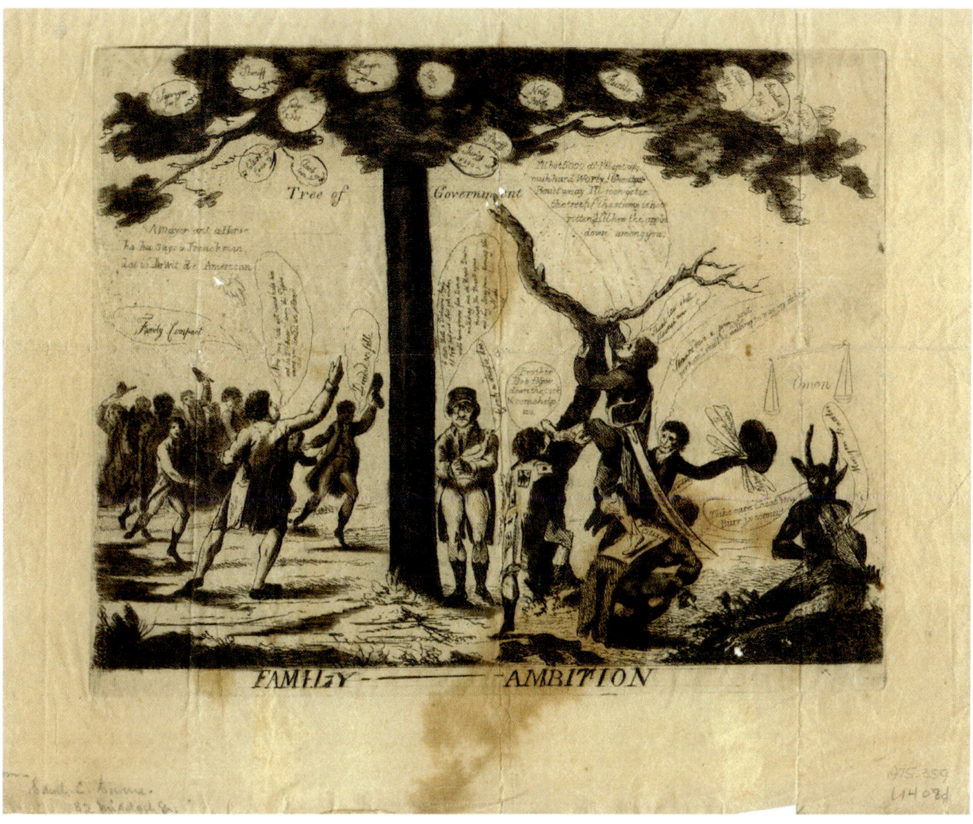

Figure 30 | Anonymous, *Family-Ambition*, n.d. [1804]. M1975.359.1, Brooklyn Public Library, Center for Brooklyn History.

things of this sort usually are. The prominent features are—the government tree loaded with offices in the shape of pippins—the family compact, with labels in their mouths—Judge Lewis climbing up a blasted tree, with the assistance of Maturin Livingston and James Cheetham—Mr Lewis is drawn with a huge sword by his side, and declares that, if he can get up, he will cut down the pippins among them—the Devil is represented in one corner, scraping a fiddle for them, with this significant label, showing his paternal care: "Take care, Cheetham, Burr is coming."[106]

The unidentified artist responsible for this ambitious design was undoubtedly familiar with the style and formats popular in eighteenth-century British caricatures. *Family-Ambition* employs specific emblematic motifs and is similar in its layout to British caricatures in that the print is filled with figures, emblems, and speech bubbles.[107] Apples or "pippins" hang from the top of the tree and spread along the top of both the British and American examples. On either side of the tree are two groups of men, identifiable by the speech bubbles provided and from the previously quoted contemporary description of the caricature, which correctly identifies Morgan Lewis on the right side of the print. The Clinton family is depicted on the left of the "Tree of Government" and the Livingston family on the right; both groups reach toward the tree to obtain the apples, seeking political prominence.

The Audience for American Caricatures, 1789–1820s

Newspapers published mixed reactions to the growing number of American caricatures. There was dismay at the arrival of the British satirical tradition in America, as evidenced by the following opinion piece published in an 1802 newspaper: "It is with pain we observe that a species of libel has already appeared in our Country in imitation of the abominable and licentious practice of the lower English, commonly called caricature, in which the unhappy object of abuse is exposed to vulgar derision without any possibility of defence. It is a species of attack equally cowardly and brutal."[108] A decade later, in 1813, the following was published in reaction to caricatures that appeared at the start of the War of 1812:

> The practice of caricaturing, so much encouraged in Europe, is but little patronized in this country. Whether it is that those who would naturally turn their attention that way find the art of *counterfeiting* more lucrative, or whether it is that the public taste is not yet viciated, we are unable to say. Be that as it may, it will not be long before we shall add this to our long catalogue of imitated European follies. If the practice disgusts now, we shall very soon accommodate our taste to it, and caricatures will become as necessary to our amusement as a thousand other follies of the same origin.[109]

Still, some newspapers heralded the new medium, occasionally adding to their reports prompts to caricaturists noting that a particular event would make for a good print.

Newspapers also provide information as to where and how caricature could be seen and purchased. Because most caricatures were political and published by men, the audience for such imagery could be expected to be male. The venues in which caricatures could be viewed, in taverns and barbershops, support this. As a further differentiation as to who should be observing these caricature prints, a letter was published in a New York newspaper offering an opinion "on the manner of passing Sunday rationally and agreeably" for young women. Approved were "prints and drawings," being an "innocent and rational amusement," but young women should not look on "the caricatures, and political prints, with which our shops are at present crowded; they may *amuse* but cannot *instruct*; but historical prints, prints of illustrious persons, views of places, figures, of plants and animals, are at once instructive and entertaining."[110] This was one such opinion, but in reality women did look at political caricature, and in some cases prints were sent to women from male family members. On at least two occasions, Thomas Jefferson included caricatures in letters to his daughters at Monticello (in the summer of 1790 and in 1793), while Theodore Sedgwick wrote explicitly to his wife about the caricature prints in circulation, with glee and horror. Thomas Boylston Adams included a description of a caricature in circulation in a letter to his mother Abigail. That these men, and likely countless others in this period, chose to send impressions and descriptions of caricatures to the women in their lives allows for the inquiry into these prints as being of interest to all genders. Although no records have been located of women in the United States purchasing caricature, Abigail Adams purchased such prints while she was in London during the 1780s, sending at least one impression of *The Bosom Friends* to a female friend, writing that "when an object is to be ridiculed, tis generally exagerated [*sic*]. The print however does not greatly exceed some of the most fashionable Dames."[111]

Advertisements in American newspapers specified that caricatures could be seen and purchased in bookstores. No American caricature from this period has been located in which individuals are represented as spectators admiring prints in windows, but there are contemporary descriptions of individuals looking at visual material in this manner. William Cobbett wrote of the care he took in designing his Philadelphia storefront windows in 1796. He evidently took great pains to "excite" a reaction from his professional rivals by painting the exterior of his store "Tory blue" and exhibiting engraved portraits of George III in his windows.[112] Cobbett described the opening of his bookstore and his choice of prints displayed in the windows: "I put up in my windows, which were very large, all the portraits that I had in my possession of *kings, queens, princes,* and *nobles*. I had all the English Ministry; several of the Bishops and Judges; the most famous Admirals; and in short, every picture that I thought likely to excite the rage in the enemies of Great Britain."[113] One newspaper notice referred to a crowd of spectators looking at a caricature in a shop window: "Observed a number of people gazing at a print in the window— It appeared to be a caricature."[114]

Barbershops were a popular venue in the late eighteenth- and early nineteenth-century for displaying caricatures. This was a distinctively male venue, in which men congregated and discussed current political events.[115] As a place where women were not expected to disrupt the conversations of customers waiting for service, a barbershop might double as a makeshift committee room.[116] British caricaturists have represented

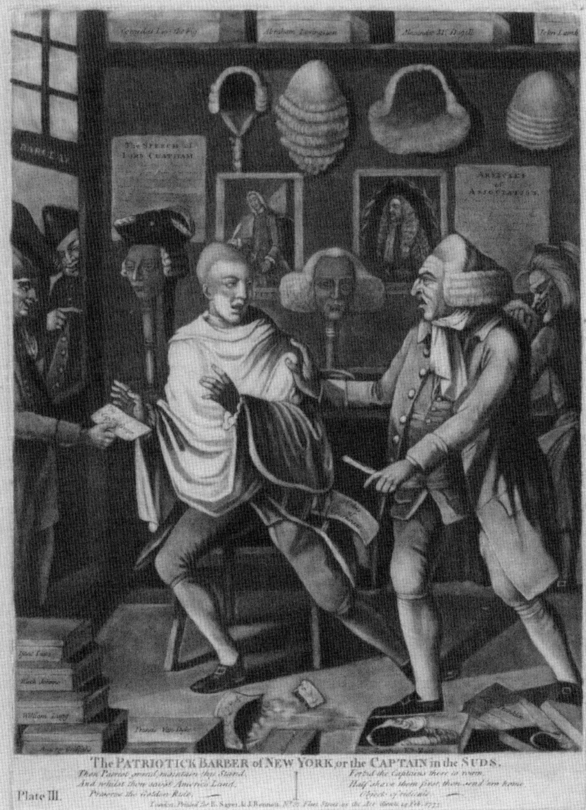

Figure 31 | Anonymous (attributed to Philip Dawe), *The Patriotick [sic] Barber of New York, or the Captain in the Suds*, February 14, 1775. Mezzotint, plate 13 7/8 × 10 in. (35.3 × 25.4 cm), sheet 16 1/2 × 11 9/16 in. (41.9 × 29.3 cm). Gift of William H. Huntington, 1883. The Metropolitan Museum of Art, New York.

the interiors of barbershops as venues for political discussion and debate since the 1770s. Published in London by Robert Sayer and John Bennett, a popular example from the revolutionary period was *The Patriotick [sic] Barber of New York, or the Captain in the Suds* (fig. 31). The caricature depicts the interior of a New York barbershop owned by Jacob Vredenburgh that includes wigs and various accoutrements in addition to the prints adorning the walls, although there are no caricatures displayed. Other late eighteenth-century British caricaturists such as Thomas Rowlandson and Robert Dighton also published caricatures that depict the interiors of barbershops, with men gathered around one another reading newspapers or pamphlets.[117]

Barbers utilized the reach of newspaper advertisements by informing potential clients of newly received and entertaining caricatures to be had at their shops. One newspaper advertisement for a barbershop in northern New Jersey announced to its male clientele that the shop "was embellished with a variety of caricatures ... to beguile the tedious moments of operation."[118] Another notice described a caricature of Napoleon

Bonaparte that adorned the walls of a barbershop in Virginia: "*Bonaparte.*—There is a caricature of this extraordinary man suspended in a Barber's shop in town. His *Imperial Majesty* is represented, as a dernier resort, to be knocking at the Gates of Hell, and his *Satannic* [*sic*] Majesty refuses to give him admittance."[119] The barbershop also provided a metaphor for caricature; an account published in an 1803 newspaper in Essex County, Massachusetts, described Thomas Jefferson ("Great Personage") depicted as a barber: "*Caricature.* The wits of New Haven have lately executed a most excellent *caricature*, for which they ought to be bound over to the peace, or thrown into jail. A certain Great Personage is represented with a razor, in the act of performing the operation of shaving upon one seated in a barber's armchair; at the same time is seen entering the door a man in the habit of a collegian, and under the device the following *keen* verses."[120]

The most "fashionable barber in New York" in the first decade of 1800s, John Richard Desborous Huggins, displayed prints and caricatures in his shop. Huggins attended to both male and female clients; in newspaper advertisements he addressed the two genders separately, as seen in an 1803 advertisement that was directed at his male customers: "To The Gentleman. He returns his sincere thanks for their past favours and assures them that he has spared neither trouble nor expense to adorn his Dressing Academy with elegant engravings, caricatures, and fanciful decorations."[121] In July 1805, Huggins advertised the following: "Just received and for sale, a large collection of European and American Caricatures."[122] His competitors followed his successful example by decorating their barbershops with caricatures and advertised that their storefronts were also stocked with prints and newspapers. When the New York barber Henry J. Hassay, a rival of Huggins's, changed his display of prints, he announced, "The eye might be gratified with a new collection of caricatures, by the latest and ablest masters, exhibiting the moral character rendered ridiculous by the adoption of fugitive folly."[123]

American caricatures published between 1789 and 1820 were primarily sold separately in bookshops, but there is at least one example of caricature prints having been bound in folios to be rented out and advertised specifically for women. London publishers such as Samuel W. Fores, Thomas Tegg, and William Holland continued to sell individual caricatures, but they had found bound portfolios of caricatures to be a lucrative market.[124] In 1788, William Holland was not only exhibiting caricatures but was also targeting "Caricature Collectors" who could "be supplied with the greatest variety in London, of political and other humorous Prints, bound in Volumes, and ornamented with an engraved Title, and a characteristic Vignette."[125] Only one bound portfolio of caricature prints is known to have been available in the United States during this period. This enterprise was advertised by the Portsmouth, New Hampshire bookseller Charles Peirce. In 1807, Peirce announced the availability of his bound book of caricatures, considered to be perfect as "Entertainment for Tea Parties, etc."[126] Peirce's book of caricatures included

48

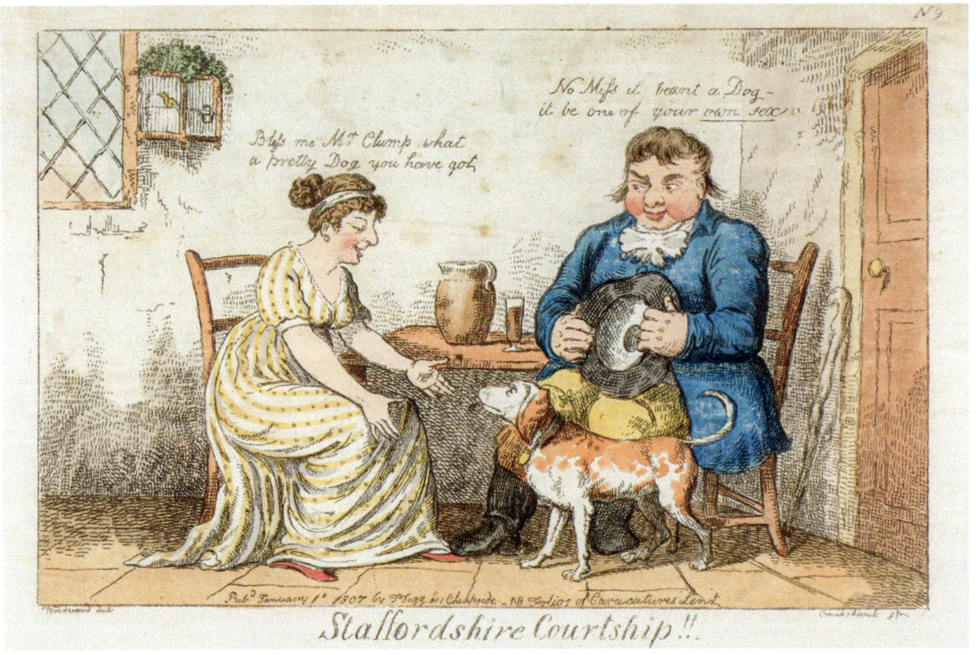

Figure 32 | Isaac Cruikshank and George Woodward, *Staffordshire Courtship!!*,
January 1, 1807. Courtesy American Antiquarian Society.

American and British caricatures, with publication dates ranging between 1797 and 1806. One of the British caricatures found within the Peirce collection is *Staffordshire Courtship!!* (fig. 32) by Isaac Cruikshank and George Woodward, published for Thomas Tegg, the publication line of which includes "Folios of Caracatures [*sic*] Lent."

Contemporary sources such as newspapers and letters provide great detail and context regarding the caricatures published during the 1790s and the early 1800s. Many of the caricatures from this period were issued anonymously, but their scope and appeal helped them to reach many different citizens in various venues. Previous scholarship has often dismissed these caricatures; however, in the discovery of new anonymously published satires from this period, along with descriptions of caricatures not known to have survived, it is possible to build a stronger narrative for the American audience of such visual humor. As the following chapters on James Akin and William Charles reveal, there was little amusement for those that found themselves attacked in caricature.

CHAPTER 2

James Akin's Career Before Caricature

James Akin stands out among the anonymously published caricaturists. His career as an engraver spanned more than fifty years, from the 1790s until his death in 1846, and he was the first American-born artist and engraver to design, publish, and sign his caricature prints. His output in this medium forms the foundation that enabled later caricaturists of the nineteenth century to become effective in producing lithographic caricature prints. Before Akin published caricature, he was a copperplate engraver of portrait and book illustrations. His inclination to the arts was nurtured in the 1780s and early 1790s. Fortunate financial circumstances allowed him to leave his birthplace of Charleston, South Carolina, to pursue an artistic education in England. His time in London, although brief, can be considered an important phase that influenced how he approached his career in subsequent decades. There, he had the opportunity to observe a thriving print market that included an abundance of shops and exhibitions containing caricature. Other American artists in London must have been aware of the saturation of caricature, but it was Akin who first brought this kind of visual satire to the United States. Although the majority of Akin's career was spent in Philadelphia, between 1804 and 1807 he was based in Newburyport, Massachusetts. There he published caricatures primarily in response to a professional dispute with his employer. These engravings were popular with a local audience; buoyed by a newfound confidence, he turned to caricaturing political subjects and changed his career trajectory.

Politics were an important factor in Akin's life. As he matured as an engraver, he targeted his prints for an audience engaged with the politics of the day, publishing portraits of Thomas Jefferson and George Washington, images that would sell. In this, Akin was not unique: other engravers, following the lead of Charles Willson Peale, also published engravings of leading politicians. A position early in his career as a clerk in the John Adams administration may have provided assurance in the political arena while cementing an early allegiance within the Federalist Party to Washington and Adams. A connection to politics, coupled with his skill as an engraver and his knowledge of caricature, shaped an awareness for propaganda at an early stage in his career.

Akin, a keen self-promoter, was consistent in using newspapers to publicize his profession. The contemporary newspapers referenced in the previous chapter are important to understanding both the sparseness and vibrancy of the culture and market for caricature prints during this period. This was the environment Akin entered with his first caricature prints. He relied on the power and reach of early American newspapers. Beginning in the late 1790s, Akin advertised subscriptions for prints, the availability to purchase recently published engravings, and announced his arrival and departure from cities. In newspapers spanning the first two decades of the nineteenth century, his name appears more often than that of his contemporary, William Charles. He was also an avid writer, sending letters to artists and politicians, and the breadth of this correspondence indicates that Akin understood the necessity of networking to expand his circle of colleagues and friends. Throughout his career, Akin strove for prominent positions and recognition as an artist of merit within the world of American art at a time when the republic was in its infancy.

Akin's Early Life in Charleston

James Akin was born in either 1772 or 1773, into an affluent family, the first child of Thomas and Ann Christie.[1] His paternal grandfather, also named James, died in 1758 having amassed substantial wealth that included sizeable acreage and enslaved people. Akin's birth came during a turbulent period in Charleston as the city fell under British occupation in the late 1770s during the Revolutionary War, prompting Thomas Akin to finalize his will and establish a plan for the future care of his three young children. His instructions to his wife were to liquidate most of their estate after his death, the profits of which would provide an inheritance to be applied to their support and education. His prudence was well founded: Thomas died in 1780, leaving his three young children in the care of the Reverend Dr. Robert Smith of St. Philips Parish in Charleston, one of three guardians named in the will.[2] The two other guardians were family members, one of whom had already died and had left an additional bequest to James and his siblings. The details of the arrangement, though, are not clear because Ann Christie survived her husband to live another fifty years. It can be assumed that Smith's role was that of a male advocate for Akin and his siblings in patriarchal Charleston, and one domain where Smith would have had significant influence was Akin's education. He presumably enrolled James and his younger brother Thomas into the academy he founded in 1785, where the brothers would have been taught English, Latin, Greek and French, writing, arithmetic, and geography.[3] It is clear from surviving letters that James was educated: his letters were well written with good penmanship and few (if any) mistakes, and he had some command or knowledge of Latin and literature, inserting quotes from literary sources and Latin references on his caricature prints. Likewise, his younger brother Thomas submitted his doctoral thesis in medicine (written in Latin) at the University of Edinburgh in 1799.[4]

Smith also provided Akin with opportunities to meet politicians through his own family and network. His reputable standing in Charleston society included a strong connection to local politics, especially to the influential Rutledge family. John Rutledge Sr. represented South Carolina in national affairs, was governor of the state during the Revolutionary War, and served as a justice on the United States Supreme Court, while his son John Rutledge Jr. was a lawyer and a member of House of Representatives. Smith's relationship to the Rutledge family was further strengthened in 1791 when his daughter Sarah Motte Smith married John Rutledge Jr. It was likely through Smith that Akin met Rutledge Jr., who recommended Akin as a clerk to secretary of state Timothy Pickering, thus providing Akin with the opportunity to work in Philadelphia in the new government in the late 1790s.[5]

His father's will provided James with a better start than many in his situation: he had the well-connected Smith as a guardian and financial stability with an inheritance. The city of Charleston also played a crucial role in Akin's development, offering a cultured environment for him to follow his artistic pursuits. According to art historian Carolyn Weekley, Charleston was an important hub of artistic activities immediately before and after the Revolutionary War.[6] The fourth-largest city in the United States and the largest city in the South, Charleston had close to fifteen thousand inhabitants and an abundance of wealthy citizens who were strong employment prospects for portraitists. There were opportunities in Charleston to take lessons in drawing, painting, and engraving. Henry Benbridge (1743–1812) and Thomas Coram (1756–1811) are two important artists in Charleston at this time that can later be linked to Akin. Benbridge arrived in Charleston 1772 with his wife Hetty Sage (d. 1776) after almost a decade in Europe, where he had studied in London under Benjamin West.[7] Although there are no advertisements for Benbridge as an instructor, it is thought that he provided Thomas Coram with lessons. Coram later opened his own drawing school in 1784, "for the purpose of instructing youth in that useful and pleasing art; and having a large collection of prints, and studies of every kind."[8] In that same year, the artist David Oliphant also opened a school, "for the purpose of teaching young gentlemen the art of DRAWING in Black Lead, Indian Ink and Water Colours, &c."[9] Oliphant stated that ladies were also welcome but felt it prudent to teach them in their own homes. In a subsequent advertisement, Oliphant added that classes would operate in the evenings.[10] The market for the arts and art instruction was so competitive in Charleston that shortly after Oliphant's notice, Coram announced he too would provide additional hours for instruction in the evening: "His Drawing School, is still continued in his house, and for the benefit of those who cannot spare time in the day, he has devoted his evenings to that purpose."[11] With Coram, Oliphant, and Benbridge available for instruction, Akin would have had his choice of tutors. Akin likely met Coram and Benbridge at this time, because in the following decade he included the names of Coram and of Henry Benbridge Jr. (b. 1773), a minor artist and son of Henry Benbridge, on a subscription list for an engraving project.[12]

Artists from Philadelphia were also attracted to the city of Charleston. John Trumbull and brothers Raphaelle and Rembrandt Peale came to Charleston in the 1790s, and like Coram and Benbridge these artists are later connected to Akin and his career in Philadelphia.[13] Trumbull was based in Charleston for three months between February and April 1791, painting portraits of local figures to be used in a subscription series of prints dedicated to Revolutionary War heroes.[14] The sons of Charles Willson Peale, Rembrandt and Raphaelle arrived in Charleston in December 1795 and brought copies of these works. According to a newspaper announcement, the Peale brothers carried with them "a large collection of portraits of those patriots who most distinguished themselves in securing the Independence of these States, many of whom are now dead; which they propose to exhibit, with a number of other pieces, as soon as a convenient room for the purpose can be procured."[15] Akin's whereabouts in 1795 are generally not known: he may have already left Charleston by this time, although it is also possible that Akin's relationship to the Peale family began in Charleston. By 1797, when Akin is in Philadelphia, he lists all three Peale names in newspaper advertisements for an uncompleted engraving project.

These artists likely provided some form of instruction and counsel to Akin, as his career choices in the 1790s show that this artistic community influenced him. By 1794, the decision to leave Charleston might have been made when Akin completed the engraving of text for the Philadelphia print publisher Mathew Carey. Akin was roughly twenty-one years of age in this year, and he must have sufficiently acquired the skills of a draftsman and engraver to gain an introduction to Carey and to receive a commission to engrave 763 words on the plate for "Map of Scotland."[16] This is Akin's first known engraving project, and it was neither a simple nor an entry-level task. Akin would have proved himself worthy of it, either by way of an introduction, perhaps from one of the artists in Charleston, or by examples of his engravings, or both. Sometime afterward, Akin made the bold decision to go to London. By doing so, Akin was taking part in an established tradition of young male American artists who had gone abroad to receive instruction in the arts, including a number of artists connected to him, such as Charles Willson Peale, Henry Benbridge Sr., and John Trumbull.

Akin's Professional Circles in London

In a letter written to the British engraver Thomas Bewick when he was twenty-three or twenty-four years of age, Akin stated that he was in London in 1796.[17] By his twenty-first birthday Akin likely received access to his inheritance, which would have provided the funds to self-finance his international trip. The timing of his travel to London could have also aligned with his younger brother's educational plans. In December 1796, Thomas was enrolled as a medical student at the University of Edinburgh, and perhaps the brothers traveled together.[18] For James, the destination was London and the Royal Academy, where his circle included Benjamin West, James Heath, and Thomas Stothard. It is known he entered this network of established artists from two separate newspaper notices in the first decade of the nineteenth century. In an 1804 notice, Akin claimed that he had "completed his professional studies in London under an eminent master."[19] Sometime later, Akin expanded on this with further details by stating that he "was instructed in LONDON, by *James Heath*, Esq. his present *Majesty's Engraver*, during which time he received considerable improvement from the criticisms of his countryman, Mr. *West*, who sanctioned his attendance *to the Royal Academy*. Possessing a testimonial of the above, he hopes by attentive endeavours to please, that he will satisfy those who favour him with their commands."[20] A ticket for an evening lecture at the Royal Academy, dated January 8 and signed by West, with Akin's name on it, has survived and supports his claims of having a connection to the Royal Academy.[21] How Akin gained entry into Benjamin West's circle is not clear: perhaps Smith or one of the artists he had come to know in Charleston and Philadelphia provided Akin an introduction.

While he may have attended classes and lectures at the Royal Academy through Benjamin West, "who sanctioned his attendance," Akin's name does not appear in the student matriculation records from this period. Martin Myrone, who has extensively researched the history of students at the Royal Academy, reveals that a high proportion of West's pupils asserted that they had attended classes despite not being officially registered and there being no record of their attendance. Akin is to be included in this group. Myrone has established a detailed demographic history of the American artists in West's circle,

54

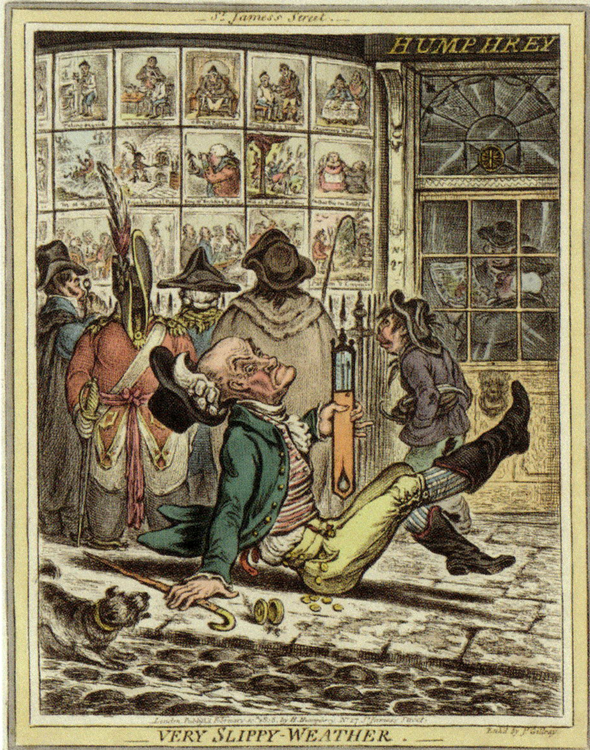

Figure 33 | James Gillray, after the Rev. John Sneyd, *Very Slippy-Weather*, February 10, 1808. Hand-colored etching and graving on wove paper, plate 10 1/4 × 8 1/16 in., sheet 11 × 8 1/8 in. Gift of the Arcana Foundation, accession number 1996.51.1, National Gallery of Art, Washington, DC.

the majority of whom had financial resources and were "unusually well-educated."[22] Akin fits within these parameters: his background was similar to other American artists in London. Akin likely found a welcome environment in West's company. The Royal Academy president had a reputation as a gracious mentor to visiting Americans.[23] Although it is possible Akin was introduced to West, Charles Willson Peale later wrote that simply being an American was enough to gain entry to West's studio.[24] West's home and studio was located in a four-story Georgian townhouse at 14 Newman Street and served as both a showplace and museum for his impressive art collection.[25] The physical location of West's studio held other advantages: Newman Street was later referred to as a "street of artists."[26] Akin would have been in close proximity to this community of peers. He had only to walk left or right on Newman Street to meet neighboring artists and Royal Academicians James Heath and Thomas Stothard.[27]

In this environment, Akin experienced the myriad opportunities only available in a major global city with an established and flourishing art market. It would have been impossible for Akin to ignore London's thriving print commerce, a scene unlike what he had witnessed in Charleston and Philadelphia. By the time Akin arrived in 1796, London

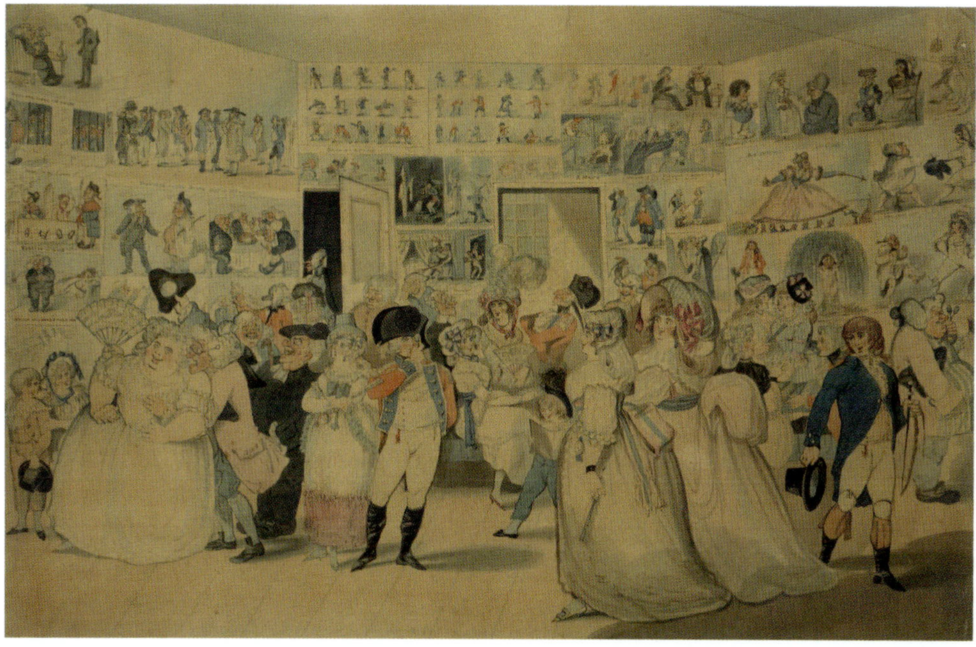

Figure 34 | Richard Newton, *Holland's Exhibition Room*, n.d. [ca. 1794]. British Museum. © The Trustees of the British Museum.

was the most important city for the European print trade, sustaining a range of shops that sold prints of all kinds.[28] The London printshops sold caricatures, their windows often plastered with caricatures facing outside for a passing audience and potential sale. West's home and studio on Newman Street was a short distance from William Holland's shop on Oxford Street and not far from Somerset House, where the Royal Academy was then located. Holland's shop had the largest collection of humorous prints in Europe; while he charged an entrance fee for customers interested in purchasing, the caricatures displayed in his windows were freely available for anyone on the street to view.[29] A number of British caricatures from this period depict the window displays of caricatures, showing groups of figures gathered, as seen in James Gillray's *Very Slippy-Weather* from 1808 (fig. 33). Although there are fewer examples that provide interior details of London caricature shops and exhibitions, Richard Newton's watercolor of the exhibition rooms of Holland's print shop (fig. 34) was completed in 1794, just prior to Akin's arrival in London. Newton's depiction shows walls covered in caricatures of all sizes in a space crowded with well-dressed men and women, groupings that would not look out of a place at an exhibition held at the Royal Academy. Holland's competitor,

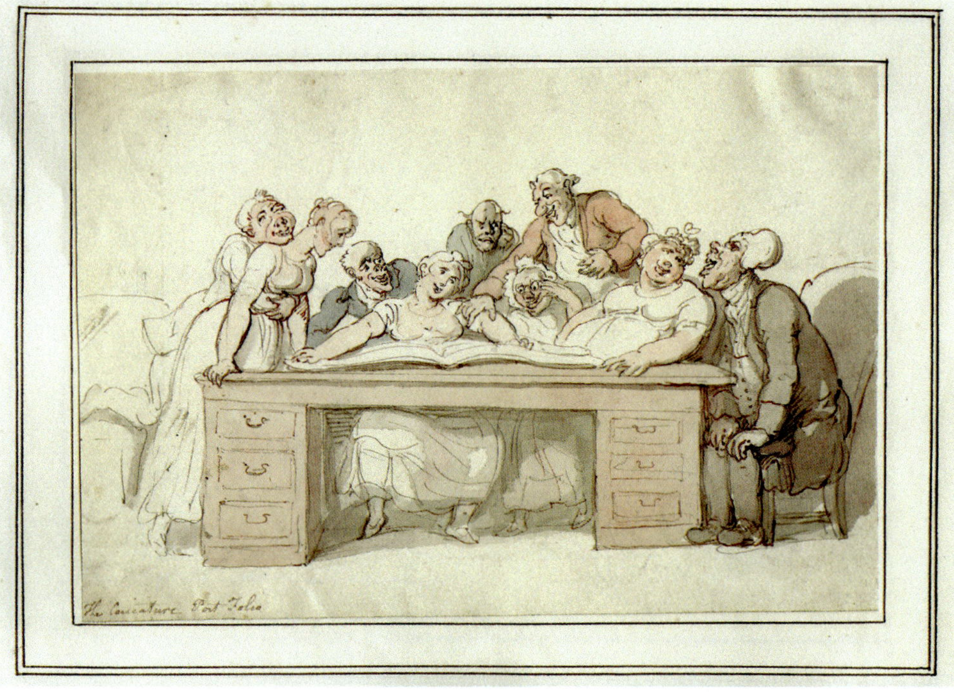

Figure 35 | Thomas Rowlandson, *The Caricature Port Folio*. n.d. Pen and watercolor.
British Museum. © The Trustees of the British Museum.

Samuel Fores, had strategically moved his printshop in 1795 to 50 Piccadilly to accommodate his increasingly affluent and upmarket clientele. The shop had two large front windows that were ideal for displaying caricatures. Like Holland, Fores also charged a fee (one shilling) to enter his shop. Such shops were not the exclusive province of men. Hannah Humphrey had a successful professional and personal relationship with Gillray and was the proprietor of a shop on Bond Street. Humphrey adhered to the models of Fores and Holland by also selling a wide variety of prints and books, so a customer did not necessarily have to be looking for a caricature print to enter these venues. Most of the caricature prints found in these shops were separately published and individually sold; however, some publishers bound caricatures in portfolios or books and offered them to rent. In 1793, Fores advertised this with the statement on the bottom of a caricature print that he was now offering lending folios of caricatures for the evening.[30] Customers would pay a deposit and a fee for the loan of the portfolio, receiving the deposit back upon its safe return. Rowlandson immortalized this practice in a watercolor in which men and women are depicted at a table with a large folio of caricatures open in front of them (fig. 35).

The availability of visual material on view would have been difficult for Akin to ignore on his walks from West's studio to the Royal Academy. Evidence of Akin's exposure to British caricature can be seen several years later: a number of his caricature prints were directly influenced by specific visual satires published in London. Akin's awareness of how London print publishers operated may have also remained with him, inspiring him in 1806 to advertise his own book of bound prints. In London, Akin would have had the opportunity to see how print sellers and publishers functioned, how they addressed their audience, how they gained patronage, and the ways they adapted their designs to their clients. He was able to use what he had seen as a template once he began to draw and publish his own caricature prints.

The (Un)successful Revolutionary War Prints, 1797

Akin returned to the United States, settling in Philadelphia in 1797 "at Powell Street, 4 doors from 5th st. between Spruce and Pine Streets."[31] Energized by his time abroad, Akin announced in newspaper advertisements his intention to publish prints after paintings depicting American Revolutionary War battles (fig. 36). These advertisements were published between June and September 1797 and were placed strategically in newspapers in New York City, Philadelphia, and Charleston. If these advertisements were only brief notices for the engravings, they would not merit further investigation, especially as it does not appear that the project was completed. However, the information provided by Akin reveals that he recognized that such public announcements were an important introduction to potential patrons.

This proposal was ambitious. The advertisement stated his intention to produce three historical engravings after paintings: two of them, *The Eutaw Springs* and *The Cowpens*, depicted battles fought during the Revolutionary War in South Carolina, and the third depicted *The Capture of Major Andre*. Two of the paintings to be engraved, *The Eutaw Springs* and *The Capture of Major Andre*, were by the British artist Thomas Stothard and were owned by Akin. If this initial project were to be successful, Akin planned to publish "other important scenes from our revolutionary war." Publishing historical prints after paintings was not unique to Akin in this period. The subject of revolutionary battles was popular in the new nation, and advertisements similar to his can be found in other contemporary American newspapers. In proposing this project, Akin was demonstrating his awareness of what was current, but he was also responding directly to what he observed from his time in London. Benjamin West had long been a proponent of publishing engravings of historical prints after paintings and had suggested to John Trumbull that he should pursue such projects.[32] In 1790, Trumbull advertised in American

THE FINE ARTS.

To the CITIZENS of the UNITED STATES.

HAVING employed a confiderable part of my life in acquiring a knowledge of the fine arts, from the moft celebrated and efteemed mafters in Europe, and being highly ambitious in tranfmitting to pofterity, portraits of fome of thofe illuftrious characters, whofe heroifm contributed greatly to the eftablifhment of the liberties of America; and alfo of fome of thofe brilliant battles, which will forever be regarded as mafter pieces in the military art, and which placed the United States amongft the freeft and moft independent nations of the earth, I purpofe engraving reprefentations of the two very important battles fought at

THE EUTAW SPRINGS and THE COWPENS,

In the ftate of South-Carolina.

I have this day opened a fubfcription for publifhing the above pieces, and if my undertaking fhall receive the patronage and fupport which I flatter myfelf one fo interefting to my countrymen may expect, I will be enabled to continue my plan of publifhing other important fcenes from our revolutionary war.

That of the Eutaw Springs was painted by the much celebrated STOTHARD; and a few very valuable picture I have which were painted by this diftinguifhed artift, and which may be feen in my poffeffion, will ferve as fpecimens of my friend's great talents to thofe who are unacquainted with his works. The prints will be engraved in the line manner from two original pictures, and their fize will be 2 feet 1 inch, by 1 foot 6 inches.—The price for each print will be 15 dollars; one half to be paid at the time of fubfcribing, for which a receipt will be given. The prints will be delivered in the order they fhall be fubfcribed for, fo that perfons wifhing to have firft impreffions, muft be early in giving in their names. The receipt to be transferable, and the holder entitled to all its advantages as it ftands on the lift.

In addition to the above prints, I propofe engraving, as a centre piece,

THE CAPTURE OF MAJOR ANDRE.

From *Stothard.*

This event being one of the moft interefting which occurred during the American war, and the reprefentation having ftrong likeneffes of André and his brave captors, the print will, I hope, be valued highly by my fellow-citizens. The price will be eight dollars—payment as above. The fize will be 1 foot 2 inches, by 1 foot.

JAMES AKIN, of South-Carolina,

Powell-ftreet, 4 doors from Fifth-ftreet, between Spruce and Pine ftreets.

SUBSCRIPTIONS for the above prints, or either of them, will be received by C. W. Peale, at his mufeum; Thomas Dobfon, and John Ormrod, bookfellers, and Henry Benbridge, jun. South Front-ftreet, near the Drawbridge, Phildelphia; by C. Tiebout, engraver, No. 29, Goldenhill-ftreet, New-York; by R. and R. Peale, at the Mufeum, Baltimore; and by major Shubrick (who was aidde-camp to general Greene, at the Eutaw Springs), and Thomas Coram, Charlefton, S. C.

May 27, 1797.

newspapers for subscriptions of engravings after two of his historical paintings, *The Death of General Warren at the Battle of Bunker Hill* and *The Death of General Montgomery in the Attack of Quebec*, and included the names of other battle scenes proposed to be engraved, including *The Battle of Eutaw Springs*.[33] Trumbull's engraving project brought him to cities along the East Coast to paint portraits of the men represented, eventually arriving in Charleston in 1791, when Akin was at the beginning of his career. Trumbull's project was not completed, nor was a similar project that the New York engraver Cornelius Tiebout announced in 1797, the same year as Akin's, of his intention to publish by subscription engravings after paintings depicting specific battles from the American War of Independence.[34] Tiebout's advertisement listed six battles to be engraved "from original paintings and drawings, by . . . American Artists" and included *The Battle at the Cowpens*.[35] Although Tiebout did not complete this project, he did publish at least one engraving in the series, *The Battle of Lexington* after a painting by the artist Elkanah Tisdale.[36]

Akin's engraving proposal relied on the paintings by Thomas Stothard that he had obtained in London, in addition to "a few very valuable pictures I have, which were painted by this distinguished artist, and which may be seen in my possession, will serve as specimens of my friends great talents, to those who are unacquainted with his work."[37] Although the current locations of these paintings are not known, *The Battle of Eutaw Springs* and *The Capture of Major Andre* were both painted by Stothard, who was already known to a Philadelphia clientele, as he is referred to as "the admired artist" in at least one 1795 advertisement.[38] Akin lent his Stothard painting of *The Battle of Eutaw Springs* to an exhibition at Peale's Museum, suggesting that at this time there existed a professional relationship between Peale and Akin.

If the proposal was bold, so too was the advertisement. It served an important function in providing evidence of the impressive network of artist friends that Akin had constructed in Charleston, Philadelphia, and London. He listed eight men available to take subscriptions for the project, with five of those individuals having already having some established connection to Akin: Charles Willson Peale ("C. W. Peale, at the Museum"); Henry Benbridge Jr. ("South Front-Street, near the Drawbridge, Philadelphia"); Rembrandt and Raphaelle Peale ("at the Museum Baltimore"), and Thomas Coram ("Charleston, South-Carolina"). Akin also named Tiebout, whom he may have met in London when both men had received instruction from the engraver James Heath.[39] Akin described himself in the advertisement as "highly ambitious in transmitting to posterity, portraits of some of those illustrious characters whose heroism contributed greatly to the establishment of the liberties of America." Although he was not able to receive enough subscriptions to see this proposal to completion, Akin would transmit "for posterity" engraved portraits of politicians in the coming years.

Why Akin was unsuccessful in this endeavor is not known, although some theories can be considered. Akin may not have appreciated just how expensive and time-consuming the printing of engravings would be in Philadelphia. In London, where the printing industry had existed for generations, there were artisans to prepare the plates and established print shops to handle the trade and sale of prints.[40] It was a different situation in the United States in the late eighteenth century. The engraver David Edwin described some of the hardships he had encountered in attempting to establish himself as an engraver. Edwin arrived in Philadelphia from London in December 1797 without any tools to practice his trade. Although he quickly received commissions, he complained about the equipment and presses available to him. Engraving tools were not readily available in Philadelphia, and he was forced to make his own, while "copperplates were finished rough from the hammer." For engravers without access to their own press, working conditions were dismal.[41] Akin likely did not own a copperplate press at this time and his experience might have been similar to Edwin's complaints: "Often have I, in extreme cold weather, waited hours for a proof, till the paper, oil, and even the roller could be thawed. The workshop of the principal printer in Philadelphia was little better than a shell, open to winds."[42] If Charles Willson Peale had continued to work as an engraver in 1797, he might have commiserated with Akin and Edwin. Ten years prior, in 1787, Peale had entered the printmaking market but found conditions unsustainable. Unable to procure polished copperplates, Peale soon realized that he had would have to perform all the labor necessary for production and marketing: he prepared the plates, engraved the designs, completed the printing, and finalized the sale of the prints. Peale published only a handful of mezzotints and etchings before stopping entirely to resume his portrait painting and museum work.[43] What emerges from these contemporary accounts are the difficulties and frustrations faced by young, ambitious engravers such as Akin in Philadelphia at the turn of the century.

Another factor that might have exposed Akin's inexperience and aided in the lukewarm reception to the subscription was the high price he established for the prints. He proposed to sell each of the two battle engravings at "15 dollars: one half to be paid at the time of subscription," and *The Capture of Major Andre* for "8 dollars." When compared to the engravings of the same subject matter proposed by Tiebout—three dollars per print for subscribers, five dollars for nonsubscribers—Akin's prices appear far too expensive.

An Engraving Business in Philadelphia, 1798–1803

Despite the failure of his subscription proposal, Akin persevered. In November 1797 Akin married Eliza Cox.[44] This personal milestone might have been his motivation to obtain a stable position with a consistent income outside the arts. During this period, Akin was a clerk for Secretary of State Timothy Pickering, a Massachusetts Federalist, a position he received after an introduction from a Charleston connection, John Rutledge Jr.[45] One official document has been located, dated December 6, 1798, to support evidence of Akin's employment with Pickering, although it remains unclear as to what his duties entailed.[46] From this document, the time he spent in London in 1796, and his engraving activities during the following period, it can be presumed that Akin's position as a clerk was brief and likely coincided with the failure of the subscription proposal and with his marriage. The position with Pickering nevertheless elevated Akin's status, providing opportunities to meet a variety of important influential political leaders and to once more expand his network. Indeed, the connection likely led to the commission to design and engrave a seal for the United States Navy.[47] Akin did not complete this engraving alone, instead partnering with Philadelphia engraver William Harrison Jr. (ca. 1750–1803). The collaboration between Akin and Harrison might have been an attempt to address the challenges of a fledgling printmaking business referenced in the previous section; together they would have been equipped to handle the costs related to engraving, printing, and purchasing ink and paper. Akin and Harrison collaborated on at least four engravings, published between 1798 and 1800. In May 1799 they published a print of Charles Cotesworth Pinckney, after a portrait of the general by the Charleston artist James Earl that was in the possession of Major Thomas Pinckney.[48] In response to Jefferson's election as president, in January 1800 Akin and Harrison advertised "a portrait of the Hon. Thomas Jefferson from the picture now in the Museum painted by C. W. Peale" (fig. 37).[49]

Their most successful engraving was a memorial print of George Washington, published on January 20, 1800, several weeks after his death on December 14, 1799 (fig. 38). Unlike the engravings of Jefferson and Pinckney, both of which were after paintings, this was an original design and was not copied directly from a painting, although they were inspired by other portraits of Washington. The print was especially significant because it was the first published memorial engraving dedicated to the president after his death.[50] The Akin and Harrison print was published in three different states, copied and interpreted by other artists, and its popularity led to impressions of it transferred onto Liverpool pottery.[51] As Wendy Wick Reaves has noted, Akin and Harrison understood the necessity for engraved Washington memorials first, and they anticipated the inevitable competition that would ensue among other artists and engravers. They promoted their engraving, advertising frequently in newspapers and in published broadsides, where they appealed to different audiences and classes by offering the print to be colored. They even provided details on how best to display the print in the home, writing that it was "admirably calculated to ornament a parlor, or hang as a centre-piece between any two other prints."[52] While newspapers advertised to the general public, Akin and Harrison took the added initiative of sending an impression to President John Adams. On January 28, 1800,

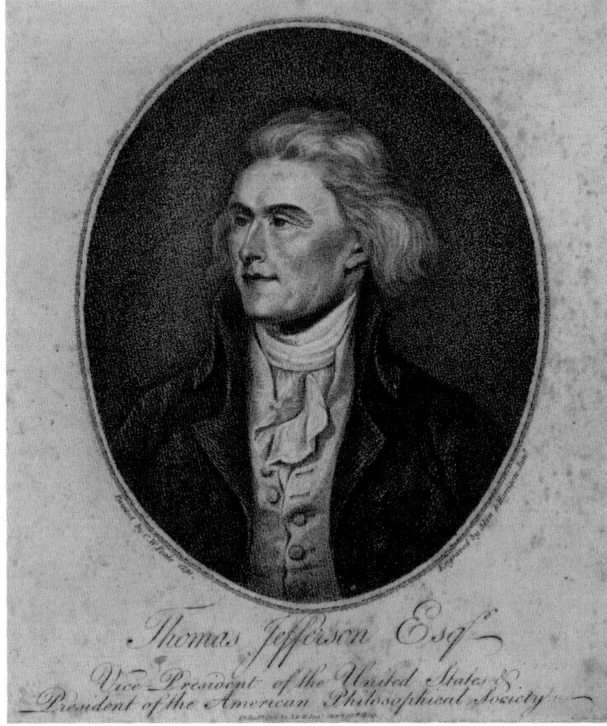

Figure 37 | James Akin and William Harrison Jr., after Charles Willson Peale, *Thomas Jefferson, Esq.*, January 10, 1800. Stipple engraving and etching on cream paper, 5 7/16 × 4 1/4 in. (13.76045 × 10.795 cm). John S. Phillips Collection, 1876.9.1. Courtesy of the Pennsylvania Academy of Fine Arts, Philadelphia.

Akin and Harrison wrote to Adams, "Permit us in the humble movement of Artists to present you with a specimen of Engraving, done in remembrance of our late illustrious and most Amiable General Washington."[53] Although signed with their two signatures, the handwriting in the text of the letter is similar to Akin's as found in other documents from this period.

This engraving's popularity was likely Akin's first taste of commercial success. Soon after its publication, his partnership with Harrison dissolved, with no other engravings attributed to their collaboration. Akin might have chosen to use this triumph to propel his own career forward. In March 1800, Akin published an engraving of the Philadelphia physician Benjamin Rush, after an oil painting by the Philadelphia artist Jeremiah Paul Jr (ca. 1760–1820).[54] There are two versions of the engraving. One version has this inscription below the portrait: "To the Gentlemen of the Faculty & Medical Students throughout the United States, this plate Engraved with the Drs Permission & at the request of the Pupils from the Original Picture in the Proprietor's Possession is Inscribed by their Obed[ien]t Humble Serv[an]t James Akin" (fig. 39).[55] This reference described the "Original Picture in the Proprietor's Possession" would indicate that Akin had this painting by Paul in his collection, joining the paintings he owned by Thomas Stothard.

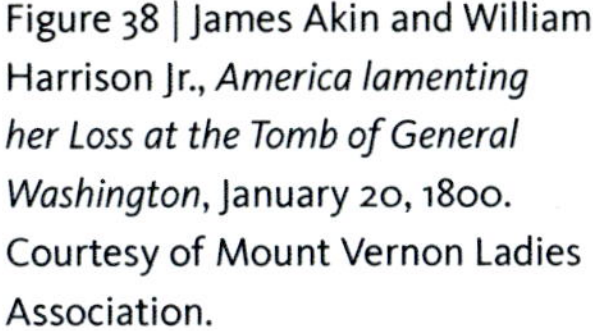

Figure 38 | James Akin and William Harrison Jr., *America lamenting her Loss at the Tomb of General Washington*, January 20, 1800. Courtesy of Mount Vernon Ladies Association.

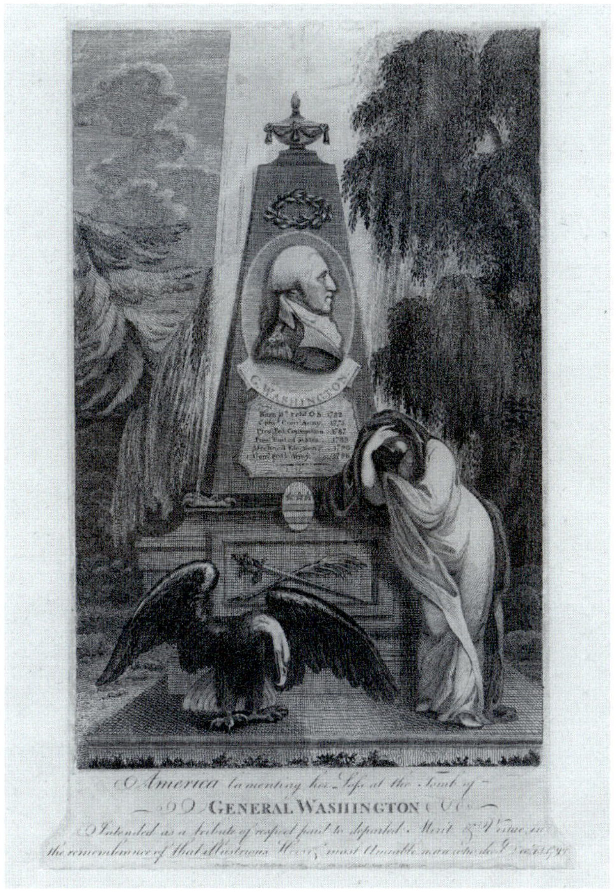

Akin's growing interest in medicine might have led him to the commission of Benjamin Rush. A prestigious physician in Philadelphia, Rush had fought both the 1793 and 1798 epidemics of yellow fever in Philadelphia by a practice of depletions (bleedings). Akin and Rush became acquainted during the latter epidemic, when Rush attended to a mutual friend at Akin's home.[56] Two years after the publication of the Rush engraving, Akin advertised that he had entered the medical field, practicing bleeding and cupping. He boasted in the *Philadelphia Gazette* that he "had the advantage of attending Courses of Anatomical Lectures, in Europe, and of receiving much instruction in the use of the Lancet and Cups, from an eminent practical anatomist in this city, whose friendship and great attention he begs leave this publicly to acknowledge."[57] Rush is potentially the "eminent practical anatomist" who instructed Akin, while the assertion of having attended courses on anatomy in Europe might allude to opportunities he had through his younger brother Thomas, a medical student in Scotland in the late 1790s. His understanding of

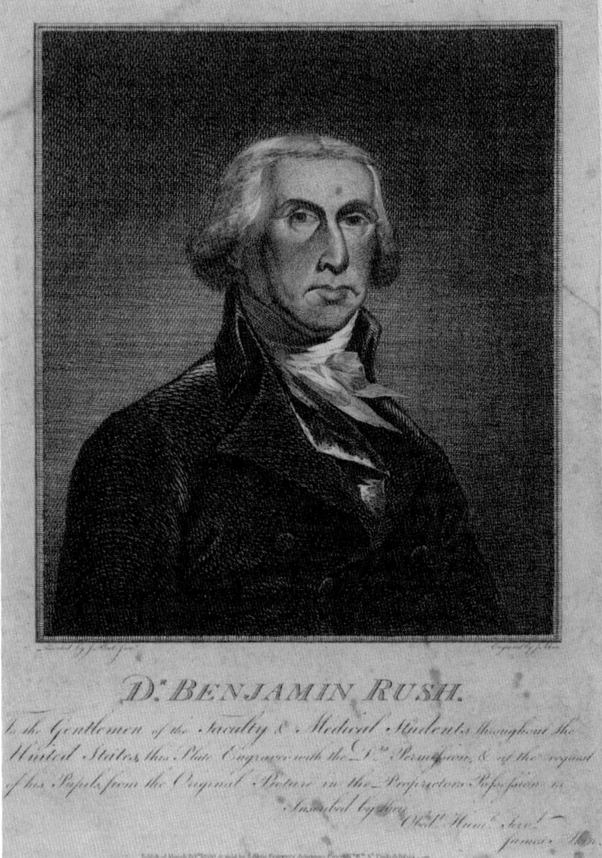

Figure 39 | James Akin, after Jeremiah Paul Jr., *Dr. Benjamin Rush*, March 20, 1800. Etching and engraving on cream paper, 7 3/8 × 6 1/4 in. (18.7325 × 15.875 cm). John S. Phillips Collection, 1876.9.3. Courtesy of the Pennsylvania Academy of Fine Arts, Philadelphia.

medicine and anatomy was also related to his art. His mentor Benjamin West strongly believed that artists should have a thorough knowledge of anatomy, writing in a letter to Charles Willson Peale, "Correctness of outline, and the justness of character in the human figure are eternal; ... color, manners, and costume: they are the marks of various nations; but the form of man has been fixed by eternal laws, and must therefore be immutable."[58] Akin's knowledge of anatomy was another skill applicable to his engraving career.

Akin's medical interest did not go unnoticed. John Uhle, a fellow Philadelphian, penned a notice several days after Akin's advertisement stating that "Akin is an engraver by trade, but having found some equal, if not superior in that art, he has turned his thoughts to bloodletting—Beware Ladies and Gentlemen of this Carolinian.... Is it not surprising that two of eminent physicians should (as he says) have encouraged him to undertake this new trade? It cannot be true!"[59] Uhle must have viewed Akin's new

Figure 40 | *Philadelphia Gazette and Daily Advertiser*, June 16, 1802. Courtesy American Antiquarian Society.

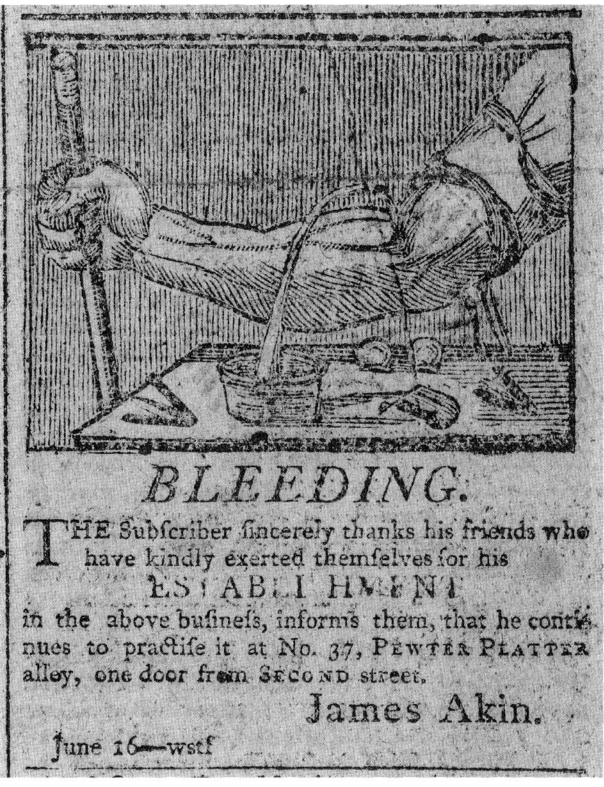

interest as a threat to his own business of bleeding and cupping; meanwhile, Akin may have read Uhle's negative endorsement, because the following month he omitted the word "cupping" from an advertisement.[60] While Uhle's advertisement contained only text, Akin's skill as an engraver enabled him to illustrate his advertisements with a woodcut of his endeavor, which depicted an arm open and blood spouting into a cup (fig. 40). Akin announced his ability to perform this medical procedure; however, perhaps in a sly rebuttal to Uhle, with the image he was also reminding Philadelphia customers of his proficiency in engraving.

During the period between 1797 and 1803, Akin found some success at engraving trade cards and illustrations in books.[61] Akin also appears to have incorporated his wife Eliza into his business, as she contributed at least one engraving to *Lessons for Children Part II*, an illustrated book by Anna Barbauld, signing "Eliza Akin fecit" below the image of a rooster.[62] James's professional relationship with the Peale family was further strengthened in the late 1790s. In 1799, Akin produced engravings of fossil bones after drawings by Titian Peale (d. 1799), and in late 1801, Akin completed an engraving for letterhead and subscriptions for Peale's Museum (fig. 41).[63] The museum engraving should

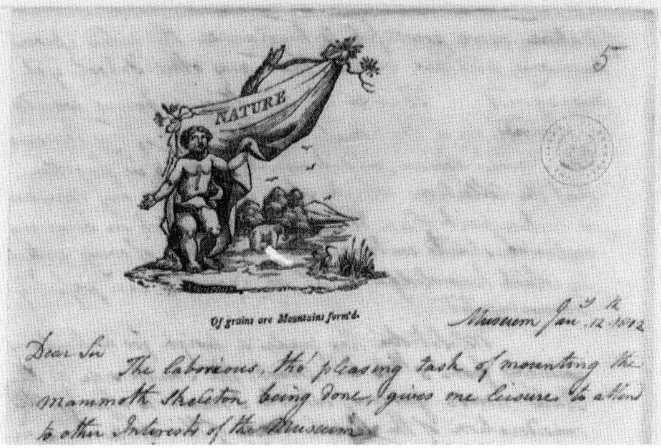

Figure 41 | Charles Willson Peale to Thomas Jefferson, letter with engraving titled *Nature* by James Akin (ca. 1801), January 12, 1802. Thomas Jefferson Papers at the Library of Congress: Series 1: General Correspondence, Manuscript Division, Library of Congress.

have been one of Akin's most important projects, propelling his career to some level of prestige. There is no doubt Akin would have been aware of the potential audience for his engraving and, with it, Peale's seal of approval, which is perhaps why Akin included his name so prominently within the vignette. However, no other engravings or artwork can be found after this date that connect Peale and Akin; their relationship appears to have ended sometime in 1802. Even without a connection to Peale, Akin remained active in engraving and continued to receive commissions, working with other artists, publishers, and engravings.

By the end of 1802 Akin hired an apprentice, William Kneass (1780–1840).[64] A surviving invoice lists the various engraving projects commissioned to Akin and the assignments allocated to Kneass, who was responsible for such tasks as engraving text on certificates and labels for vials of medicine at Akin's apothecary shop.[65] The invoice offers an insight into the engraving work that someone with Akin's skill would be hired to perform: for example, his clientele was diverse, ranging from the fine arts ("Portrait of Wesley," "View of the City of New York for Birch," "A Map of South Carolina for J. Drayton") to more mundane tasks ("a tooth powder label"). During his seven-month apprenticeship, Kneass worked on nineteen different engraving projects, including "4 bank notes for Mr. Pain of Boston." Banknotes had been a specialty of Akin's since at least 1799. Akin might have become interested in engraving currency as early as his time in Charleston, since Thomas Coram had been hired to engrave interest bills. Akin could have also learned this skill while in London from James Heath, who at that time was responsible for engraving banknotes.[66] The experience engraving currency opened other professional doors. Although based in London, Heath is potentially the connection that links Akin to Jacob Perkins (1766–1849), the Newburyport, Massachusetts, goldsmith, inventor, and mechanical engineer. Heath and Perkins, though separated by the Atlantic Ocean, corresponded at some length. In 1799, Perkins published notices in Philadelphia and Newburyport announcing his invention of a method of detecting counterfeit bank paper. He cited the approbation of "James Akin, Engraver," along with two other Philadelphia-based engravers, James Smither and Robert Scot.[67] Because Perkins lived and worked in Newburyport, he may have been an important factor in Akin's decision to move there. In the ensuing years, as Akin published caricature prints, Perkins would be his closest ally.[68]

CHAPTER 3

America's First Caricaturist

In Newb'ryport, a famous place
For trade and navigation . . .
—James Akin, "The Skillet. A Song," 1805

The small but thriving coastal city of Newburyport, Massachusetts might appear to be an unusual spot for the first grouping of published caricature prints in the United States signed by an artist, James Akin. Removed from the national politics of Philadelphia, New York, and the new capital of Washington, DC, Newburyport had its advantages. As an engraver, Akin fit in well in the city that, in the nineteenth century, had a reputation for attracting "craftsmen, artists, engravers, publishers, and entertainers."[1] Painters and printers arrived; some stayed for a period of time while others passed through on their way to Boston or New York. Accommodation for these itinerant artists was plentiful. Rooms were offered at Davenport's Tavern located on State Street, while Samuel Richardson ran a boardinghouse in Union Hall as early as 1799 before removing his "Genteel" establishment first to Water Street and soon after to Market Square.[2] Richardson's was the preferred accommodation for the miniature painter John Roberts in January 1801 and for the profile cutter William King in January 1805.[3] Art materials were readily available at a number of establishments. "An assortment of Painters Colours, wholesale and retail" was sold by Benjamin Tucker, an artist and engraver who also offered instruction in drawing and painting, from his store on State Street.[4] Joseph Noyes offered paint required by artists, while Samuel Goodhue sold copperplates.[5] Those that stayed in town were spoiled for choice of things to purchase: Newburyport's waterfront allowed for shipments of all kinds of domestic and foreign goods, sold in stores along State Street and Market Square. In considering a sample of advertisements from one page of the *Newburyport*

Herald published in May 1802, there are rich examples of the diverse quality of items on offer, from the regional to the exotic: parasols and silk handkerchiefs could be purchased from O'Brien and Toppan on Water Street; William W. Proust had for sale "articles in the English and West India Goods line"; while Mark Coffin at his establishment on Market Square offered "fresh supply of EUROPEAN GOODS."[6] John Barnard offered "fresh raisins, figs . . . and a few jars of excellent olives."[7]

The bookselling and publishing business was especially lucrative in Newburyport in the early 1800s, with four proprietors clustered near the waterfront at Market Square and State Street. Edmund March Blunt's bookstore was located on State Street, next to the printing offices of the *Newburyport Herald*, established in 1797 with the merger of two forerunner newspapers.[8] Blunt's occasional partner in the bookselling business, Ebenezer Stedman, ran the "Newburyport Book, Chart, and Stationery STORE," and in April 1804 he moved to the same address as Blunt's store.[9] On Market Square were two other bookstores, Angier March's "Essex Bookstore" at 13 Market Square, and in June 1803 Isaiah Thomas Jr. announced his "New and Cheap Bookstore," operated with local partner Charles Whipple.[10] Nearby, Jacob Perkins was perfecting his patent for stereotype plates, to be used for the engraving of banknotes, and was to be influential in national banking in the years to come.[11]

This was the Newburyport that James Akin and his wife Eliza found when they arrived in late 1803 or early 1804.[12] James had been persuaded to move from Philadelphia by Edmund March Blunt with the promise of steady employment. Blunt had been actively looking for printing help since April 1803, perhaps because of problems he had encountered with the 1802 publication of the first edition of *The New American Practical Navigator* by Nathaniel Bowditch. A lecture delivered in March 1803, and subsequently published in New York, claimed to present "genuine principles of common refutation of the false and spurious principles ignorantly imposed on the public in the 'New American practical navigator.'"[13] Corrections were needed for the next edition, and this likely prompted Blunt to search for four "journeymen printers" in April and May 1803, placing advertisements in the local newspaper with the promise of "constant employ for two years and cash paid when due."[14] Blunt's business was productive, his name consistently found in newspapers noting the availability of new books, pamphlets, and a variety of domestic and imported goods on offer. Blunt also announced vacancies and the need for journeymen printers and bookbinders, which was relatively frequent. His print shop on State Street must have been chaotic and boisterous from the printers who worked on the presses churning out the various publications.

In June and July, Blunt repeated separate advertisements for an individual proficient in copperplate engraving: "Any person who is acquainted with the different branches of *Copperplate Engraving* may have constant employ and good wages."[15] While Blunt may have been more fortunate in hiring journeymen printers, he was unable to find a local copperplate engraver. As the months went on, he must have felt increasingly desperate to hire someone to complete the work required, especially as his indentured apprentice, George Franklin Williams, had left a void by running away.[16] At least eight months passed between the date of the initial advertisement and February 3, 1804, when Akin signed a contract with Blunt. In order to entice Akin to leave Philadelphia, Blunt provided him with additional incentives to agree on the contract. The agreement stated that while Akin was to be a resident in Newburyport, Blunt would offer constant employment for at least five years and pay Akin the rates he would have charged and received in Philadelphia for the same work; in cases when there had been nothing comparable, "the price of the same should be estimated according to the difficulty of the work and the time necessarily employed in executing it valuing time at the same rate it was usually valued by the said James in said city of Philadelphia."[17] Despite these terms, Akin was hesitant to make a permanent move, as he kept an address in Philadelphia through 1805.[18]

Akin did not announce his arrival in Newburyport until April 27, 1804, almost three months after the contract was signed. Ambitious, he did not limit the notice of his arrival to Newburyport, placing notices in newspapers in cities in Massachusetts, Maine, and New Hampshire, declaring he was proficient in "Engraving in General" having "completed his professional studies, under an eminent master [Benjamin West]."[19] He also provided as his reason for leaving Philadelphia an outbreak of yellow fever. While Akin had at least two reasons to move to Newburyport—his association with Jacob Perkins and a position with Blunt—the yellow fever story might have been a more convenient tale to hide emerging fractures in his Philadelphia network. The surviving William Kneass invoice referenced in the previous chapter was used in a lawsuit against Akin and is evidence that there might have been difficulties within his professional circle. As well, his recent venture of practicing bloodletting may allude to him needing to find an alternative income. Further to this, as an engraver in the city of Philadelphia, Akin had trouble obtaining tools and copperplates. Blunt's contract with Akin specified that he would provide him with the necessary tools and equipment to complete his engravings, "furnishing plates and such things as the work was to [be] executed upon."[20] The poor conditions for individual printers in Philadelphia could indicate why this this was included. Blunt's offer held the potential in Newburyport of a new start for himself and Eliza, whose own engraving might have the opportunity to flourish there.

Blunt, with Akin's help, must have initially addressed the shortcomings in the first edition of Bowditch, because in March 1804 Blunt secured copyright for *An Appendix to the New American Practical Navigator*; its tables were to be calculated "by a new method" and "all corrections … additive."[21] The publication in May of the *Appendix*—"Illustrated with Copperplates"—corresponded with another project introduced

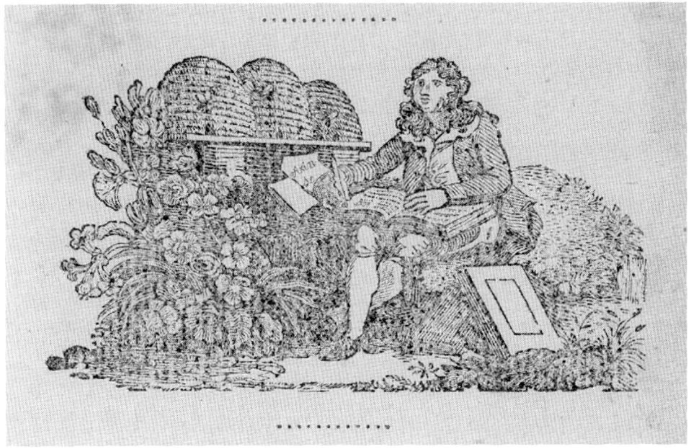

Figure 42 | James Akin, engraving on the title page of *A New System of Mercantile Arithmetic*, by Michael Walsh, published by Edmund March Blunt, Newburyport, Massachusetts, 1804. Courtesy American Antiquarian Society.

by Blunt, a subscription for engraved profiles of "the late Right Reverend Edward Bass, D.D. Bishop of the Episcopal Churches of Massachusetts, New-Hampshire and Rhode Island … to be executed by an eminent Artist," presumably Akin.[22] Also in that same month, Blunt announced that in his store "specimens of Copperplate Engravings may be seen" that were "executed in a style of elegance unequalled in [Massachusetts]."[23] On the cover of Blunt's 1804 publication *A New System of Mercantile Arithmetic* (fig. 42) Akin displayed his name prominently on a piece of paper found in the middle of the engraved vignette. The start of the partnership between Akin and Blunt appeared to have been productive. However, between June and October 1804, their professional relationship was unravelling, leading to accusations related to inconsistencies of payment. By October 27 Akin had "ceased … working in said art or profession and neglected and refused to do the work," resulting in delays to Blunt's publications.[24] Tensions continued between the two men in early November, with Blunt accusing Akin of being a "thief" for stealing a copperplate and paper from him. Akin countered Blunt's accusation with a request for a duel, "with sword or pistol."[25] Akin had accepted work in November from Blunt's occasional business partner, fellow bookseller Ebenezer Stedman, to produce "elegant" engravings for *A Perpetual Almanac*; Akin may have used Blunt's materials for this project, perhaps prompting Blunt's name-calling.[26] Akin and Blunt filed at least five lawsuits against one another between late 1804 and early 1807.[27]

Through this tumultuous time, Akin continued to promote his engraving business, aligning his services with the Newburyport publisher and bookselling proprietors Thomas and Whipple. In January 1805 he moved his business to the center of town, "directly over Thomas and Whipple's Bookstore, Market Square," where he continued to make "Copper-Plates neatly printed."[28] The following month Akin advertised that he was producing profile cuts and paintings, in preparation for the imminent removal of itinerant artist William King (active 1804–9).[29] The use of a "physiognotrace," which Akin referenced in his advertisement, may have further reflected his previous connections to Peale and his Philadelphia museum. A physiognotrace, an instrument used to trace a person's physiognomy to profile, had been installed by Peale at his museum, where it held the public's fascination.[30] The method continued to be of interest in- and outside of Philadelphia and, with King's departure leaving a void for profiles in the city, Akin absorbed the demand from his patrons. He informed the public that the prices charged for paintings ranged from "2 to 4 dollars" and for "cutting 6 cents each," and that he was available at all hours, "from 9 o'clock till 9 in the evening at his house."[31] This proved a lucrative business, and he continued to produce likenesses, reporting two months later that he was working "upon an improved plan" and that he was "highly obliged to those Ladies and Gentlemen, who have repeatedly called to patronise his undertaking[.] Ladies attended thro' out the day, and gentlemen in the evening only."[32] Akin found success in this and had a growing patronage, as evidenced by a notice placed by Akin for a customer that, having his profile traced, had forgotten his "Great Coat."[33]

Akin traveled outside of Newburyport when necessary for commissions. He went, for example, to Hampton, New Hampshire, to make profiles of Thomas and Hannah Leavitt and engrave a map of the town.[34] Akin's ability to solicit customers was successful, as seen with the commission from the Leavitts, but he also received interest from some individuals engaged in nefarious acts. In November 1804, Akin was contacted by a man named Baxtor Lyon to make counterfeit banknotes for the Manhattan Company bank and others, a job Akin refused and about which he notified the local authorities.[35] In June 1805, he received a letter from John McKown of Portland, Maine, with a request for an impression of a horse on metal or wood. This order resulted in Akin filing a suit against McKown for lack of payment after he refused to pay Akin's price.[36]

While Akin endeavored to make his time in Newburyport a success, he was embroiled in court cases with Blunt, and this was exacerbated by an altercation involving a skillet that occurred sometime between October 1804 and May 1805.[37] Although not referenced in the court cases, according to the antiquarian F. B. Sanborn, Blunt and Akin met in the hardware shop of Josiah Foster located on State Street, where an argument between the two men resulted in Blunt throwing a nearby skillet at Akin.[38] The skillet missed its intended target and hit Nicholas Brown, a local ship captain. Contemporary accounts of this have not been located, but Akin might have subtly referred to it in a November 9 advertisement when he stated that he "continues to carry on the Engraving Business in a variety of branches" and that he had "furnished himself with a Press."[39] For Akin, armed with his own printing press and no longer dependent on Blunt, the skillet incident was the impetus for his career as a caricaturist.

Caricature in Newburyport: The Beginning, June 1, 1805

74

Previous to the caricatures that Akin first produced, engravers and artists had primarily been prompted by political episodes. For Akin, though, it was personal. Blunt had attacked his character and thus became both target and inspiration. The caricatures that relate to the infamous skillet incident are thought to be Akin's first attempts in the medium. Published and offered for sale on June 1, 1805, *Infuriated Despondency!* (fig. 43) depicts Blunt, alone and without a background, except for a few engraved lines at his feet. Akin provided Blunt with two attributes: bulging eyes (a trademark Akin would use in future caricatures as well) and a mangled right hand. While the feature of the skillet alluded to the incident at Josiah Foster's hardware store, it is not clear why Akin chose to make Blunt's hand disfigured, as no reference (either factual or mocking) has been located to Blunt having any problems with his hands. Around this time, either before or after the caricature was printed, Akin also produced a broadside consisting of thirteen verses that mocked Blunt and the incident, titled "The Skillet. A Song. Written in the Iron Age," to the tune of "Yankee Doodle" (fig. 44). Akin helpfully included at the top of the sheet an image of a three-footed skillet similar to the one seen in *Infuriated Despondency!* Akin initially advertised the print for sale in the *Newburyport Herald* in July 1805, soon after it was published. It was "calculated for Writing Book Covers for Children and adapted with singular taste to amuse their Juvenile Fantasy."[40]

The popularity of this print or Akin's desire to annoy Blunt, or both, persisted, and soon afterward the caricature design was placed on pottery. No contemporary information survives regarding the background of this venture, but it was reported by Sanborn that Akin sent impressions of *Infuriated Despondency!* to England with Nicholas Brown, the local ship captain who had been hit by the skillet, to arrange for the image to be transferred on to pottery. After this, pitchers and chamber pots were sent back from England to Newburyport.[41] This endeavor was successful for what it was likely intended to do: aggravate Blunt, who had his family and friends retrieve and destroy as many pieces of the pottery as they could find. At least two pitchers have survived, with the placement of the Blunt caricature different on each.[42] One of the pitchers was a private commission for the family of Captain Nicholas Brown that included a small version of Blunt below imagery relevant to the family (fig. 45). Perhaps Akin saw an entrepreneurial opportunity, because the other pitcher, which may have been a production piece, has Blunt's image on one full side of the pottery below the title "A Droll Scene in Newbury Port."[43]

On the same day that Akin published the caricature of Blunt in *Infuriated Despondency!* he also produced two further caricatures of Blunt, designed also to be book covers. Both *An Edict from Saint Peter* (fig. 46) and *A Confidential Intrigue!!!* (fig. 47) include

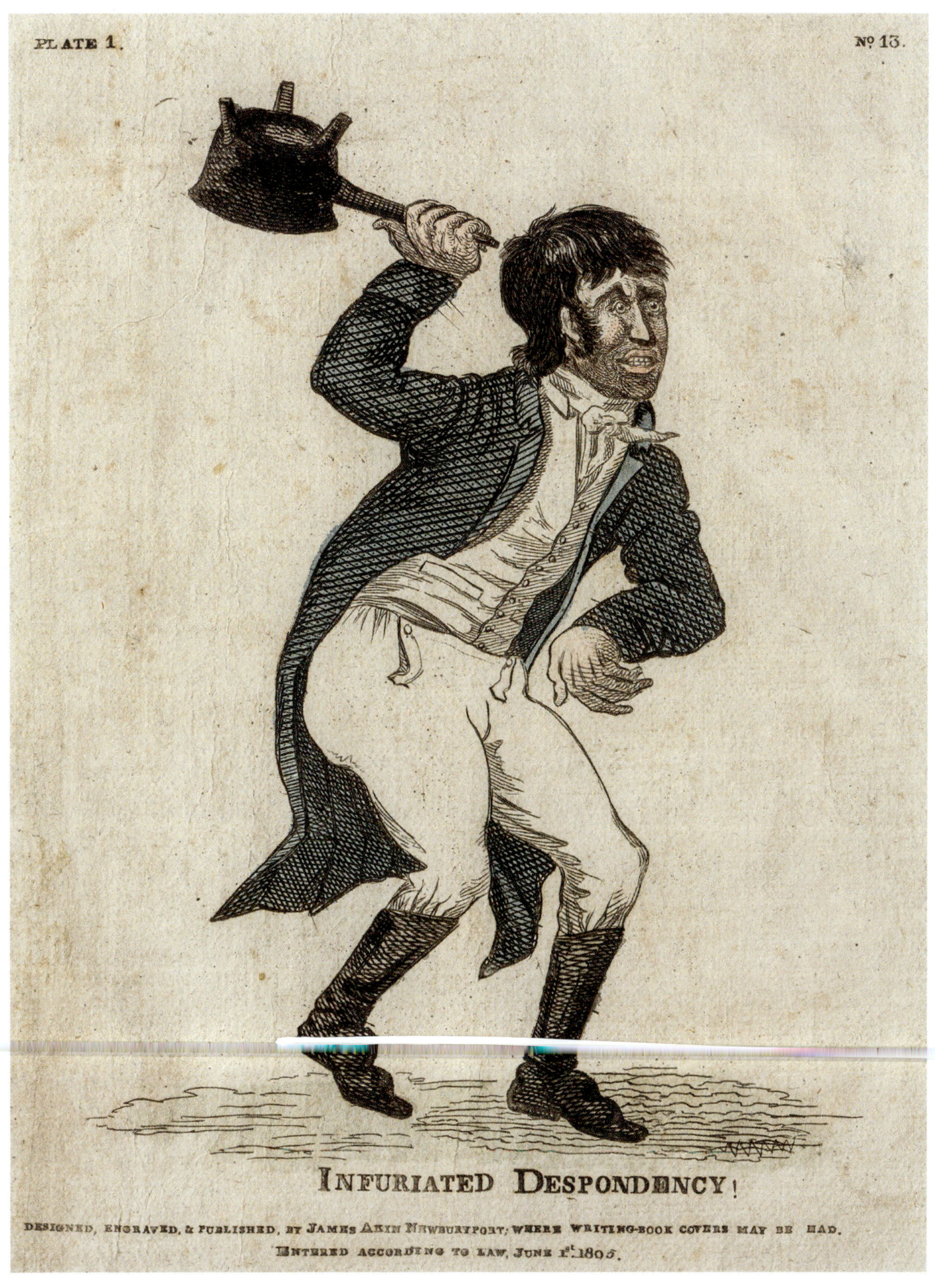

Figure 43 | James Akin, *Infuriated Despondency!*, June 1, 1805. Hand-colored wood engraving, 20 × 16 cm. Courtesy American Antiquarian Society.

76

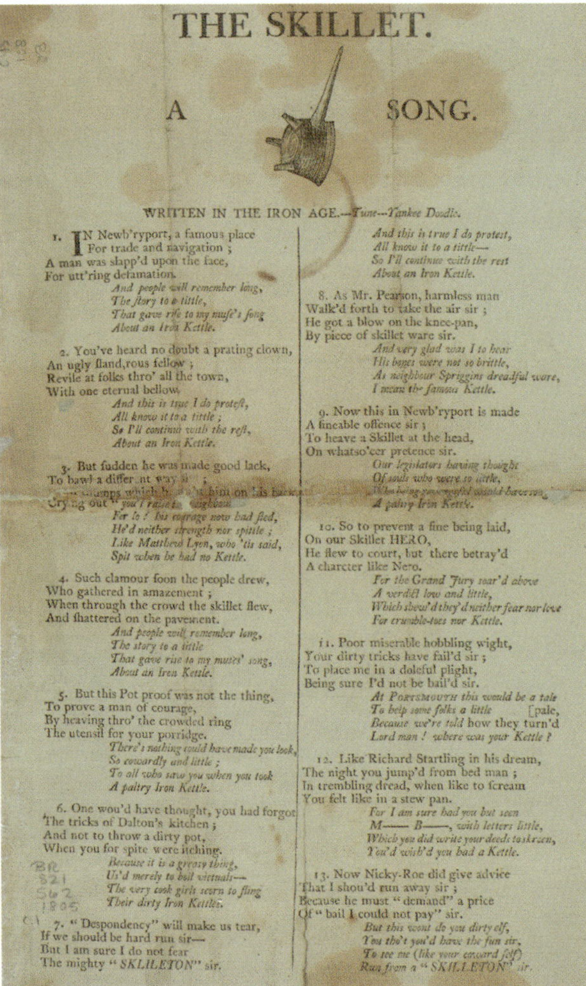

Figure 44 | James Akin, "The Skillet. A Song," n.d. [1805]. Courtesy of Phillips Library, Peabody Essex Museum, Rowley, MA.

the copyright statement "Entered according to Act of Congress June 1st 1805." These two caricatures are stronger in subject matter than *Infuriated Despondency!* and show greater artistic skill and originality. Akin has taken great liberty in depicting Blunt, especially in *A Confidential Intrigue!!!* Considering that Blunt took Akin to court for slander and libel for writing letters in November 1804 to business colleagues in Philadelphia, Baltimore, and Alexandria, Virginia it is surprising that these prints are not referenced in the court cases, or that Blunt did not file further suits against Akin.[44] In *A Confidential Intrigue!!!* Blunt's arm is raised as if the skillet has just left his hand and is already shattered in front of him. His face in this caricature is wilder than in the others, his hair spiked and his eyes even more bulging and round. Blunt kneels while a skeletal, devil-like figure of

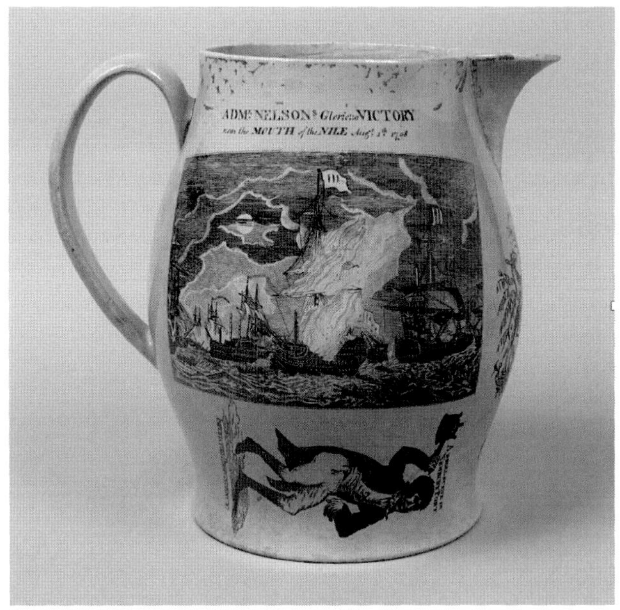

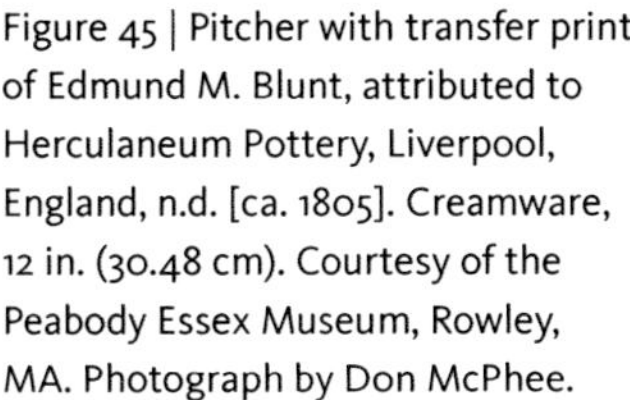
Figure 45 | Pitcher with transfer print of Edmund M. Blunt, attributed to Herculaneum Pottery, Liverpool, England, n.d. [ca. 1805]. Creamware, 12 in. (30.48 cm). Courtesy of the Peabody Essex Museum, Rowley, MA. Photograph by Don McPhee.

Blunt leans in, joined by the words "Your skillets broke, your bond you'd have to pay. Unless by my advice the fool runs away." Akin's *An Edict from Saint Peter* depicts Blunt with both hands deformed. In these two caricature prints, Akin has provided Blunt with words "Rascal" or "Rascals" emanating from his mouth. Perhaps this was a name yelled at Akin during one of their arguments; in a later caricature print, the focus of which was on national politics and had nothing to do with the situation between Blunt and Akin, he included a figure of Blunt, with bulging eyes and skillet, in a group, with the word "Rascal" coming out of his mouth once again. The slur must have meant a great deal for Akin to continue to include it with depictions of Blunt.

During the ensuing court cases, which lasted until 1807, Akin might have felt a strong urge to leave Newburyport but nonetheless stayed. He resumed a friendship with Timothy Pickering. In the fall of 1805, Akin had produced a portrait drawing of Pickering that was to be the basis of a print, and in November he announced in local papers that he intended to offer by subscription an engraving of Timothy Pickering. This engraving does not appear to have received support: the drawing and engraving, if they were ever completed, have not been located.[45] Perhaps Pickering's concern for Akin's interest in producing caricature prints was correct. In response to Akin's request for a recommendation (likely to be used in the various court cases against Blunt), Pickering stated that a letter of reference would not be of help to Akin, that instead it was his artistic output that would be his best recommendation. "I much doubt whether any letters

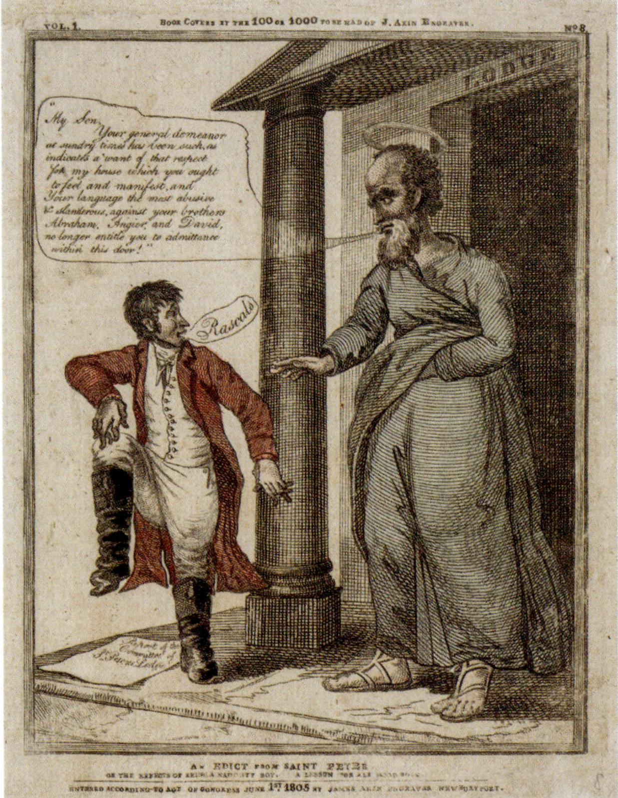

Figure 46 | James Akin, *An Edict from Saint Peter*, June 1, 1805. Hand-colored engraving, 20.5 × 15.5 cm. Courtesy American Antiquarian Society.

from me will be as useful as you imagined. But as an artist, your work must be your best recommendation. Elegant specimens of drawing will be better than a thousand letters to those whose patronage you desire. I cannot however forbear to trust that most persons are afraid ... in a moment of resentment, or ill-humour, they become subjects of [Akin's] tongue, [Akin's] pencil or [Akin's] pen." Even if Akin considered his "forte to lie in satirical drawings," he advised Akin to return to his "elegant drawings" and encouraged him to leave Newburyport for Boston, citing prominent citizens in that city as potential patrons: "'All is the gift of industry': a regular, steady application is essential to success in my profession. The implication in these remarks is obvious."[46] Pickering's advice was not warmly received by Akin, whose response reflected how deeply wronged he felt by Blunt. Akin wrote of "the infamous manner in which I have been basely persecuted" and that "I was maliciously prosecuted by a corrupt Justice and ... an enemy fraught with every species of malevolence, to destroy my reputation & bring upon [me] utter ruin and destruction!"[47] This correspondence between Pickering and Akin lasted from October 1805 until January 1806. The final letter was an apology from Akin to Pickering

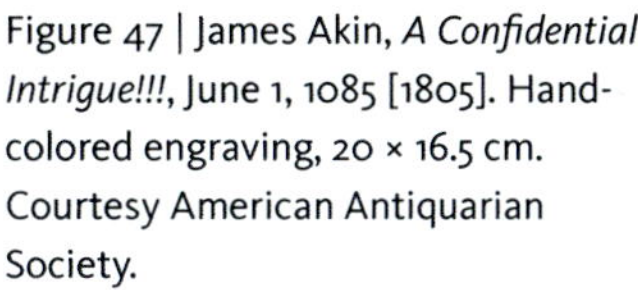

Figure 47 | James Akin, *A Confidential Intrigue!!!*, June 1, 1085 [1805]. Hand-colored engraving, 20 × 16.5 cm. Courtesy American Antiquarian Society.

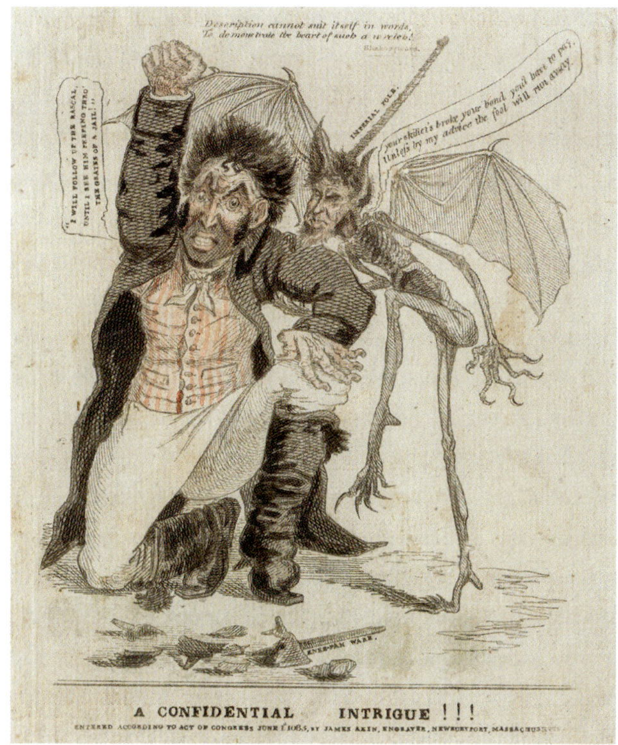

for a previous impassioned message: "I thank you Sir indeed for the services intended me, and I trust that times and facts will prove to you how much I value your advice and character."[48]

A Philosophic Cock and Political Caricature in Newburyport, 1804–1807

Pickering's advice to discontinue making caricature prints did not influence Akin. He completed at least six more caricature prints before he left Newburyport. Four of the six caricatures satirized broader political issues of the day. Two of the caricatures in this group, *A Philosophic Cock* and *The Prairie Dog sickened at the sting of the Hornet— or a Diplomatic Puppet exhibiting his Deceptions!*, depicted President Thomas Jefferson, while *A Bug-a-boo to frighten John Bull, or the Wright mode for kicking up the Bubbery* and *"The Bloody Arena"* were commentaries on sensational political events. The caricature print *All in my eye!* focused on a specific situation in Newburyport concerning Akin's friend Jacob Perkins. No impressions have been located of the sixth caricature, *The Mandate* ["Whiskerandos"], although the copperplate has survived.

Akin included a date of publication on only one, *"The Bloody Arena,"* which was deposited for copyright on May 15, 1806. Without dates on the other prints, determining the exact time when Akin published these caricatures is problematic. This is especially true for the most widely known and reproduced today of Akin's caricatures, *A Philosophic Cock* (fig. 48). Despite this, contemporary descriptions or references in newspapers, letters, or archival documents have not been located. Akin himself did not refer to it and did not sign it: the only surviving impression of *A Philosophic Cock* does not have a signature. The subject matter of the caricature, a depiction of Jefferson with Sally Hemings, would suggest that it was made between 1801 and 1803, when rumors of their intimate relationship were noted in newspapers.[49] James Callendar, a former Jefferson ally, was the first to publish an explicit report linking Jefferson and Hemings in 1802. Callendar, disgruntled at having been passed over for a position in the Jefferson administration, attacked the president in his newspaper, the *Richmond Recorder*: "It is well known that the man, whom it delighteth the people to honor, keeps, and for many years past has kept, as his concubine, one of his slaves. Her name is SALLY."[50] Akin may have known of this report at the time it was published, but it can be theorized that Akin waited some time before producing the caricature. There are no known references to the caricature in Philadelphia newspapers or in archival papers connected to Philadelphia; however, the caricature can be linked to other prints he made while in Newburyport. The surviving impression was discovered in an album containing the caricatures Akin produced in Newburyport, among them the three Blunt prints: *The Prairie Dog, A Bug-a-boo, "The Bloody Arena,"* and *All in my eye!* The policies of Jefferson's administration were regularly attacked by those residing in the Federalist-leaning region of Newburyport, and the caricature might have been made for a local audience that would have appreciated the subject matter. If the piece was seen outside of New England, it is not known.

The design and format of *A Philosophic Cock* was influenced by the earlier Blunt caricatures of June 1, 1805. For example, both Blunt, Jefferson, and Hemings are presented on a thin patch of earth, without any background. As in *A Confidential Intrigue!!!* Akin also included a quotation at the top of the print. For the Blunt caricature, it was "Description cannot suit itself in words, to demonstrate the heart of such a wretch," misquoting from the fourth act of Shakespeare's *Henry V*: "Description cannot suit itself in words, / To demonstrate the life of such a battle." For *A Philosophic Cock* Akin included, without attribution, lines from the first act of Joseph Addison's *Cato*: "Tis not a set of features or complexion or tincture of a skin that I admire." The inclusion of these literary references elevated the nature of his caricature prints. Akin was also inspired by the output of engravings by the British artist Thomas Bewick. Some years before Akin completed either work, he wrote a letter to Bewick that his "admirable specimens . . . long ago ravished my eyes," having purchased Bewick's *Land Birds* in Philadelphia.[51] In

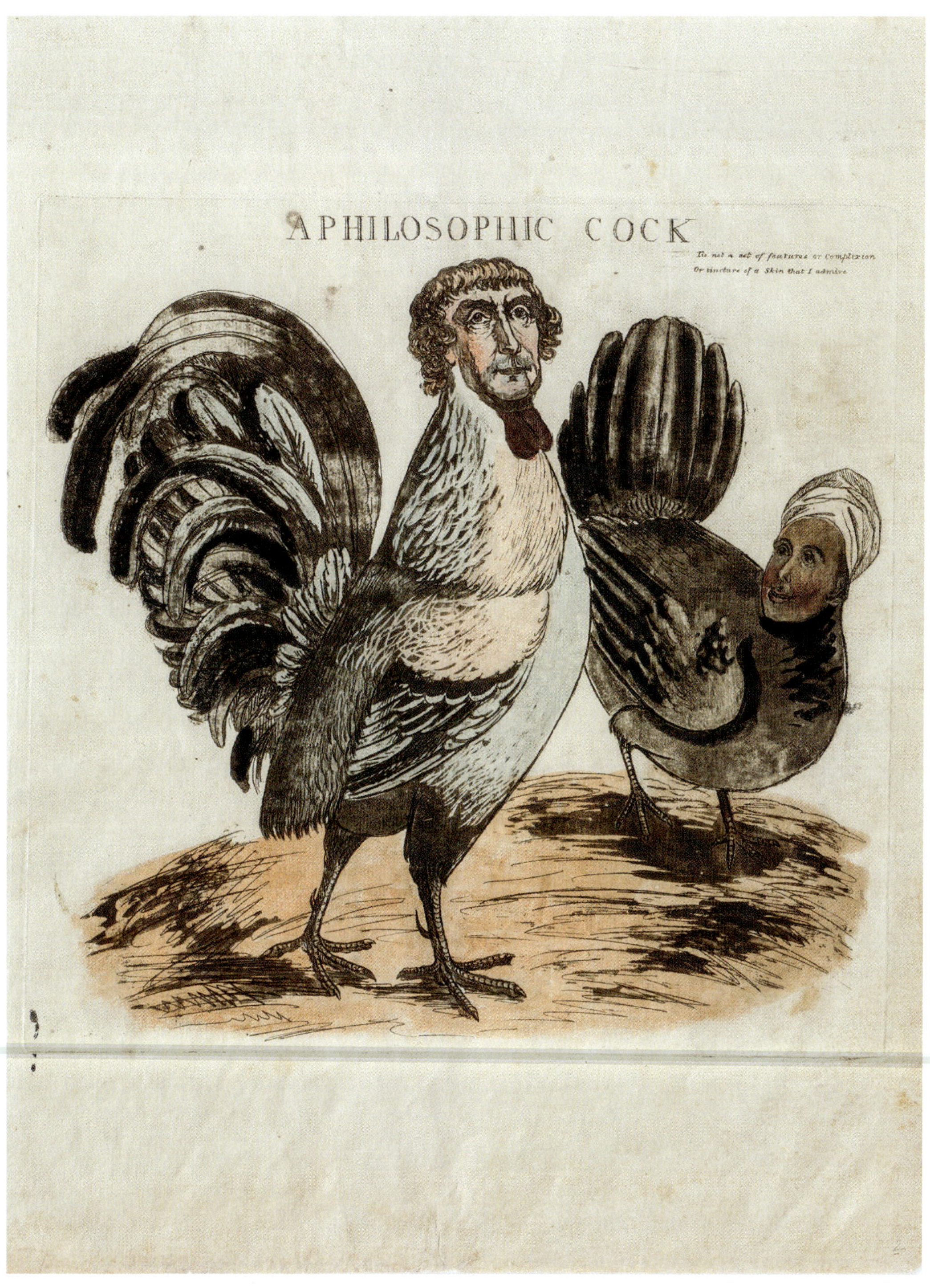

Figure 48 | [James Akin], *A Philosophic Cock*, n.d. [ca. 1804–7]. Hand-colored engraving, 42 × 33.5 cm. Courtesy American Antiquarian Society.

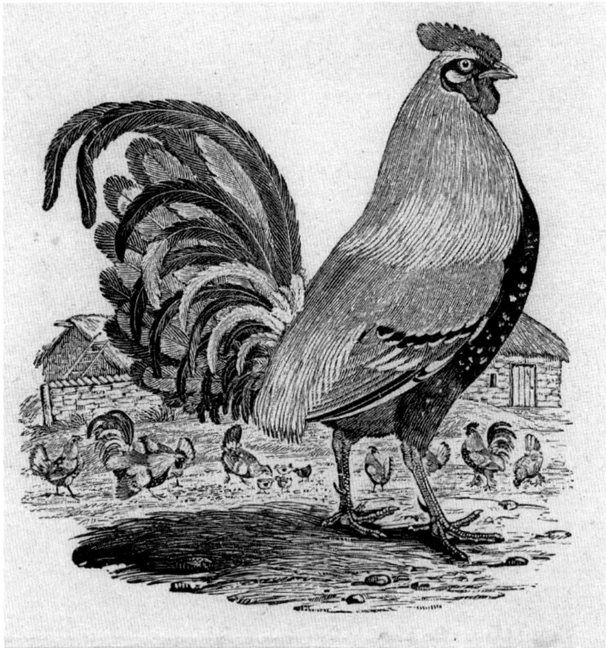

Figure 49 | Thomas Bewick, "The Domestic Cock" in *A History of British Birds*, 1797. British Museum. © The Trustees of the British Museum.

light of this letter, what becomes quite interesting is the strong similarity between Akin's representation of Jefferson and Bewick's *The Domestic Cock* (fig. 49). Included in *History and Description of Land Birds*, the first volume of *A History of British Birds*, it was also one of two illustrations chosen for the prospectus that announced the title's publication.[52] While it is not known if Akin saw the prospectus, he owned Bewick's two-volume set.[53] In both Bewick and Akin's designs, the image of the cock is not placed within a boundary or a frame but rather exists on a slim patch of earth. Strikingly, Akin's depiction of Jefferson as the rooster is almost an exact copy of Bewick's depiction: both face to the right, with comparable placement of feathers, chest, and feet. It is likely that this design influenced Akin's caricature print. Numerous British caricature prints could have inspired Akin's depiction, but one example is difficult to ignore: Robert Dighton's *The Royal Cock=Pitt* was published in the summer of 1796 and was available when Akin was in London (fig. 50). Akin's caricature shares similar qualities to Dighton's, particularly the placement of the cock, the feathers, and even the feet of the bird, and of the hybrid human-bird, comprising a human head placed on the body of a bird.

It is easier to determine when Akin produced the second Jefferson caricature, *The Prairie Dog sickened at the sting of the <u>Hornet</u>—or a Diplomatic Puppet exhibiting his Deceptions!* (fig. 51). The New York barber John Richard Desborous Huggins placed a notice in May 1806 stating that his shop had "lately been graced with the Prairie Dog."

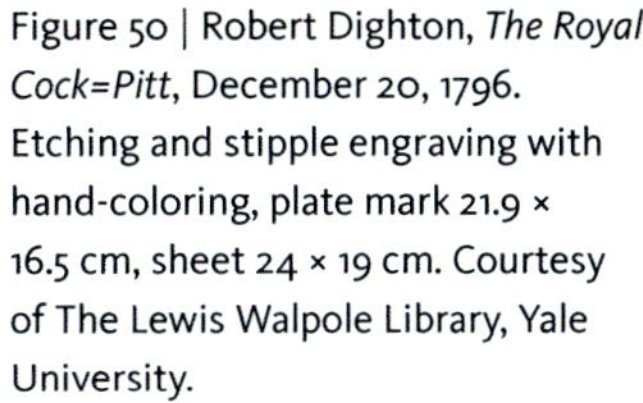

Figure 50 | Robert Dighton, *The Royal Cock=Pitt*, December 20, 1796. Etching and stipple engraving with hand-coloring, plate mark 21.9 × 16.5 cm, sheet 24 × 19 cm. Courtesy of The Lewis Walpole Library, Yale University.

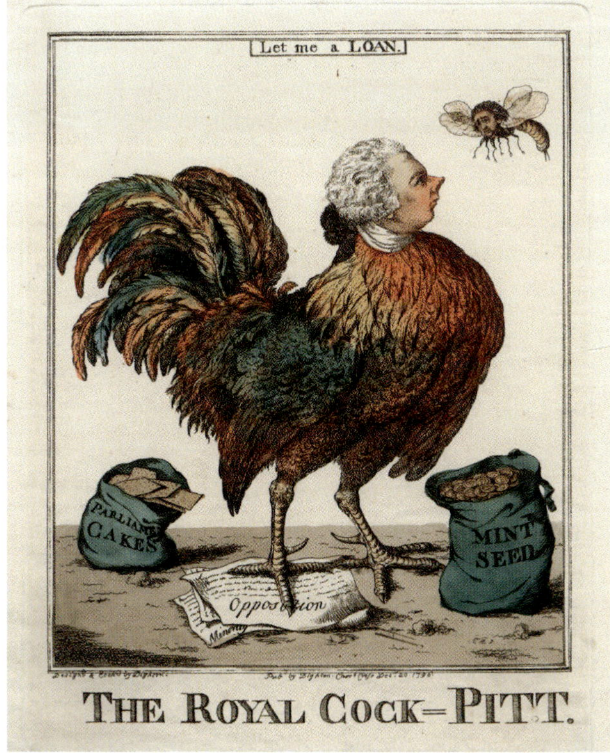

He continued, "This historical piece is from the hands of a master, and may be seen every day. It may not be amiss to give a short description of this inimitable performance, which by some ill-natured folks, has been called a caricature."[54] In the caricature, Akin once again represented the human head of Jefferson (coughing up coins) on an animal's body, this time an emaciated dog, while a hornet with the human head of Napoleon stings the dog's backside.[55] Unlike with *A Philosophic Cock*, Akin has included his name on this print, signing it "J. Akin."

Akin published five further caricatures while in Newburyport, a pace he would not match until the 1830s when he worked in lithography. Among the caricatures was *A Bug-A-Boo to frighten John Bull, or the Wright mode for kicking up a Bubbery*. Neither Murrell nor Weitenkampf knew of this caricature. The only reference earlier scholars had to it was Akin's notice in the *Newburyport (MA) Herald* on November 14, 1806, in which he claimed to be the "author of 'Prairie Dog' / 'Infuriated Despondency' / 'Bug A Boo.' &c &c." Two impressions of this caricature are currently known, one in London at the British Museum and the other in Worcester, Massachusetts at the American Antiquarian Society (figs. 52 and 53). British historian M. Dorothy George included this caricature

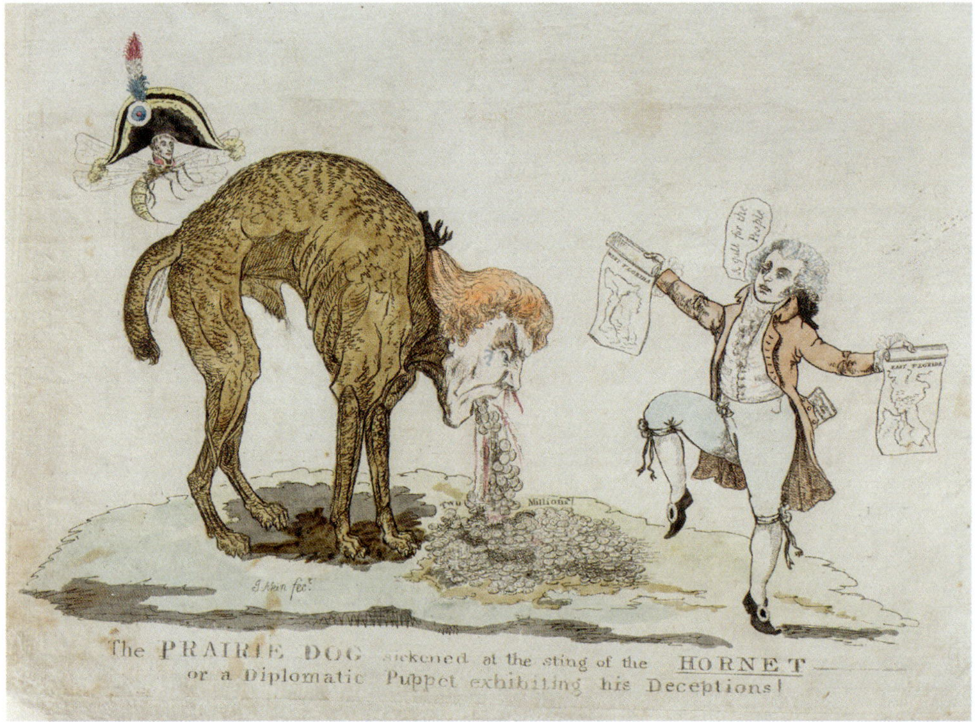

Figure 51 | James Akin, *The Prairie Dog sickened at the sting of the <u>Hornet</u>—or a Diplomatic Puppet exhibiting his Deceptions!*, n.d. [1806]. Hand-colored engraving, 34 × 46 cm. Courtesy American Antiquarian Society.

in the multivolume *Political and Social Satires* and referred to the print in her 1953 article in the *William and Mary Quarterly*.[56] Maureen Quimby, writing in 1972, included in her catalogue the title Akin provided in the notice and dated it to "ca. 1805" with the statement that the collection was "unknown."[57] In this caricature, the large group of figures on the ship includes Blunt with his distorted hand and skillet and the word "Rascal" issuing from his mouth. Even in this caricature, in which a national issue is being represented and whose audience outside of Newburyport would have little knowledge of Blunt and the skillet incident, Akin was not ready to let go.

Around the same time as *The Prairie Dog*, Akin published *"The Bloody Arena"* (fig. 54) in May 1806. Part of the design was copied from an 1802 British caricature, *The Balance of Justice*, by Charles Williams (fig. 55). That Akin adapted sections of the Williams design implies that this caricature was either imported to the United States as one of the many anonymous British caricatures referenced in newspapers for sale in bookstores of this period; or that Akin was personally receiving caricatures from a

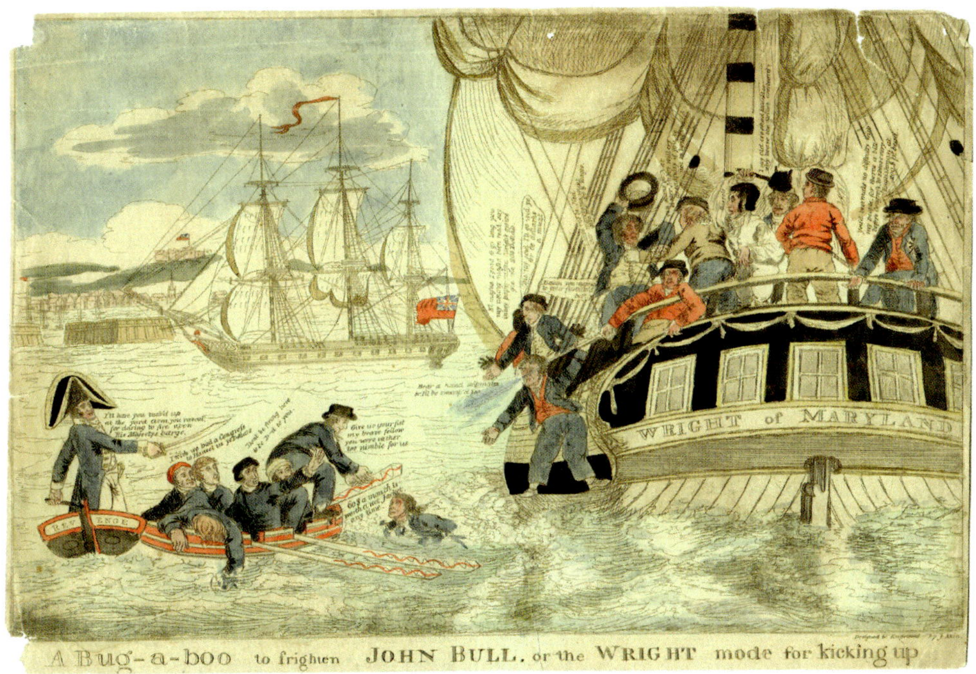

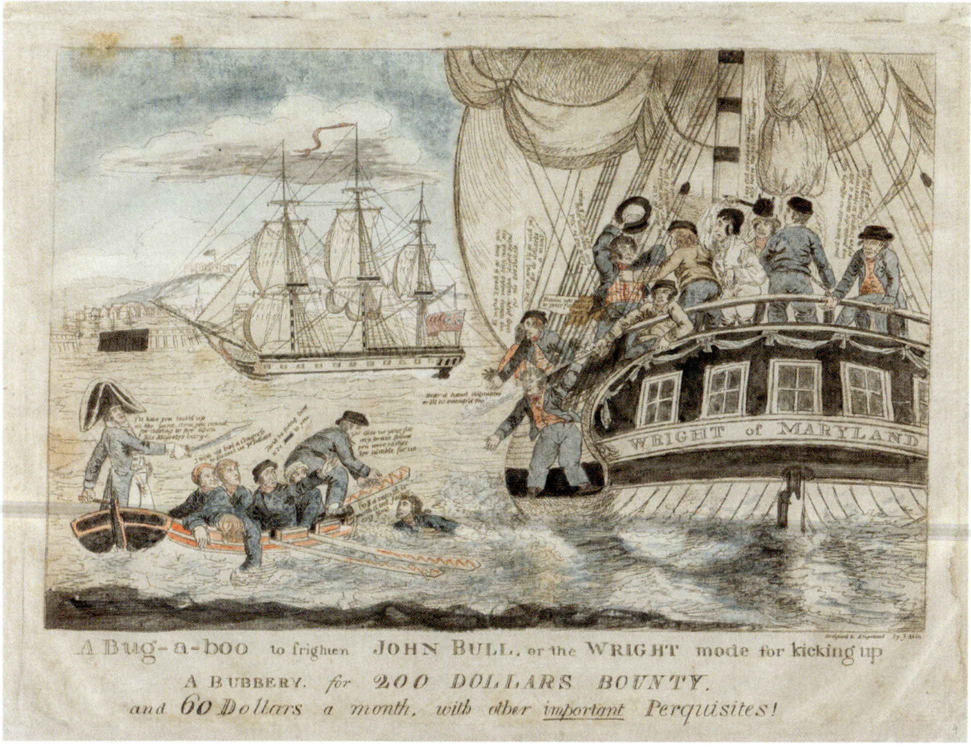

Figure 52 (*top*) | James Akin, *A Bug-a-boo to frighten John Bull, or the Wright mode for kicking up*, n.d. [1806]. British Museum. © The Trustees of the British Museum.

Figure 53 (*bottom*) | James Akin, *A Bug-a-boo to frighten John Bull, or the Wright mode for kicking up a Bubbery for 200 Dollars Bounty, and 60 Dollars a month, with other <u>important</u> Perquisites*, n.d. [1806]. Hand-colored engraving, 35 × 45.5 cm. Courtesy American Antiquarian Society.

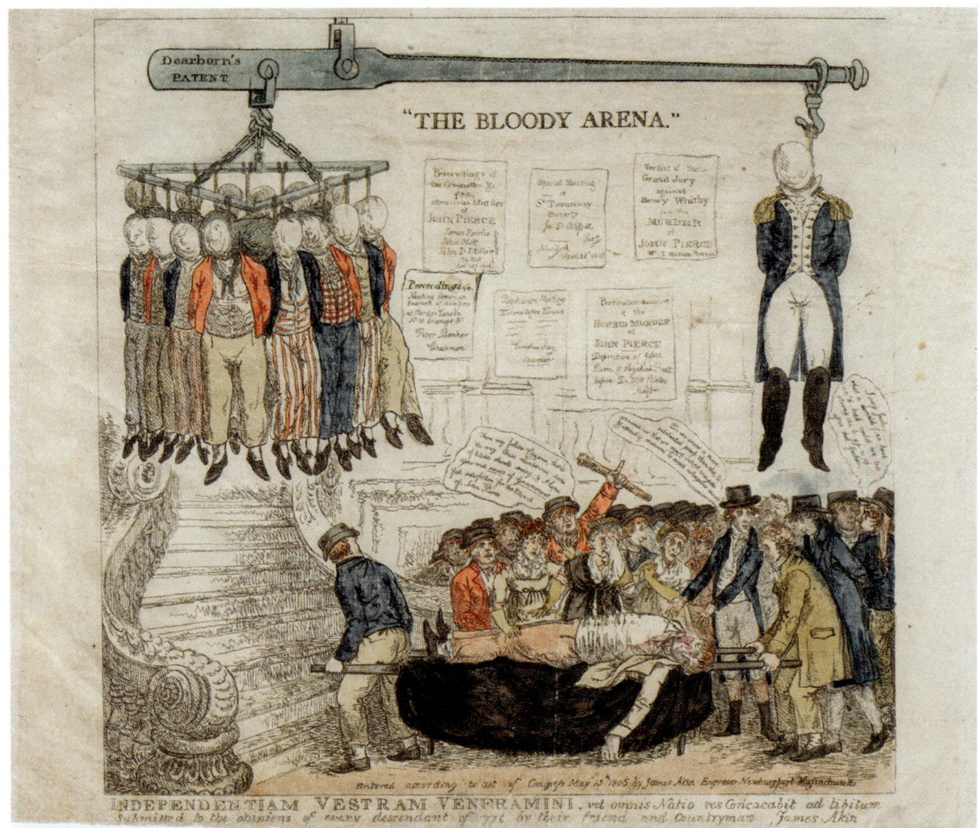

Figure 54 | James Akin, *"The Bloody Arena" / Independentiam Vestram Veneramini, vel omnis Natio vos Concacabit ad libitum Submitted to the opinions of every descendant of 1776 by their friend and Countryman James Akin*, May 15, 1806. Hand-colored engraving, 34 × 40.5 cm. Courtesy American Antiquarian Society.

supplier or friend in London. Akin has taken the general design of the Williams caricature but tailored it for an American audience with a contemporary American event. In the Williams version, thirteen men are shown hanging from a triangular steel frame on the left, while one man hangs on the right-hand side. All fourteen men have their hands behind their backs and their eyes covered with cloth. Akin's print varies slightly. The Akin caricature is of a New York City street scene featuring a procession carrying the body of John Pierce, an American sailor murdered by Henry Whitby, the captain of the British vessel *Leander*. Broadsides can be read above the group of mourners announcing the death of Pierce and the trial of Whitby that alert the audience to the scene's subject. This subtle hint may not have been necessary: the news of the murder and Jefferson's proclamation in response was issued the first week of May and widely published in newspapers

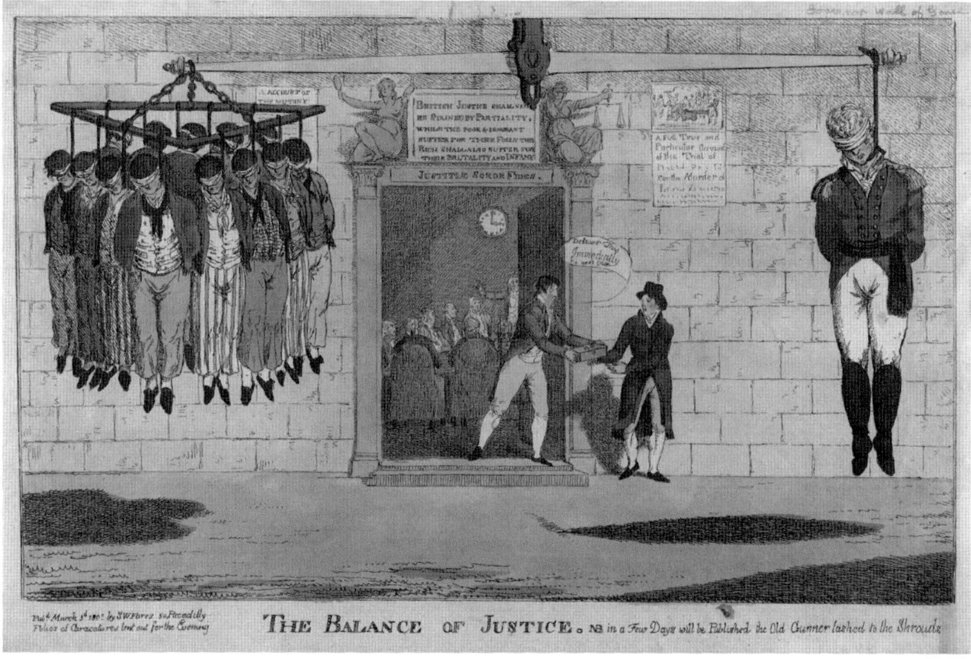

Figure 55 | Charles Williams, *The Balance of Justice*, March 3, 1802. Engraving on laid paper, hand-colored, plate mark 269 × 405 mm. Courtesy of The Lewis Walpole Library, Yale University.

along the Eastern Seaboard, especially in Vermont, Rhode Island, Massachusetts, New York, Virginia, Maryland, and South Carolina. This was a well-executed caricature with skill and artistic knowledge: the New Yorkers are depicted mourning the death of Pierce while broadsides announce the news regarding the murder. The balance seen in the Williams image is depicted as "Dearborn's Patent," a reference to Secretary of War Henry Dearborn, and from the triangular steel frame on the left hang fourteen men, their entire heads covered. Below this, Akin has included mourners, some praying and others weeping over the fallen American soldier lying on a stretcher with blood covering his face.

No impressions have survived of *The Mandate* ["Whiskerandos"], although the engraved copperplate has been located (fig. 56). Reference to the caricature can be found in newspapers in New York that would date it to before March 1807. The notice reads, "We have received from a correspondent at the eastward a caricature representing a great emperor with a drawn sword."[58] The engraving depicts Napoleon and the king of Spain, who is referred to as "Whiskerandos" in the newspaper notice. On the reverse of the plate is Akin's engraving for a Newburyport entrepreneur, Jacob Coburn, who opened the Sun Hotel on State Street in May 1807.[59]

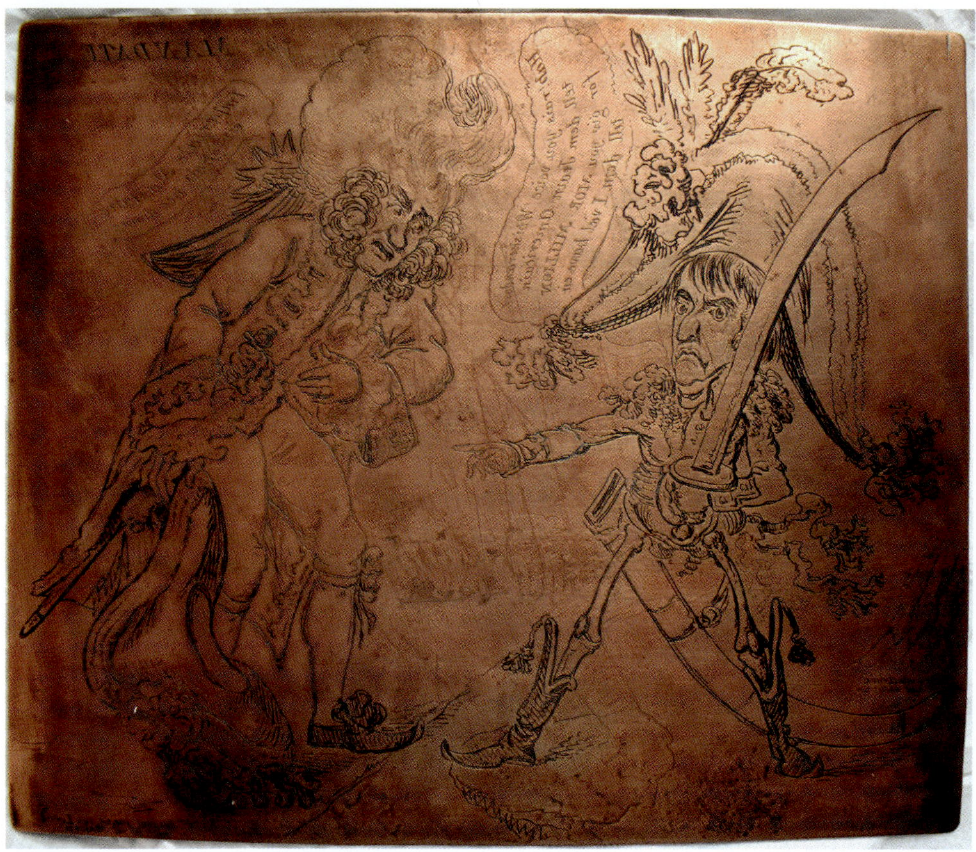

Figure 56 | Copperplate, with engraving by James Akin, *The Mandate* ["Whiskerandos"], n.d. [March 1807]. Historical Society of Old Newbury Collection.

While it is clear Akin was aware of British caricature and copied from examples published in London, perhaps no work of his from this period better represents his knowledge of the tradition and history of British caricature than *All in my eye!* (fig. 57), published in late March or early April 1806. Akin's signature can be found in the lower right-hand corner of the framing device. Other caricatures made by Akin usually had a sparse background or depicted an outdoor space, whereas in this caricature Akin presented the interior of a Newburyport barbershop. Is it an imagined barbershop? Potentially. Listings for barbershops in Newburyport are rare, although Samuel Davis's barbershop was located on Federal Street, two blocks from State Street.[60] Much like the caricatures of Blunt that featured a local personage, this example supports Akin's friend and fellow printer Jacob Perkins.[61] It is unlikely to have been intended for an audience beyond Newburyport, as its subject matter would not have been of interest to those not

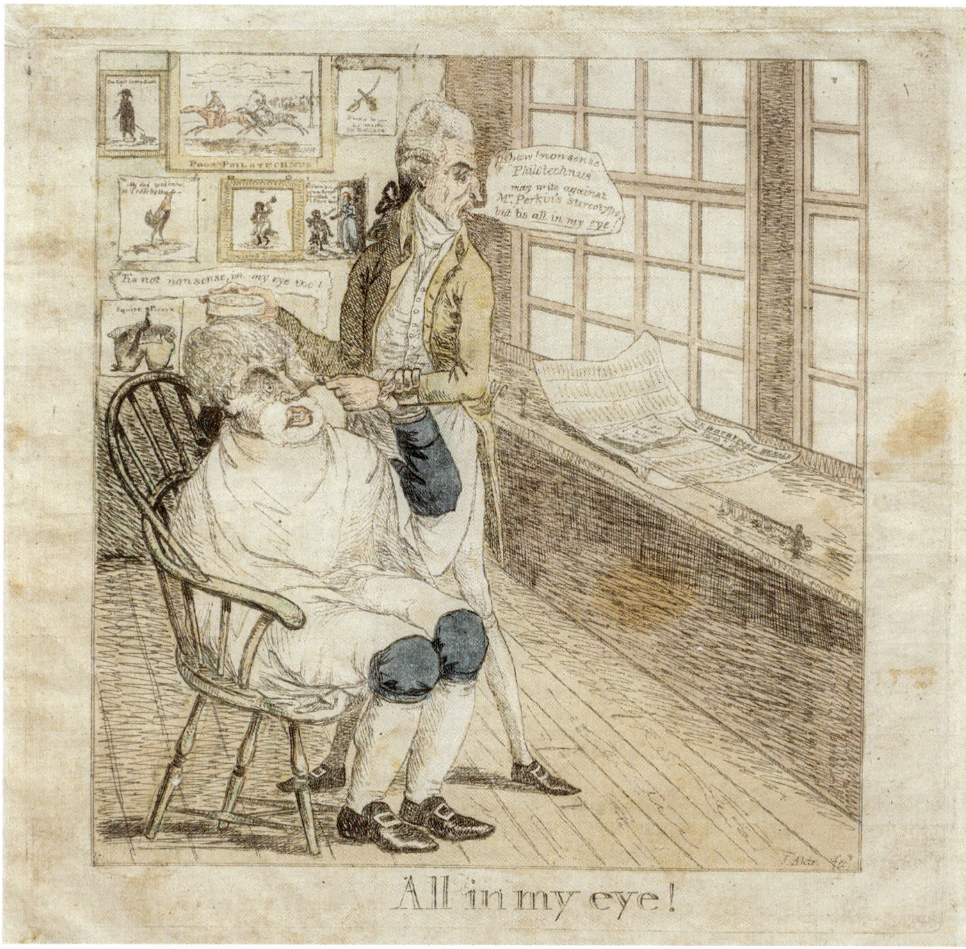

Figure 57 | James Akin, *All in my eye!*, n.d. [March or April 1806]. Hand-colored
engraving, 32.5 × 33 cm. Courtesy American Antiquarian Society.

in the know. This print is innovative as Akin uses it as a visual business card by including on the wall behind the barber and his customer examples of engravings and caricature prints he made in Newburyport. At least three of the seven prints on the wall are
known to be by Akin. The remaining four are likely also by him, although impressions
of them or references to them have not been located. On the wall are two of the Blunt
caricatures, *Infuriated Despondency!* and *An Edict from Saint Peter,* as well as an engraving of Lord Timothy Dexter (fig. 58). Although there are rarely impressions of interiors
that show caricatures in British prints, Akin might have been aware of the images published in London in which window displays could be seen (fig. 59). Akin's preference for

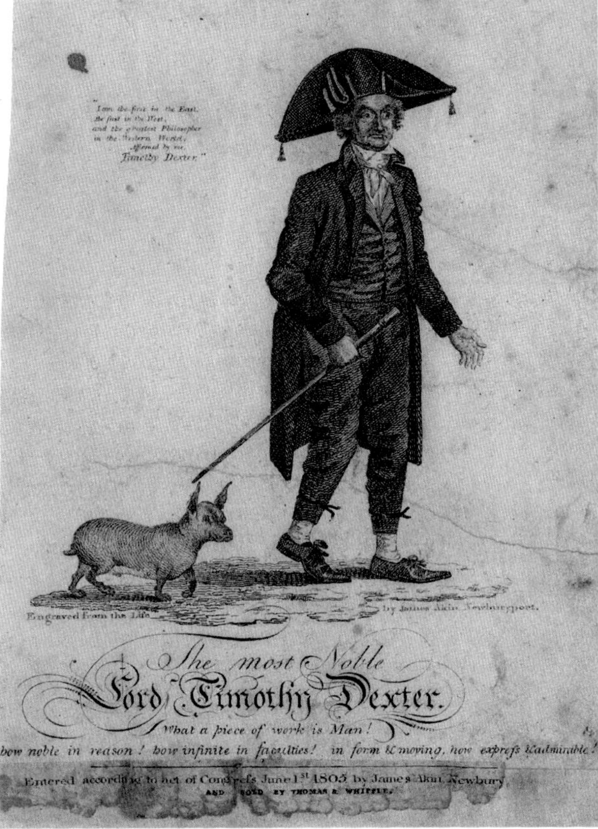

Figure 58 | James Akin, *The most Noble Lord Timothy Dexter*, June 1, 1805. Courtesy American Antiquarian Society.

Infuriated Despondency! is revealed by its prominent position and the fact that it is hanging in a frame, not tacked to the wall, as some of the other prints are.

Akin's experience in London provided him with further insight as to how to monetize and make available his prints. One option he considered was selling his caricatures in a bound portfolio. In February 1806, Akin submitted for copyright protection in Massachusetts the title for a book of twenty-five plates. Akin appears to have at the very least started to print some of these caricatures with the intention of binding them: a number of surviving impressions of caricature prints discussed in this chapter have plate numbers corresponding to the advertisement.[62] For example, the three caricatures of Blunt were intended for inclusion, as they were listed in the advertisement: *An Edict from Saint Peter, Infuriated Despondency!*, and *A Confidential Intrigue!!!* A surviving impression of *An Edict from Saint Peter* has numbers corresponding to those found in the newspaper notice: "Vol. 1 / No. 8." *Lord Timothy Dexter* was also included in this notice, but not *"The Bloody Arena,"* which had not yet been completed, nor *A Bug-a-boo* or *The Prairie Dog*, which

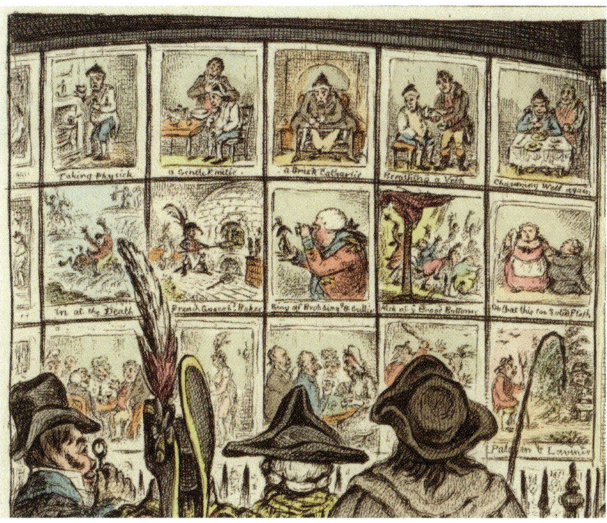

Figure 59 | Detail of James Gillray, after the Rev. John Sneyd, *Very Slippy-Weather*, February 10, 1808. Hand-colored etching and engraving on wove paper, plate 10 1/4 × 8 1/16 in., sheet 11 × 8 1/8 in. Gift of the Arcana Foundation, accession number 1996.51.1, National Gallery of Art, Washington, DC.

were likely made soon afterward. Searches for the titles listed in the advertisement have not been successful, so it is possible they were planned but not completed. Akin continued to seriously consider putting together a book of plates through November, when he announced his intention to leave Newburyport (fig. 60). In the notice, he acknowledged his dispute with Blunt as a "public curiosity" and that he was motivated

> from a sense of duty which I owe to the reputation of my family and to my honour, to lay before the public, with a rigid adherence to truth, minute details of the abuse of power that has been practiced towards me by the imprisonment and unconstitutional demands for excessive bail, the effect of a shameful collusion oppressively intended and wickedly exercised, for pretended offences presumed to have been committed by me, against the peace and dignity of the Commonwealth of Massachusetts, after all which the Grand Jury was discharged without finding a bill of indictment against me.
>
> *"Vivat respublica" "vivent la liberté et L'Egalité."*

Upon arriving in Philadelphia, Akin stated that he would publish his account of the wrongdoing, with engraved plates, at a cost of one dollar for a subscription. Then "the politician, the moralist and the critic shall find a record of events as strange as they are true."[63]

Akin did not leave Newburyport until the following year. During this time, Akin was expanding his networks in preparation for his move and locating print sellers and

92

> **"*Secret History*" a la mode "*St Cloud.*"**
>
> AS publick curiosity has been greatly excited relative to the very peculiar situation in which I have been placed, by a controversy of three years standing, and as rumour has caused much speculation in inquiries respecting my character, which from various causes has alternately become the theme of conversation at the fire-side, in the stage, and upon the ocean, perhaps with few or none of the connecting circumstances to give truth its proper colouring—I am actuated from a sense of duty which I owe to the reputation of my family and to my honour to lay before the publick, with a rigid adherence to truth, minute details of the abuse of power that has been practised towards me by imprisonment and unconstitutional demands for excessive bail, the effect of a shameful collusion oppressively intended and wickedly exercised, for pretended offences presumed to have been committed by me, against the peace and dignity of the Commonwealth of Massachusetts, after all which, the Grand Jury was discharged without finding a bill of indictment against me.
>
> "*Vivat respublica*" "*vivent la liberté et L'Egalité.*"
>
> As soon as I can coveniently remove to Philadelphia, it will be put to press, and shall contain the full value of One Dollar, at which price subscribers are solicited.
>
> Many Plates from entire new and original designs, made expressly for the occasion, shall accompany the work; and the politician, the moralist and the critick shall find a record of events as strange as they are true.
>
> JAMES AKIN,
> Author of the "Prairie Dog"
> "Infuriated Despondency,"
> "Bug a boo," &c. &c.
> Newburyport, Nov. 21, 1806.

Figure 60 | *The Repertory* (Boston), November 21, 1806. Courtesy American Antiquarian Society.

venues interested in displaying his caricature. In August 1806, "Hair Dresser and Cutter, to Ladies and Gentlemen," Edward Quirk announced that he was due to receive from Newburyport a collection of caricatures, to be delivered gratis on application, "to all who love a good joke."[64] While Akin is not named here, his previous connection with Huggins provides evidence that Akin was sending impressions of his caricatures to barbers in New York. Further to this, his caricature prints were available to be rented in the bound portfolio organized by Charles Peirce of Portsmouth, New Hampshire. In spring 1807, Peirce likely acquired from London a selection of fifty-five British caricatures by Gillray, Cruikshank, and Charles Williams, dating from 1796 to April 1807; he advertised that his "Book of Caricatures, consisting of *handsome* figures, *pleasing* likenesses;

ugly, but *necessary* positions, etc. etc." could be rented out by the hour, day, or evening. It is possible that since Akin had already decided to leave Newburyport, he sold Peirce remainders of the prints in his possession—including *A Philosophic Cock, The Prairie Dog, Infuriated Despondency!, A Confidential Intrigue!!!, An Edict from Saint Peter, A Bug-a-boo, All in my eye!,* and *"The Bloody Arena"*—to add to his bound collection. In support of this theory, four months after Peirce's initial advertisement he announced that "His Book of Caricatures is now completely filled with new BEAUTIES! And ready to let for 20 cents an hour." These two advertisements alone would mean little if not for the fact that Peirce's "Book of Caricatures" survived intact through the nineteenth and twentieth centuries and was donated to the American Antiquarian Society in 1991.[65] The first ten prints in Peirce's "Book of Caricatures" are of American subject matter, featuring nine caricatures by Akin. Both the British and American prints were bound in a similar fashion, with the caricature sheets mounted on a rough, sturdy canvas and sewn together.[66] Akin may have reevaluated his plan to publish a book of caricature prints in Philadelphia and decided that the nine caricatures reflected a specific moment, and a New England audience would therefore have a greater interest.

The closest to a public acknowledgment that Blunt's employment of Akin had ended was a notice published in May 1805, in which Blunt announced that "he has now completed the arrangement he so long wished & procured a person of good character, and one who bears the credit of being industrious and punctual to his engagements, so that he can with propriety promise to deliver so such as please to employ him, work in the above branches in a style of elegance not surpassed by any one in New-England."[67] Six weeks later Blunt stated that copperplate printing was being "EXECUTED with neatness, punctuality, and dispatch."[68] In 1807, Blunt announced that he had established "an ENGRAVING ROOM, under the direction of Mr. [William] Hooker, the first artist in New-England."[69] Blunt likely had Akin in mind with the statement that to his "enemies he wishes every, satisfaction (which may result from a disappointed and envious mind) and assures them he shall not *'set down aught in malice against them.'*" Once Blunt employed Hooker, he held a monopoly in Newburyport for engraving projects.

By October 1807, Akin was ready to move on. He thanked his friends and customers and took one final opportunity to express his opinion of his former employer as he alluded to the contentious end of their business arrangement: "Those who benevolently encouraged my *Little* labors to prevent the *blunt* wearing of my *points* in *Legal executions,* will please accept my sincere thanks." He and Eliza planned to stop first in New York before settling in Philadelphia, "where, if uninterrupted health prevails, shall be *traced* and *bitten* with *acid* for their amusement, some Phantasmagorie subjects."[70] Eliza's preparation for the move included her withdrawal from membership in the Female Charitable Society of Newburyport in 1807.[71] His valued and loyal friend Jacob Perkins would continue to act as Akin's conduit in his absence and receive any outstanding claims against Akin after they left. The Akins were terminating their ties with Newburyport. This period had been Akin's most productive in engraving, leaving a trail of information in newspapers and letters and a group of important caricatures.[72]

Return to Philadelphia

By February of 1808, Akin was back in Philadelphia. He announced in a newspaper notice that he was accepting engraving commissions: "James Aken [*sic*]. Engraver: Respectfully informs his friends and the public, that he is ready to execute for them any commands in the above business."[73] Orders could be left with the Philadelphia silversmith Philip Garrett (1780–1857) at "no. 136 Market, above Fourth Street," while the address provided at the bottom of the notice ("Schuylkill, near the Upper ferry") might refer to Akin's general location at the time. His return to Philadelphia was not a success for his caricature, although three caricatures can be attributed to this period, two of which previously lacked a connection to Akin. Both these prints can be assigned to him based on the style and comparison of figures to those that Akin published in the early 1800s. Akin's first caricature of this new Philadelphia chapter, *Economical Projects, or an old Philosopher teaching his mad son* (fig. 61), can be linked to him by noting the striking similarity between the figures depicted in this 1808 caricature and those previously signed by Akin. For example, the figures are represented with similar bulging eyes, as can be seen in the prints by Akin that include Blunt (*All in my eye!* and *"The Bloody Arena"*). Akin is more ambitious in the design of *Economical Projects* compared to his earlier caricatures, in which only one scene is usually depicted. This work is multileveled, divided into three sections. The top section is the largest, taking up the entire length of the print, and depicts President Thomas Jefferson with James Madison pulling a boat toward the diminutive figure of Napoleon, while on the right side a member of Congress pulls back a curtain to show dissatisfied legislators debating the Embargo Act. Below this large section are two smaller scenes: an image of war ships and another of a man hanging himself. An advertisement for this caricature that appeared in the *Washington Federalist* on December 15, 1808, has aided in providing an accurate title and in dating its publication, as it was "FOR SALE AT THIS OFFICE, PRICE SEVENTY-FIVE CENTS. Economical Projects, or an Old Philosopher teaching his mad son—A well designed and well executed caricature."[74] Few caricatures were being designed during this period, and Akin's skill at facial expressions, his fluidity in designing figures, and his attention to providing information in the speech bubbles provides strong evidence for his authorship. The only surviving impression is in the collection of the Free Library of Philadelphia.

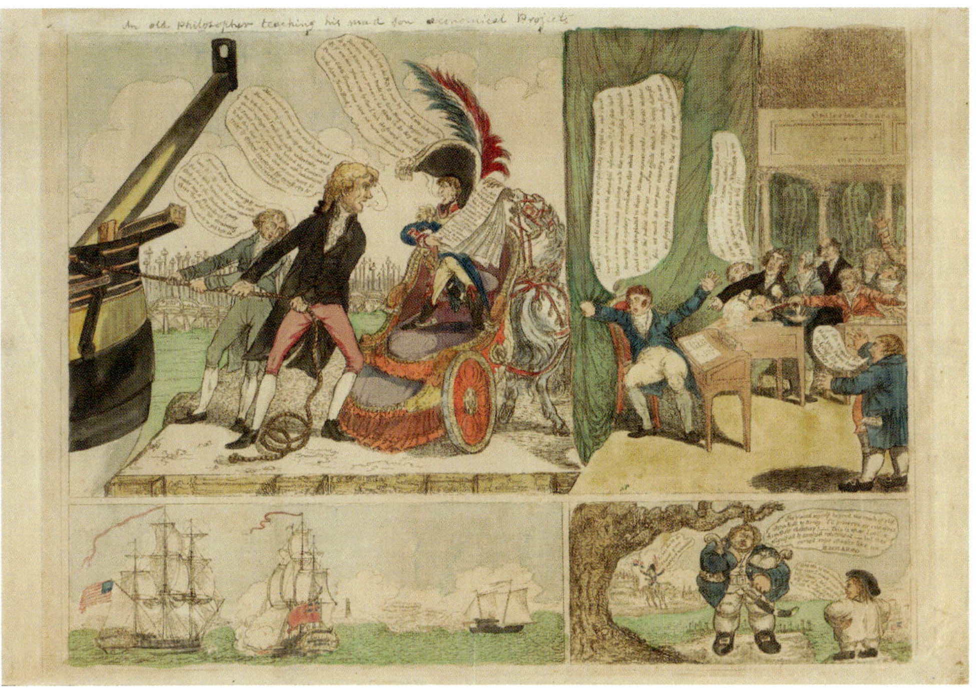

Figure 61 | [James Akin], *Economical Projects, or an old Philosopher teaching his mad son*, n.d. [December 1808]. Free Library of Philadelphia, Print and Picture Department.

A second caricature can also be attributed to Akin through newspaper advertisements. *Brazen Projectiles, or, an enforcement of the solid arguments of the Old Sceool* [*sic*] (fig. 62) was published in late summer of 1810. It was advertised as "An Elegant Expressive Caricature" in the Philadelphia satirical weekly *The Tickler*, published by George Helmbold; the listing announced that a proof could be seen in August, with impressions available for purchase on September 3, 1810.[75] Although the advertisement for the caricature does not provide an attribution to Akin, his name does appear several times in the same newspaper the following year, including an announcement that Akin had taken up residence at "No 129, Locust above 10th Street."[76] For an unknown reason, Helmbold's pseudonym "Toby Scratch'em" is found on the caricature print.

Akin published one further caricature in 1811. At least two editorials describing Akin's "Dicky Folwell" (fig. 63) appeared in Philadelphia newspapers in October. The first, published by *Spirit of the Press* on October 1, stated that the likenesses of Richard Folwell and Simon Synder, depicted as a sow, were "designed by one I. [J.]Akin."[77] Two weeks later, a detailed—and glowing—account of the caricature could be found in *The Tickler*:

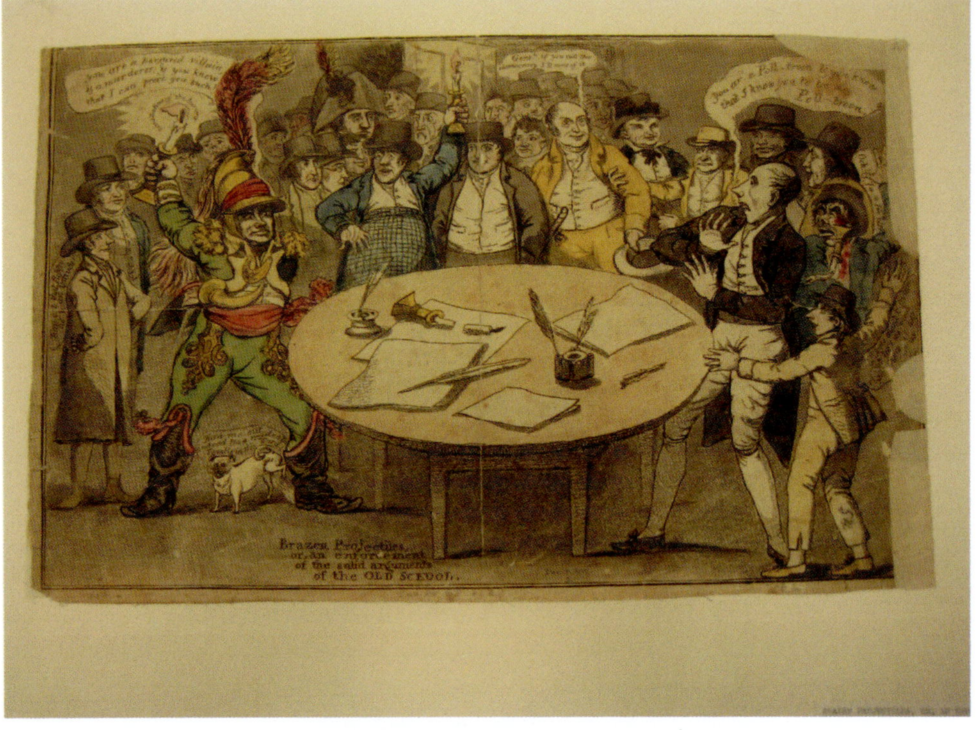

Figure 62 | Toby Scratch'em [James Akin], *Brazen Projectiles, or, an enforcement of the solid arguments of the Old Sceool* [sic], n.d. [August 1810]. Arts Department, Boston Public Library.

That ingenious artist, Mr. Akin, has executed an excellent likeness of "*Simon Synder's opponent,*" Richard Folwell, esquire. It is not as many suppose a likeness of Folwell alone, but contains an admirable hieroglyphical [*sic*] resemblance of *Folwell's opponent.* Richard is represented standing with great *grave-eye-*ty depicted in his countenance; his spectacles, costume and the lineaments of his face all proclaim the excellence of Mr. Akin's skill. In the background, and near Richard's right hand, is an *old sow*, half rising, half recumbent—this hieroglyphic is emblematical of Snyder, who is supposed to be startled at an opposition from Mr. Folwell. The reason why the artists chose the *sow* to represent Snyder is, because he suffers Jack Binns to ride and direct him; and the *teats* signify that Jimmy Carson, Doctor Porter, Ben Reynolds, Sammy Bryan, and the horde of office-holders are all *sucklings,* and derive their sustenance from the old sow.[78]

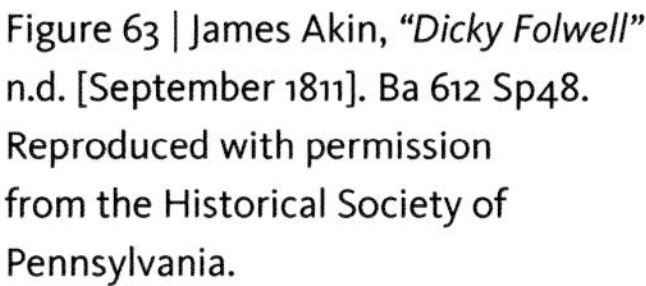

Figure 63 | James Akin, *"Dicky Folwell"* n.d. [September 1811]. Ba 612 Sp48. Reproduced with permission from the Historical Society of Pennsylvania.

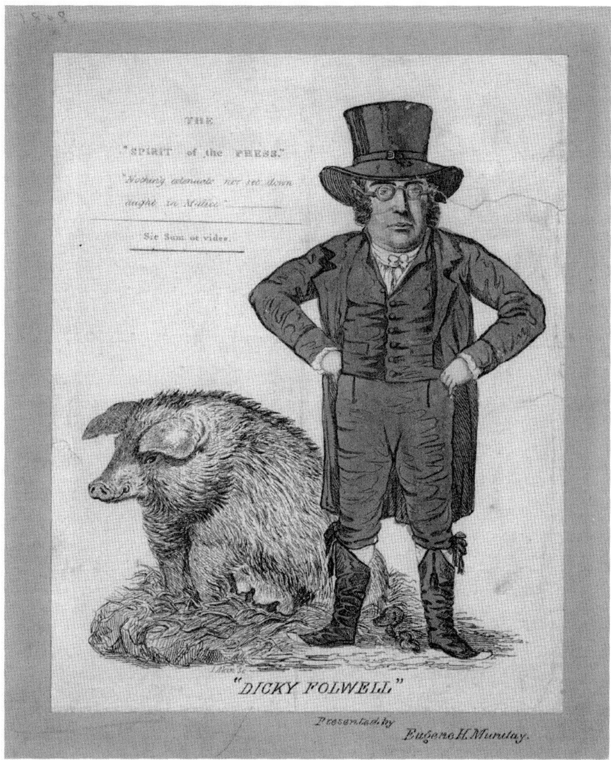

In that same year, Akin moved at least three times: from Mulberry Street, to Arch Street, to the aforementioned "no. 129, Locust above 10th street," from which he announced his intention to produce drawings for patents.[79] In addition to being a producer of caricatures and patent drawings, Akin began to consider himself a proprietor of artists. From earlier notices, Akin had already claimed to own paintings by Thomas Stothard, which he had lent to Charles Willson Peale's museum. In 1811, he exhibited paintings by Jeremiah Paul at his Mulberry Street address in an "infant attempt to found a recreative gallery" and invested a lengthy notice in Philadelphia newspapers about Paul's artistic merit, expounding that "Mr. Paul is a native genius of the United States, whose developed genius" is "unaided by foreign instruction, or the advantages of travel."[80] Akin exhibited every day and evening for an admission charge of twenty-five cents; Mondays and Thursdays were reserved for female visitors.

Between 1813 and 1817, Akin's name disappears from the public record, and no caricatures have been located that date to this period. Akin is listed as "engraver and draughtsman" in the Philadelphia directory for 1813, and in 1814 he acted as a subscription agent for the *Geographical and Military Museum*.[81] One of the final contributions Akin made

98

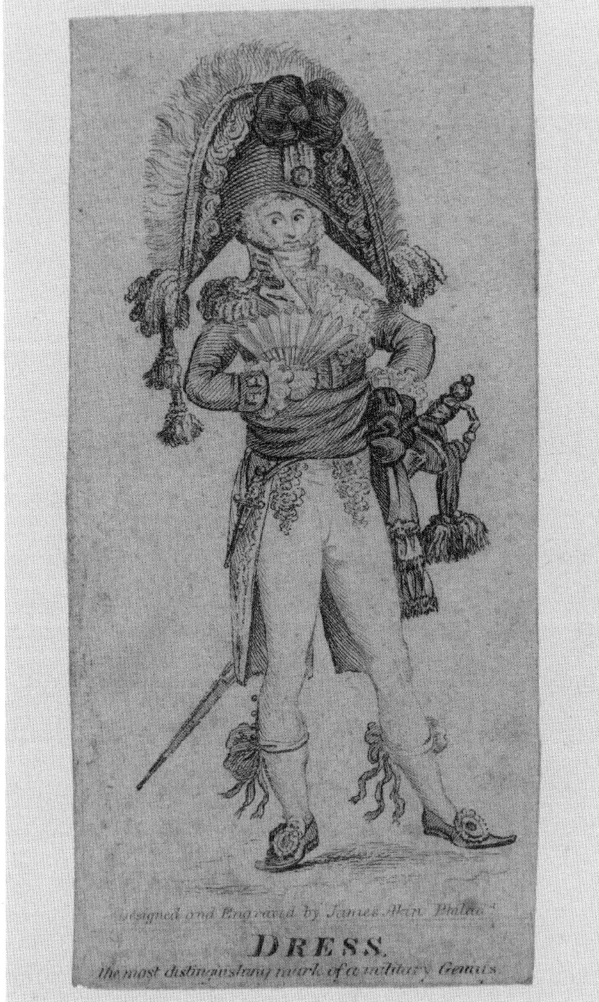

Figure 64 | James Akin, *Dress, the most distinguishing mark of a military genius*, 1813. Engraving published by Mathew McConnell Jr. in *Advice to the Officers of the Army, to the Officers of the Ordinance, and to the Secretary of War*. Prints & Photographs Division, Library of Congress, LC-DIOG-pga-05110.

was a caricature to be included in the book *Advice to the Officers of the Army, to the Officers of the Ordinance, and to the Secretary of War*, published by the bookseller Mathew McConnell Jr. in 1813 (fig. 64).[82] There are a number of possibilities as to where Akin might have been at this time, with surviving letters suggesting he was traveling in other parts of the United States. Perhaps he took on a different profession entirely before returning to caricature in the 1820s. This absence meant that Akin was not a significant contributor to the second-most important movement in early American caricature: satirical depictions of the War of 1812.

The Business of Caricature in the 1810s

William Charles arrived in New York City in late 1806 with a "large collection of modern caricatures" brought with him from London and a plan to publish new caricatures every week (fig. 65).[1] One can imagine, even from the brief description of his "Repository of Arts" provided in the newspapers, what a customer might have encountered upon entry: shelves lined with items from London such as frames for miniatures and walls covered in "a variety of prints by the first masters." Perhaps one side of the store displayed "a few superb portable writing desks on the newest construction." Charles—standing at five feet seven inches, with his "dark complexion, black hair, dark eyes"—oversaw his venture in a new country.[2] In addition to the store and its contents was the promise by Charles of weekly new caricatures. It is not clear at this time whether Charles had a printing press (he does not mention owning one in this or other notices), but if he did, it likely would have been somewhere on these premises. Number 17 Liberty Street was a two-story building: both William and his brother Henry can be associated with this address, although they don't appear to have advertised together. Perhaps the Charles brothers, along with William's wife, had leased the entire property, ensuring enough room for both a home and a business.[3]

This is the first instance in the United States of an individual promoting not only the sale of imported caricature prints but also the regular production of new caricature prints for an American audience. Charles had a clear advantage over other engravers, including James Akin. While Akin may have traveled to London and had the opportunity to see the

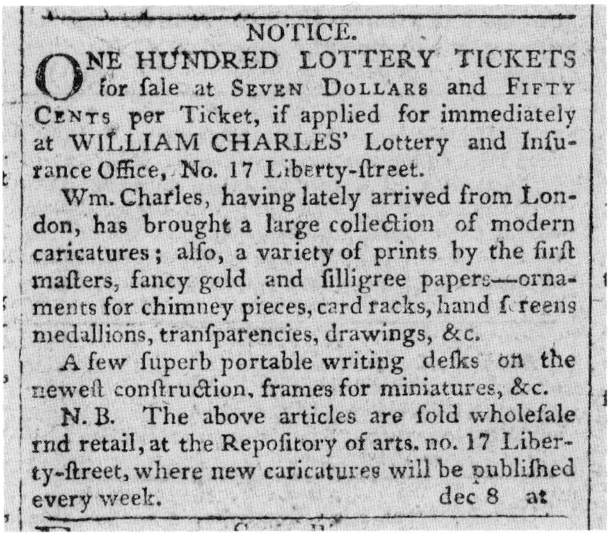

NOTICE.

ONE HUNDRED LOTTERY TICKETS for fale at SEVEN DOLLARS and FIFTY CENTS per Ticket, if applied for immediately at WILLIAM CHARLES' Lottery and Infurance Office, No. 17 Liberty-ftreet.

Wm. Charles, having lately arrived from London, has brought a large collection of modern caricatures; alfo, a variety of prints by the firft mafters, fancy gold and filligree papers—ornaments for chimney pieces, card racks, hand fcreens medallions, tranfparencies, drawings, &c.

A few fuperb portable writing defks on the neweft conftruction, frames for miniatures, &c.

N. B. The above articles are fold wholefale rnd retail, at the Repofitory of arts. no. 17 Liberty-ftreet, where new caricatures will be publifhed every week. dec 8 at

Figure 65 | *New-York Gazette and General Advertiser*, December 8, 1806. Courtesy American Antiquarian Society.

caricatures displayed in shop windows, Charles had been an active caricaturist in London and in Edinburgh; he published prints from both cities and had been a part of the chaotic and exciting caricature market, particularly in London. Charles would have been thought of in London as an amateur engraver who copied from and attempted to emulate the masters of satirical humor, such as Gillray, Rowlandson, and Cruikshank, but his new audience in New York was ignorant of this fact. Many of his caricature prints reveal his knowledge of the market: unlike Akin, Charles usually included a framing device, colored in yellow around the caricature, which was similar to the design of London caricature. Although Charles's plan to transplant a market for caricature to the United States was not successful at first (he produced only a handful of caricatures while active in New York between late 1806 and 1808), he did not give up on this endeavor. He bided his time, turned to other engraving projects, and waited for an opportune moment. The right set of circumstances presented themselves in Philadelphia during the War of 1812, and this is where Charles made his impact. A newspaper account in August 1815, about recent battles being "significant material for a new American caricature," questioned why there had not been a new caricature by Charles: "It is rather strange that Charles, the artist in this line, has not struck out something of this kind."[4]

Charles's only competitor should have been James Akin. At the time of Charles's arrival in New York, Akin was based in Newburyport. However, this would have changed when Akin left Newburyport at the end of 1807. It is curious that no references have been found that link Charles and Akin, even though they were twice in the same city at the same time. The first potential meeting could have occurred in New York in 1807, when Akin announced his plan to travel through the city on his way from Newburyport to Philadelphia. It is not clear if Akin did stop for any length of time, but if he had he likely would have visited the two barbershops that displayed his caricatures: Huggins on Broadway and Quick on Maiden Lane, both venues blocks from Charles's store on Liberty Street and his Broadway location where he moved in 1807. If the two caricaturists did not meet in New York, then their proximity to one another in Philadelphia would have provided ample opportunities to cross paths or, at the very least, to become aware of each other. In 1808, both were based in Philadelphia and actively working as engravers. By 1811, Akin had a store on Mulberry Street (now Arch Street) where he exhibited paintings by the artist Jeremiah Paul, while Charles was hired by Mathew Carey. In 1813, each produced engravings for competing publishers: Charles worked for Carey on a book that included designs after the British caricaturist Henry Bunbury (see fig. 3), while Akin engraved for the bookseller Mathew McConnell Jr. a caricature of an officer in military dress (see fig. 64). An advertisement placed by Carey announcing that he had both books for sale is the only reference that includes the work of both caricaturists.[5] When Charles partnered with Philadelphia bookseller and publisher Samuel Kennedy in May 1813 and announced their intention to publish caricatures regularly, Akin may have heard of their endeavor. However, surviving evidence suggests that he did not attempt to counter Charles's output with work of his own.

The caricatures made by Charles and Kennedy did prompt a response from at least one engraver. Charles's decision to establish an enterprise to design, publish, and elicit talent from other engravers in order to regularly publish caricatures that referenced newsworthy events from the War of 1812 evidently inspired Amos Doolittle. To promote and sell the prints he produced, he sent impressions with letters explaining them to newspaper editors. The intention was for interested editors to act as agents and sell the prints while also promoting the engravings in their newspapers, with the result that the contemporary print is the source for identifying caricatures in circulation at the time. The caricatures made were described at length in newspapers. This interest in caricatures appears to have influenced other artist and engravers to create their own offerings. This third strand of caricature production also takes advantage of the War of 1812 as a subject, but these works were anonymously published and not all of them have survived.

William Charles: "A Foreigner and an Alien"

William Charles was born in Scotland in 1776.[6] Details of his training and early professional life are not known until February 1803, when Charles was in London and married Mary Graham at St. Mary's Church, Lambeth.[7] Charles may have set up his home in

London with the prospect of entering into the caricature market because several months later, in April, he began to publish caricature at least until October of that year. These are his earliest known engravings, and at least four of the caricatures published during this period included his London address, "No. 49 Corner of Harpur St Theobalds Road."[8] By the following July he was in Edinburgh, where he established the "Emporium of Art and Produce," on a caricature with a John Bull theme.[9] Two years later, in May 1806, he and his brother, Henry, were both in Edinburgh, but at a new address when they signed two caricatures, "W. & H. Charles 7 North Bridge Edinburgh."[10] With so many pauses between the publication of caricatures, and with Charles traveling between London and Edinburgh, it is likely that he had other projects to sustain him financially. One such project was likely publishing children's books, a venture that Charles was engaged in while working in New York and Philadelphia. If Charles learned this trade in London or Edinburgh, examples have not been located. He, like Akin, might have received an inheritance or other forms of familial support, or else he was involved in other unknown business ventures.

Following other caricaturists working in London at this time, Charles primarily focused his subject matter on Napoleon Bonaparte. He copied designs and subject matter from others, adapting specific figures from recently published caricatures to fit into his own awkward styling. His output was neither technically advanced nor striking enough to make an impact among the hundreds of caricature prints published weekly in London. This is perhaps why Charles left London and returned to Edinburgh. In 1805, while in Edinburgh, he published the caricature that appears to have brought him some notoriety. *A Fallen Pillar of the Kirk* (fig. 66) depicts a woman with her chest exposed on the lap of a clergyman, who happily says, "O'h lord what good things dost thou provide for us men!" Although there is no contemporary evidence in either London or Edinburgh that this caricature triggered a fervor, it is possible to imagine that Charles used the racy subject matter to build a more exciting backstory. Soon after he had arrived in New York, Charles was described in a newspaper as "lately escaped here from Edinburgh to avoid prosecution for a caricature print."[11] Years later, Charles's friend, the engraver Alexander Anderson, then ninety-two years old, recalled that he had immigrated to the United States because of a print published in Edinburgh that "caricatured one or more of the magistrates of that city. [T]o avoid the consequences of prosecution, he left and came to the United States."[12] Some of Anderson's memories, such as the year when Charles arrived (1806, not 1801 as Anderson stated), have proven to be inaccurate, so Charles himself may have been the source of this story.

A Fallen Pillar of the Kirk is inscribed with the year "1805" without a month or day, and Charles arrived in the United States in November 1806.[13] If this specific caricature did push him to the decision to immigrate, he took his time to devise a plan. Within a

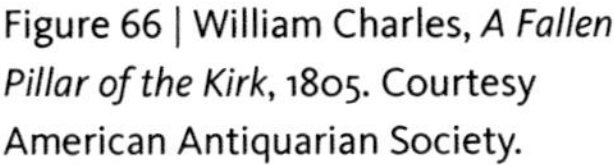

Figure 66 | William Charles, *A Fallen Pillar of the Kirk*, 1805. Courtesy American Antiquarian Society.

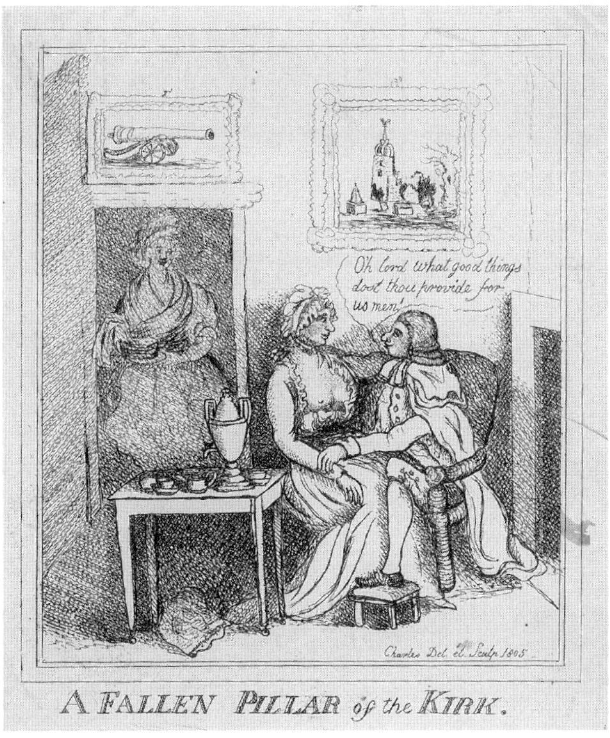

month of his arrival in New York, Charles established the "Repository of the Arts," where he would sell imported caricatures from London in addition to "a variety of prints by the first masters, fancy gold and filigree papers, ornaments for chimney pieces, card racks, hand screens, medallions, transparencies, drawings, &c." and "superb portable writing desks on the greatest construction, frames for miniatures, &c."[14] Charles must have incurred considerable expense and risk by moving to New York to set up his business. One can imagine Charles; his wife, Mary; and their young children stepping off the ship after a long journey at sea, surrounded by the boxes that held their personal possessions and the many items they planned to sell in this foreign country. Perhaps they were met by a print or bookseller in New York with whom one or both of the brothers had forged a relationship. The brothers must have had intelligence from people there to know that imported goods from London were in demand and sold well. Because no letters have been located in Charles's hand, it is not known who might have provided the newcomers with such insider information.

His New York customers might not have been aware that Charles had taken the name of his business from the London publisher and print seller Rudolph Ackermann, whose own Repository of the Arts was located on the Strand. Charles might have aspired

104

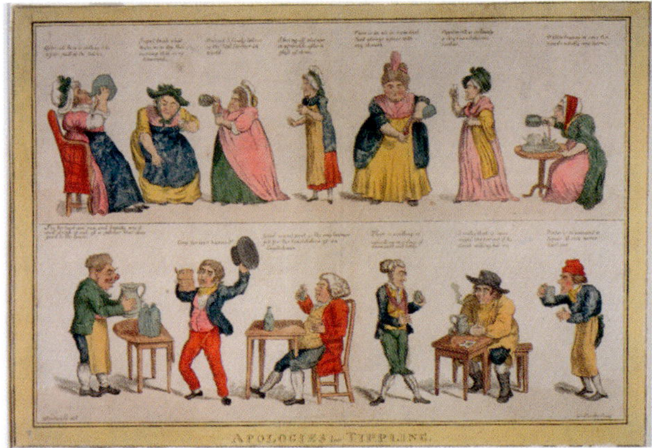

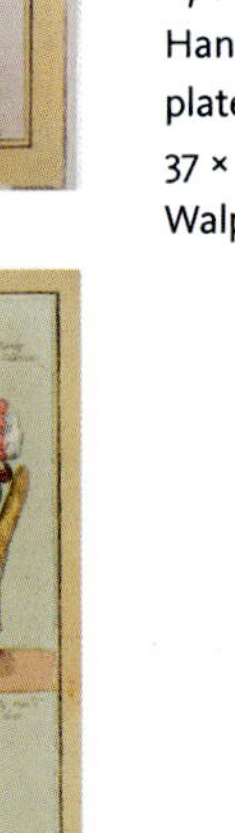

Figure 67 (*top*) | William Charles, after George Woodward, *Apologies for Tippling*, n.d. [1806–8]. Etching and watercolor, 35 × 49 cm. The Library Company of Philadelphia.

Figure 68 (*bottom*) | George Woodward, after Isaac Cruikshank (?), *Apologies for Tippling*, May 1, 1798. Hand-colored etching on wove paper, plate mark 35.6 × 47.9 cm, sheet 37 × 50 cm. Courtesy of The Lewis Walpole Library, Yale University.

to be the Rudolph Ackermann of America. In London, Ackermann was a well-respected business partner to the caricaturist and artist Thomas Rowlandson; his clientele came to his shop not only for caricatures but also for books and fine art engravings.[15] Charles may have exaggerated when he announced his intention to publish "new" caricatures. An American audience would not have known whether Charles was engraving entirely new plates and printing them off weekly. This is not to say that Charles did not do this, but the surviving caricatures from this period reveal that he sold pirated British caricature prints as his own; furthermore, few of his designs focused on American subject matter. One example is an undated caricature, *Apologies for Tippling*, signed "Wm Charles Sculp" and "Woodward del," the name of the popular British print publisher George Woodward (fig. 67 and fig. 68). Charles had an impression of the original caricature that he copied onto a copperplate either in the United States or before leaving London. Between the time he spent in London and Edinburgh, Charles had at his disposal a

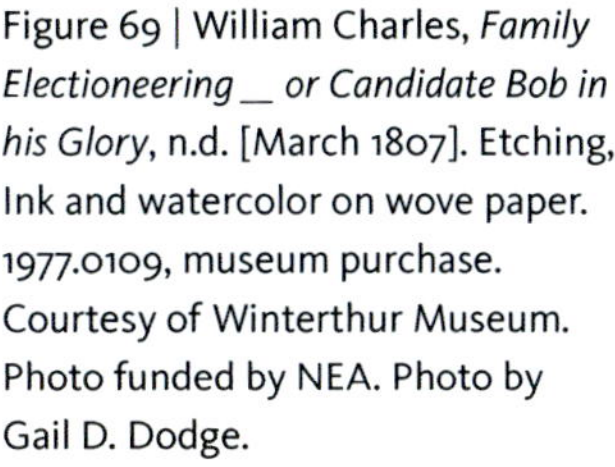

Figure 69 | William Charles, *Family Electioneering __ or Candidate Bob in his Glory*, n.d. [March 1807]. Etching, Ink and watercolor on wove paper. 1977.0109, museum purchase. Courtesy of Winterthur Museum. Photo funded by NEA. Photo by Gail D. Dodge.

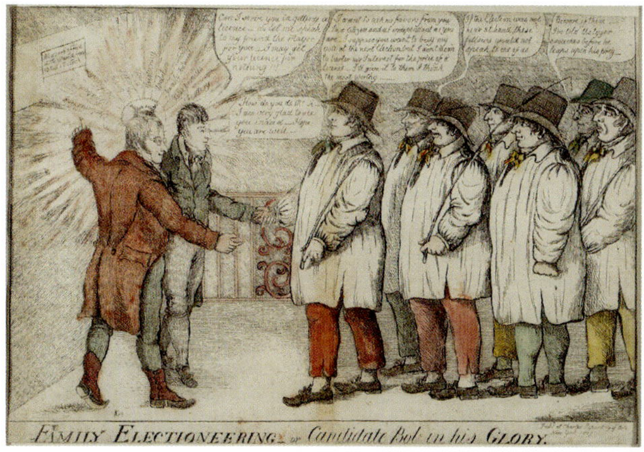

personal catalogue of British caricatures (with distinctive subjects, themes, and motifs) to be deployed for an American audience. Charles continued to copy and adapt subject matter from British caricatures well into the 1810s. The notice placed in 1806 is further evidence of Charles's entrepreneurial aspiration to introduce the regular production of caricature prints, a concept that was successful in London.

The first caricatures issued from Charles at this address were copies of such British caricatures; those that have survived contain only his name with no dates or places of publication. The first political caricature—a Charles original—was not published until March 1807, four months after establishing his business. Focused on the New York mayoral election between DeWitt Clinton, a Democratic-Republican, and his opponent, Marinus Willet, *Family Electioneering ___ or Candidate Bob in his Glory* (fig. 69) was published from Charles's Repository of the Arts in New York.[16] Newspapers were quick to criticize the print and the engraver responsible for it. According to the *People's Friend and Daily Advertiser*, "A Caricature print was yesterday in circulation, of which we can with truth say that one more infamous in the design and more worthy of signal punishment has never appeared in any country.... The lowest drab might make designs by hundreds in a day and of the drawing and engraving it may be said that [the] more execrable they are, the more suitable they are to the nature of the print." The account continued with a personal attack: "It is unworthy of an artist—a real artist would not stoop to it."[17] Charles is identified in another newspaper report as "*a Foreigner and an Alien, who lately escaped here from Edinburgh to avoid a prosecution for a caricature print ... whose name is* CHARLES; *as he carries a concealed dagger about him.* AMERICANS, *this is another attempt upon you, by the Alien gang, who infest this city.*"[18]

Charles was in New York for a little over a year; *Family Electioneering* represents the only caricature produced depicting local politics. Other caricatures that can be attributed

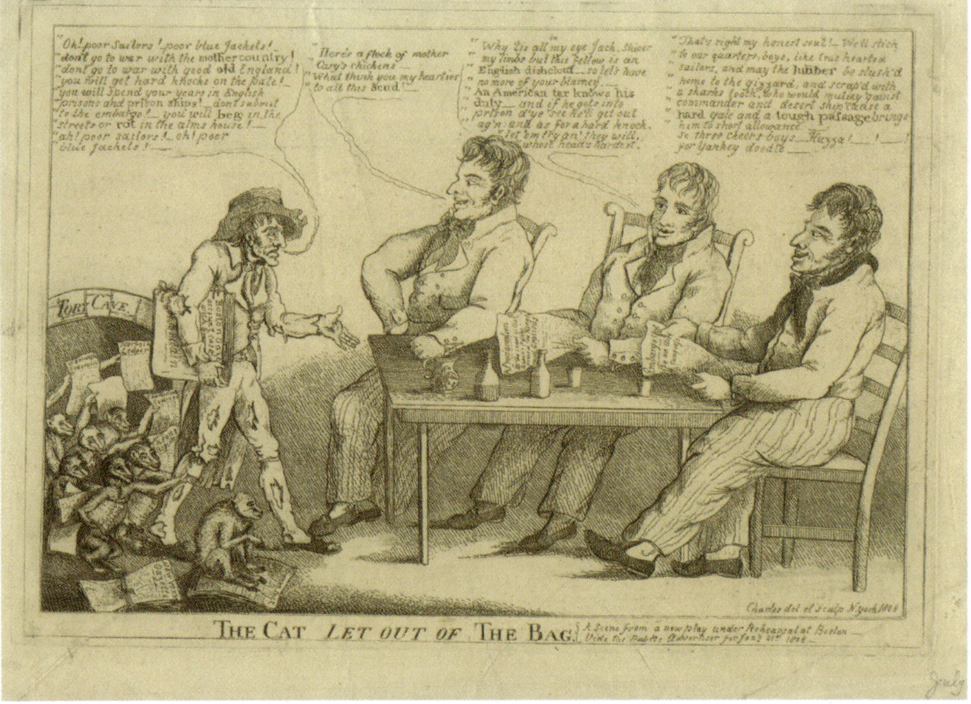

Figure 70 | William Charles, *The Cat Let Out of The Bag*, n.d. [January 1808]. Cartoon and Caricature File, PR 010, 1808-1, FF19. New-York Historical Society, image number 43347. Collection of the New-York Historical Society.

to him in this period focused on broader national issues or were copied directly from British sources. He designed and published a caricature print about the Embargo Act, *The Cat Let Out of The Bag* (fig. 70), in January 1808.[19] A British source has not been located for the general design of this caricature, and Charles took ownership ("Charles del et Sculp.," indicating that he was the artist responsible for both the drawing and the engraving). He saved the copperplate of this caricature and reissued it later during the War of 1812 with a different title, *The Tory Editor and His Apes Giveing* [sic] *Their Pitiful Advice to the American Sailors* (fig. 71). Lorraine Welling Lanmon observed that Charles exhibited a greater perspective within the image in this second state, clearly delineating a sense of space where the floor and wall meet as well as further dimension with the handling of shading. Charles changed little else, save for inserting "War" in place of "Embargo" within the speech bubbles on the far left and in the newspaper on the far right.

Another caricature that may have been published in New York was *Between Two Stools my B____ comes to the ground* (fig. 72). Although signed with the line "Charles del et

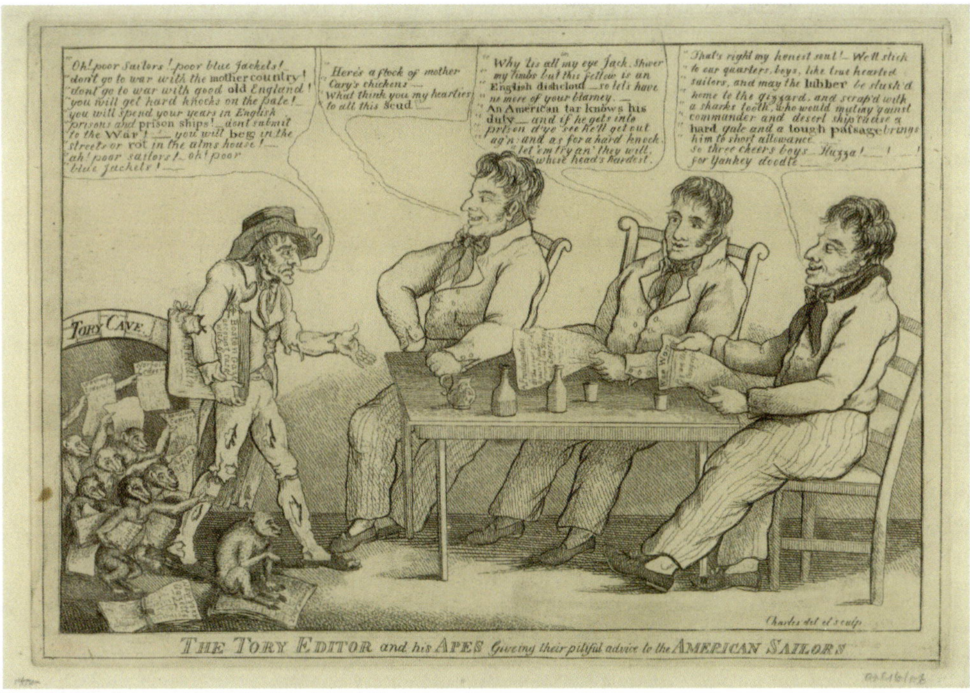

Figure 71 | William Charles, *The Tory Editor and his Apes Giveing* [sic] *their pitiful advice to the American Sailors*, n.d. [ca. 1813] Cartoon and Caricature File, PR 010, 1808-2, FF19. New-York Historical Society, image number 44811. Collection of the New-York Historical Society.

sculp," it was not a wholly original design but adapted from the British caricature *Between Two Stools the Bottom Goes to the Ground* (fig. 73) published in 1802 by Samuel Fores. Here, Charles duplicated the figure falling between the stools and the title. Because the design is different and not a complete copy, Charles might not have owned the caricature but rather remembered the title and the general scene, which he modified to depict the figure of Thomas Paine for an American audience.[20] Charles took liberties with this caricature, changing the layout by rotating the Fores design on the paper from a horizontal to a vertical orientation. Charles also adapted a figure in profile from the Thomas Rowlandson caricature, *High Fun for Iohn* [John] *Bull, or the republicans put to their last shift* (see fig. 94), leaning out the window on the far left of his print. Charles likely had this caricature in his personal collection, as he incorporated elements from it into a number of later works.

His caricature output in New York was modest, and sales from these caricatures and the imported prints were likely not enough to keep his business financially sustainable.[21]

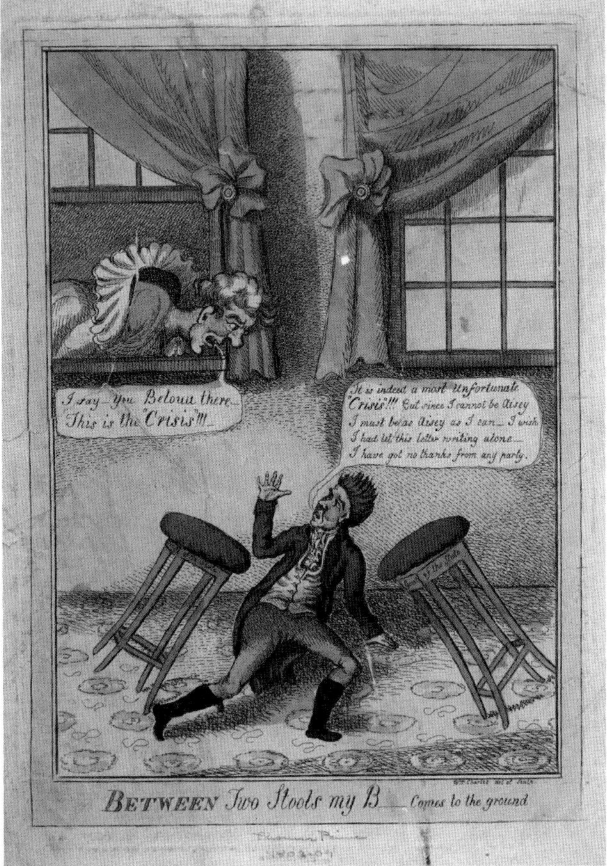

Figure 72 | William Charles, *Between Two Stools my B___ comes to the Ground*, n.d. [ca. 1808]. Courtesy American Antiquarian Society.

Attached to his "Repository of Arts" was a Lottery and Insurance Office from which he could derive additional income. Sometime in November 1807, he left his Liberty Street address and set up a shop at 195 Broadway.[22] He found other forms of employment in engraving and was responsible for book illustrations and plates etched for the *American Magazine of Wit*, published by Henry Collins Southwick on Wall Street in New York; he also published children's books.[23] By March 1808, Charles attracted the interest of the Philadelphia publisher Mathew Carey, who purchased several dozen books from him at this Broadway address.[24] By then, Charles may have recognized that patronage in New York was not as forthcoming as he had hoped; with his brother already actively working as a copperplate engraver in Philadelphia, the logical move would be to that city.[25] Perhaps Henry put Carey in contact with his brother in New York, because within months of Carey's March 1808 purchase William left New York for Philadelphia. No announcement of the move has been found in local newspapers, but by September 1808 Carey

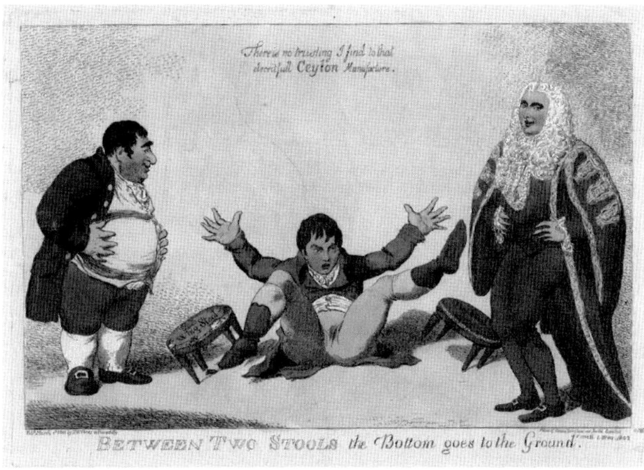

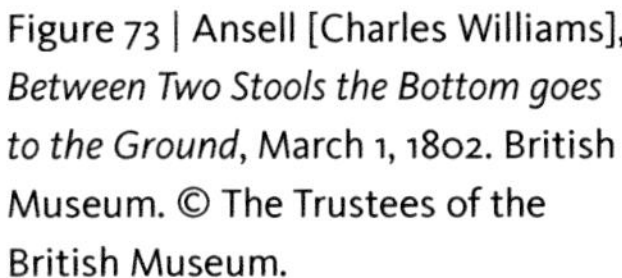
Figure 73 | Ansell [Charles Williams], *Between Two Stools the Bottom goes to the Ground*, March 1, 1802. British Museum. © The Trustees of the British Museum.

had hired Charles for "copying of caricatures."[26] In March 1809, both Henry and William were employed by Carey; however, while Henry was hired to do seven different printing jobs, William completed only one engraving task.[27] In Edinburgh, the brothers had collaborated on caricatures, but there is no evidence that they resumed a professional alliance in the United States or became partners. In addition to completing engravings for others, Charles opened a shop, from which Carey purchased several dozen items in July 1810.[28] John McAllister, who had a store on Chestnut Street in Philadelphia, wrote that he remembered "Charles and his small book-store and print-shop, which he opened in Philadelphia just before the War of 1812."[29] Charles continued to take on printing jobs, notably from Carey, who hired him to engrave plates for Mason Locke Weem's *Life of George Washington* and to add color to a number of maps.[30] Charles also was employed by other printers, with a surviving invoice providing evidence that he undertook work for William McCulloch.[31]

It was during this period that Charles may have completed the caricature signed "Wm Charles del et Sculp," *The Present State of our Country* (fig. 74). Specific British sources have not been located for this print, suggesting that generally the design and engraving were Charles's alone.[32] Although the two men on the left of the print have not been identified, a portrait in profile of George Washington can be found on the top right corner, his recognizable head revealed in the parting of clouds. In the print, Washington chastises the men with the words, "I left you with a precious casket of choicest Blessings supported by three pillars Desist my sons from pulling at them—Should you remove one you destroy the Whole." Both men on the left attempt to pull down the pillars, one labeled "Federalism" and the other "Democracy"; the wording from both explains that one wants peace, the other war. The caricature is not dated, and there are

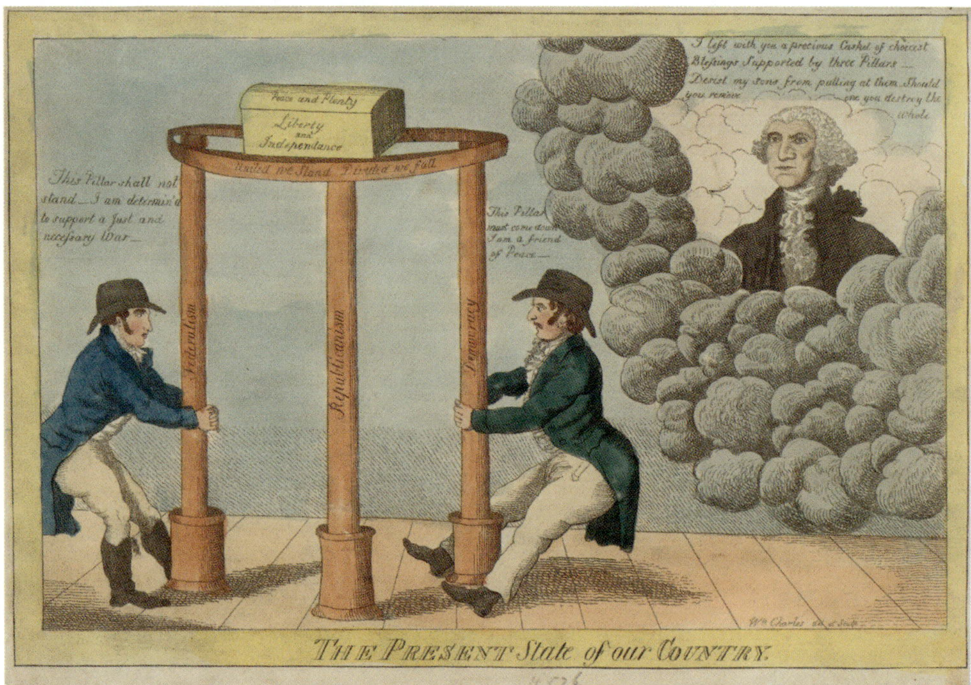

Figure 74 | William Charles, *The Present State of our Country*, n.d. [1812?]. The Miriam and Ira D. Wallach Division of Art, Prints, and Photographs: Print Collection. The New York Public Library.

no contemporary references to it, but Lanmon and Weitenkampf date the work to the beginning of the war with Britain.[33]

The War of 1812 and the Partnership Between Charles and Kennedy

Charles's experiences in London and Edinburgh, his arrival in New York, and his eventual move to Philadelphia in 1808 prepared him to take advantage of important events in the second decade of the nineteenth century. A major international situation, the War of 1812, was to provide consistent subject matter for caricaturists. Charles appreciated how caricature prints could be deployed to maximize opportunity; in 1813 he partnered with the established proprietor Samuel Kennedy to offer subscriptions and to solicit public support for this endeavor.

However, Charles was not the only engraver to see the potential of caricature at this time. There are a limited number of caricatures made by others, no doubt largely because of Charles's command of this medium. These caricatures were often signed with pseudonyms, such as three works penned by "Peter Pencil."[34] The engraver Alexander Anderson collaborated with the American portrait painter John Wesley Jarvis on at least one caricature, *Ograbme*, published in newspapers in 1814.[35] Although popular at the time, this caricature was published in a newspaper, and not separately, as were the works by Charles and Doolittle. As with other caricatures of the era, the subject matter in *Ograbme* was obscure enough that the newspaper responsible for the print's publication had to provide a description.[36] Amos Doolittle was the only engraver to publish more than one satirical print during the War of 1812 period, although he published only three caricatures.[37]

Charles likely published the first caricature of the War of 1812 in reaction to the battle between the United States naval ship the *Wasp* and the British *Frolic*.[38] *A Wasp Taking a Frolick Or a Sting for Johnny Bull* (fig. 75) was signed solely by him, prior to his partnership with Kennedy. If Charles advertised the print, these have not been located, but newspapers published lengthy reports of the "Gallant Achievement" beginning in November of 1812, and artists produced paintings, such as Thomas Birch's *The Wasp and the Frolic* that was subsequently engraved by Benjamin Tanner and James Webster. The following year, Doolittle published a caricature inspired by another American victory in February 1813. The American sloop of war *Hornet* encountered the HMS *Peacock* off the northern shore of Africa. According to newspaper reports published a month later, the battle between the two ships lasted less than fifteen minutes before the *Peacock* surrendered, having lost its commanding officer and at least seven sailors to gunfire. The American vessel took aboard the survivors of the other vessel and set a course back to Massachusetts, arriving by the middle of March. The victory inspired the publication of caricatures in the ensuing weeks and months, depicting the symbolic emblems of peacocks and hornets in battle. Doolittle's caricature, *The Hornet and Peacock, Or, John Bull in Distress* (fig. 76), was published on March 27, 1813, six weeks after the battle. To an engraver of Revolutionary War prints, the US naval victory may have been a reminder of the interest that had inspired him in the 1770s to memorialize American military victories. Doolittle, in accordance with the copyright law of 1802, inscribed the following below the title: "Entered according to act of Congress the 27th day of March 1813 by A. Doolittle of the State of Connecticut." He was not the first engraver to provide a copyright on his prints: after 1805 Akin included this line, although many artists did not.

A description of the Doolittle caricature was soon referenced in numerous newspapers, but he himself did not advertise the print for sale, a departure from what he had done for his earlier engravings.[39] A Hartford, Connecticut, newspaper notice on March 26, the day before Doolittle's caricature appeared, observed that the recent battle might be excellent subject matter for a caricature: "If, in this wild country, we had

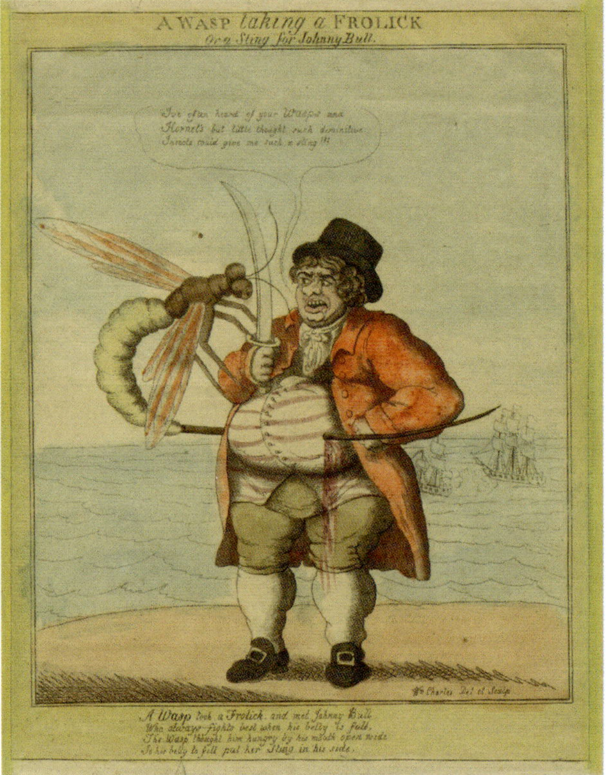

Figure 75 | William Charles, *A Wasp Taking a Frolick Or a Sting for Johnny Bull*, n.d. [1812]. PR 047, OFig lds Collection #429. New-York Historical Society, image number 98258d. Collection of the New-York Historical Society.

attained all the delicate civilization which characterises 'the bulwark of our holy religion,' and were, like our *polished* antagonists, fond of *caricaturing,* some of our geniuses might make a very tolerable representation of a Peacock (no unfit emblem of the boastful Briton) stung to death by an indignant Hornet, whose nest he had, in his magisterial strut, arrogantly invaded."[40] It is possible the newspaper editor was already aware of Doolittle's plans to produce a caricature of the battle. Less than a week later, *The Yankee* in Boston was the first of many New England newspapers to describe the Doolittle caricature: "We have seen a very diverting and ingenious caricature of the defeat of the Peacock by the Hornet, which is about to be published. The lovers of humor cannot fail to enjoy this pertinancity [*sic*] and pleasantry of the conceit, and the risiblaties [*sic*] of the most grave will be moved by its greatness. It will be a choice treat to those who are fond of fun."[41] Several days later the caricature was available to purchase from Paul Mondelly's store in Boston, with an advertisement stating that the work was "a rich treat to lovers of wit and patriotism."[42] The caricature could be purchased individually for "*twelve and an half* cents" while an enterprising book or print seller could purchase one hundred impressions for nine dollars.

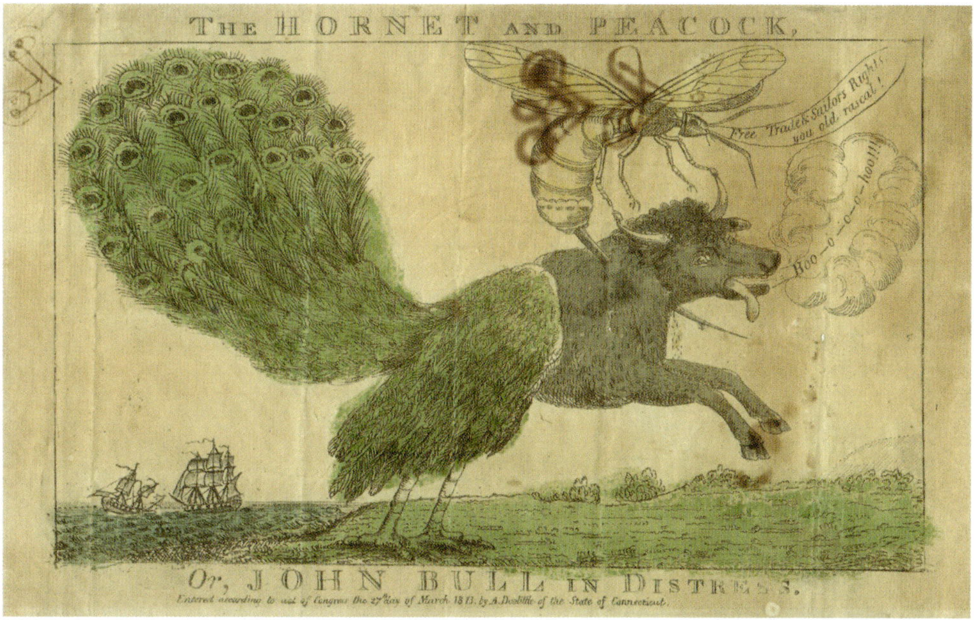

Figure 76 | Amos Doolittle, *The Hornet and Peacock, Or, John Bull in Distress*, March 27, 1813. Cartoon and Caricature File, PR 010, 1813-2, FF21. New-York Historical Society, image number 98259d. Collection of the New-York Historical Society.

Newspaper advertisements provide the opportunity to trace the circulation and availability of this caricature. Surprisingly, references at the time of the caricature's publication in Connecticut newspapers have not been found; rather, beginning in March, the caricature was frequently advertised in Boston newspapers. In mid-April, when Charles Shepherd of Hartford offered impressions of the caricature for sale, it was around the same time that impressions of the caricature were available in New York and could be purchased at "No. 90 Broadway, and at the War Office, No. 473 Pearl St." At the discretion of the editor, the language of these advertisements might embellish what had already appeared in another city. For example, one newspaper wrote, "'More is meant than meets the eye' at the first view of this print. It represents John Bull proud, like the Peacock, but at the same time his pride is receiving the mortal wound by the sting of the Hornet, and his tail flags the consequence of it."[43] Advertisements for the Doolittle caricature have not been located in newspapers south of New York; it appears that the print was sold primarily in New York as well as the New England states of Vermont, Connecticut, and Massachusetts.[44]

If Doolittle, in Connecticut, was one of the first to produce a caricature of the battles, caricaturists in Philadelphia were a close second. Newspapers hailed "the great feats of our little Navy" that were the subjects of two recently published caricatures:

114

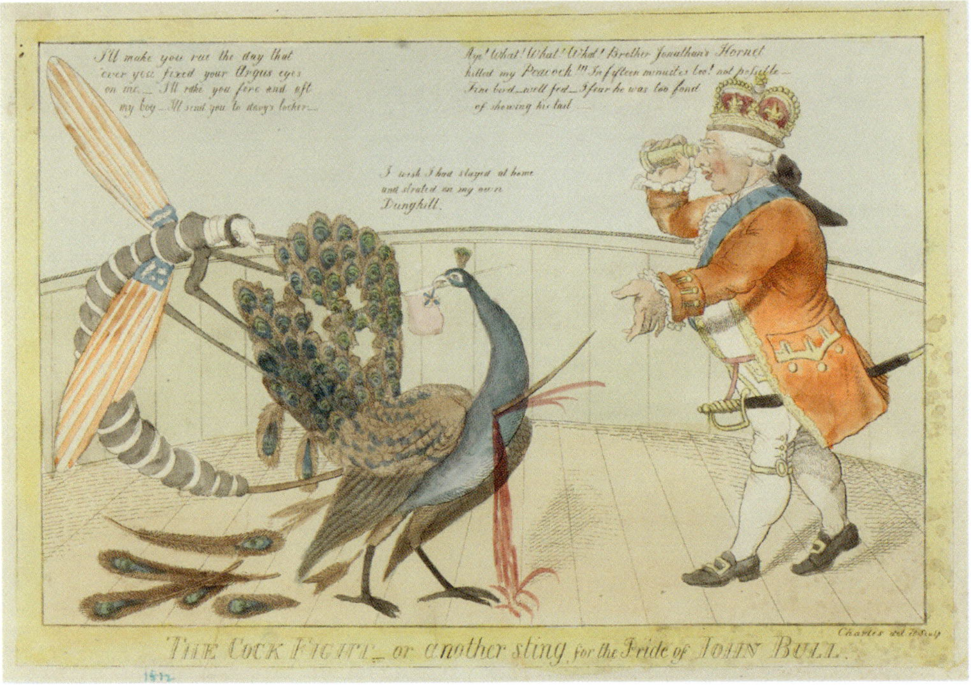

Figure 77 | William Charles, *The Cock Fight __ or another sting for the Pride of Iohn [John] Bull*, n.d. [September 1813]. Bb 612 C644. Reproduced with permission from the Historical Society of Pennsylvania.

CARICATURES.... Connected with our praise is the disgrace of our enemy. The boasts of Mr. Bull, his extravagant encomiums upon his own navy, and his insolent taunts upon our seaman, has caused us to enjoy his disgrace with additional relish. The disappointed boaster is the most ridiculous of all characters. He becomes the bull of every one, and if he is of consequence enough to deserve rebuke, is handed over to the lash of the genius of ridicule. He struts in a farce; writhes in a satire; is impaled by a pun; or figures in a caricature.

The wits of Philadelphia have already taken Mr. Bull by the horns—and with a genius happy and prompt, have depicted his agonies in Caricature. We have seen two of them, of this description.[45]

Charles's caricature is referenced in this notice, having published his response to the battle in early April with *The Cock Fight ___ or another sting for the Pride of Iohn* [John] *Bull* (fig. 77). He found inspiration in at least one British source, the 1803 James Gillray caricature *The King of Brobdingnag and Gulliver* (fig. 78). Charles took the figure of King

Figure 78 | James Gillray, after Lieutenant Colonel Thomas Braddyll, *The King of Brobdingnag and Gulliver*, June 26, 1803. Etching and aquatint on wove paper, hand-colored, sheet 37 × 28.2 cm. Courtesy of The Lewis Walpole Library, Yale University.

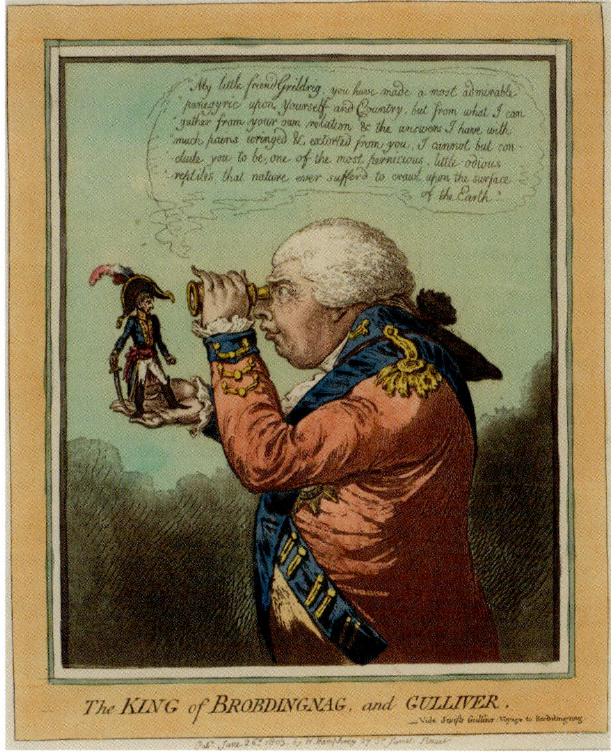

George from the Gillray print, where it was shown in profile, and placed it within his American caricature in full length. This is another British caricature that Charles relied heavily on and used in a number of the works he made while in London.[46]

Charles did show some creativity, however, in his depiction of the hornet, with its wings covered in stars and stripes and its stinger piercing the body of the peacock. Charles may have known the engraver, "S.D.F.," who likely published the second Philadelphia caricature mentioned in the notice, *Iohn* [John] *Bull stung to agony by Insects* (fig. 79), since the two works display similar features. The caricature has an unusual element, as the newspaper notice observed: "The most curious circumstance, however, in this caricature is the date on it—It was 'published in Philadelphia, 1st March, 1813': thus predicting, by a sort of inspiration, the splendid triumphs of the *Hornet*." If this was not in error, then perhaps "S.D.F.," who was likely the Philadelphia publisher and miniaturist Samuel Folwell, simply wanted his caricature to be known as the very first to depict this event.[47] Folwell's impression was copied by at least two others who made a slight change to the title (deleting "Insects" and adding the ship names, "by the Wasp and Hornet") and omitted Folwell's vignette scene to the far right (of a wasp's nest in a dying tree

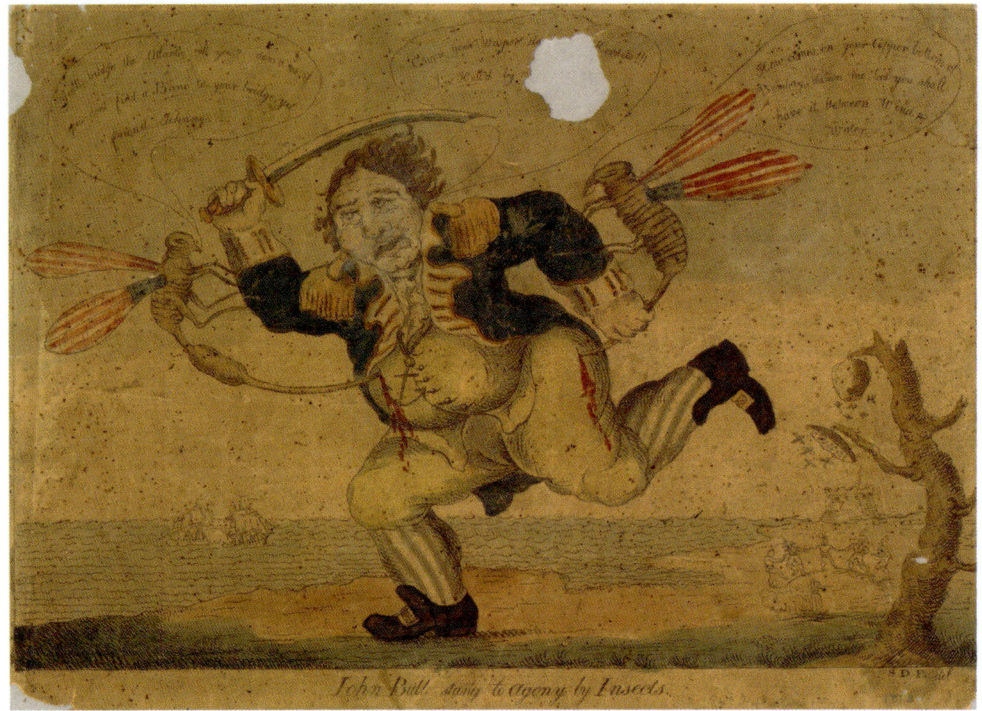

Figure 79 | S.D.F., *Iohn* [John] *Bull stung to agony by Insects*, March 1, 1813. Courtesy American Antiquarian Society.

and a group of figures in a circle). The copies survive in at least two separate states, and both are thought to have been completed in Boston. One impression includes the words "Huzza for 'Free Trade and Sailor's Rights'" above the image, while another includes the text "Huzza for the American Navy" (fig. 80 and fig. 81). These caricatures, including the one signed by "S.D.F.," feature the same text within the speech bubbles and text.

At this juncture, Charles saw an opportunity for caricature that had not been available to him in 1806 in New York: an audience that wanted visual imagery that mocked a common enemy, the British navy, and taunted their victories in battle. How Charles and Kennedy came to partner is not clear: before this time, there are no apparent connections between the two, and no caricatures can be attributed solely to Kennedy before this collaboration. Newspaper accounts and directory listings reveal that Kennedy was a respected and established Philadelphia entrepreneur, and Charles likely believed that a partnership with him would elevate the endeavor.[48] Kennedy, for example, ran a "looking glass manufactory" and store at 72 Chestnut Street, where he also sold a wide variety of items that included picture frames and prints.[49] Like Akin and his partnership with

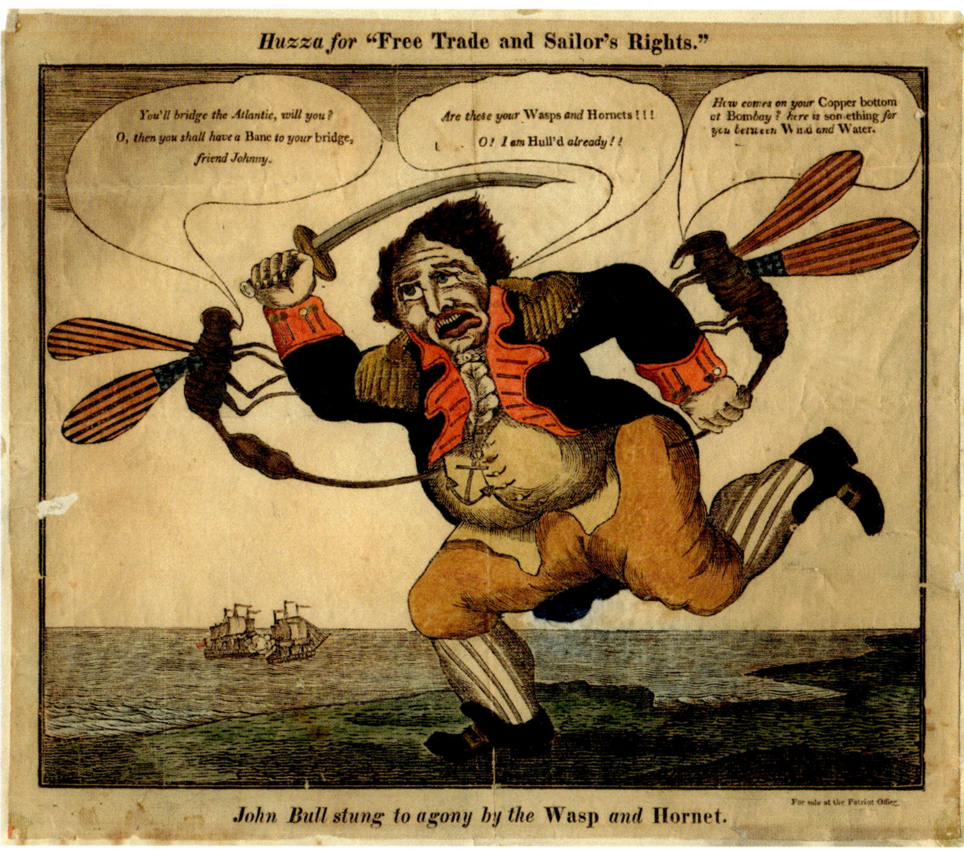

Figure 80 | Anonymous, *John Bull stung to agony by the Wasp and Hornet / Huzza for "Free Trade and Sailor's Rights,"* n.d. [1813]. Cartoon and Caricature File, PR 010, 1812-1, FF21. New-York Historical Society, image number 22851. Collection of the New-York Historical Society.

Harrison in the late 1790s, Charles understood the necessity of pairing with another to establish a stronger network and distribute the expensive and time-consuming work required of printing. In return, Charles, brought his intimate knowledge of caricature to the partnership.

In May, Charles and Kennedy announced their joint intention to publish caricature prints in a lengthy advertisement exclusive to Philadelphia newspapers (fig. 82). Referencing Horace's axiom that "a picture is a poem without words," they proclaimed that their endeavor was to "produce, ORIGINAL CARICATURES, OF THE FIRST STYLE, and [they] flatter themselves with their joint knowledge of experience in and attention thereto, will obtain public patronage, being entirely uninfluenced by party." Claiming to

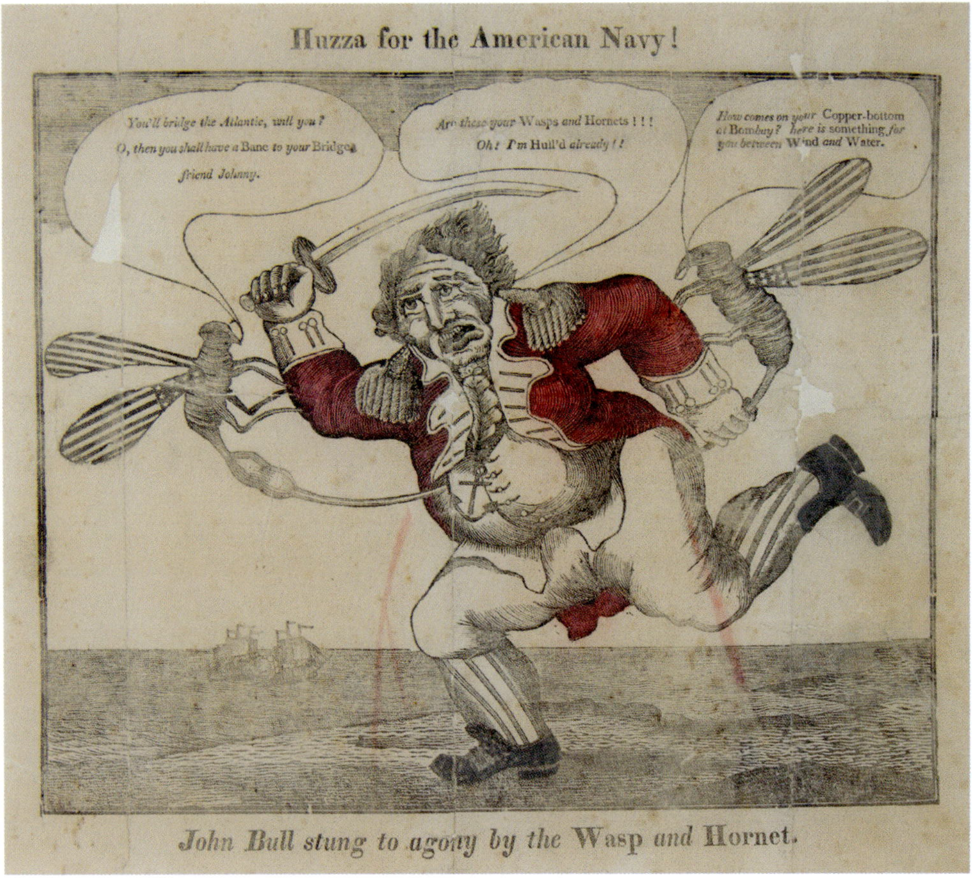

Figure 81 | Anonymous, *John Bull stung to agony by the Wasp and Hornet / Huzza for the American Navy!*, n.d. [1813]. The Connecticut Historical Society.

have no political affiliation, they offered subscriptions of four caricatures to be published each month. The partners gave readers a taste of their vision by imagining that "on this foundation, they (with public assistance) propose raising a fortress, from which they may 'shoot folly as it flies.'" Two price levels were offered: $1.50 per number or $2.00 for nonsubscribers.[50] While what is known about the engraving practices of James Akin is limited to the surviving 1803 Kneass invoice, there is no information about the assistance Akin might have enlisted to produce his caricature prints or whether he attempted to sell his caricatures wholesale or individually. However, the Charles and Kennedy advertisement reveals that they intended to work collaboratively together and that they sought artistic input in the form of sketches and drawings from other artists and engravers. They were actively searching for artists and engravers who could contribute to their venture.

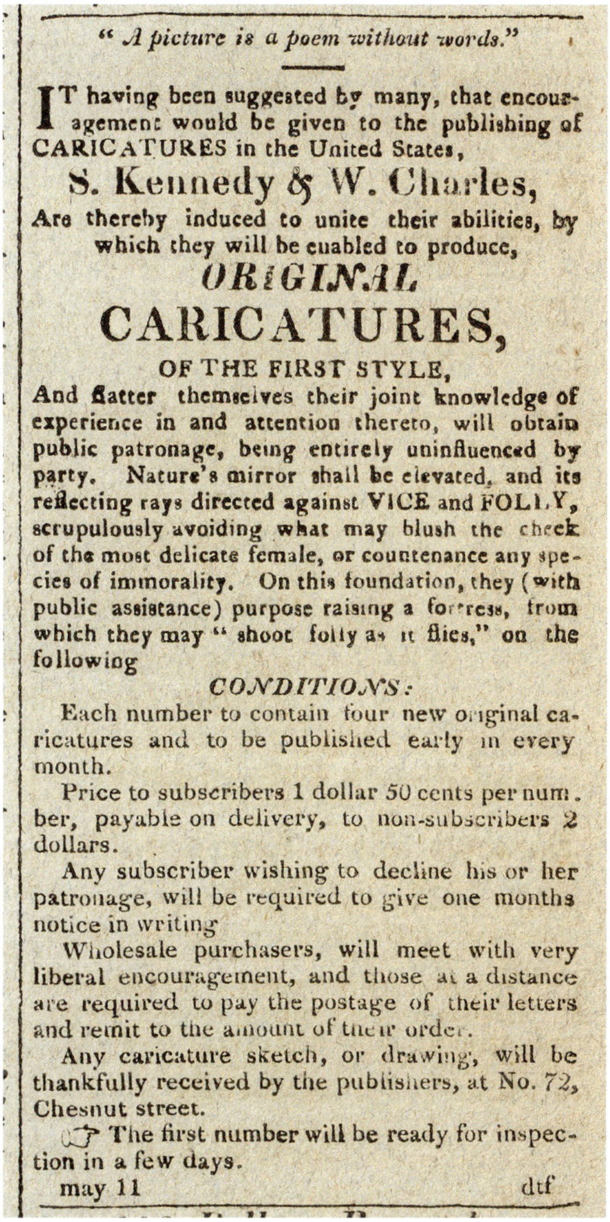

Figure 82 | *Poulson's American Daily Advertiser* (Philadelphia), May 11, 1813. Courtesy American Antiquarian Society.

" A picture is a poem without words."

IT having been suggested by many, that encouragement would be given to the publishing of CARICATURES in the United States,

S. Kennedy & W. Charles,

Are thereby induced to unite their abilities, by which they will be enabled to produce,

ORIGINAL

CARICATURES,

OF THE FIRST STYLE,

And flatter themselves their joint knowledge of experience in and attention thereto, will obtain public patronage, being entirely uninfluenced by party. Nature's mirror shall be elevated, and its reflecting rays directed against VICE and FOLLY, scrupulously avoiding what may blush the cheek of the most delicate female, or countenance any species of immorality. On this foundation, they (with public assistance) purpose raising a fortress, from which they may " shoot folly as it flies," on the following

CONDITIONS:

Each number to contain four new original caricatures and to be published early in every month.

Price to subscribers 1 dollar 50 cents per number, payable on delivery, to non-subscribers 2 dollars.

Any subscriber wishing to decline his or her patronage, will be required to give one months notice in writing

Wholesale purchasers, will meet with very liberal encouragement, and those at a distance are required to pay the postage of their letters and remit to the amount of their order.

Any caricature sketch, or drawing, will be thankfully received by the publishers, at No. 72, Chesnut street.

☞ The first number will be ready for inspection in a few days.

may 11   dtf

This may explain why some of the prints that can be associated with the Charles and Kennedy name or address vary in skill and style: these were contributions engraved and printed without reference to the original designer.

The partnership of Charles and Kennedy worked intermittently, with long pauses followed by bursts of activity around specific events resulting in groupings of caricatures.

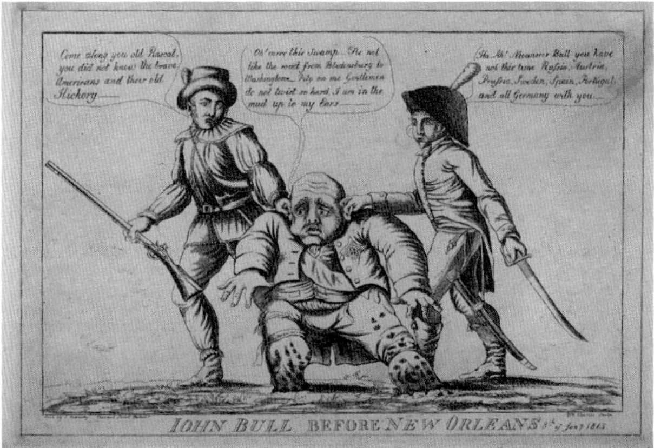

Figure 83 | William Charles, *Iohn [John] Bull before New Orleans*, January 8, 1815. Courtesy American Antiquarian Society.

The total number of works published by the partnership is not fully known, as more caricatures might be located, although at least six known presently bear either the Kennedy and Charles names or the 72 Chestnut Street address, as listed in the advertisement: *Columbia Teaching John Bull His New Lesson, Queen Charlotte and Johnny Bull Got Their Dose of Perry, Iohn* [John] *Bull before New Orleans* (fig. 83), *Johnny Bull in a Fret, A Boxing Match,* and *The Hartford Convention or Leap No Leap.*[51] The sequence in which caricatures were issued from the partnership is generally not known, because none of their caricatures provides a date of publication. The first caricatures were likely published in May 1813, as an advertisement promised that "the first number will be ready for inspection in a few days." Publication attributions can be made for some of the caricatures, based on advertisements that have been located in newspapers and by examinations of the subject matter is relation to historical events.

One further caricature was *Johnny Bull in a Fret* (fig. 84), which does not include a publication date but does include additional information on the print linking it to Charles and Kennedy and to Kennedy's Chestnut Street address. *Johnny Bull in a Fret* inscribes the location of publication as "Pubd at 72 Chestnut St. Phila.," the premises of Kennedy's looking glass factory and print store, below the title.[52] The similarities found in the inscription on this caricature and *John Bull Stung to Agony by Insects* suggest the attribution of both to S.D.F. (Samuel Folwell). Perhaps Folwell submitted a drawing for publication and his name was omitted when published.[53]

Subject matter of this kind remained in the memories of many and enjoyed wide appeal. Newspaper editors printed reports of naval battles urging caricaturists to take up their engraving tools and publish new prints. An account of the capture of the British ship *Epervier* by the American *Peacock* off the coast of Florida on April 29, 1814, is one such example: "The subject will doubtless occasion another punishing caricature for the

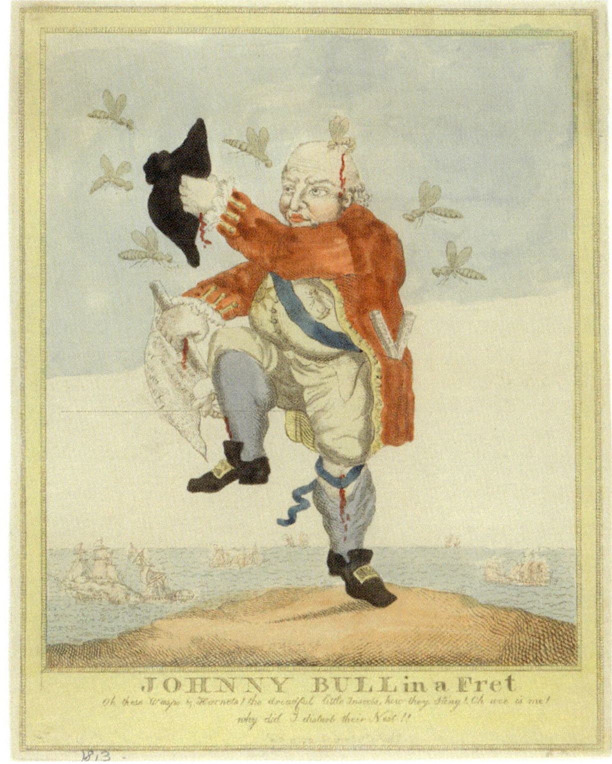

Figure 84 | Anonymous [William Charles or S.D.F?], *Johnny Bull in a Fret*, n.d. [1813]. Bb 612 J616. Reproduced with permission from the Historical Society of Pennsylvania.

print shops."[54] As no prints have been located that might have been published in commemoration of this battle, it does not appear that caricaturists took this particular bait.

From the start of their partnership, Charles and Kennedy were enthusiastic that their ambitious and unique plan would be well received. They aspired to publish a series of caricature prints under its own title, although they did not mention this plan in their initial May announcement. At the end of May they advertised that "on the 1st day of June, the Public will be presented with the first number of the 'Caricaturist's Magazine,' with a specimen available at 72 Chestnut Street."[55] However, their enthusiasm for the project quickly soured because support for the "Caricaturist's Magazine" did not materialize; in July they announced that "in consequence of not receiving the encouragement they were induced to expect, they decline publishing Carricatures [*sic*] in periodical numbers, but will as eligible subjects may offer, publish single Caricature Prints."[56] They added that they continued to welcome drawings of caricatures and that a new caricature print was due to be published within days. With this announcement, their partnership appears to have lost its momentum. Because they were publishing caricatures "as eligible subjects may offer," it is possible to understand why the works that have survived appear

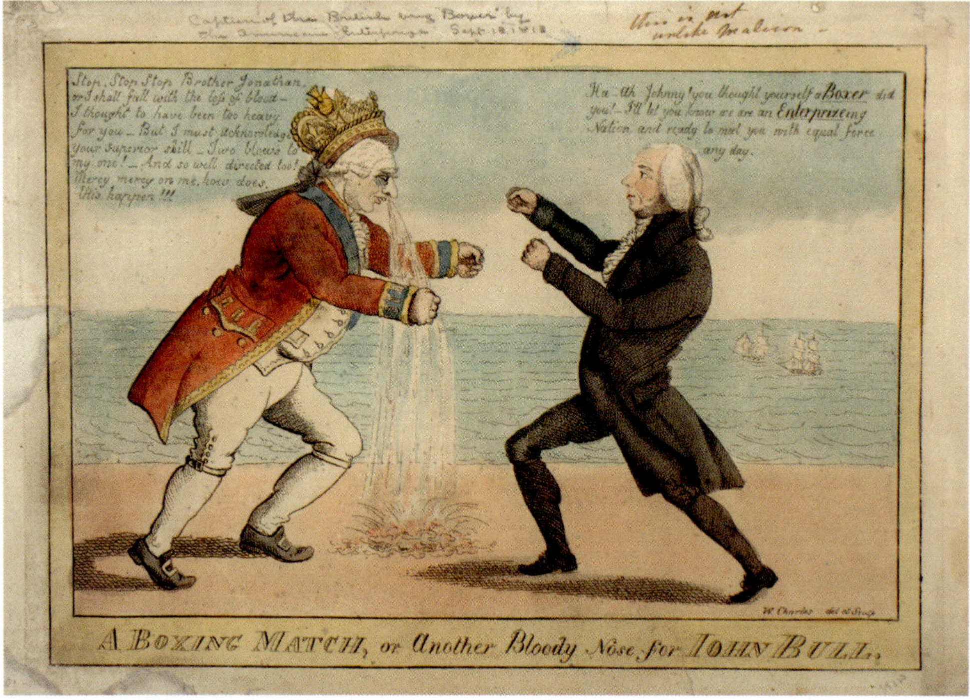

Figure 85 | William Charles, *A Boxing Match, or Another Bloody Nose for Iohn* [John] *Bull*, n.d. [September 1813]. Hand-colored etching, printed area 24.2 × 33.7 cm, sheet 25 × 34 cm. Courtesy American Antiquarian Society.

to have been published infrequently. Their partnership continued in reduced form and with intermittent pauses between May 1813 and December 1814.[57] Indeed, after the July 1813 notice announcing the failure of the "Caricaturist's Magazine" their names are not found together in newspaper notices, and advertisements that provide titles of caricatures include either Kennedy's Chestnut Street address or Charles's name but not both. Around this time Charles made the decision to become a naturalized citizen, which his brother had done in 1811.[58]

Between 1813 and 1815, Kennedy continued to advertise his varied businesses and partnerships frequently in newspapers. For example, in March 1814 Kennedy advertised that he was selling busts of Washington by Houdon and was still accepting subscriptions for a "Bust of Commodore Bainbridge."[59] Charles placed considerably fewer advertisements, and they often omit his name, giving either the title of a caricature for sale or an address associated with him. By 1814, it was the "corner of George and Broad streets."[60]

In June 1814, Kennedy advertised a collaboration with "J. Webster" that operated out of the Chestnut Street address and announced the sale of a print of Russian emperor

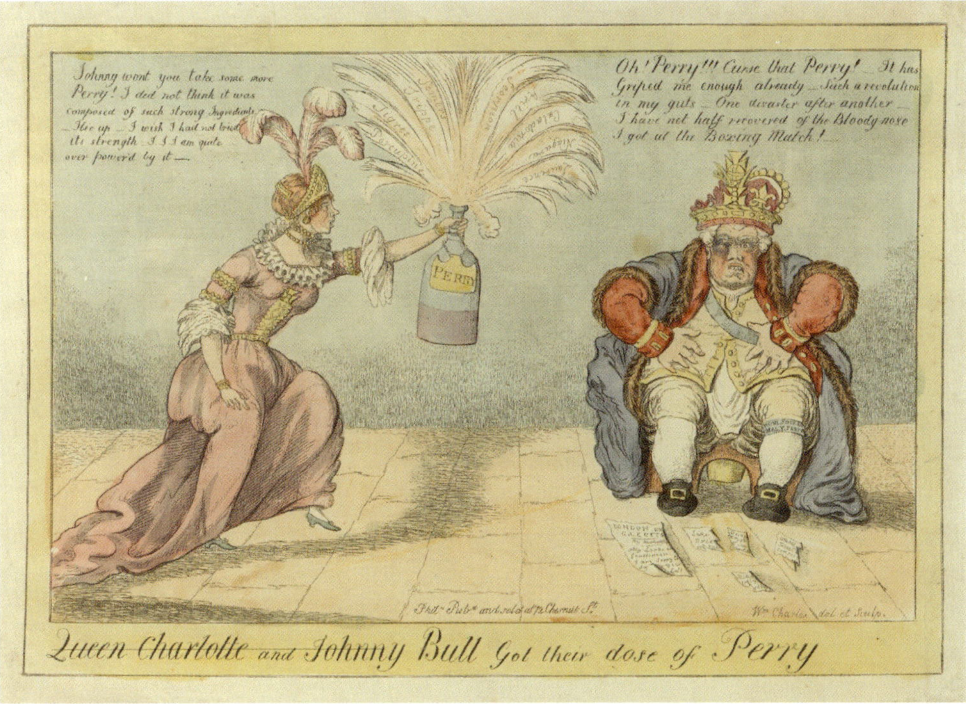

Figure 86 | William Charles, *Queen Charlotte and Johnny Bull got their dose of Perry*, n.d. [September 1813]. Bb 612 Q31. Reproduced with permission from the Historical Society of Pennsylvania.

Alexander I by David Edwin.[61] He also noted that he had for sale impressions of two prints that depicted victories from recent battles on Lake Erie, which could be purchased from the "Bookstore of R. P & C. Williams." He did not indicate whether these prints were caricatures (e.g., by providing titles or noting a connection to Charles), although it is possible that they were. The previous year the next collection of caricatures published by their partnership celebrated another American victory against Britain, the Battle of Lake Erie in the fall of 1813. It was considered one of the more important naval battles of the War of 1812 as it ensured American control of the lake for the rest of the conflict. With a small fleet of specially built ships led by Admiral Oliver Hazard Perry, the Americans were able to capture the British ship *Queen Charlotte*. On September 16, Charles and Kennedy published the first of two caricatures, *A Boxing Match, or Another Bloody Nose for Iohn* [John] *Bull* (fig. 85), announcing it as "The Boxer—A Caricature of the Engagement between the Enterprize & Boxer."[62] Two weeks later, *Queen Charlotte and Johnny Bull Got Their Dose of Perry* (fig. 86) appeared and was advertised as "Queen Charlotte and her Bottle of Perry, A Carricature [*sic*]" at the Chestnut Street address.[63] The caricature

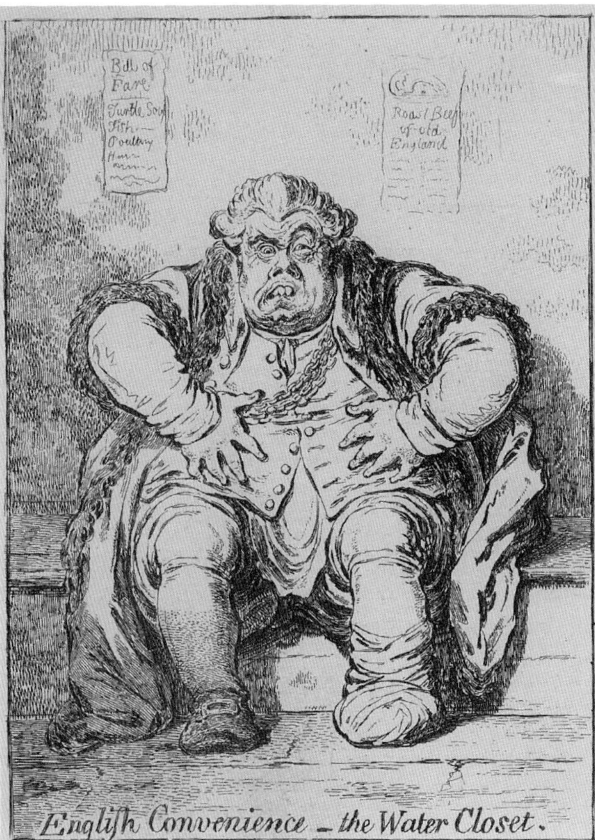

English Convenience _ the Water Closet.

Figure 87 | James Gillray, *National Conveniences. English Convenience__ the Water Closet*, January 25, 1796. British Museum. © The Trustees of the British Museum.

of Queen Charlotte was greatly influenced by British caricature prints by Gillray. The figure of John Bull, seen on the right of the Charles caricature, was copied from a section of Gillray's 1796 caricature *National Conveniences. English Convenience_____ the Water Closet* (fig. 87), while the spray emitting from the bottle of Perry with a text bubble in the Charles caricature can be traced to Gillray's 1805 *Uncorking Old Sherry* (fig. 88). In the Charles caricature, John Bull is depicted saying to Charlotte, "Oh Perry!!! Curse the Perry! It has griped enough already—Such a Revolution in my guts—One disaster after another I have not yet recovered of the Bloody-nose I got at the Boxing Match!" This reference to *A Boxing Match* also provides the order in which these prints were made.

Kennedy may have had remainders from this group of caricatures still on hand in June of the following year, as he sold four caricatures to Mathew Carey on three separate occasions. In October and November 1813, Carey paid two dollars for twelve works in total.[64] Kennedy may have had the Lake Erie caricatures for sale, although it is also entirely possible that Kennedy and Charles had published other caricatures in the fall of

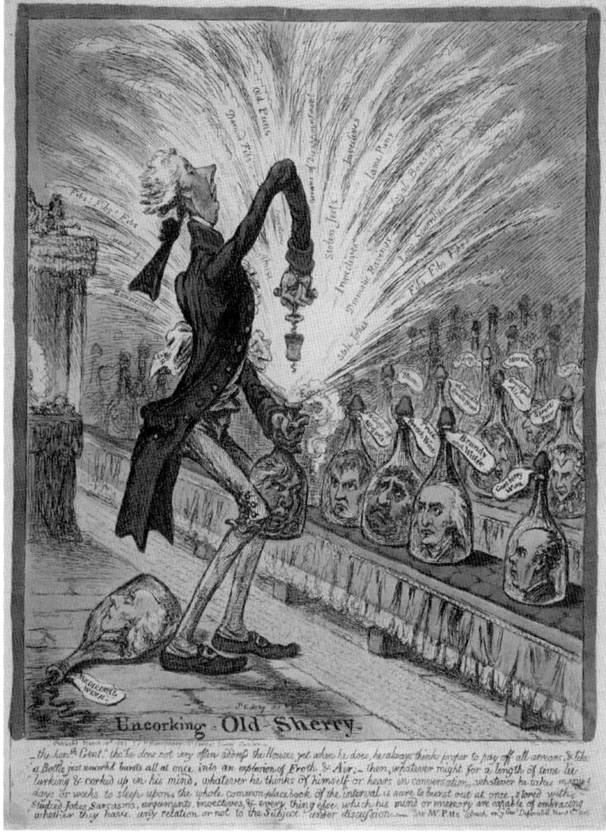

Figure 88 | James Gillray, *Uncorking Old Sherry*, March 10, 1805. Plate 14 1/16 × 10 in. (35.7 × 25.4 cm), sheet 15 3/8 × 11 1/2 in. (39.1 × 29.2 cm). Gift of Adele S. Gollin, 1976. The Metropolitan Museum of Art, New York.

1813. If so, these could include *Columbia Teaching John Bull His New Lesson* (fig. 89) and *Bruin Become Mediator or Negociation* [*sic*] *for Peace* (fig. 90).[65] Neither caricature bears a date of publication, and newspaper references have not been located. The inscription on *Columbia Teaching John Bull His New Lesson* indicates that Kennedy was responsible for the design and Charles the engraving. The inscription on *Bruin Become Mediator* names only Charles, who must have been aware of the Isaac Cruikshank print with the same title, first published in London in 1803. It is unlikely that he had an impression with him in Philadelphia, as the figures are not directly copied. The speech bubbles in this carica-ture refer to the battle of the *Hornet* and *Wasp*, indicating that its publication followed the caricatures from the spring. *Columbia Teaching John Bull* is stylistically different from other caricatures made by Charles, but this could reflect the involvement of Kennedy or an unknown engraver.

The following year, three caricatures are dated to October 1814 with only Charles as engraver: *Iohn* [John] *Bull making a new Batch of Ships to send to the Lakes* (fig. 91), *John*

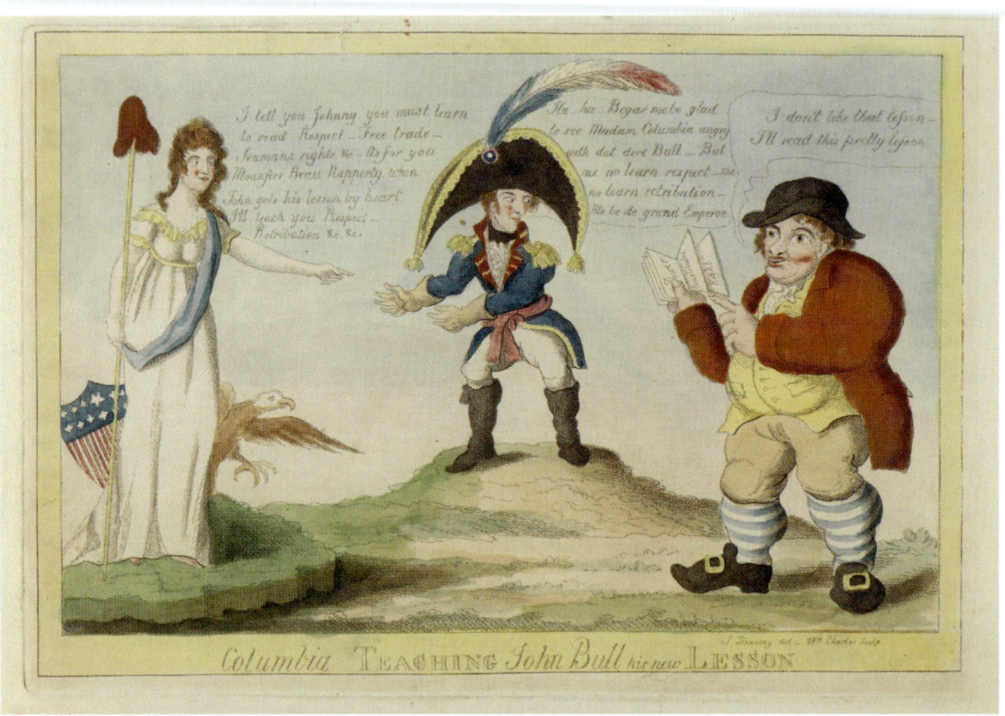

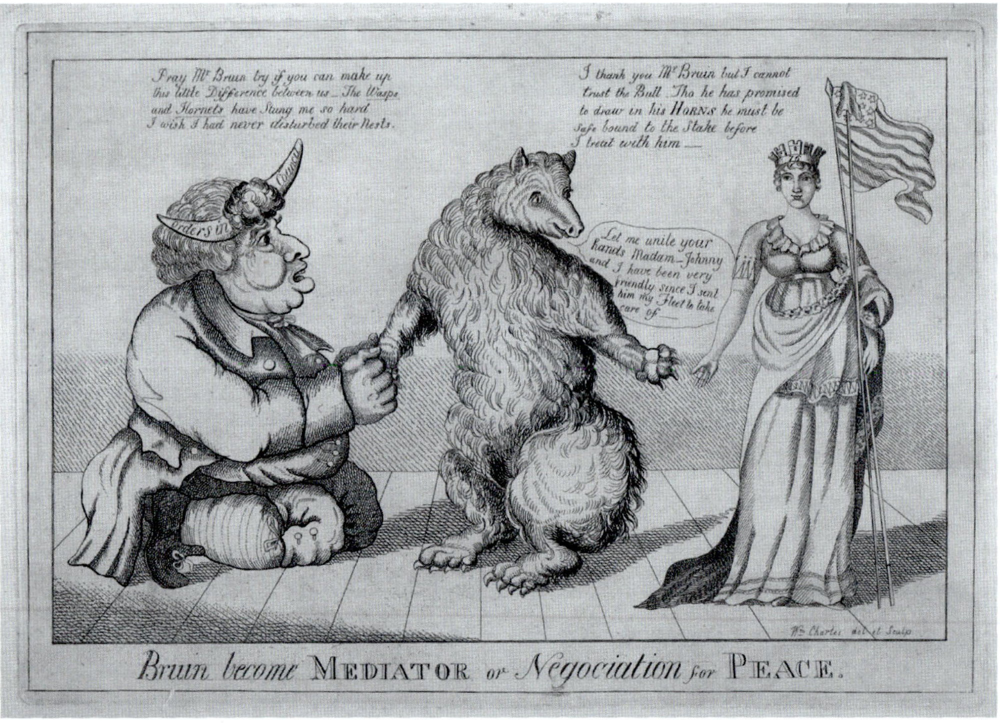

Figure 89 (*top*) | William Charles, *Columbia Teaching John Bull His New Lesson*, n.d. [1813]. Bb 612 C723. Reproduced with permission from the Historical Society of Pennsylvania.

Figure 90 (*bottom*) | William Charles, *Bruin become Mediator or Negociation* [sic] *for Peace*, n.d. [1813]. Courtesy American Antiquarian Society.

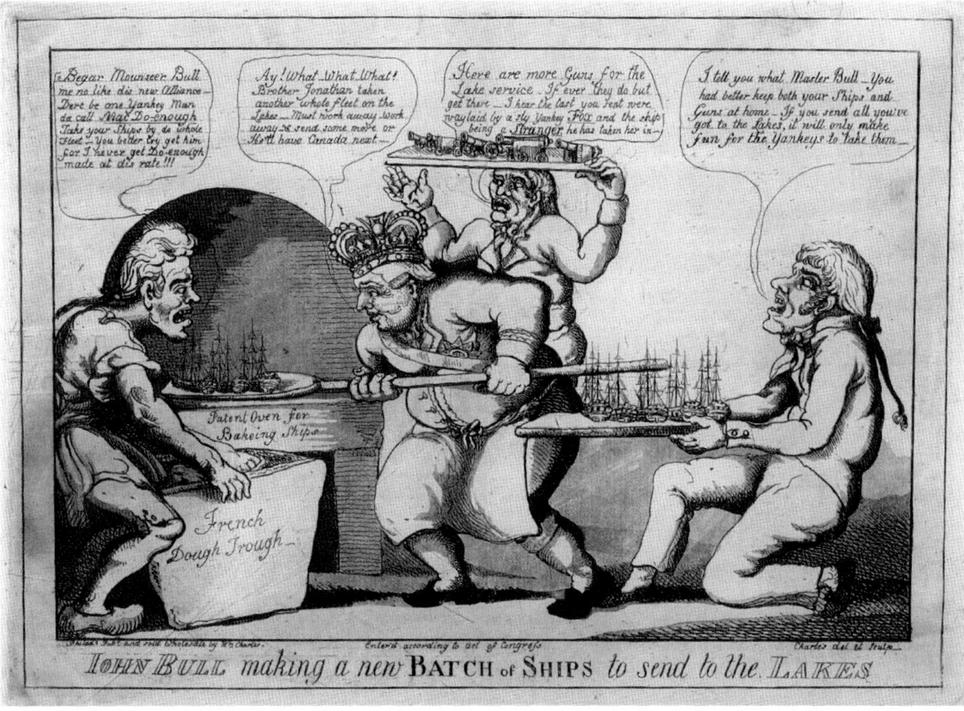

Figure 91 | William Charles, *Iohn* [John] *Bull making a new Batch of Ships to send to the Lakes*, n.d. [October 1814]. Courtesy American Antiquarian Society.

Bull and the Baltimoreans (fig. 92), and *Johnny Bull and the Alexandrians* (fig. 93). Inscriptions on these caricatures state that they were published in Philadelphia and sold wholesale by William Charles ("del et sculp") and include the copyright statement that they were "enter'd according to Act of Congress." Indeed, Charles did deposit all three caricatures for copyright. The Library of Congress has an impression of each work with the date of deposit recorded: *Johnny Bull and the Alexandrians* and *John Bull and the Baltimoreans* (October 21, 1814), and *Iohn* [John] *Bull making a new Batch of Ships to send to the Lakes* (October 24, 1814). On October 2, Charles announced the publication of "John Bull and the Alexandrians" and "John Bull and the Baltimoreans" from the "Corner of George and Broad Street, and for sale at John Melish's Map & Print Store."[66] These caricatures continued to be offered for sale well into the following year, when advertisements can be located in Wilmington, Delaware, from October 1814 until July 1815 listing the price as "50 cts. each."[67] Because only Charles can be associated with these three caricature prints, it is possible that he (not Kennedy) was solely responsible for these prints.

Charles continued to borrow from his collection of British source material. For example, the design for his *Iohn* [John] *Bull making a new Batch of Ships to send to the*

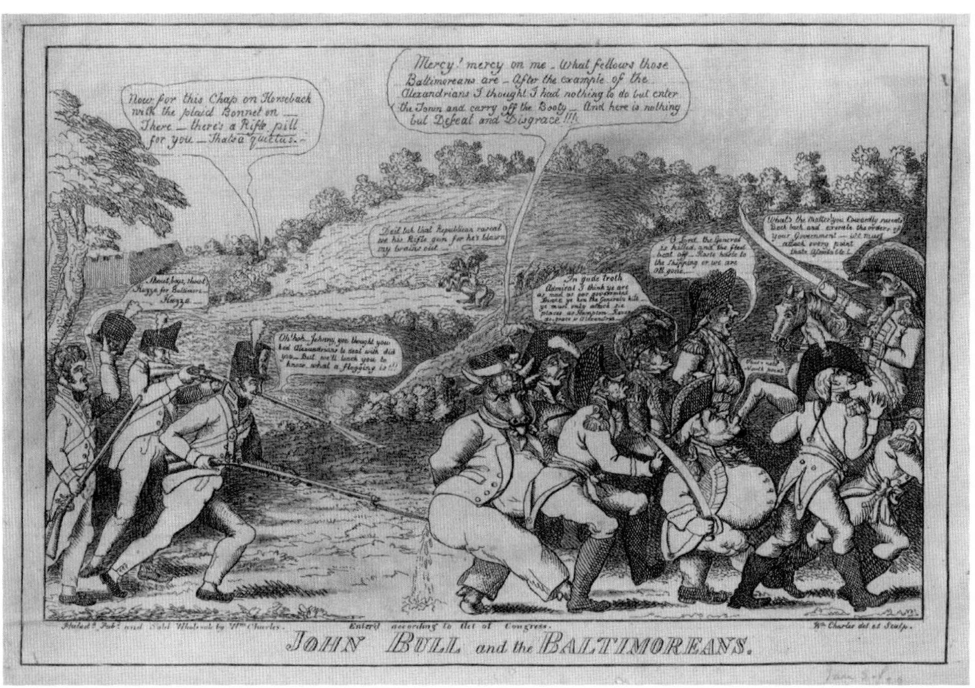

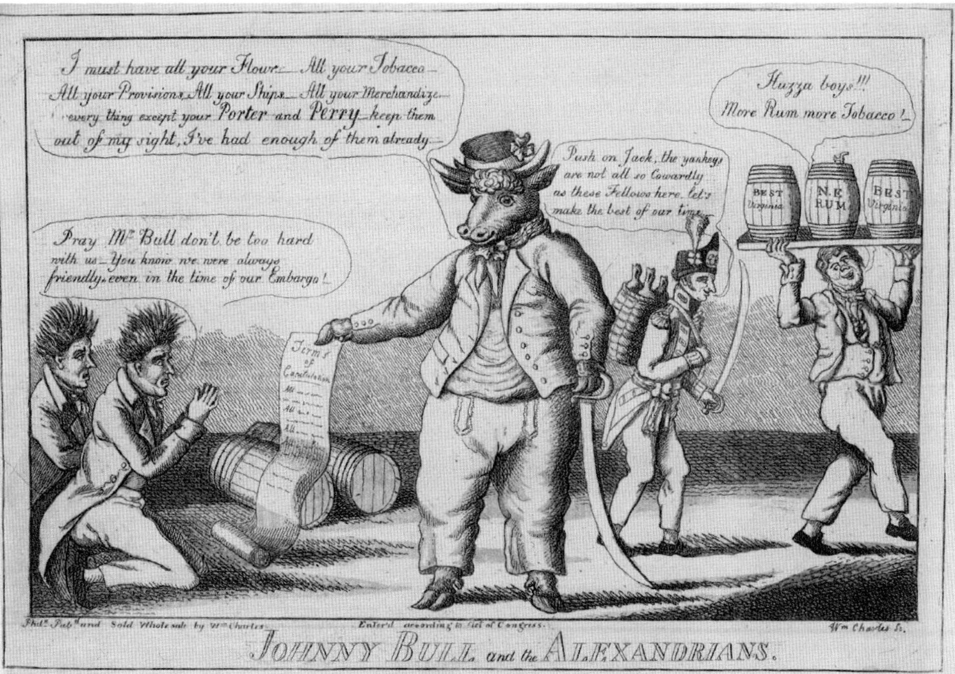

Figure 92 (*top*) | William Charles, *John Bull and the Baltimoreans*, n.d. [October 1814]. Caricature and Cartoon File, PR 010, 1813-6, FF21. New-York Historical Society, image number 98260d. Collection of the New-York Historical Society.

Figure 93 (*bottom*) | William Charles, *Johnny Bull and the Alexandrians*, n.d. [October 1814]. Etching and aquatint on laid paper, plate mark 24.8 × 34 cm. Courtesy of The Lewis Walpole Library, Yale University.

Figure 94 | Thomas Rowlandson, *High Fun for Iohn* [John] *Bull, or the republicans put to their last shift*, November 12, 1798. Hand-colored etching and aquatint, sheet 11 × 14 1/8 in. (28 × 35.9 cm). The Elisha Whittelsey Collection, The Elisha Whittelsey Fund, 1959. The Metropolitan Museum of Art, New York.

Figure 95 | Richard Newton, *A Batch of Peers*, January 6, 1792. Etching on laid paper, hand-colored, plate mark 27.3 × 40.3 cm, sheet 30 × 43 cm. Courtesy of The Lewis Walpole Library, Yale University.

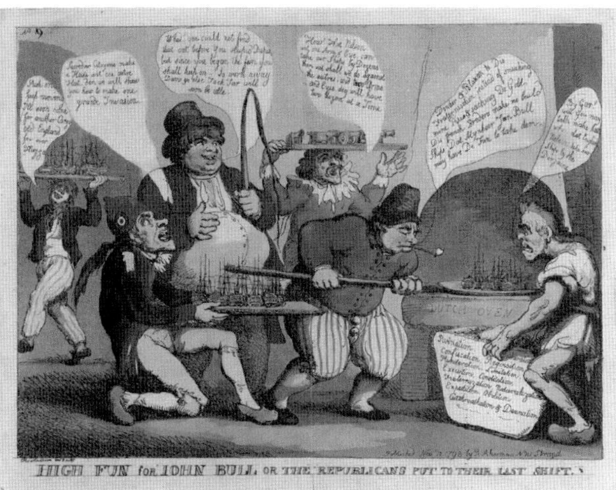

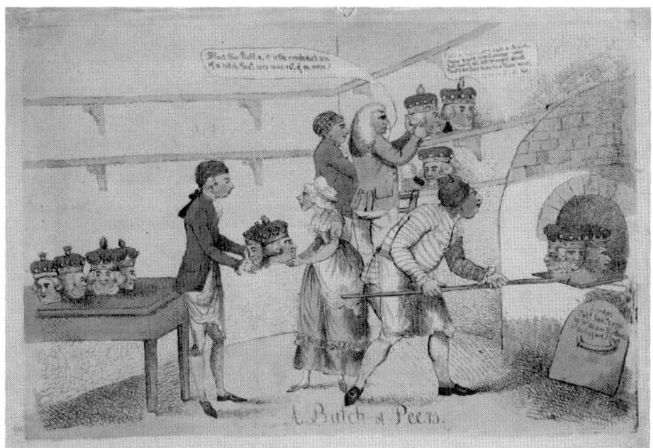

Lakes was copied directly from Thomas Rowlandson's 1798 *High Fun for Iohn* [John] *Bull, or the republicans put to their last shift* (fig. 94). Rowlandson's design was already a copy, taken from Richard Newton's 1792 *A Batch of Peers* (fig. 95), with the same basic format and design. The influence of both caricature prints is also seen in Gillray's 1806 *Tiddy-Doll, the great French-Gingerbread-Baker; drawing out a new Batch of Kings* (fig. 96), which Charles might well have seen as it was published just before he immigrated to America. Charles's design for *Johnny Bull and the Alexandrians* includes four of the six characters from the Rowlandson impression, depicted in reverse; the male figure holding a tray containing small ships above his head is also a Rowlandson creation. Charles's *Soldiers on a march to Buffalo* (fig. 97) is a reverse impression of Rowlandson's 1808 caricature *Soldiers on a March* (fig. 98), but Charles changed the words found in the speech bubbles to relate to the current war and inscribed "U.S." on the soldiers' satchels to appeal

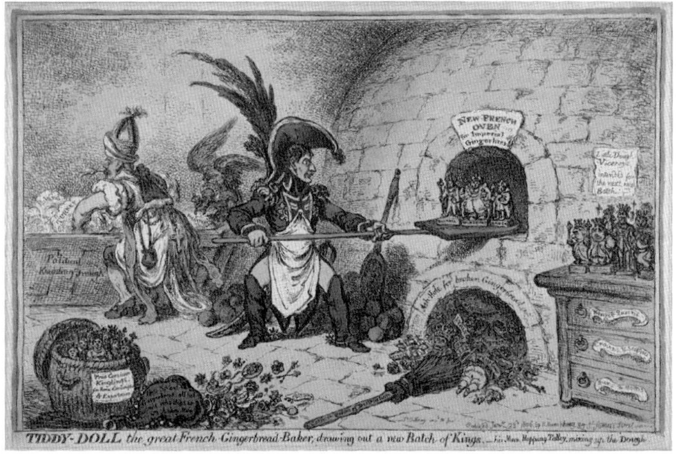

Figure 96 (*top*) | James Gillray, *Tiddy-Doll, the great French-Gingerbread-Baker; drawing out a new Batch of Kings*, January 23, 1806. Hand-colored etching, sheet 10 1/4 × 15 1/16 in. (26 × 38.3 cm). Gift of Philip van Ingen, 1942. The Metropolitan Museum of Art, New York.

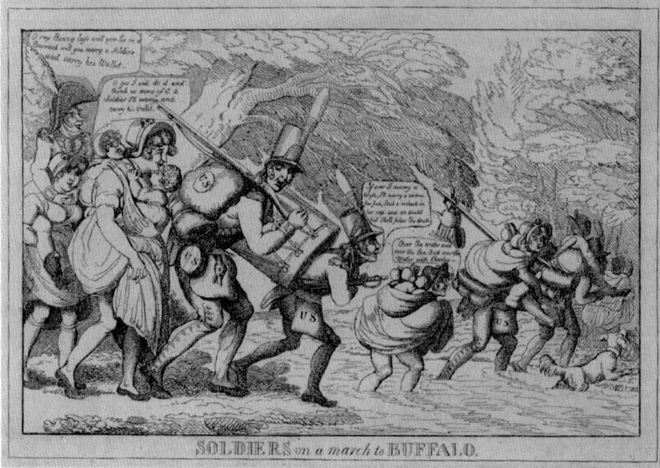

Figure 97 (*middle*) | William Charles, *Soldiers on a march to Buffalo*, n.d. [1813]. Etching, 29 × 41 cm. The Library Company of Philadelphia.

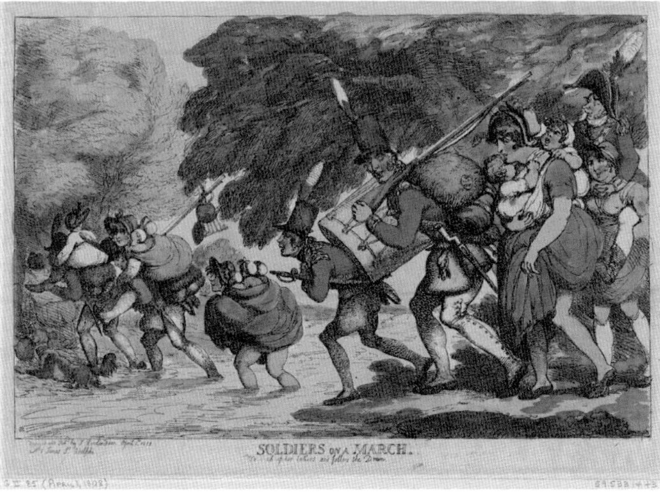

Figure 98 (*bottom*) | Thomas Rowlandson, *Soldiers on a March*, April 1, 1808. Hand-colored etching, 9 3/4 × 13 5/8 in. (24.8 × 34.6 cm). The Elisha Whittelsey Collection, The Elisha Whittelsey Fund, 1959. The Metropolitan Museum of Art, New York.

to an American audience. It is clear that Charles found a way to continue to acquire British caricatures, perhaps from remaining family members or from contacts he maintained in London.

Charles likely had impressions of the George Cruikshank caricature print *Louis XVIII climbing the <u>Mât de Cocagne</u>* (fig. 99), published in London by William Hone in October 1815.[68] The caricature was popular, with descriptions of it found in American newspapers two months after publication in London mistakenly stating that it was a "French Caricature . . . which is privately sold, and which is pretended to have been brought from London."[69] Perhaps the correspondent was responding to Cruikshank's notice inscribed on the top of the caricature: "New French Caricature selling privately in Paris." Charles's impression is, interestingly, not reversed and upon a quick glance the impressions appear to be identical. However, there are subtle differences, which can be found primarily in the speech bubbles: while the text is the same, the lines of text are presented differently. It seems unlikely that Charles would have had access to the plate that would have allowed him the opportunity to add his own name. Charles sold the caricature as his own from his print shop in Philadelphia (fig. 100). The publication line reads, "Philada. Pub. & Sold by Wm. Charles 32 So. Third St.," the address where Charles operated a bookstore between 1817 and 1819.[70] Although the print has no date, it was likely published sometime in early 1816. The longevity of this caricature persisted; more than fifty years after its publication, in 1871, *Harper's Magazine* referred to it as "one of the best caricatures ever issued by Charles."[71]

Promoting Caricature: Amos Doolittle

Amos Doolittle's first contribution to the War of 1812, *The Hornet and the Peacock Or, John Bull in Distress* (see fig. 76), had been published in March 1813, with the naval war as its subject. It was followed in October by a second caricature, *Brother Jonathan Administering a Salutary Cordial to John Bull* (fig. 101). The impression at the American Antiquarian Society not only reveals how Doolittle promoted his caricature (by approaching newspaper editors as agents) but also states his reasons for creating caricature. Also on the same sheet as the caricature is a letter, addressed to the editor of the *Democratic Press* in Philadelphia in Doolittle's hand and stamped New Haven, October 27 (fig. 102). He writes, "Sir, Although a stranger to you, I take the liberty of sending you a Caricature Print, entitled 'Brother Jonathan administering a Salutary Cordial to John Bull.'" He continued with his opinion of contemporary caricature prints: "Although many caricatures extant are of no use, and some of them have immoral effect, I flatter myself that this will not answer that description. At the present time, it is believed, it will have a tendency to

132

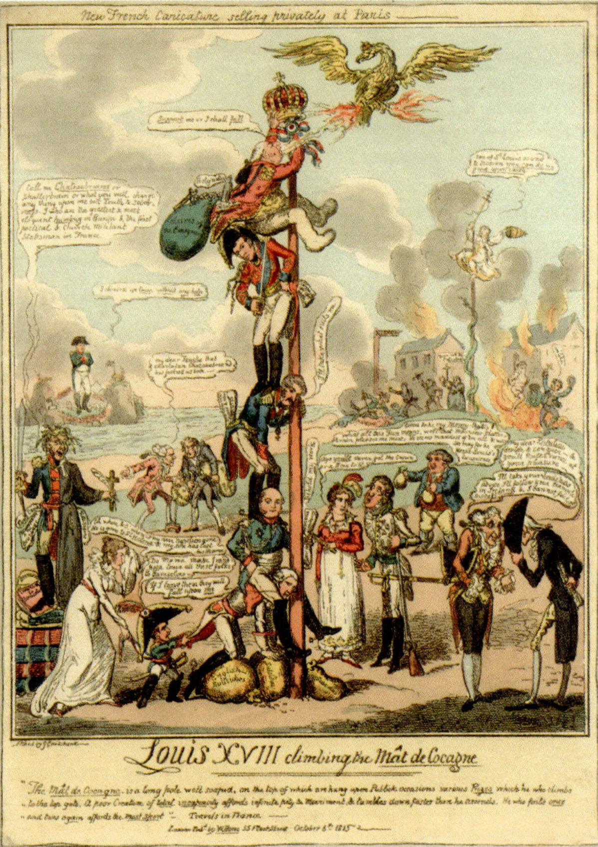

Figure 99 | George Cruikshank, *Louis XVIII climbing the <u>Mât de Cocagne</u>*, October 6, 1815. University of Washington, Special Collections, UW40987.

inspire our countrymen with confidence in themselves, and eradicate any terrors that they may feel as respects the enemy they have to combat."[72]

Addressing the uncertainty of obtaining the prints from a distance, Doolittle assured potential customers that the roads were safe. He also requested that if the recipient was not interested in receiving copies of the print for resale, he show it to others as a "favour on me" with the knowledge that anyone who agreed to purchase impressions would be given "the exclusive sale in the town where he resides." Doolittle's price of seven dollars for at least one hundred impressions or eight dollars for less than one hundred was comparable to the prices advertised by Charles and Kennedy in May 1813. He concluded with the suggestion that if the editor thought "it proper to give a concise description of the design of the print," the caricature would "entertain your readers, even though they should not see the design."

Doolittle's strategy of including the letter alongside an impression of his caricature renders it possible to determine the names of other editors he contacted. Charles Holt,

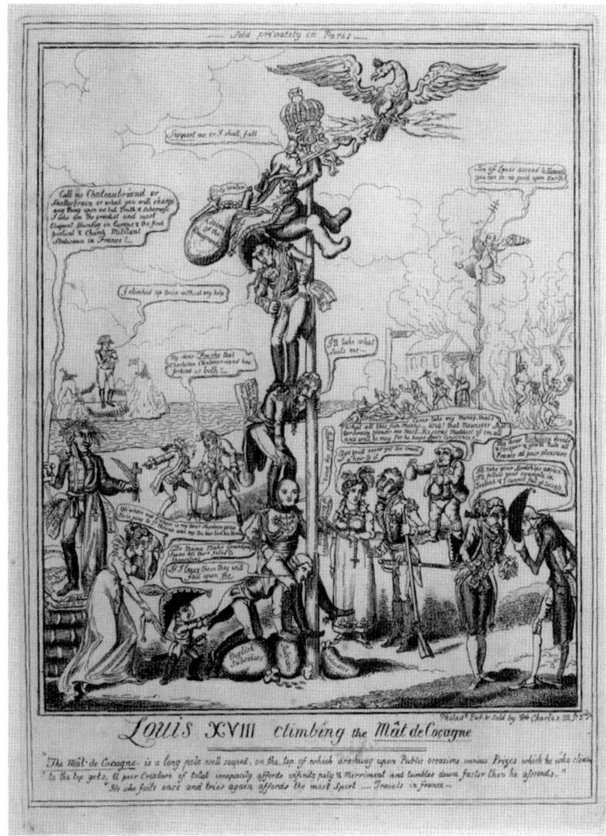

Figure 100 | William Charles, *Louis XVIII climbing the Mât de Cocagne*, n.d. [December 1815]. Courtesy American Antiquarian Society.

editor of the New York paper *The Columbian*, published an advertisement in November stating that it was an "Excellent Caricature."[73] While not naming Doolittle as the artist, the advertisement stated that it was "the production a true son of *Brother Jonathan*, in New-Haven, Connecticut; and its execution, the ingenuity of its design, and the popular subject from which it is taken, places it above the level of common caricatures." The "humorous emblematical Print" was exhibited and could be purchased at 90 Broadway in New York, the same location that sold Doolittle's first caricature:

> "Brother Jonathan *administering a salutary cordial* to John Bull." This is the title of an ingenious Caricature Print, in which *Brother Jonathan* is represented in the act of pouring a cup of *American* Perry down the throat of John Bull, which the old gentleman is compelled very reluctantly to swallow. Out of the mouth of John issues the following words: "O! don't force me to take it Brother Jonathan! Give me *Holland* gin, *French* brandy—anything but this d—d *Yankee* Perry—it has

134

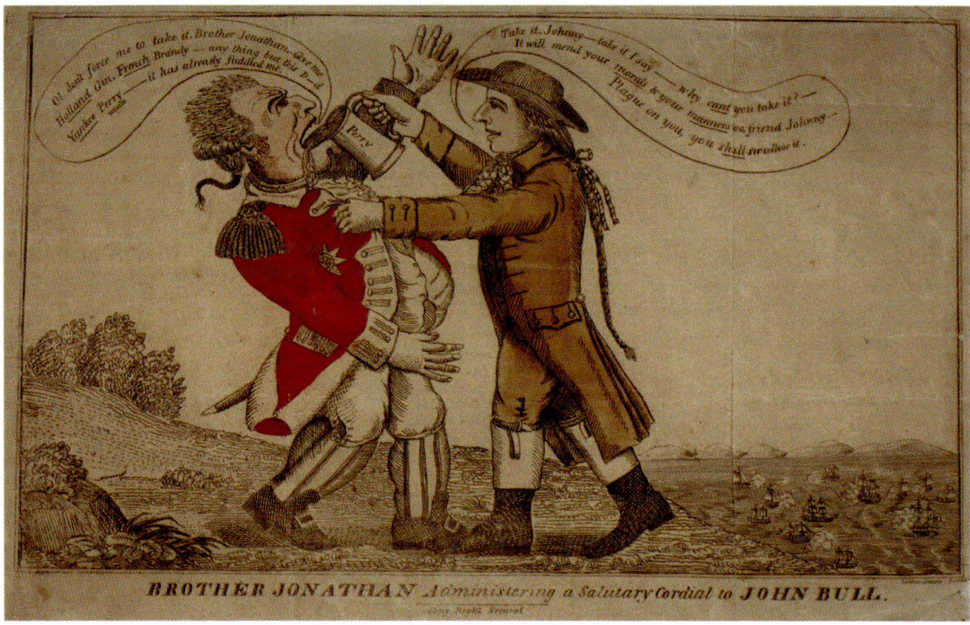

BROTHER JONATHAN *Administering a Salutary Cordial to* JOHN BULL.

Figure 101 | Yankee Doodle Scratcht [Amos Doolittle], *Brother Jonathan <u>Administering</u> a Salutary Cordial to John Bull*, n.d. [October 1813]. Courtesy American Antiquarian Society.

already fuddled me!" To which *Jonathan* rejoices, "Take it Johnny—take it, I say—why can't you take it?—it will mend your *morals* and your *manners* too, friend Johnny. Plague on you, you shall take it!" The Print also contains a neat perspective view of the naval engagement on Lake Erie.

The *Baltimore Patriot* also likely received a Doolittle letter and caricature, as this newspaper published a description of the piece: "A Caricature, Representing *Brother Jonathan* administering a dose of Perry to *John Bull*, . . . it was engraved by Doolittle, of New-Haven, and is an extremely humorous illustration of the *effects* of the battle of Erie." For anyone interested it was noted that "this ingenious device may be seen at our reading-room; and copies engaged."[74]

The New York and Baltimore advertisements are similar to each other and reference the patriotic nature of the caricature design, a prompt from the last sentence of Doolittle's letter ("to inspire our countrymen with confidence in themselves, and eradicate any terrors that they may feel as respects the enemy they have to combat"). Although the surviving letter at the American Antiquarian Society was addressed to John Binns (fig. 101) in Philadelphia, no newspaper advertisements or descriptions have been located that

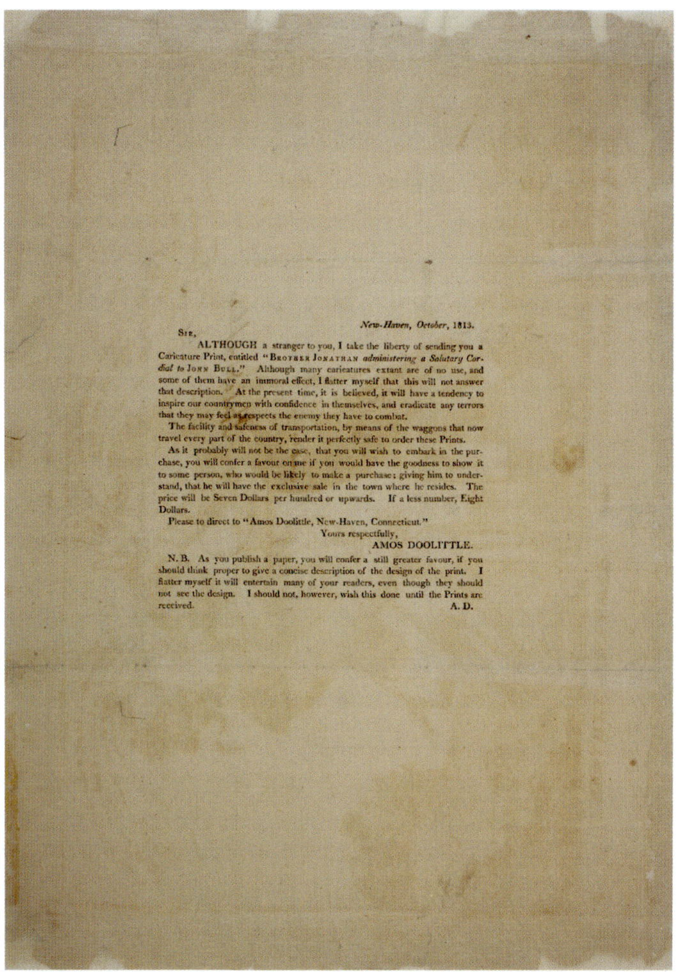

New-Haven, October, 1813.

SIR,

ALTHOUGH a stranger to you, I take the liberty of sending you a Caricature Print, entitled "BROTHER JONATHAN *administering a Salutary Cordial to* JOHN BULL." Although many caricatures extant are of no use, and some of them have an immoral effect, I flatter myself that this will not answer that description. At the present time, it is believed, it will have a tendency to inspire our countrymen with confidence in themselves, and eradicate any terrors that they may feel as respects the enemy they have to combat.

The facility and safeness of transportation, by means of the waggons that now travel every part of the country, render it perfectly safe to order these Prints.

As it probably will not be the case, that you will wish to embark in the purchase, you will confer a favour on me if you would have the goodness to show it to some person, who would be likely to make a purchase; giving him to understand, that he will have the exclusive sale in the town where he resides. The price will be Seven Dollars per hundred or upwards. If a less number, Eight Dollars.

Please to direct to "Amos Doolittle, New-Haven, Connecticut."

Yours respectfully,

AMOS DOOLITTLE.

N.B. As you publish a paper, you will confer a still greater favour, if you should think proper to give a concise description of the design of the print. I flatter myself it will entertain many of your readers, even though they should not see the design. I should not, however, wish this done until the Prints are received.

A. D.

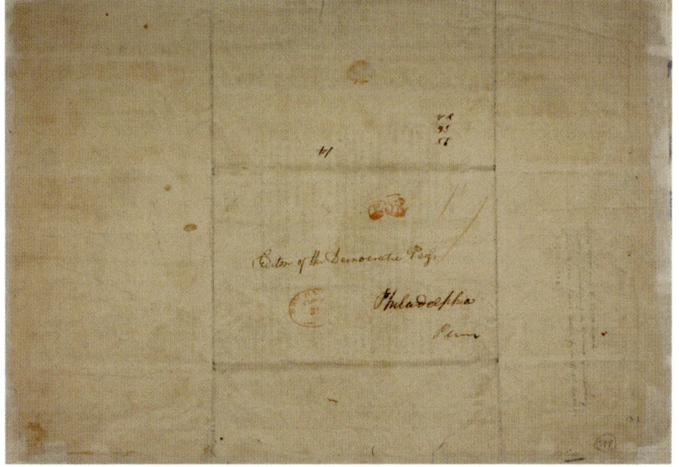

either describe the caricature or offer it for sale there. Perhaps Binns and other Philadelphia newspaper editors ignored Doolittle's appeal because they were partial to Charles, the caricaturist in their own city. Doolittle's name does appear in the Mathew Carey account book in 1813 and 1814, but there are no references to Carey purchasing caricatures from Doolittle.[75] Baltimore is the closest city to Philadelphia where Doolittle's caricature appears to have been sold; Charles may have had a strong support in his city.

There is little from this period on Charles and Doolittle beyond their caricatures and other newspaper references. Doolittle's letter to Binns provides information that explains the interaction between newspaper editors and caricature prints. Doolittle's prints appear to be responding directly to the output by Charles. The proximity of New Haven to New York suggests that word of Charles would have reached Doolittle. Descriptions of Charles's caricatures from 1813 appeared in newspapers at least as far north as New York, and while advertisements have not been discovered in Connecticut papers, it is possible they have yet to be located. The output of caricatures by Charles and Kennedy meant that even if they were not advertised, it is probable that a traveler journeying from Philadelphia to New York or New Haven would have had impressions of the print and could have distributed them or shown them to friends. This conjecture is based on previously cited examples that provide evidence that caricatures had a varied market and audience. They were bought, passed around the city of production, and sent with letters to family and friend for amusement and entertainment. The caricatures published by Charles and Kennedy during the War of 1812 were numerous, and it is likely that Doolittle was aware of them and would seek to balance their message with his version of patriotism. Doolittle made it clear that his caricature prints were made for a moral purpose rather than to achieve widespread fame and success.

Doolittle's final known caricature was *Bonaparte in Trouble* (fig. 103), published between 1814 and 1815 after Napoleon's abdication by the Treaty of Fontainebleau. Neither Weitenkampf nor Murrell knew of the print, but in the 1960s New-York Historical Society print curator Wendy Shadwell noted the date of publication as "circa 1814."[76] Only for *Bonaparte in Trouble* did Doolittle sign his full name below the image ("A. Doolittle del et Sc") and not with a pseudonym.[77] This could be because the print isn't entirely a caricature but is largely allegorical. Doolittle inserted an image of the devil on the left and an angel on the right, while only Napoleon is represented as a human figure. Doolittle included an explanation of the scene with numbers corresponding to the figures: "1. The Infernal spirit enticing Bonaparte with the Crown of Rusia [*sic*]. 2. Bonaparte arrested in his progress by the Russian Bear. 3. The British Lion attacking him in the rear, having already wrested from his power the Crowns of Spain & Portugal. 4. The Confederated Eagles of Austria & Prussia, plucking the feathers of the Rhiniste Confederation.

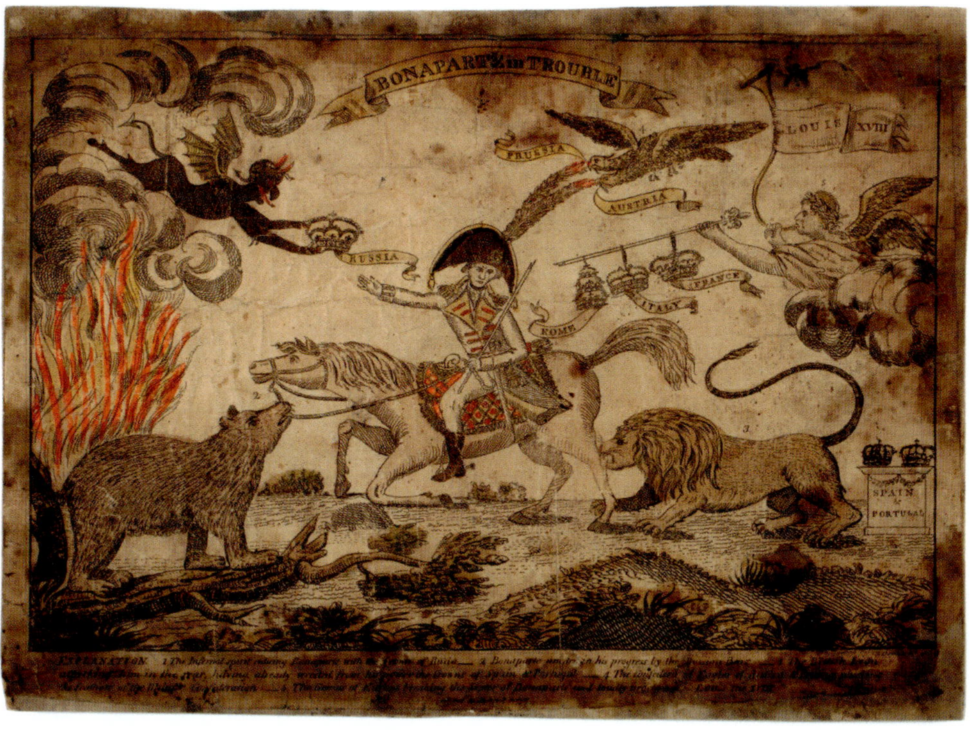

Figure 103 | Amos Doolittle, *Bonaparte in Trouble*, n.d. [1814–15?]. Courtesy American Antiquarian Society.

5. The Genius of Europe breaking the sceptre of Bonaparte and loudly proclaiming Louis the XVIII." The Connecticut firm of Shelton and Kensett published this caricature in addition to a number of Doolittle's other plates after 1813.[78] This is the last caricature known to have been completed by Doolittle. Perhaps because his caricatures were unsuccessful or because the war had ended, he returned to engraving historical subjects and left the satirical humor to Charles and other anonymous caricaturists in New England. Sometime after publication, the Doolittle impression was copied (fig. 104). Recently discovered, it is signed at the bottom "Drawn, by, Elezebeth, Edgar." The circumstances under which this copy were made are unknown; this might have been for a school project, or perhaps she was copying an impression that her family owned.[79] Such a copy by a relatively young woman is reminiscent of F. B. Sanborn's boyhood recollections of seeing Akin caricatures owned by his grandfather. Sanborn recounted that the caricatures were kept in a desk for "grandchildren to tumble over and destroy."[80] Although Napoleon was a frequent feature of British caricatures, his appearance in American works is

138

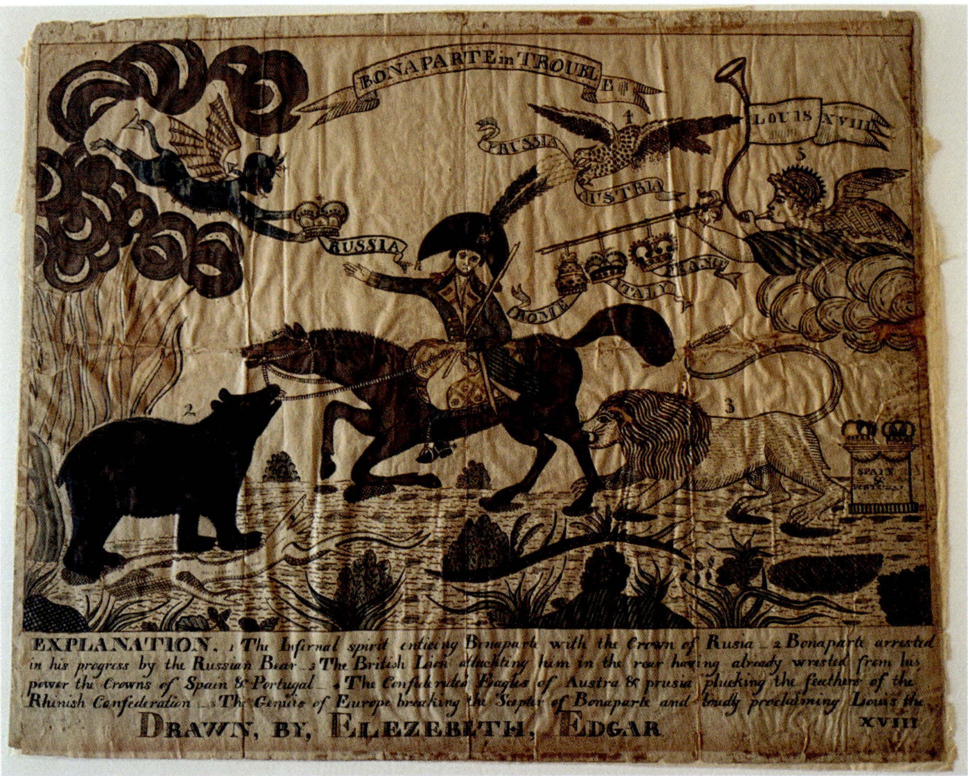

Figure 104 | Elezebeth Edgar, after Amos Doolittle, *Bonaparte in Trouble*, n.d. Jay Heritage Center, New York.

relatively rare.[81] There is reference to another caricature that is unlocated but was evidently published in Boston in 1814 in which "the figure of BONAPARTE is seen hovering over the whole, looking down with indignation, and swearing vengeance."[82]

The War of 1812 and "The Boston Wits"

Another prompt for caricaturists in the second decade of the nineteenth century came in the form of the Massachusetts representative Josiah Quincy, whose outspoken politics and frustration with Thomas Jefferson sparked their interest. Quincy was vocal in his disapproval of the Embargo Act of 1807 that closed American ports and called for the impeachment of President Jefferson, who had signed the bill into law. The impeachment effort was defeated by an overwhelming majority, 117 to 1 (Quincy had the lone negative vote). He vehemently opposed the war with England and in 1813 left Congress

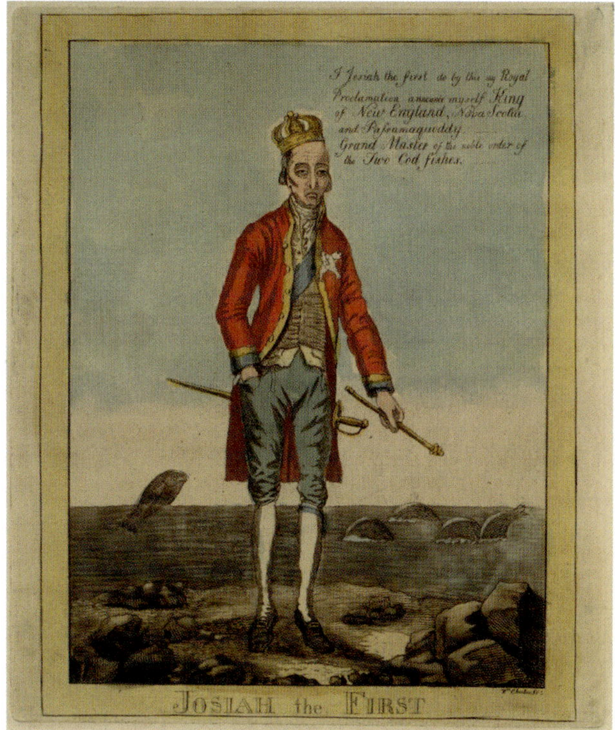

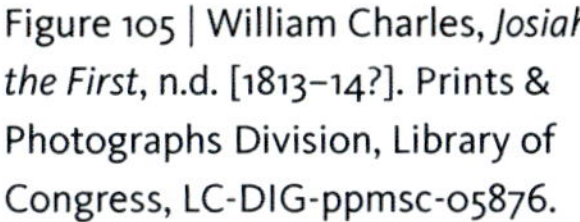

Figure 105 | William Charles, *Josiah the First*, n.d. [1813–14?]. Prints & Photographs Division, Library of Congress, LC-DIG-ppmsc-05876.

to return home to Massachusetts, where he soon became a target for caricaturists. Two caricatures of Quincy were described in Boston newspapers, and there may have been others. In February 1814, a description of a caricature focused on Josiah Quincy as "the would-be-king, Josiah the First" and "an American senator."[83] A second caricature of Quincy was described in the same Boston newspaper in July, in which "Josiah the First" was depicted as one of several autocratic figures, including John Bull, Prince Louis, and the "Hero of Lexington" Andrew Jackson.[84] Although these two prints have not been discovered, they reflect a demand for and interest in satirical images of Josiah Quincy that likely influenced Charles (perhaps in partnership with Kennedy) to publish his print in Philadelphia around this time, *Josiah the First* (fig. 105).[85]

These descriptions found in newspapers allude to an emerging market for political caricatures in New England, particularly in Boston. However, as with the two unlocated Josiah Quincy caricature referenced above, few impressions appear to have survived. An 1813 newspaper notice alludes to this with the statement, "The Boston wits are very prolific in Caricatures." Caricaturists were particularly drawn to the Federalist governor of Massachusetts, Caleb Strong. A caricature "representing *Governor Caleb-Pious* opening up the Gates, and delivering the Keys of *Fort Bulwark* to *John Henry*" was advertised as

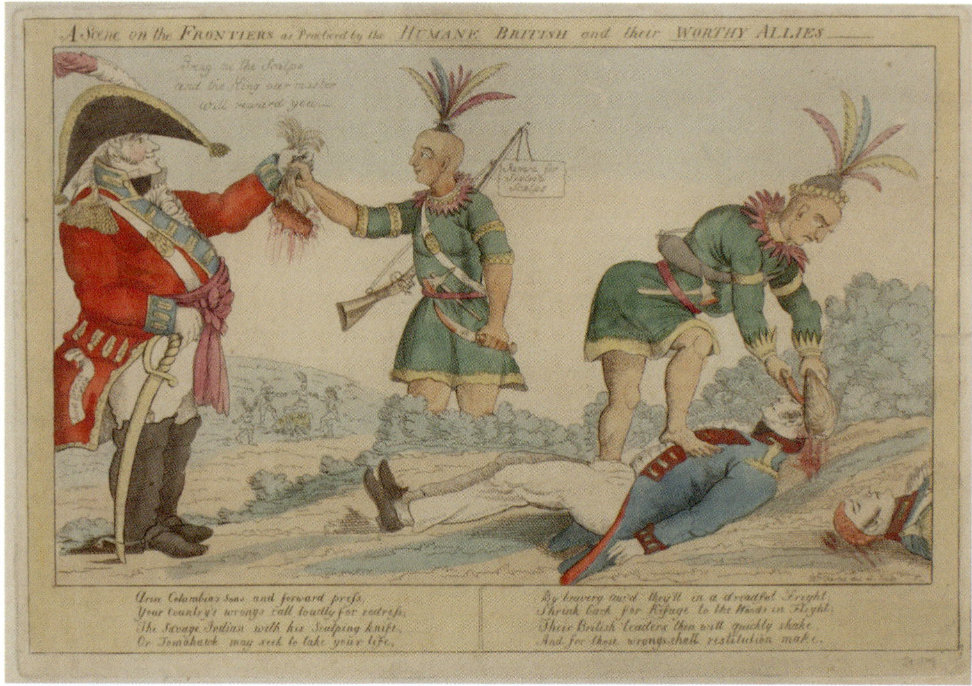

Figure 106 | William Charles, *A Scene on the Frontiers as Practiced by the <u>Humane</u> British and their <u>Worthy</u> Allies*, n.d. [1813–14]. Courtesy American Antiquarian Society.

available for "public inspection." In this caricature, "*Commodore Perry* is seen looking over Caleb's shoulder, and with a tremendous voice calls out—'DON'T GIVE UP THE FORT.'"[86]

Such descriptions have proved important in allocating attributions of publication dates to caricatures made by Charles and Kennedy. The caricature *A Scene on the Frontiers as Practiced by the <u>Humane</u> British and their <u>Worthy</u> Allies* (fig. 106) is one example. Previous scholarship to include this caricature has attributed a publication date of 1812, prior to Charles's partnership with Kennedy. However, in November 1813 references to caricatures with similar subject matter can be found in newspapers. Further to this, there appears to have been a specific request for works in which Native Americans were depicted in the act of scalping the heads of militia members. A description of a print published in London during the Revolutionary War, *The Allies. ___ Par nobile Fratrûm* (fig. 107), specifically asked that if any readers had it in their collections they should copy and redistribute them:

A Caricature Engraving was published in London, during our Revolutionary War, and had a pretty general circulation in this country, which represented

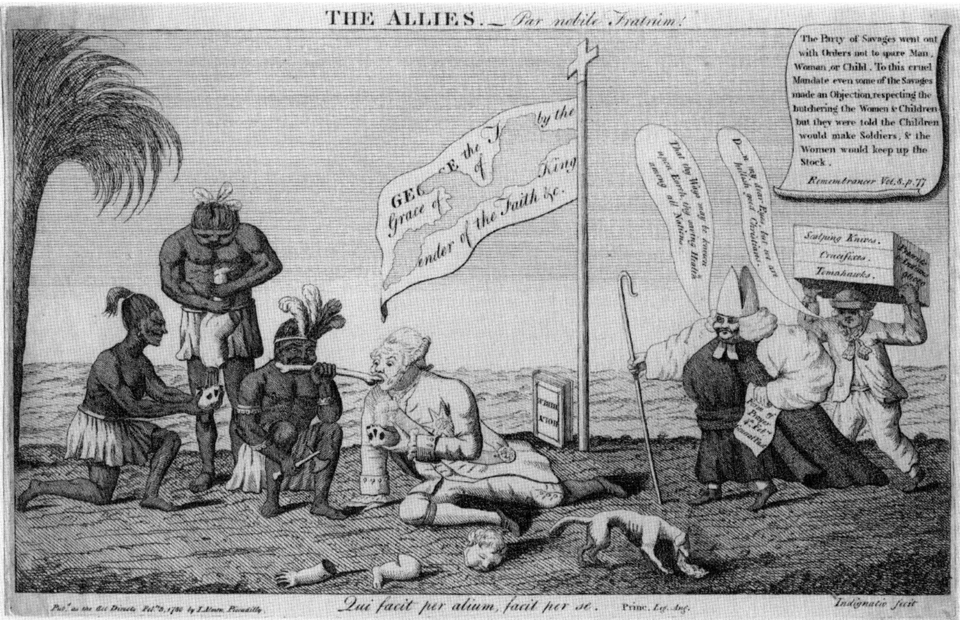

Figure 107 | Anonymous, *The Allies. _ Par nobile Fratrûm!*, published February 3, 1780. Etching with engraving, sheet 24 × 37 cm. Courtesy of The Lewis Walpole Library, Yale University.

a Savage feast. In the middle of a circle of Savages, was a striking likeness of George III, with his star and garter, gnawing at the leg of a child, while the Indians were eating some other parts of it, some the head, some the heart, and others the legs, &c. &c. A dog was represented in the act of vomiting. The British flag was seen in the background with some sailors bearing bales, and packages, of which was written presents for the Indians—Tomahawks and Scalping Knives. On the right was pictured an English Bishop in his full robes, mitre and crosier, and the words "thy saving health among all nations" from his mouth; and from the mouth of one of the sailors—"D—m me, Jack, but we are hellish good christians." Over the whole was written Qui facit per allum, facit per me He who does a thing by the hand of another, does it himself.—If any person has one of these English engravings, a second edition of it here might serve to show the friends of the "Bulwark of our Religion" what the English themselves thought of their King, Bishops, and Savages, thirty years ago.[87]

This request might very well have inspired engravers, because there appears to have been a number of caricatures prepared for publication during this period depicting such subjects (although if they were indeed completed, impressions have not been located). For example, three notices appeared in Vermont newspapers providing descriptions of caricatures believed to be in preparation. One described "a CARICATURE [that] we understand is in preparation, representing a British Indian, scalping an American Officer. A Peace-Party Man is seen near the spot, trembling, with a loaf of bread in his hand, in the act of presenting it to the Indian; in his other hand he holds this inscription.—'Spare a Washington Benevolent Peace Party Man, but scalp the War Hawks.' They both sit down together and smoked the calmut of peace."[88] Another account reported plans in December 1813 for "a CARICATURE, it is said will soon be got up, exhibiting a group of American officers (*alias white Savages,*) lately returned from Canada, and represented sword in hand pursuing the *Little Rebel John,* his bag-pipe Ben, and the sprout of the common-sewer *Horatio,* who luckily made their escape and take refuge in a *British office* in state-street, and thereby save their ears.[89] A week later, another notice promised, "A CARICATURE will soon be ready representing Gov. *Shelby* at the head of his troops, with sword in hand pursuing and defeating the Indians and British at the River Thames. After the battle the Governor is seen surrounded by the inhabitants—men, women, and children with grateful hearts, bestowing their benedictions on him for his patriotism; his nobleness of soul and God-like humanity, in relieving them from the Tomahawk and Scalping Knife of the Indians and British Savages. The Governor exclaims with extasy [*sic*]—'*How delightful it is to defend our Country and its Laws.*'"[90]

As no impressions have been located, it is unclear whether any of these caricatures were ever completed and published. Conversely, there are surviving impressions of two versions of the caricature *A Scene on the Frontiers as Practiced by the <u>Humane</u> British and their <u>Worthy</u> Allies*: one that is signed by Charles and the other with only the initials "L.G.," although descriptions or advertisements have not been located in newspapers (figs. 106 and 108). These are the only caricatures from this period that have survived to represent Native Americans in the act of scalping military officers and were likely published around the same period as the descriptions above. It is unclear which impression was published first: although Charles included "del et Sculp" after his name, this not necessarily mean he was the first to produce the image. The other impression, by L.G., is in reverse, but both are similarly brightly colored.

The Hartford Convention in Caricature

The final caricature to be published by Charles and Kennedy, *The Hartford Convention or Leap No Leap* (fig. 109), has frequently been used to illustrate that event in American history texts and journals. Published in December 1814, a colored impression of it was

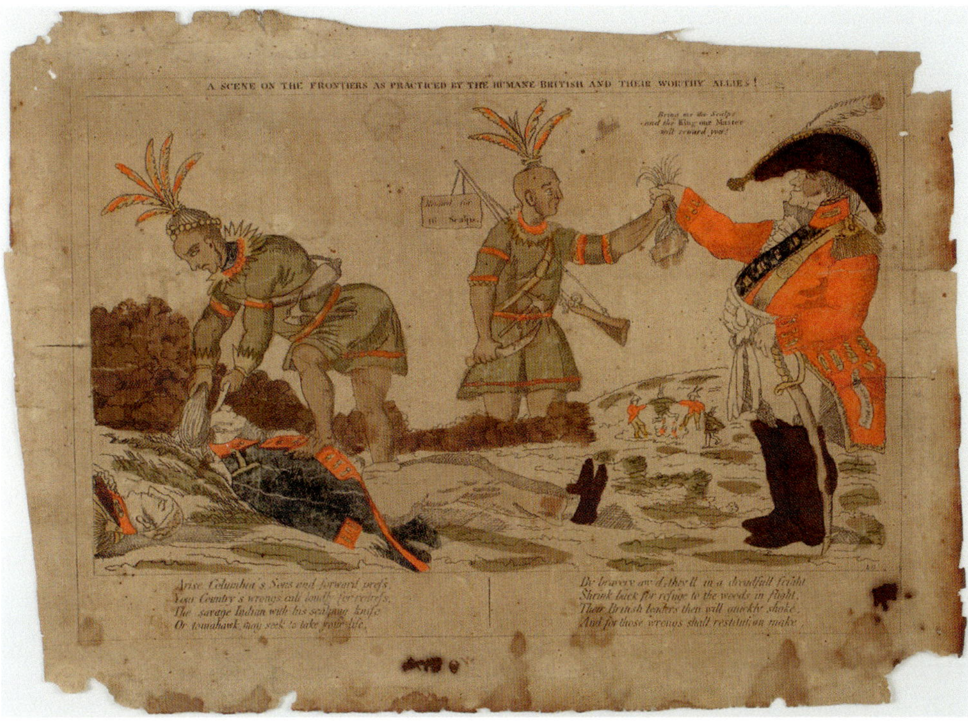

Figure 108 | L.G., after William Charles, *A Scene on the Frontiers as Practiced by the Humane British and Their Worthy Allies!*, n.d. [1813–14?]. Etching, hand-colored, image and sheet 23 × 33 cm, sheet 28 × 39 cm. Courtesy American Antiquarian Society.

deposited for copyright on December 10 by Kennedy (who provided his occupation as "proprietor"). Several days later, the print was advertised for sale for "50 cents, or $4 per dozen."[91] A large number of impressions, both uncolored and colored, have survived.

Despite not publishing together for several months, Charles and Kennedy may have seen the potential in the news surrounding the Hartford Convention, which held great interest and provided much anxiety for the nation facing recovery from a difficult war. Between December 1814 and January 1815, twenty-six delegates from the five New England states (New Hampshire, Vermont, Rhode Island, Connecticut, and Massachusetts) attended the meeting at the Old State House in Hartford. Outwardly, the meetings had an innocent purpose—the protection of states' rights after the war—although there were rumors that secession was under consideration. New England was the last bastion of the Federalist Party, which opposed the policies of Thomas Jefferson and his successor, James Madison. The caricature by Charles and Kennedy depicts King George III encouraging three members of the New England delegation to jump into his waiting

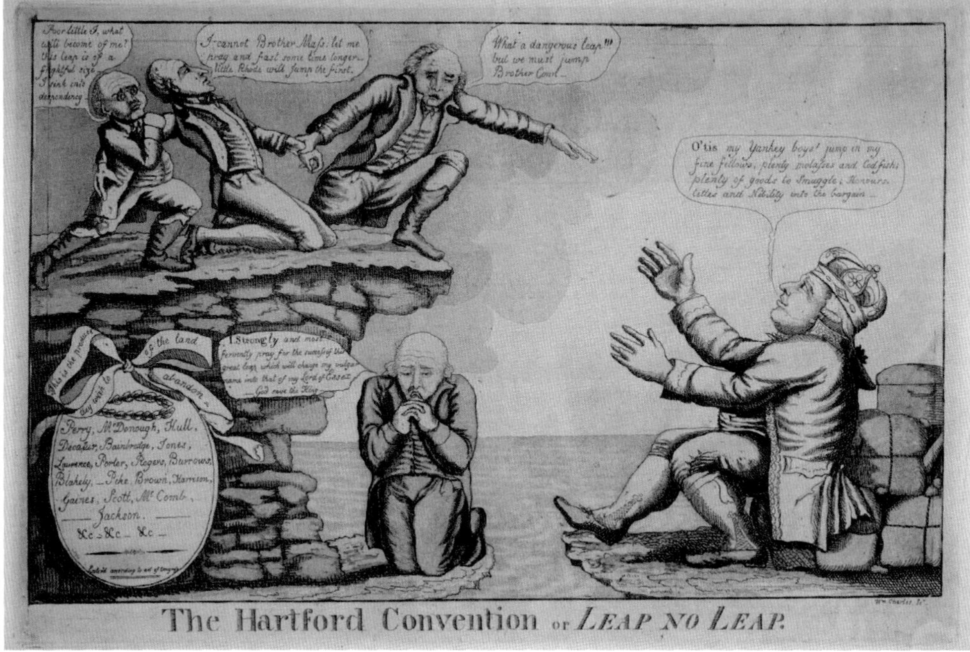

Figure 109 | William Charles, *The Hartford Convention or Leap No Leap*, n.d. [December 1814]. Courtesy American Antiquarian Society.

arms, lured by numerous promises of fish and honor: "O 'tis my Yankey boys! Jump in my fine fellows, plenty molasses and codfish; plenty of goods to smuggle; Honours, titles and Nobility into the bargain ___." Harrison Gray Otis, a Federalist leader from Boston, is shown on the rock, along with Governor Roger Griswold of Connecticut and William Jones of Rhode Island. Lanmon identified the figure kneeling in prayer as Timothy Pickering, but a more likely attribution is Caleb Strong, then governor of Massachusetts, whose name is alluded in his speech bubble: "I Strongly and most fervently pray for the success of this great leap, which will change my vulgar name into that of the Lord of Essex ___ God save the King." Beneath this grouping are the names of land and ship owners who had gained recognition during the War of 1812.

The caricature prompted copies, including an impression published in 1815 (fig. 110). This impression is the reverse of the original, although it includes additional figures within the image, such as a barrel and fish between the figure of King George and that of Caleb Strong, as well as three smaller figures seen above the British monarch. To the right, outside the image, are a man and a young girl. The man says, "Oh I'm Un-Dun H a m! Do give me a seat!!!" as the young girl tugs on his coattail and says, "Go home, and enquire who sent you!" It has been suggested that this print was a copy after Charles

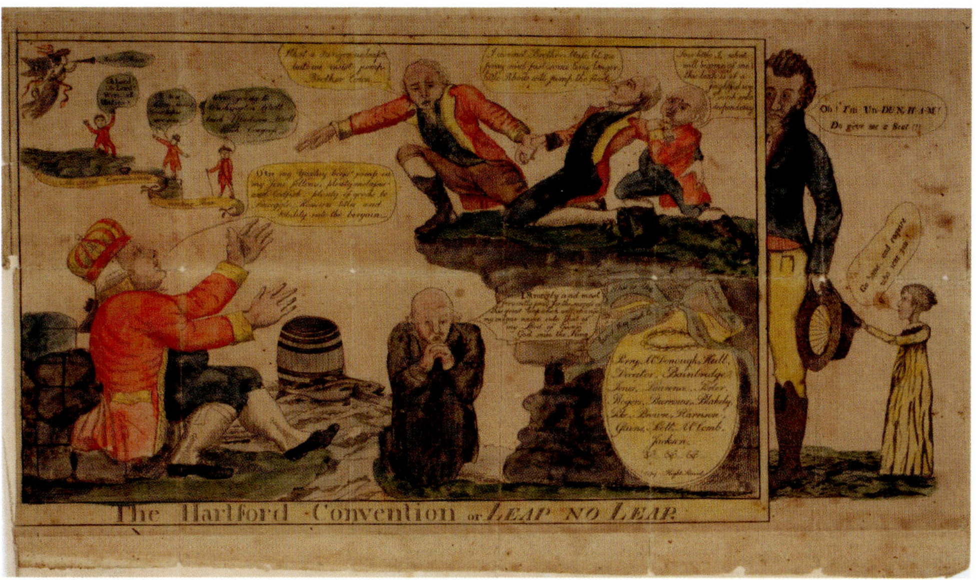

Figure 110 | Anonymous, *The Hartford Convention or Leap No Leap*, n.d. [1815?].
Courtesy American Antiquarian Society.

made in Vermont by Isaac Eddy.[92] A further impression has been located at the Connecticut Historical Society (fig. 111), where it was included on a larger sheet of paper with a broadside that discusses the Hartford Convention.

Two previously unknown caricatures inspired by the Hartford Convention are housed in the collection at the Connecticut Historical Society. As they were unknown to either Murrell or Weitenkampf, the discovery of these prints suggests that there was wider market in New England for such visual commentary of the period and that more prints might yet be found. *The N. England Convention or the Prophecy of J. Henry Fulfilled!!!!* (fig. 112) is not dated or signed, although information found on the lower left-hand corner referring to the Hartford Convention does include the date "May, 1815." The design includes a large image of John Bull surrounded by six figures; the devil wears a crown, and the speech bubbles allude to the identities of the figures and the states they represent. The title refers to John Henry, who revealed to the British that the New England states were unhappy with the situation in Washington and planning an antidemocratic takeover. Henry reported in an 1809 letter that in the event of war with England, "the legislature of Massachusetts will declare itself permanent until a new election of members; incite congress, to be composed of delegates from the Federal States; and erect a separate government for their common defence and common interest."[93] The Connecticut Historical Society has two impressions of this caricature, with different

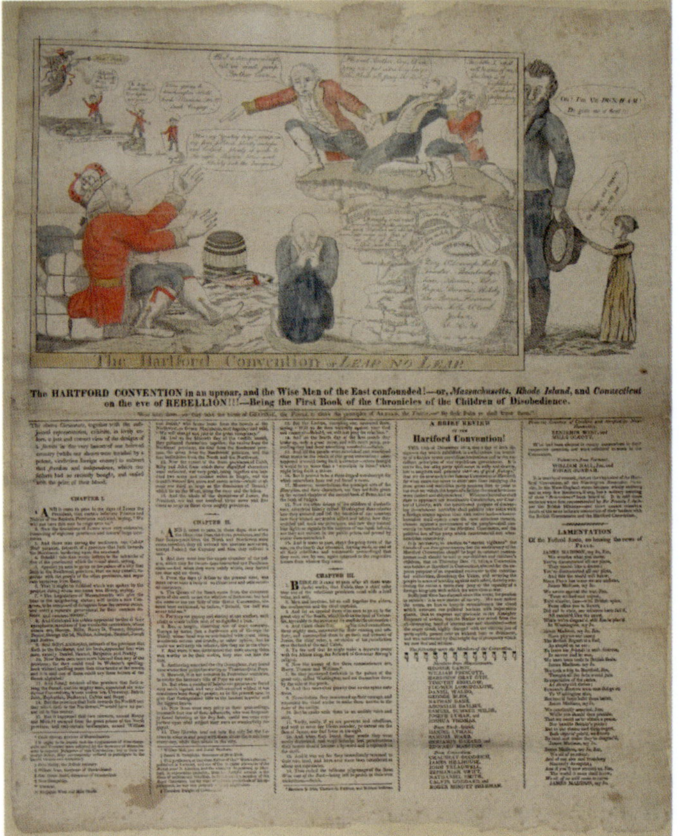

Figure 111 (*left*) | Anonymous, *The Hartford Convention or Leap No Leap*, n.d. [1815?]. The Connecticut Historical Society.

Figure 112 (*below*) | Anonymous, *The N. England Convention or the Prophecy of J. Henry Fulfilled!!!!*, n.d. [after May 1815; 1816–17?]. The Connecticut Historical Society.

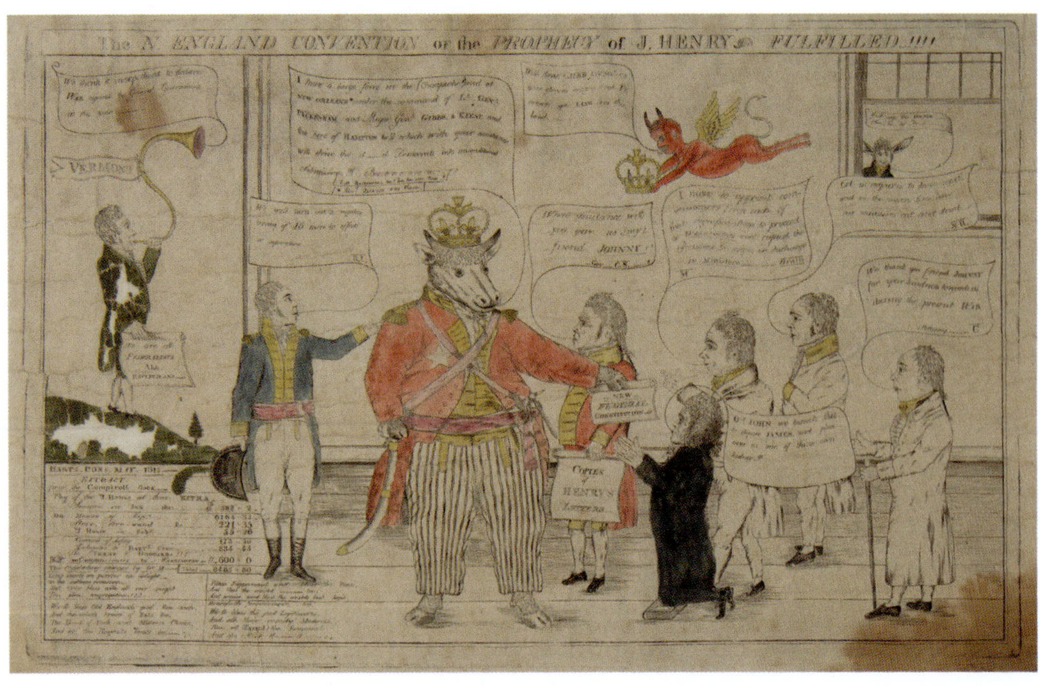

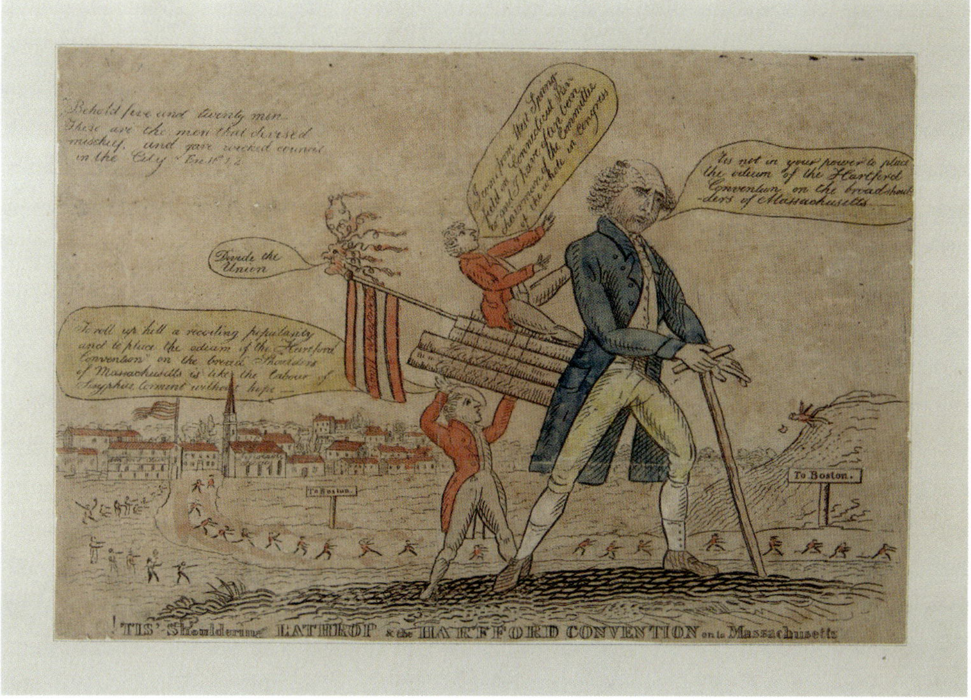

Figure 113 | Anonymous, *!Tis' Shouldering Lathrop & the Hartford Convention on to Massachusetts*, n.d. [1815?]. The Connecticut Historical Society.

hand-coloring. One of the impressions lacks the descriptive text on the lower left-hand side. Although no advertisements for this caricature seem to have been published, a jocular notice in a Boston newspaper appears to refer to this caricature, with a description of John Bull holding the Federal Constitution in his hand: "Strayed, stolen or run away from this office some time in February last, a Caricature of the 'Hartford Convention' representing John Bull and his associates; said Bull when he went away was dress'd in his regimentals, holding the new federal Constitution, acting as commander in chief over the 'kingdom of New England'—whoever will take up said Bull and Co. and return them to the subscriber will be handsomely rewarded."[94] The subject matter of the caricature *!Tis' Shouldering Lathrop & the Hartford Convention on to Massachusetts* (fig. 113) is difficult to interpret. The large figure is perhaps Samuel Lathrop, whom the title references, who was a member of the Massachusetts delegation at the Convention. In his speech bubble, he responds to the two smaller figures pushing him forward, "Tis not in your power to place the odium of the Hartford Convention on the broad shoulders of Massachusetts." The two figures hold books that bear the words "The Hartford Convention," while a flag with medusa-like hair pronounces, "Divide the Union." The background depicts a procession of men in red coats and the city profile of Boston. Although the meaning and message are not explained, the discovery of both caricatures underscores the value of seeking descriptions of caricatures in newspapers; such mentions indicate not only that the market for such prints was widespread but also that there were localities in which independent engravers were using their skill to depict local affairs and events in caricature.

The 1820s welcomed the new printing technology of lithography, and caricaturists began to focus their subject matter on satirizing national events and American politicians. But William Charles, who had been the dominant figure in the production of wartime caricatures, would not live to be a part of this. His life was unexpectedly cut short when he drowned in Philadelphia harbor on August 9, 1820.[95] He had been on a ship that was bound for Boston, evidently journeying north to promote the sale of his toy books and illustrations, which had been his primary work between 1817 and his untimely death. By 1819, Charles may have been struggling financially as the 1820 Philadelphia directory shows that he had moved from the address of his bookstore on 32 South Third to "North 6th above Vine."[96] He died without a will, leaving his wife Mary, mother of their eight children, to sell off the remaining inventory of prints and children's books. William Dunlap remembers Charles in his 1834 history with a brief notice: "William Charles, engraver and caricaturist, native of Scotland; died in Philadelphia, in 1820. He was a prolific engraver and publisher of caricatures and juvenile literature, both in a style similar to contemporary English productions. He worked in line, stipple and aquatint."[97] Charles's obituary was republished in newspapers outside of Philadelphia, a reflection of how well-known he had become in his adopted country.[98]

CHAPTER 5

Copperplate to Lithography, 1820–1830

In the history of caricature in the United States, 1820 was a pivotal year. William Charles died, and James Akin resumed publishing caricatures in Philadelphia after a brief absence. Instead of the patriotic wartime caricatures by Charles and Doolittle, subject matter turned inward, focused on national and state election campaigns and American politicians. Akin made caricatures for the elections of 1820, 1824, and possibly 1828, but the work of a new competitor, David Claypoole Johnston (1799–1865), brought a change in the field of American caricature.[1] Akin and Johnston are the only two caricaturists active during this period who have been identified, though there are a number of unsigned caricatures from the period that have yet to be attributed. The style found in these anonymous prints is not uniform or consistent, so the identities of those responsible are not known.

As in previous decades, caricatures made at the start of this decade were primarily copperplate engravings, with print runs relatively low and surviving impressions generally rare. This decade also ushered in a change in printing technology. Lithography, invented by Aloïs Senefelder (1771–1834) in Munich at the end of the eighteenth century, allowed for the production of mass impressions.[2] With some level of control by the artist, the engraved plate was replaced by drawing with special crayons directly onto the lithographic stone, which was inked over and printed.[3] Although this method was known in the United States as early as 1803, it was not until the 1820s that lithography was adapted by American artists and caricaturists. The merits of the lithographic stone were initially described in newspapers as the artist "makes a drawing on paper in the ordinary way, excepting that he uses a peculiar ink; this is transferred to the stone by simply passing it through the press, and the stone, without further preparation, is ready to print off thousands of proofs, all equally perfect."[4] Such descriptions heralded the ease of the technology and the opportunity it afforded to print large number of impressions. Newspapers soon shifted from printing descriptions of the process to announcing the availability of lithographic prints for sale in major American cities. Bass Otis (1784–1861) is believed to have been the first artist in the United States to use lithography in 1819.[5] Stores offering lithographic prints opened in Boston and New York in 1825 and in Philadelphia in 1828.[6] Lithography would soon become the preferred printmaking method for producing caricatures.

The presidency of Andrew Jackson (1829–37) prompted the publication of more caricatures than any of the previous six administrations, and the majority of these were lithographs. Murrell acknowledged this, although he expressed uncertainty that lithography was the reason for caricature's explosion in the 1830s. It is an "open question," he wrote, "whether the flood of cartoons that began with and covered the Jackson administration was the result of the new, simple, and cheap method of reproduction or whether it came of the intense interest and protest Old Hickory's acts and policies aroused."[7] The question posed by Murrell seems less one of precedence, but rather that both factors contributed to the rising number of caricatures. Akin and Charles provided a strong foundation on which a new generation of artists trained in the age of lithography could readily pursue caricature. Akin worked in lithography, but from the 1830s until his death in 1846 he had to compete with a new, younger group of artists. Although Akin and Charles did not caricature the same events and are not known to have responded to one another's output, this is not the case for Johnston, who was predominantly active in Boston after 1824. At least one newspaper acknowledged both Akin and Johnston in the same notice, comparing their prints against one another during a campaign cycle, but Akin and Johnston did not become rivals. Johnston's career in the 1830s and beyond eclipsed that of Akin, who suffered professional setbacks until his death in 1846. Although its subject matter extends slightly beyond the stated framework of this book, this final chapter posits how caricature developed with the aid of lithography; it also examines how the career trajectory of Akin, the established caricaturist born in Charleston before American independence, compares with that of Johnston, born in 1799 in Philadelphia to a father who worked in newspapers and publishing.

Issues of Slavery in Pennsylvania Politics: A Caricature of Joseph Hiester

With the exception of Akin's *A Philosophic Cock*, no other caricatures have survived from the period before 1820 where the subject matter focused on people of color or slavery.[8]

There is evidence, however, that in 1809 a caricature was published in New York in reaction to the trial of the upholsterer Amos Broad and his wife, who were accused of beating their slave Betty and her three-year-old daughter Sarah: "The Caricature, now in circulation, relative to the conduct of Amos Broad, and his wife, towards their slaves."[9] A further reference can be located for a caricature prompted by legislation signed by President James Monroe in March 1820, known as the Missouri Compromise. The new law allowed for the admission of Missouri as a state with legalized slavery, while Maine was admitted as a free state. Newspaper notices mention at least one caricature, titled *A Rider!*, although this has not been located in public collections. The description of the caricature was reprinted verbatim in at least sixteen newspapers, from Maine to Kentucky: "Maine is represented as a young *Dandy* of 21, with the constitution in his hand, walking fearlessly over the steps of the Capitol, in pursuit of his patrimony. Virginia and other Slave States, aware of his approach, and determined to deprive him of his inheritance, had placed themselves at the threshold; at the moment of his entrance, they placed a fat *Negro Wench* astride his shoulders, and toppled him to the earth."[10] The caricaturist responsible for this image was not named in the newspaper description; however, because the notice was first printed in New Hampshire, it is possible the caricature was published in New England. The presence of this description in so many geographically dispersed newspapers between February and April 1820 indicates that while impressions may have had limited circulation, knowledge of it was widespread.

A caricature by James Akin focused on the pro-slavery tendencies of a Pennsylvania politician has survived. *Joseph Hiester's claims to the votes of a Christian People, or the Reformer of 1820 exhibiting his love of Liberty and Country / Instruere el servare populum* (fig. 114) was published in reaction to the candidacy of Joseph Hiester (1752–1832) for governor of Pennsylvania on the Federalist ticket in 1820, running against the Republican incumbent William Findlay. Politics had been an important aspect throughout Akin's life. He was now in his mid-forties, and his political leanings had aligned with the Republican Party. Akin had gravitated toward an area of Philadelphia where he became active in meetings of the "democratic citizens of Locust Ward." This district voted overwhelmingly for the Federalists, so Akin was part of the minority. At a meeting held in September 1820, Akin was elected to represent the ward and party as "inspector"; four resolutions were unanimously adopted at the meeting, including two that focused on Hiester's treatment of fellow Americans:

> *Resolved,* That Joseph Hiester's vote to prevent the sons of poor men from exercising the inestimable right of suffrage is hostile to every principle of republican equality, and is sufficient reason, together with his total want of capacity, why he should not receive our support for the office of governor.

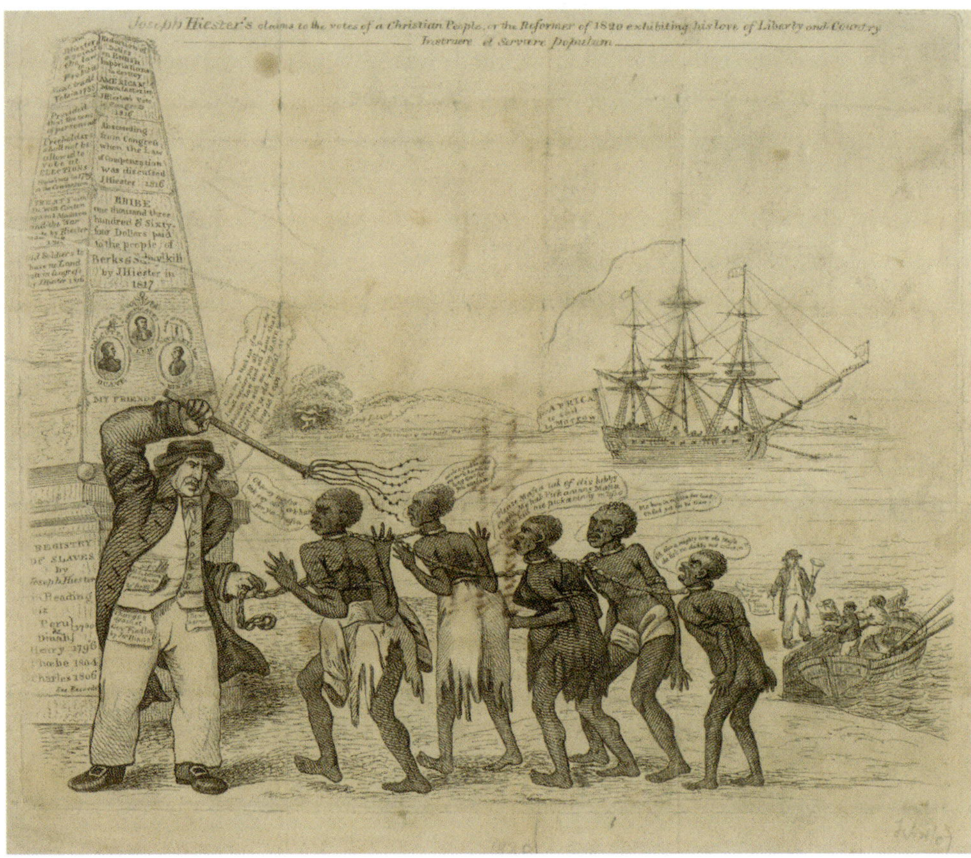

Figure 114 | [James Akin], *Joseph Hiester's claims to the votes of a Christian People, or the Reformer of 1820 exhibiting his love of Liberty and Country / Instruere el servare populum*, n.d. [1820]. Cartoon and Caricature File, PR 010, 1820-1, FF23. New-York Historical Society, image number 23682. Collection of the New-York Historical Society.

> *Resolved,* That we know Joseph Hiester to be a slave holder and we abhor the principle; and inasmuch as the great question of slavery is considered as yet undecided, we cannot give our support to a man who, if elected, would render any instruction to our representatives in congress on that important question on a contemptible farce.[11]

During this election, slavery was a contested issue, brought to the forefront by discussions on the Missouri Compromise. One Philadelphia newspaper published lengthy opinion pieces on both candidates and their history with slavery, one providing a column divided by the headings "Hiester and Slavery" and "Findlay and Freedom."[12]

Akin's decision to focus on Hiester's treatment of slaves reflects the amount of text devoted to this topic in newspapers. He did not sign the caricature, but it is undoubtably his work. The style of the print, the depiction of the main figure of Hiester, the lettering of words within the image, and the inclusion of a Latin phrase in the title all resemble Akin's earlier prints. Similarities can be found in *"The Bloody Arena."* (fig. 54), in which the facial expressions of the figures are comparable to Hiester's and where Akin also included an inscription in Latin. At least three uncolored impressions of the caricature of Hiester have survived, and an impression was known to Murrell, whose observation was short, stating only "There is no humor in this, but doubtless his political opponents guffawed loudly as, looking at it, they had mental pictures of Hiester writhing impotently under the savage attack."[13] It is unlikely that the audience for the caricature was large. Without Akin's name on the print, it may be understood that it was made for those within his local Republican Party, perhaps for those in attendance at the meetings in Locust Ward. Individuals aware of Akin would not need a signature to know who created it. No reference to this caricature has been found in newspapers or private papers from the period, another indication that this may have been made for a small and intimate audience.

The subject matter is problematic in its depiction of race. Akin has crowded the image, not wholly unlike other caricature prints; however, the figures of the enslaved people in particular require attention. Akin has depicted Hiester in the foreground, shown on the left with a whip in his hand, facing five enslaved Africans, all bound together by chains around their necks, their arms constrained from behind. Four of the slaves wear rags; the fifth slave appears to be naked. Rags are wound around the chest of the middle figure, perhaps suggesting that she is a woman. The figures, especially the faces, of these five individuals are crudely presented. Where Akin found source material for his depiction of the figures is not known, but he may have drawn from memories of his youth. He was raised in the South; his family owned slaves; and it is likely he witnessed the public sale of slaves in Charleston in the 1780s and 1790s.[14] Unlike the enslaved figures, Hiester is not altogether satirically represented. Akin could have chosen to portray Hiester, age sixty-eight at the time of the election, as stooped and elderly. Rather, Akin has depicted him as strong and fit, wielding a whip referred to as a cat o' nine tails. Akin included next to Hiester an obelisk that lists his wrongdoings. Noteworthy is the attention that Akin placed on Hiester's voting record: against the law to prohibit the slave trade in 1788, against allowing the sons of those not freeholders to vote in elections, and against providing older soldiers the right to own land. Akin included the bribes Hiester was believed to have taken, a list of slaves owned, and the names and portraits of three friends, including the newspaper editor John Binns. A large ship in the background flies a flag that reads, "For AFRICA to sail tomorrow," and to the far right another vignette includes a figure standing onshore beside a rowboat with two men on board. He holds a bullhorn and a document. In a speech bubble, Hiester says to the figures, "D[am]n the Abolition Laws and all Laws that interfere with me and my SLAVES. I'll hold you ye old rascal as long as I can." Akin's caricature also included a reference to Hiester's participation in the Revolutionary War in the form of a figure in the background attempting to hide behind some trees. Revealing that Akin was aware of Hiester's past, this likely alludes to his capture during the war, as does the identification of "Long Island" and the statement "Oh that they would take me a prisoner and not hurt me." These attacks on Hiester's morality did not derail his bid for governor, as he won by a margin of almost four thousand votes.[15] The Federalist candidate for inspector also won, ending Akin's bid for that office without success.[16]

Both Murrell and Weitenkampf included *Joseph Hiester's claims to the votes of a Christian People* in their publications without an artist attribution and with the incorrect date of 1817, despite the year 1820 being part of the title.[17] It is possible this was because the earlier gubernatorial campaign between the same two candidates had generated a print by William Charles, *Democracy ___ against the ___ Unnatural Union. Trial Oct. 14th 1817* (fig. 115). In the Charles caricature, Hiester is represented as a humpbacked older gentleman, standing atop the Philadelphia newspapers *Aurora* and *U.S. Gazette* that are perched preciously on two blocks of wood labeled "Federalism" and "Old Schoolism." On the left, Findlay ascends to the seat of the power. The governor's throne floats in the air surrounded on both sides by crowds of supporters. Charles's style in this 1817 caricature is similar to *Family Electioneering* (fig. 69), designed ten years earlier. The date found within the title refers to the day of Findlay's win over Hiester. Charles did not sign his name to this caricature print; rather, he inscribed it with words that might have alluded to his having become a naturalized United States citizen, forsaking his Scottish origin: "Designed and executed by one who has neither place nor pension."

The Anonymous Caricatures of the Presidential Campaigns of 1820 and 1824

The presidential election of 1820 was uncontested. The influence of the Federalist Party had weakened over the previous years to such an extent that the organization was unable to back a promising presidential candidate. The only evidence of a political caricature comes from descriptions in contemporary newspapers. A caricature that depicted Monroe's vice president, Daniel Tompkins, was described in newspapers along the East Coast in March and April: "A Caricature. . . . representing the Vice President, in military costume, his sword on the wrong side, approaching the treasury (a large chest), and demanding $600,000 for extra services. . . . We have never seen a caricature better conceived or

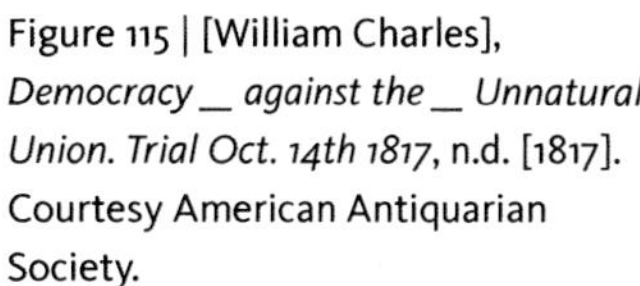

Figure 115 | [William Charles], *Democracy __ against the __ Unnatural Union. Trial Oct. 14th 1817*, n.d. [1817]. Courtesy American Antiquarian Society.

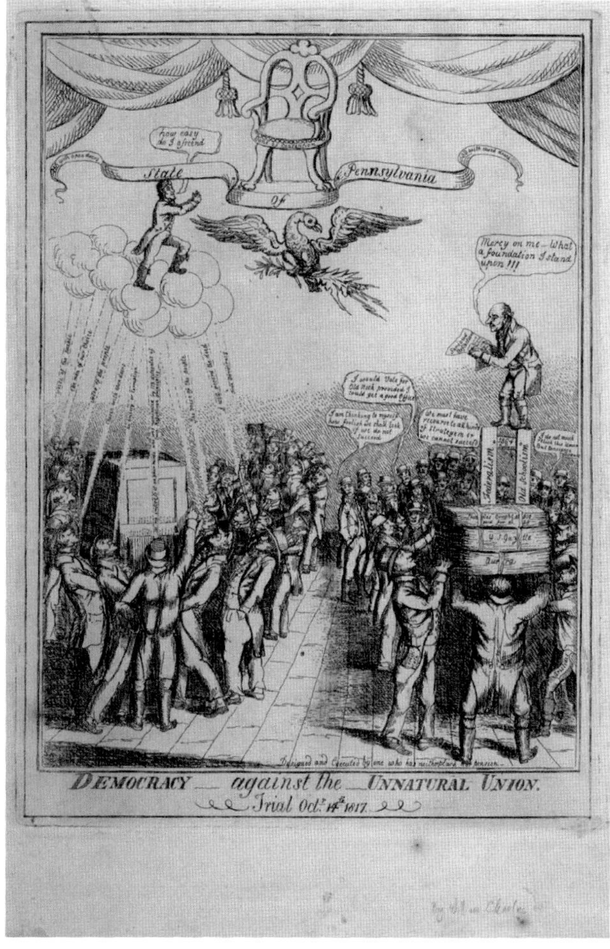

more appropriate."[18] Running unopposed for a second term, President James Monroe received all electoral votes cast with the exception of one, held to preserve the memory of George Washington who had gained support from all.[19]

The next presidential election prompted at least four known caricatures. While Monroe had run unopposed in 1820, the field in 1824 was crowded initially with six strong contenders: Secretary of State John Quincy Adams of Massachusetts, Secretary of War John C. Calhoun of South Carolina, Secretary of the Treasury William H. Crawford of Georgia, Henry Clay of Kentucky, Andrew Jackson of Tennessee, and former governor of New York DeWitt Clinton. The first caricature to be published during this campaign cycle was *The five aspirants* (fig. 116), of which only one impression is known.[20] The work was completed without a signature, and so its artist is unknown, although the publication date can be attributed to before November 1823, based on a lengthy newspaper

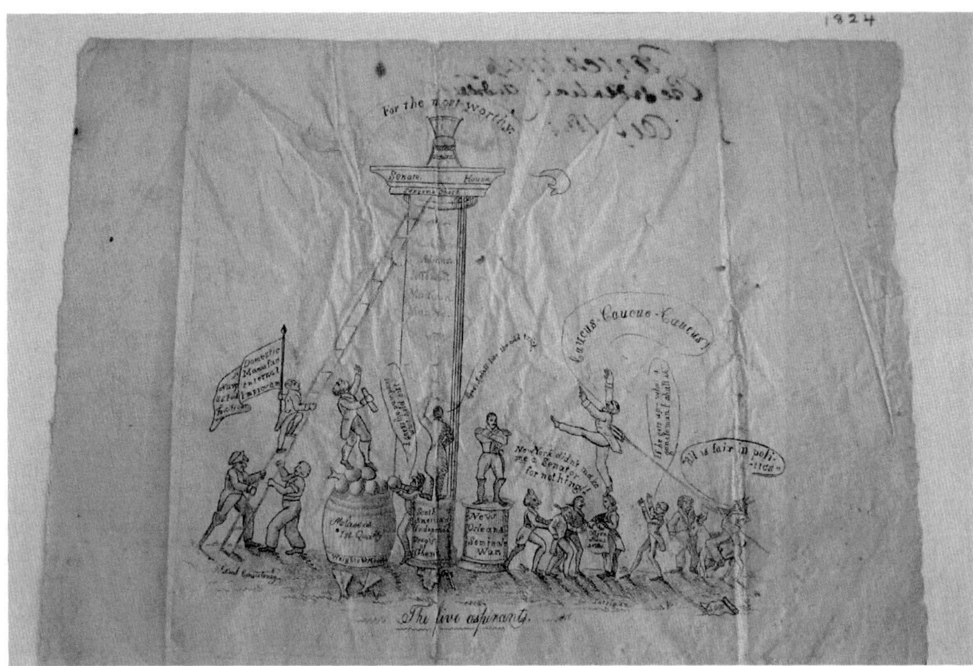

Figure 116 | Anonymous, *The five aspirants*, n.d. [1823]. American Prints, Houghton Library, Harvard University.

description that stated that the caricature was "circulated in New-York."[21] Five of the six contenders were depicted: Crawford, Calhoun, Jackson, Adams, and Clay. Clinton was not included, perhaps because early in the election he was not taken seriously and was mocked as "a candidate for president only in his own imaginings and those of his most devoted followers."[22] New York State is represented by its senator, Martin Van Buren, who has been provided with a speech bubble in which he proclaims, "New York did not make me a senator for nothing." The newspaper reported a full description of the caricature so that even without seeing the physical work a reader would have known the point of the print: "Nearly in the centre of the plate rises a lofty column, on which are engraved the names of Washington, Adams, Madison, and Monroe; on the capital are the words 'Supreme Court, Senate, House' and above these is the Presidential Chair, yet vacant, surrounded by rays of glory, and over it the words 'for the most worthy.'"[23] This imagery may have served as inspiration for the caricature published for the following election cycle of 1828, which is also untitled and lacking any form of date or inscription (fig. 117). This work depicted a presidential chair and a ladder for the "aspirants." In this rendering Andrew Jackson is shown being assisted by an unidentified figure

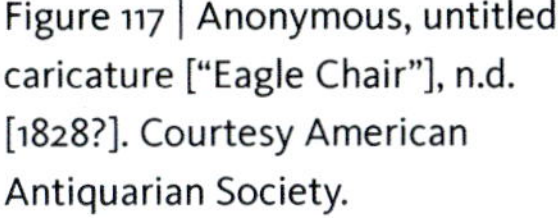

Figure 117 | Anonymous, untitled caricature ["Eagle Chair"], n.d. [1828?]. Courtesy American Antiquarian Society.

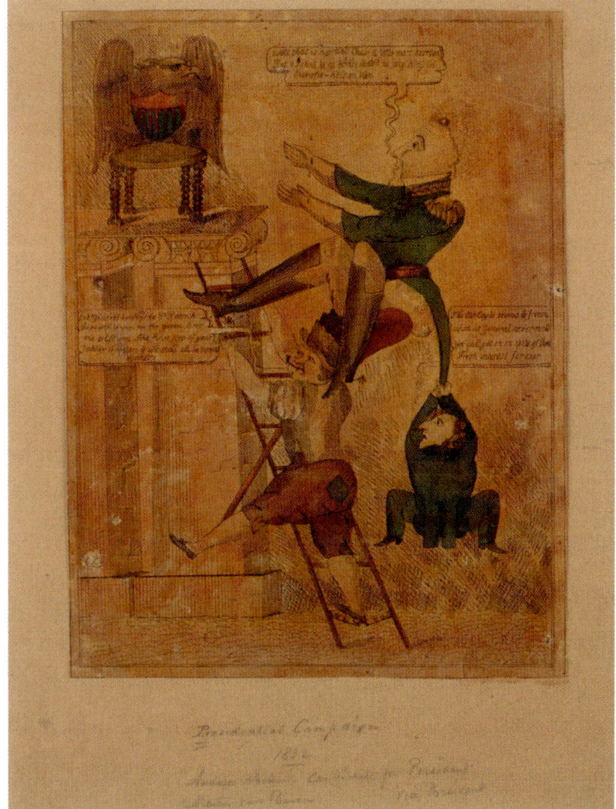

in climbing the ladder to reach the presidential chair. Holding on to his coattails is the politician Martin Van Buren; an eagle frowns down on them both.[24]

DeWitt Clinton, who had been New York governor for two terms (1817–22), was the subject of a caricature that hinges on the notion of unintended consequences. Clinton was out of office but remained involved in a variety of volunteer projects, such as supporting the New-York Historical Society, the Academy of Fine Arts, and the University of the State of New York. From 1810 onward, he was also a member of the Erie Canal Commission that took almost fifteen years to create a waterway between Lake Erie and the Hudson River.[25] In the spring of 1824, Clinton's political opponents, termed the "Bucktails," conspired against him and successfully voted to remove him from the commission. Clinton, who had been with the commission since its inception and served as its president since 1816, was suddenly ousted from a project he had worked on for fourteen years. The caricature that was published shortly afterward, *A Caucus held at Albany on Sunday Evening April 11th 1824 by the N.Y. city members* (fig. 118), appears to depict

158

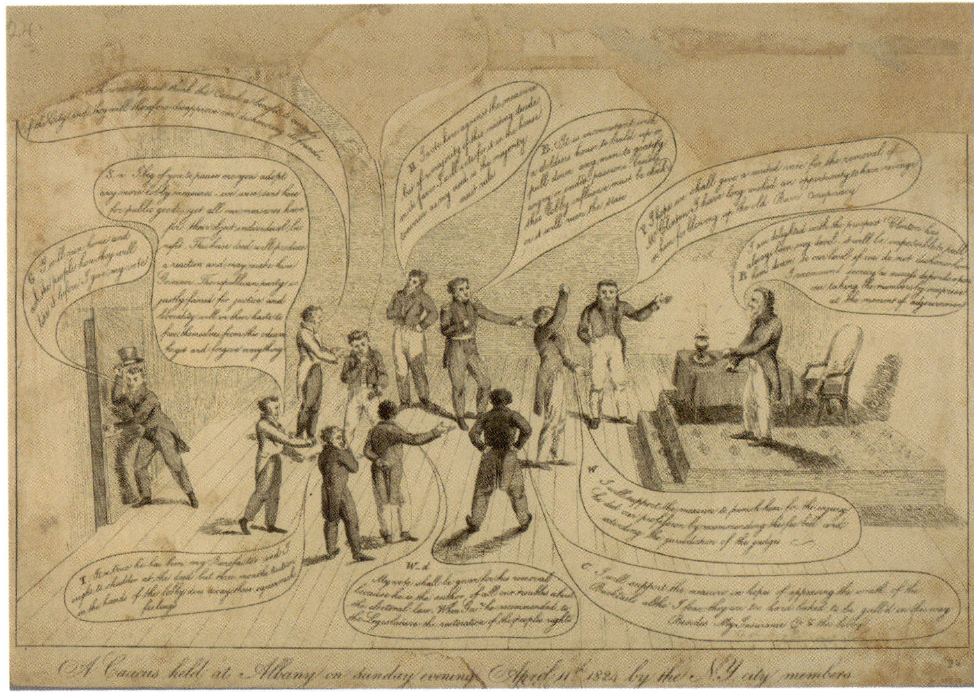

Figure 118 | Anonymous, *A Caucus held at Albany on Sunday evening April 11th 1824 by the N.Y. city members*, April 1824. priAPC 0018, American Social/Political Caricatures Collection, The Huntington Library, San Marino, California.

either a secret or an imagined meeting held the day before the Bucktails convened to oust Clinton. Newspaper accounts reported on the official meeting that was held on April 12: "A resolution from the Senate removing De Witt Clinton from the office of Canal Commissioner, was received—After a few remarks by Mr Conningham, in opposition to the resolution, the question was taken and carried, ayes 64, noes 34." Another report characterized the absurdity of the removal in the following terms: "as gross and foolish an abuse of power was ever recorded."[26] Clinton's removal caused such a controversy among New York voters that he was nominated for another term as governor, to which the caricature alludes. One of the speech bubbles reveals the consequences of removing Clinton from office: "I beg of you to pause once you adopt any more lobby measures—we were sent here for public good—yet all out measures have for their object individual benefit. This base deal will produce a reaction and may make him Governor." The design and format are reminiscent of caricatures published decades before; however, unlike previous American caricatures, the viewpoint is from above, looking down on the scene, and the figures are not represented in a linear fashion. Members of the Bucktails depicted here are each identified by their initials within their speech bubbles. On the upper right-hand side is an allegorical image of Liberty, flanked by an eagle and an American flag, emerging from a grouping of clouds to say, "I renounce them and their ways." Thirteen figures are included in the scene, and all with lengthy speeches supporting their cause. The caricaturist responsible was likely an amateur, as he relies heavily on text to enable his "image" to be read. As predicted by one of the figures in the caricature, Clinton won the election and as governor presided over the festivities celebrating the opening of the completed canal.

The Presidential Campaign of 1824: David Claypoole Johnston and James Akin

The crowded field of candidates for the presidency in the fall of 1824 caught the attention of Akin and Johnston, who each published a caricature on the topic. By the 1820s, the metaphor of a presidential race had become popular imagery, with candidates jostling for the top of a ladder or running against one another to reach the "presidential seat." By the fall of 1824, three contenders remained, down from the original six of the previous year: John Quincy Adams, William Crawford, and Andrew Jackson. Akin, the elder caricaturist, published his print in support of Jackson, *Caucus Curs in full Yell, or a War-Whoop to Saddle on the People, a Pappoose President* (fig. 119), in Philadelphia that November. It was Johnston—whose print *A Foot-Race* (fig. 120) was published a month earlier than Akin's—who received the first press in newspapers. Johnston's caricature is crowded with the many candidates for office, helpfully accompanied by text in speech bubbles to enable his audience to better understand the depictions. In the background is situated the Capitol and the White House. Johnston's caricature favored John Quincy Adams, who is seen in the lead beside Andrew Jackson, identifiable by his military dress. Johnston's print names the "spoils of winning": the coveted presidential chair and the annual salary of $25,000. Johnston signed with the pseudonym "Crackfardi Del et Sct."

Johnston had spent the year prior in Baltimore working for the theater and retained a close connection to that city. When his caricature was published in Boston, the *Baltimore Patriot* was enthusiastic about Johnston, identifying him as "DC Johnson, of the Theatre, lately of Baltimore, now of Boston." The paper added, "We have just had a glance at one of the finest pieces of caricature engraving that ever threw the visibles of human nature into convulsions. The several candidates are all real likenesses, in the face, and equal, if not superior, to any we ever saw. . . . There is something so inexpressibly humorous throughout the whole piece, so characteristic, and so true to nature."[27] Advertisements announcing the availability of the caricature print are found in Boston newspapers, where impressions were available to purchase for 25 cents beginning on October 6.[28]

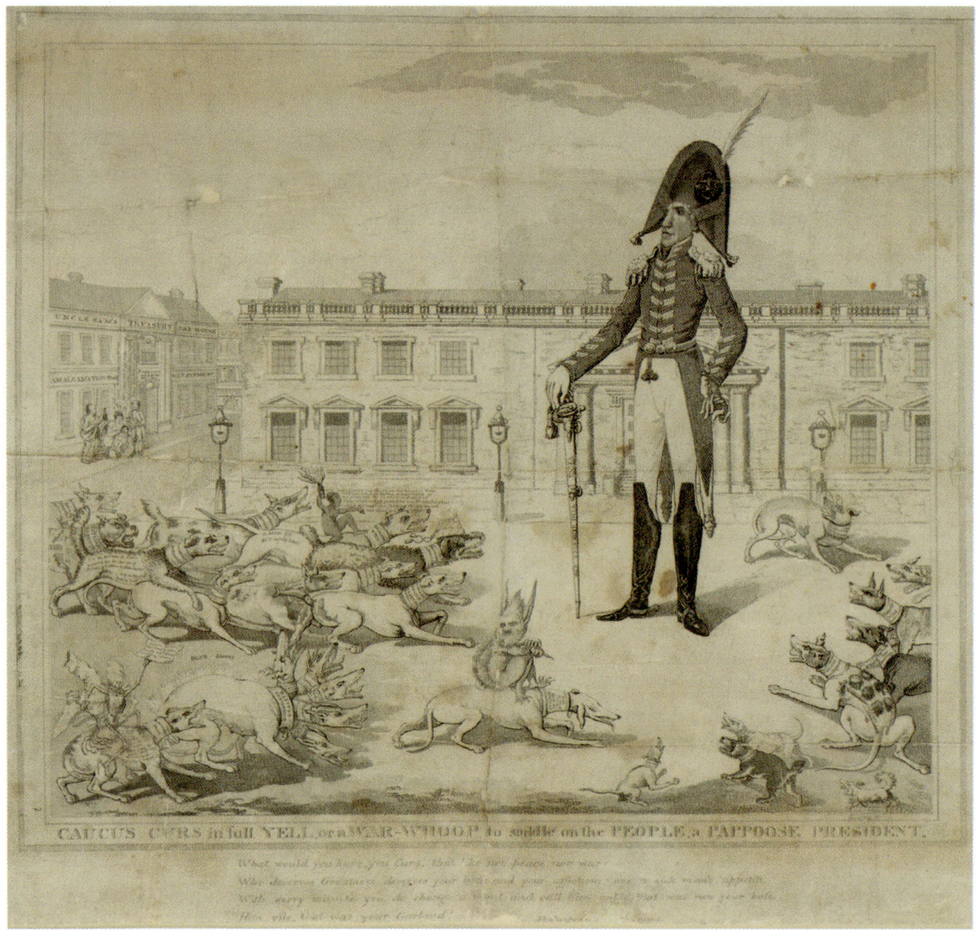

Figure 119 | James Akin, *Caucus Curs in full Yell, or a War-Whoop to Saddle on the People, a Pappoose President*, n.d. [1824]. Prints & Photographs Division, Library of Congress, LC-DIG-pga-00005.

Later that month the caricature was exhibited in New York and could be seen in Rhode Island in November.[29]

A Foot-Race was completed as a copperplate engraving, but soon afterward Johnston turned to lithography for his caricatures. Johnston, who came of age as an engraver and printer in the 1810s, was twenty-six years younger than Akin and able to capitalize on the market for caricature established by Akin and Charles. Johnston's reputation in the medium was acknowledged and celebrated during his lifetime, as he was included in William Dunlap's *History of the Rise and Progress of the Arts of Design*. In the 1830s, when the New Yorker Dunlap began research for his book, he displayed a bias toward those artists

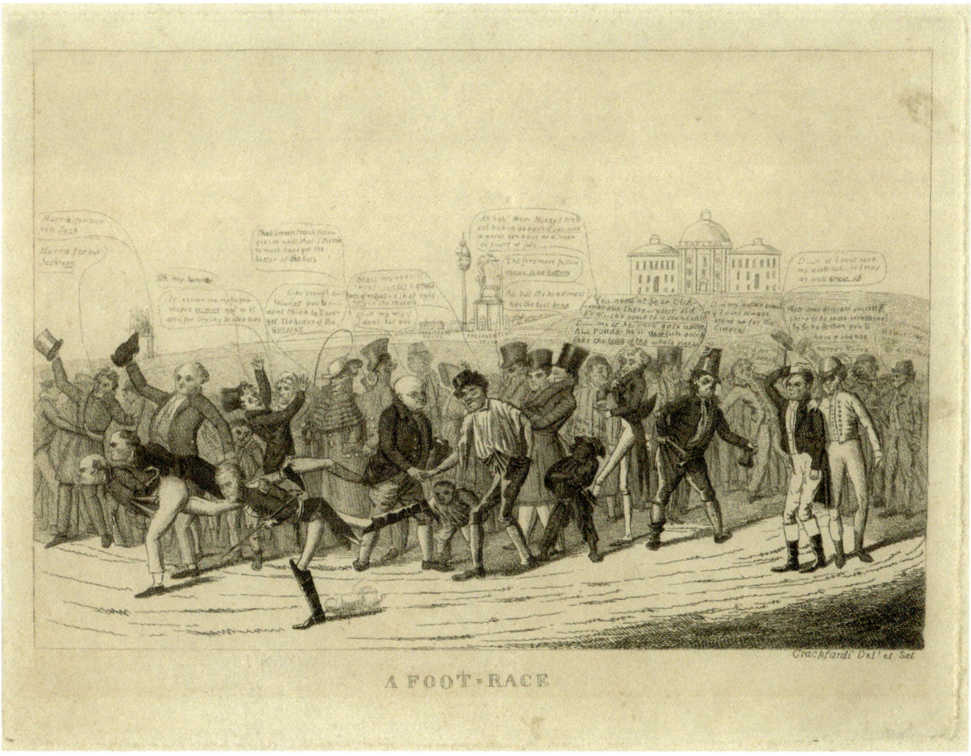

Figure 120 | "Crackfardi" [David Claypoole Johnston], *A Foot-Race*, n.d. [October 1824]. Cartoon and Caricature File, PR 010 1824-1, c.1, FF23. New-York Historical Society, image number, 23681. Collection of the New-York Historical Society.

from his home city. He wrote letters of interest to those living artists whose work he respected—and who lived in the North.[30] This did not include southerner James Akin, who was based in Philadelphia in the 1830s. Dunlap contacted Johnston, who replied with a lengthy, six-page answer in which he gave a detailed account of his life from 1815 to 1834. Skepticism regarding Johnston's autobiography was urged by Clarence Brigham, who wrote on Johnston in the early twentieth century that "not more than a dozen lines of real fact" could be found.[31] Johnston's dismissive thoughts on his career in caricature might well be truthful: he described how he "occasionally put forth a caricature of dandies, militia trainings, etc. In these efforts I succeeded so far, that sundry well-known characters in each department were readily recognized, the prints met with ready sale."[32]

From the number of descriptions found in newspapers, it can be concluded that it had become common practice for caricaturists such as Johnston and Akin to contact editors with letters of inquiry and impressions of their prints. Although no contemporary letters have been located for either Johnston or Akin, it can be assumed from the newspaper descriptions that their methods were similar to Amos Doolittle's in 1813. The description found in the *Baltimore Patriot* for *A Foot-Race* indicates that it is likely that both Johnston and Akin sent proof sheets. The paper published an account that named both caricatures, one in support of Adams and the other of Jackson:

> ANOTHER PRESIDENTIAL CARICATURE.—The laughing Deity must have taken us into his particular favor; for it is but a short time since he favored us with a subject for laughter sufficient to cure the most confirmed melancholy—nay the most obdurate attack of the blue devils; we allude to the Presidential Foot Race in which Adams takes the lead in the last round; and now he has put us in possession, through one of its prime ministers, James Akin of Philadelphia, of another, which is absolutely a bolus of provokative [*sic*]. We recommend it, nay we prescribe it, in all cases of melancholy produced by the pending presidential election. It is a proof sheet of a print entitled,
>
> "CAUCUS CURS in full yell, or a WAR WHOOP to saddle on the PEOPLE a PAPOOSE PRESIDENT."[33]

The description of the Akin caricature ran the full length of the newspaper page, filling one column and part of the next. It paid special attention to the print's size and subject matter: "This print is about 24 inches square, handsomely engraved, and of very superior execution throughout, and is altogether an antidote, and we recommend it to be used as such, for the ensuing epidemic—the Presidential ennui. Those who are curious enough to examine this print, can do so by calling at this office, and we especially invite the friends of General Jackson. If it does not excite their risible faculties, they can at least look upon it 'with composure.'" However, there was a limit to the generosity of the press. Such glowing endorsements were not forthcoming from newspapers that were represented in the caricature as dogs, each wearing a collar that named a publication biting at Jackson's feet.[34] The *Salem Gazette* observed that "caricaturing, on a general scale, produces no good, and carries no point.... That these presses have an undoubted right to oppose the general can not be questioned."[35] The *Baltimore Patriot* punned on the reaction of New York's *National Advocate*: "The first growl we have heard from any of animals, whose likenesses are drawn in the caricature print, of which we gave a description the other day, is by the National Advocate, which has conspicuous place in the kennel."[36]

The appearance of Akin's caricature is striking in its resemblance to "high art," particularly the depiction of Jackson. Perhaps Akin had provided a hint to the editor of the *Baltimore Patriot* to highlight this: "The Likeness is excellent, and affords a good representation in full length of the General." Akin took the subject of engraving Jackson seriously, using as his template a full-length portrait of the general that he had seen some years before, at the Nashville Museum of Ralph Eleaser Whiteside Earl (ca. 1788–1838).[37] Earl was a confidant of Jackson and had produced so many paintings of him that he was referred to as the "King's Painter."[38] Their relationship was further cemented when both became widowers and Jackson sought comfort in Earl's continued loyalty. He acted as Earl's benefactor, often financially supplementing the artist when commissions were slow to materialize.[39] How Akin and Earl came to know each other is not clear. They were both in Massachusetts in 1804 (Akin in Newburyport, Earl in Boston) and it is possible their paths crossed at that time.[40] Alternatively, the Philadelphian James Earle might have been the individual who brought the two together.[41] A mutual friend of both artists, Earle ran a gallery and store where he exhibited paintings and sold imported prints from London.[42] Akin's trip to Tennessee might have been prompted by the opening of Earl's Nashville Museum, which was founded in 1818 with Earl's growing art collection that included portraits of Jackson.[43] From surviving letters to Earl, it is possible to trace Akin's movements after his visit to Tennessee to Lynchburg, Virginia, in December 1818, and on to Washington "City" in February 1819. In this letter, Akin wrote to Earl to express outrage for "the virulent abuse from certain members in Congress against the character of Genl Jackson." Akin was referring to the controversy over the Seminole War, in which Jackson was under investigation by the House Committee on Military Affairs for his handling of the executions of two British subjects, Robert Ambrister and Alexander Arbuthnot, who had both been found guilty by a military court of aiding and abetting the Seminoles. This news had even reached London, where later that spring George Cruikshank portrayed the executions from the British perspective in a caricature titled *American Justice!! or The Ferocious Yankee Genl. Jack's Reward for Butchering Two British Subjects!!!* (fig. 121).[44] Jackson was cleared on February 8, 1819; with his image, "scarcely . . . blemished," he embarked on a three-week trip that "became a grand triumphal tour."[45] Akin's letter was written after Jackson's acquittal was secure and interest in portraits of him was growing. He may have wanted to join this movement by adding his own brand of caricature and was inspired to request of Earl a sketch of the general. Akin's remarks make it clear that upon his return to Philadelphia he was planning to design and publish a work in support of the war hero and that his print would not intrude on any plans Earl might have to publish prints of Jackson. Akin requested that Earl "furnish me an outline of the Generals visage, & figure, that I may accomplish my purpose—I merely want the strong outlines of feature & figure, required in caricature. . . . I have all the materials to begin, & shall look for your answer on my arrival in Philadelphia. The sketch can be made on a large sheet, & folded in the letter form, & the postage will only be made for a single letter."[46] Akin had evidently seen Earl's portrait paintings when he visited the Nashville Museum, as he referenced "recollections of your commanding whole length

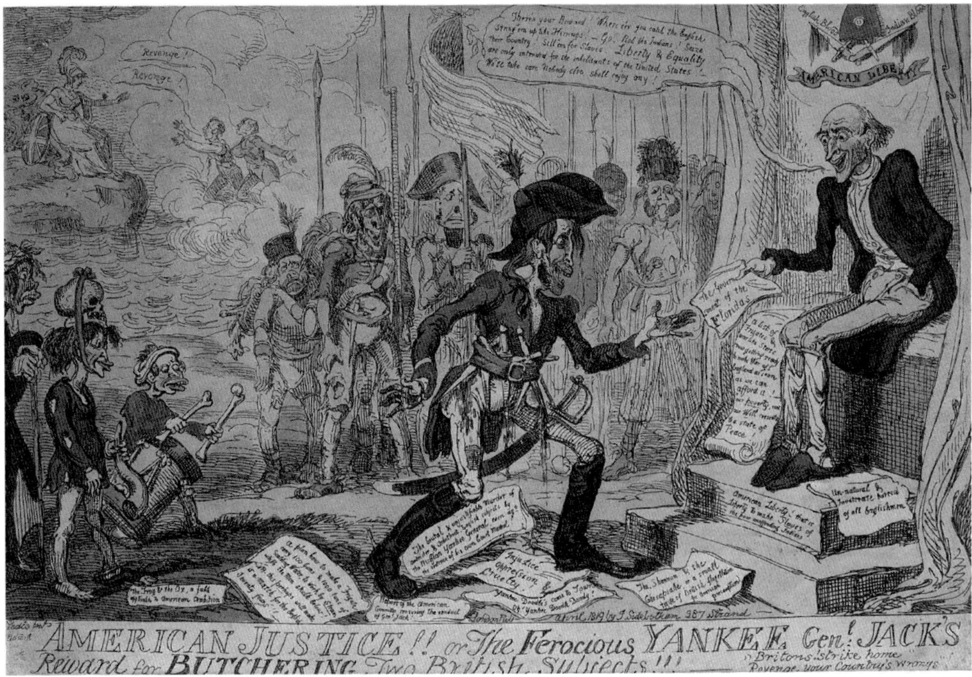

Figure 121 | George Cruikshank, *American Justice!! or The Ferocious Yankee Genl. Jack's Reward for Butchering Two British Subjects!!!*, April 1819. Hand-colored etching. Tennessee State Museum.

attitude."[47] For the print to be successful, Akin sought an image with "the strong outlines of feature and figure, required in caricature." Akin's attention to detail and his desire to be furnished with a portrait of Jackson recalls the practice of James Gillray in London. When confronted with the prospect of designing a caricature in which new politicians were to be included, Gillray would attend the visitors' gallery at the House of Commons to make a rapid sketch of the new figure.[48] Perhaps Akin had also attended public hearings and seen Jackson while in Washington. As such, he had all the materials necessary and was ready to begin once Earl sent the image to Philadelphia.

Earl was not forthcoming, however, as Akin wrote again in March, likely to request once more the portrait. Although the exact contents of this letter are not known, Earl responded to the March letter in November 1819 with no direct reference to Akin's request, only that he had written to their mutual friend James Earle: "As he will unquestionably advise you of my sentiments, touching the proposition I have been able to make to him, with respect to publishing a print of general Jackson &, I think it superfluous here to repeat here."[49] Based on this letter, it is not possible to know whether Earl provided Akin with a sketch of Jackson, though it seems likely that he did not. Perhaps there was concern that it would appear as if Jackson himself had approved the caricature, and Jackson did not want to be involved. Furthermore, the tone of the Hiester caricature (were the work known to them) might have deterred either Earl or Jackson at this time. Akin did not have a finished caricature of Jackson to send Earl until 1824. "My dear Sir," he wrote, "I enclose you a Caricature in favour of Gen. Jackson, in opposition to the miserable herd of wretches who publish their pitiful resentments against the Man who saved them from the Grasp of British Tyranny. Accept as testimony of my high respect this feeble Effort to put down the clamours of so base a herd."[50] If Earl or Jackson responded to seeing the caricature, no reference has been located.

As Johnston had seemingly foretold in *A Foot-Race*, Jackson lost the 1824 election to John Quincy Adams. But four years later Jackson beat the incumbent to become the sixth president of the United States, taking the oath of office in 1829. Akin electioneered for Jackson during the campaign, hopeful that this latest effort would result in a position in the new administration.[51] Akin was convinced the position of superintendent of the Patent Office, vacant since the death of Dr. William Thornton in 1828, was to be his. According to a surviving letter and petition, "Akin's friends endeavoured to procure for him the recent situation; but unfortunately for him, his political creed had too deeply involved him in defending the unprincipled slanders during the Jackson Contest, so as not to be considered by the reigning party."[52] With Jackson elected, Akin began campaigning for the Patent Office position by placing a timely notice in a Philadelphia newspaper titled "Patents and Patentees," in which he announced he was offering his services to "individuals unacquainted with the business" of submitting patents, having prepared, "during many years, all papers pointed out by obtaining patents, without one solitary instance of having a petition, drawing, or specimen ever rejected at the Patent Office."[53] In March, Akin requested consideration for the position of the office of superintendent of the Patent Office: "Should you, Sir, be pleased to honor me with your notice in any way you may think proper, to aid my success, in my application It will be to me one of the most fortunate events of my life, and the greatest proof of your good opinion."[54] This, in addition to the many letters and petitions of support written on behalf of Akin, might have come at an inconvenient time for Jackson.[55] He expressed his frustration with the competition for government jobs to Ralph Earl: "It seems to me from the thousands that Press for office, that every man who voted for the cause of the people, think they ought to be rewarded with office. Having but few offices to bestow, compared with the many that apply, many must go away dissatisfied."[56] When Jackson did not respond to his initial letter, Akin turned to Secretary of State Martin Van Buren, who had been tasked with making the appointments. Akin sent at least two letters in April and May 1829, each frantic. The impetus for the tone of these letters came from rumors that Jackson intended to appoint the Baltimore teacher John D. Craig the next superintendent.[57] Writing to Van Buren, Akin was incredulous that the position would go to a foreigner: "I have the honor, Sir, to claim birth rights from the same state as yourself, a Carolinian. . . . My efforts have long been directed to serve my country's cause, and it is painful to see strangers from foreign lands, enjoying honors . . . to the exclusion of those . . . whose political feeling is consistent with the spirit of the constitution & laws of our country." He went on to ask, "Should another Englishman from recommendation, be favoured, might it not be reflected upon American sons of arts, if not weakening the character of our country, that we were constrained to depend upon a nature at all times variant with us, for aid in the departments of science connected to the fine arts?" Akin continued, "I speak patriotically, Sir, but at the same time with the most profound respect towards you, because I am assured that the impressions of Amor Patriae are alive in the breast of every American who feels disposed to serve the country of his birth."[58] When Van Buren did not respond, Akin wrote once more, this time with more emotion: "I am however particularly situated in being under the necessity of advocating my own cause with you. . . . I hope sincerely that my application will be received favourably from the circumstances of my cause." Perhaps he felt that by then he had nothing to lose. Akin was fifty-six years old and weathering a period of financial instability. The superintendent position would be the "spoils" of a career of working by all means necessary to survive. In his impassioned plea to Van Buren he remained emphatic that as an engraver he had aided in the successful Jackson campaign:

> It is I believe freely admitted by all who have interested themselves in my behalf, and to whom I am known, that I have long since warmly supported Democratic principles; my pens, my gravers, and my pencil, have always been actively employed and proved a great annoyance to political opponents generally, but more particularly to those, who endeavoured hard to overthrow the late glorious triumph. My efforts effectively rebutted the stale but frequent man sore of descriptive Coffin hand bills,[59] which my skill in caricature completely overwhelmed and silenced. For this, Sir, believe me I have been frivolously oppressed and misfortune heaped in bitterness upon my head, with the severest persecution.[60]

The importance of these letters to Akin's narrative at the end of the decade is revealed in the last known missive from Akin to Van Buren in 1829. Still desperate for patronage from the government he believed he so ably assisted, Akin recognized that his satires were "a great annoyance to political opponents generally, but more particularly to those, who endeavoured hard to overthrow the late glorious triumph." Akin claimed to have

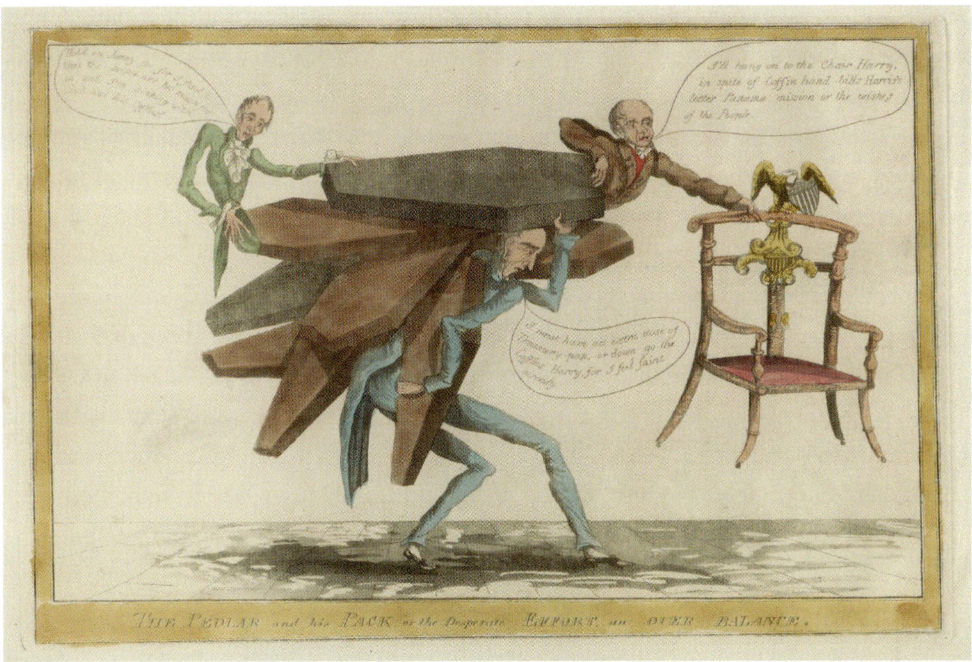

Figure 122 | Anonymous, *The Pedlar and his Pack or the Desperate Effort, an Over Balance*, n.d. [1828?]. Prints & Photographs Division, Library of Congress, LC-DIG-ds-00847.

defended Jackson, having responded to the aggressive assaults against him. The best known of those attacks were the aforementioned "coffin" handbills. The handbills had been published in 1828 by the newspaper editor John Binns, who alleged to have factual details on six militia members who had fought in 1814 and whose length of service was in dispute. After these men were found guilty of dissension, Jackson had ordered the death penalty for them all. The original handbill reproduced images of six coffins to represent the executed soldiers. As early as April 1828, a Virginia newspaper had noted the arrival of these handbills: "The Coffin Handbill—is among the principal tricks to which the parasites of the Administration are resorting. Few of our intelligent readers will believe how many of these handbills have been strewn through the Northern and Western States."[61] Although Akin claimed to have "rebutted the stale but frequent man sore of descriptive Coffin hand bills," no caricatures made during this time have been located.[62]

An unsigned caricature, *The Pedlar and his Pack, or the Desperate Effort, an Over Balance* (fig. 122), directly focused on the publication of the coffin bills, depicting Binns buried under six coffins, but this cannot be attributed to Akin. The caricature shows President John Quincy Adams holding his presidential chair, while Henry Clay is seen on the far left.[63] The figures in this anonymous print are angular, poorly executed, and unlike any other Akin caricature figures. The unknown caricaturist was not as skilled as Akin, as can be seen in the arm of John Binns, which is awkwardly placed.

An example of a caricature's contribution to a heightened political environment appeared months afterward, when political supporters of Adams and Jackson fought, punching one another, over the appearance of a caricature:

> during the heat of the late election in this city, we sauntered towards one of the ward polls, and found that a complete battle-royal was raging. Three or four strapping fellows were at it, with bloody noses, pommelling [*sic*] each other unmercifully; while several in the ring were encouraging the combatants with "give it to him Kentuc [*sic*]—strike him under the fifth rib," "mind his bread basket," and much of such mild and encouraging applause. When we had got in the midst of them, they all ceased by common consent. "By the powers, here he is himself," said one of the combatants, "say it to his face. Oh, honey, you dar'nt—hurra for our side." We soon found that the fight was between the Adams and Jackson men about a caricature, which they brought us, and to our surprise, and no small amusement, we discovered that the caricature was ourselves, mounted on an ark—at the bow was [Churchill C.] Cambreleng, and at the stern Mr Colman [William Coleman], with labels containing political declarations; in the water was Van Buren swimming for life; the whole was so well executed, that we indulged in a hearty laugh at it, which set the beligerents [*sic*] in a good humor, and restored peace and harmony.[64]

Despite all his efforts, Akin's application for the Patent Office job was not successful, and this rejection turned his already fragile emotions against Andrew Jackson. At a crossroads in his career, he was without a government position, a stable income, or the prestige that comes with such a role. Between 1824 and 1830, Akin changed his address at least three times; in all instances he was the proprietor of a boardinghouse or tavern, even operating a cellar for oysters and refreshments.[65] Oyster cellars were popular in this decade, and Akin's establishment would have been one of many in Philadelphia. An oyster spread also turned out to be the subject of a caricature and what might be Akin's foray into working in lithography with *Philadelphia Taste Displayed. Or, Bon-Ton Below Stairs* (fig. 123). The subject may refer to a competitor in the oyster business, perhaps the African American restaurateur James Prosser, although this is also unclear.[66] While the caricature does not include a date, Akin did sign his name, noted that it was "Drawn from Stone," and provided the names of "Kennedy & Lucas, Lithographic Printers." Akin might have received some form of tutorial from David Kennedy and William

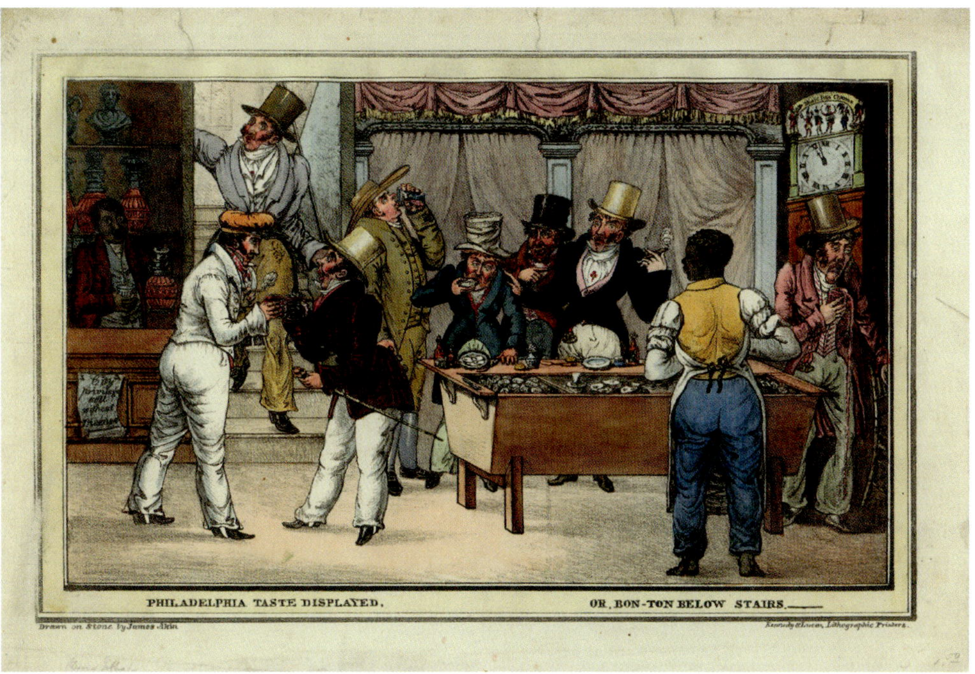

Figure 123 | James Akin, *Philadelphia Taste Displayed. Or, Bon-Ton Below Stairs*, n.d.
[1828?]. Lithograph, hand-colored, 29 × 41 cm, Bb38 097. Reproduced with permission
from the Historical Society of Pennsylvania.

Lucas, who opened the first lithographic establishment in Philadelphia in 1828.[67] As the
pace of production was speeding past him with Johnston's application of lithography to
caricatures in Boston, Akin joined his competition.

Lithography Prevails: A Brief Account of Johnston in Boston

While Akin struggled in Philadelphia, David Claypoole Johnston's career gained momentum in New England. At the start of 1827, Johnston was in Portland, Maine, where he
attempted to establish an engraving career, but in April he returned to Boston: "Having made a fair trial, and receiving but slender encouragement, he takes the liberty to
inform the Public, and those, especially, who wish to obtain any description of engraving, that he shall remain here but a short time longer."[68] In Boston, Johnston's career
focused on publishing caricatures and book illustrations. One of his first lithographic
caricatures was of Andrew Jackson and Henry Clay, *Symptoms of a Locked Jaw, Plain Sewing Done Here* (fig. 124).[69] A preliminary sketch for this caricature has survived and is one

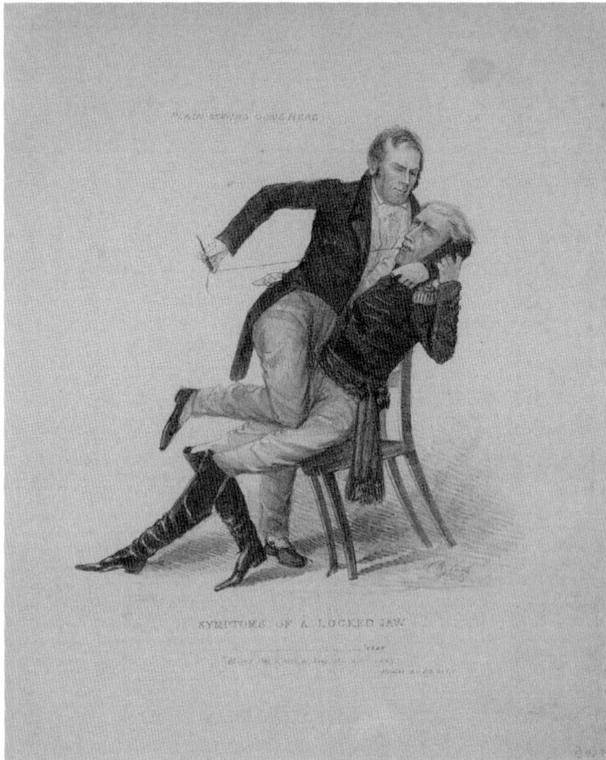

Figure 124 | David Claypoole Johnston, *Symptoms of a Locked Jaw, Plain Sewing Done Here*, n.d. [August 1827]. Courtesy American Antiquarian Society.

of the earliest known drawings made for an American caricature (fig. 125); no sketches by Charles or Akin are known.[70] Few differences can be observed between the sketch and the finished print. The caricature depicts a seated Jackson attacked by Clay, who has Jackson's head in a grip with one hand while the other sews Jackson's mouth shut. Descriptions of this caricature could be found in newspapers as early as August 1827. Generally, the notices for this caricature were similar, frequently taken from the *Baltimore Patriot* and the *Boston Advertiser* because Johnston may have sent impressions and letters to those editors. "We received this morning an admirable satiric lithographic engraving, entitled 'Plain Sewing Done Here.' It is a representation of Gen. Jackson and Henry Clay both excellent likenesses." The notice from the *Baltimore Patriot* took great satisfaction in announcing that "this admirable piece of lithographic caricature, is from the hand of DC Johnston, formerly of the Baltimore theatre, and the one who executed 'the Foot Race.'"[71] News of the caricature was noted in Washington, DC: "A caricature has just been published at Boston with the title of 'Symptoms of a locked jaw' and the depiction of Jackson, 'is a good likeness; but he looks as if he had received a stich in his side, as well as his mouth.'"[72]

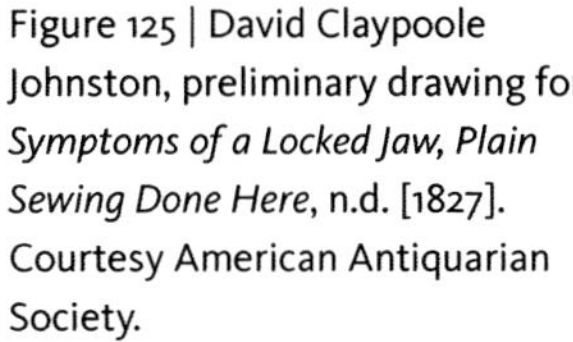

Figure 125 | David Claypoole Johnston, preliminary drawing for *Symptoms of a Locked Jaw, Plain Sewing Done Here*, n.d. [1827]. Courtesy American Antiquarian Society.

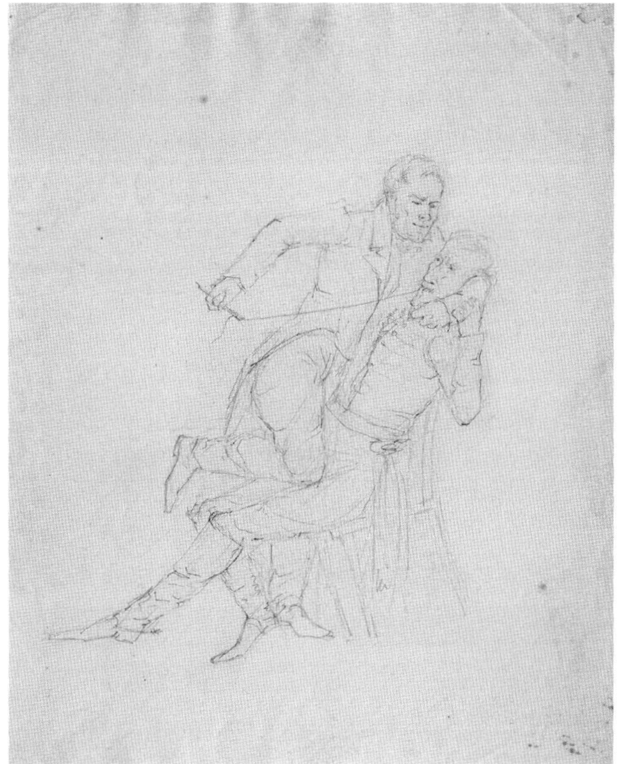

A description published in a Rhode Island newspaper noted, "We have been much amused with a lithographic caricature very neatly hitting off the most important event of the day Mr. Clay's and General Jackson controversy. The General in military costume, booted and spurred, is seated in a chair with his head thrown back, and exhibited a woful [*sic*] expression of countenance."[73] Weeks later, another description was published announcing that that caricature was available for purchase in Boston shops. This description offers Johnston's name and connects him to his previous caricature, *A Foot-Race*:

Plain Sewing. A Humorous caricature, with the label Plain Sewing done here, suggested by Mr. Clay's speech at the Lexington dinner, representing him in the act of sewing up the mouth of the military candidate for Presidency, has been some days in the shops of this city, and has attracted a good deal of attention for the felicitous manner in which a strong likeness of the actors, is combined, with attitudes strikingly expressive and the relative situations into which they are supposed to have brought themselves. The instrument with which the operation is performed is a pen, but the stitches appear to be taken with a steady hand, a strong thread, and a determination to do the work thoroughly. The ingenious artist to whom the public is indebted for this piece is Mr. D. C. Johnson [*sic*], who is also the author of the Presidential Foot Race, published two or three years since, and many other humorous productions.[74]

Although published in the summer of 1827, the print continued to be mentioned in newspapers until the New Year:

In the absence of facts and arguments suited to their necessities, the Adams party have become notorious for their caricatures. They appear to have derived at times much encouragement and consolation, from the caricature which represented Clay sewing up Jackson's mouth with a pen. It was found that Clay could not in his writings represent the design sufficiently intelligible, and hence the necessity of their caricature to help them along. . . . Last, and what is not least disgraceful to them and their cause, they have taken pains within a few days past, to issue from their press a considerable quantity of hand-bills.[75]

Johnston's caricature proved to be difficult for some historians to date. Although it can be firmly traced to 1827, the print had been frequently reproduced in publications relating to the Bank War, and the attributed date of 1834 has generally been accepted (with the subject matter presumed to focus on Henry Clay and Andrew Jackson's antagonism over the rechartering of the Second Bank of the United States).[76] Weitenkampf and Nevins were so positive of the attribution of that date that they wrote in the caricature's catalogue entry in *A Century of Political Cartoons*, "Nobody in the late thirties could have missed the point of this picture."[77]

Conclusion
"The First Will Grumble and the Last Will Laugh"

In 1825, a printer named Robert Smith wrote a letter to the former president of the United States Thomas Jefferson. Smith believed that he had played an influential role in Jefferson's successful 1800 presidential campaign and, having found himself in desperate circumstances, he demanded payment for past services. The tone found in these letters is not unlike the letters written from Akin to Jackson and Van Buren, requesting a position in compensation for efforts to secure the presidency. Smith had a plan: wait for Jefferson's letter and payment, upon which he would "go to London and set up a Caracature [*sic*] print shop &c &c."[1] It is not known if Smith did in fact travel to London for his endeavor, but it appears he considered that the answer to his financial woes rested in a caricature shop. This statement by the printer Smith reflects a general acceptance and knowledge that matured by the middle of the 1820s for caricature prints in the United States. The efforts of James Akin, William Charles, and the anonymous makers of caricatures in the decades preceding provided this printer and likely countless others with an alternative printmaking business.

In researching the prints published between 1789 and 1828, it has been impossible to ignore the two personalities that emerged from this period, Akin and Charles. In considering who they were through primary documents, the history of caricatures in early America is better revealed. Akin and Charles were both greatly ambitious and brave: they moved for their art to new environments (Akin to Newburyport, Charles to America). They developed this medium as a form of art that would further their own careers while also establishing something new and unique. Designing and publishing caricature was a difficult profession. As can be observed, Akin produced a regular number of caricatures while in Newburyport, but designing caricatures did not provide a steady income or necessarily a respected livelihood. He dabbled in many different careers, from medical apprentice to boardinghouse landlord, and appeared to fight his own inner demons with respect to his art. From his letters it is clear Akin was keenly confident in his ability as an engraver, an artist, and a caricaturist, but how such an art form could potentially propel him into a career as a respected artist appears to have bothered him greatly. On the opposite end of the spectrum is Charles, who left for the United States to make a fresh start. Charles took to his pen almost on arrival in New York. During the War of 1812, he and his partner, Samuel Kennedy, dominated the market with political caricatures, though Charles put little creative imagination into his caricatures as they were often copied from British sources. As an artist and a respected newspaper engraver, Doolittle appears to fit between Akin and Charles; his patriotic sensibilities drove him to publish satirical images that would counteract the caricatures of 1812.

Akin's short time in London allowed him to witness a world that celebrated artists: the welcoming environment that Benjamin West offered visiting Americans in his London studio, along with the daily publication of hundreds of caricature prints, enabled Akin to visualize such an environment in America. Upon Akin's return from England, his level of vigorous networking could be likened to an early form of today's social media platforms. Akin's frequently published newspaper advertisements boasted relationships to great artists on both sides of the Atlantic, announcing to potential customers his acceptance into a world of fine art made important by Charles Willson Peale and others. The way Akin set about to make caricature in early America stood in sharp contrast to the methods of the European Charles. While Akin elevated the caricatures he made by applying his acquired skill as an engraver, Charles introduced caricature to the American people by selling impressions of British caricatures from his New York and Philadelphia print shops. Charles had produced a limited number of his own caricatures while in London, but the time he spent in London was long enough for him to become familiar with successful designs and figures, elements he would later incorporate into his own caricatures. Charles also introduced the first attempt at caricature subscriptions and a regularity of caricature production to an American public. The interest generated by the War of 1812, in addition to Charles's ability to adapt British motifs for an American market, allowed Charles and Kennedy to attempt this innovation.

Without an understanding of these two individuals, caricature might have continued to serve merely as illustrations in history texts. Instead, by considering Akin and Charles and eliciting specific details of their lives and contemporary responses to their work, it is possible to study their visual imagery within a broader field of printmaking and art history. In the United States, caricature was politically motivated and publication was influenced by important, sensational events of the day. However, it was through the specific lens of Akin and Charles that these caricatures became something more: less naïve in their artistic conception, building on layers of imported knowledge that refer to other art-historical trends. Caricature made in America, like the early republic itself, was in its infancy, seeking the rhythm and routine that had already been established in London; however, that does not mean that the prints were less advanced than any other forms of contemporaneous American art.

This survey has focused on providing a context and a narrative to the caricatures published in America between 1789 and 1828. But it cannot be the definitive study of the genre in that period: there is still a great wealth of information to discover on Akin, Charles, and the caricatures made by them and by anonymous artists. Rather, it is my hope to present an introduction to this collection of previously ignored visual and textual documents. This study began with an investigation of contemporary information. Just as the caricaturists that made these satirical prints did not work in isolation, neither can a thorough history of these works treat them as only one kind of source: caricatures are art objects as well as political and historical documents. Information on caricatures gleaned from contemporary newspapers and archival documents allow these prints to be situated within a wider cultural world.

In 1789 a line was written in a private letter about the circulating caricatures of George Washington: "The first will grumble and the last will laugh."[2] It was a reference to the fact that politicians might be alarmed at seeing their likenesses in caricature, while enemies and friends would find humor in the picture. Did this happen at any point in the period? An opinion piece from 1813 did not see the humor in such circulating caricatures:

Caricatures—There are in all governments base factionists who eagerly adopt the absurd doctrine, that "ridicule is the test of truth." By them sound reason and fair argument are abandoned, and things most sacred are assailed. With them truth has no charms, virtue no admirers, civil order and political harmony no advocates. They are spirits of discord. Therefore the doctrine of ridicule is eminently calculated to carry on their great work—the work of disorganization. Caricaturists are factionists. For certainly no man of common sense and pure motives will, after he has exhausted his arguments with an opponent attempt to ridicule him, and especially by the low and puerile means of caricatures.

To excite the feelings and irritate the passions, is certainly illy calculated to demonstrate the existence of error, either in morals or politics; surely, then, it cannot be expected to produce conviction, which is the object of every honest person. But on the contrary it is calculated to produce schisms and

factions—a state of society adapted to the turbulent and rebellious disposi-
tions of caricaturists. If, then, caricaturists serve only to exasperate those who
are the subjects of them; and, inasmuch as exasperation tends to anarchy and
confusion, society cannot certainly calculate on any good resulting therefrom.
Consequently men of virtue and liberal minds will neither resort to caricatures,
nor applaud those who do.

As palpable instance of the abursdity [*sic*] and futility of carricatures
[*sic*], and as conclusive evidence that they are resorted to by the factious and
rebellious.[3]

This description was written during the War of 1812, when caricatures by Charles
could be found in shops all along the East Coast. Other accounts found in newspapers
from the late 1780s to the early 1830s also refer to caricatures in a derogatory manner.
As more caricatures were designed and sold and lithography took off, print numbers
steadily increased. These caricatures caused varying levels of annoyance and glee and are
today important documents, representing public opinion, political history, and significant examples of early American art. This book has sought to provide a more nuanced
approach to understanding the role these caricatures played in the early republic.

Appendix: Catalogue of Caricatures Published in America Between 1780 and 1828

The following is a checklist of separately published caricature prints in the United States between 1780 and 1828. The list contains caricatures in public collections, in addition to those caricatures referenced in contemporary documents but are not known to have survived or that cannot be found presently in public collections. The entries for these caricatures are preceeded with an asterik.

This catalogue format is similar in organization to Frank Weitenkampf's *Political Caricature in the United States in Separately Published Cartoons,* and the entries are arranged chronologically by date. If known, the following information is provided: title, artist, place of production, date, and collections with impressions of the caricature. References include, if located, the following: contemporary newspaper notices or advertisements, the corresponding page number from Weitenkampf's catalogue entries, the page and figure number from Murrell, and from both Lanmon and Quimby the corresponding catalogue entries and figures numbers. This is an updated list, amending and updating entries from Weitenkampf.

Brackets have been used when titles are not known, with a short description of the print, and when an artist has been assigned to a print without a signature.

Entries in bold have been reproduced in this book and corresponding figure numbers for those prints are included.

Abbreviations

Please note that an asterisk after the abbreviation has been used when I have been unable to verify a repository from Weitenkampf's original entry.

AAS	American Antiquarian Society, Worcester, Massachusetts
APS	American Philosophical Society, Philadelphia, Pennsylvania

BA | Boston Athenaeum, Boston, Massachusetts
BHS | Center for Brooklyn History, Brooklyn, New York (formerly Brooklyn Historical Society)
BM | British Museum, London
BPL | Boston Public Library, Boston, Massachusetts
ChHS | Chicago Historical Society, Chicago, Illinois
CHS | Connecticut Historical Society, Hartford, Connecticut
CLM | Clements Library, University of Michigan, Ann Arbor, Michigan
CW | Colonial Williamsburg Foundation, Williamsburg, Virginia
FLP | Free Library of Philadelphia, Philadelphia, Pennsylvania
HEH | Henry E. Huntington Library, San Marino, California
HSP | Historical Society of Pennsylvania, Philadelphia, Pennsylvania
HU | Houghton Library, Harvard University, Cambridge, Massachusetts
JCB | John Carter Brown Library, Brown University, Providence, Rhode Island
Lanmon | Lanmon, Lorraine Welling. "American Caricature in the English Tradition: The Personal and Political Satires of William Charles." *Winterthur Portfolio* 11, no. 1 (1976): 1–51.
LCP | Library Company of Philadelphia, Pennsylvania
LOC | Library of Congress, Washington, DC
LWL | Lewis Walpole Library, Yale University, Farmington, Connecticut
MdHS | Maryland Center for History and Culture (formerly Maryland Historical Society), Baltimore, Maryland
MMA | Metropolitan Museum of Art, New York, New York
Murrell | Murrell, William. *A History of American Graphic Humor, Vol. 1: 1747–1865.* New York: Whitney Museum of American Art, 1933.
NYHS | New-York Historical Society, New York, New York
NYPL | New York Public Library, New York, New York
OSU | Billy Ireland Cartoon Library and Museum, Ohio State University, Columbus, Ohio
PEM | Peabody Essex Museum, Salem, Massachusetts (formerly Essex Institute)
PMM | Independence Seaport Museum, Philadelphia, Pennsylvania (formerly Philadelphia Maritime Museum)
PU | Princeton University Art Museum, Princeton, New Jersey
Quimby | Quimby, Maureen O'Brien. "The Political Art of James Akin." *Winterthur Portfolio* 7 (1972): 59–112.

WAM   Worcester Art Museum, Worcester, Massachusetts

Weitenkampf   Weitenkampf, Frank. *Political Caricature in the United States in Separately Published Cartoons.* New York: New York Public Library, 1953.

WM   Winterthur Museum, Garden, and Library, Winterthur, Delaware

YAG   Yale University Art Gallery, Yale University, New Haven, Connecticut

1778 or 1780

* [George Washington on a throne and King George III on bended knee]; artist unknown, place of production unknown, n.d. [1778 or 1780].
Collection: Unknown.
References: Murrell, 34; Weitenkampf, 11.

1787

The Siege of Zion or *Zion Besieged and Attacked*; artist unknown, Philadelphia, n.d. [January 1787].
Medium: Etching.
Collections: FLP, HSP, LCP, LOC.
References: *Pennsylvania Journal or Weekly Advertiser* (Philadelphia), January 31, 1787; Murrell, fig. 26, p. 32; Weitenkampf, 11.

The Looking Glass for 1787, A House divided against itself cannot stand; artist unknown, Connecticut, 1787.
Medium: Line engraving with watercolor.
Collections: AAS, CHS, LOC
Reference: Weitenkampf, 11.

1789

* *The Entry*; artist unknown, New York, March/April 1789.
Collection: Unknown.
References: Contemporary description in letter from John Armstrong Jr. to Horatio Gates, April 7, 1789 (NYHS); Murrell, 34; Weitenkampf, 11.

1790

Figure 9. *What think ye of C_o_n_ss now / View of C_o_n_ss on the road to Philadelphia*; "Y.Z. Sculp" [artist unknown], New York, n.d. [1790].
Medium: Line engraving.
Collections: HSP, NYHS.
References: *New-Hampshire Gazette, and General Advertiser* (Portsmouth), July 15, 1790; Murrell, fig. 39, pp. 45–47; Weitenkampf, 12.

Figure 10. *Con-g-ess Embark'd on board the Ship Constitution of America bound to Conogocheque by way of Philadelphia*; artist unknown, New York, n.d. [1790].
Medium: Etching.
Collections: HSP, LOC.

180

References: Murrell, fig. 40, pp. 46–47; Weitenkampf, 12.

Figure 11. [Robert Morris moving the capital]; artist unknown, New York, n.d. [1790].
Medium: Engraving with hand coloring.
Collection: AAS.
References: Murrell, fig. 38, p. 45; Weitenkampf, 12.

* [Untitled Robert Morris caricature; similar in design to Robert Morris moving the capital; politicians represented include Thomas Jefferson and Alexander Hamilton]; artist unknown, New York, 1790.
Collection: Unknown.
References: contemporary description in letters in the Sedgwick Family Papers, MHS; and the Clinton Family Papers, NYHS.

1792

* [New York political caricature]; artist unknown, New York, July 1792.
Collection: Unknown.
Reference: *Daily Advertiser* (New York), July 6, 1792.

1793

* *The Funeral of George Washington & James Wilson, king and judge &c.* [caricature representing President George Washington and Supreme Court Judge James Wilson]; artist unknown, Philadelphia, July 1793.
Collection: Unknown.
References: *American Minerva* (New York), December 16, 1793; "Notes of Cabinet Meeting on Edmond Charles Genet, 2 August 1793." *Founders Online*, National Archives, Washington, DC, https://founders.archives .gov/documents/Jefferson/01-26-02 -0545 (original source: Jefferson, *11 May– 31 August 1793*, 601–3.)

Figure 15. *A Peep into the Antifederal Club*; artist unknown, place of production unknown [Philadelphia or New York], August 16, 1793.
Medium: Etching.
Collections: AAS (believed to be a restrike), BA, CLM, FLP, JCB, LCP.
References: *Federal Gazette and Philadelphia Daily Advertiser* (Philadelphia), August 20, 1793; Murrell, fig. 31, p. 38; Weitenkampf, 11.

1794

Allied Despots, or the Friendship of Britain to America; Valentine Verax, Philadelphia, 1794.
Medium: Etching.
Collection: WM.
Reference: *Columbian Centinel* (Boston), March 12, 1794.

1795

No Wooden Houses; Or, A New Way to speculate; artist unknown, Philadelphia, May 1795.
Collection: Unknown.
Reference: *Aurora General Advertiser* (Philadelphia), May 20, 1795.

1796

* [Caricature print of a man tied to a post]; artist unknown, place of production unknown, April 1796.
Collection: Unknown.
Reference: *American Telegraphe* (Newfield, CT), April 20, 1796.

Figure 20. *Porcupine, a Print* [previously titled *See Porcupine in Colours Just Portray'd*]; artist unknown, Philadelphia, n.d. [August 1796].
Medium: Line engraving.
Collections: AAS, HSP*.
References: *Minerva & Mercantile Evening Advertiser* (New York), September 9, 1796; Murrell, fig. 34, p. 42; Weitenkampf, 12.

1798

Figure 27. *Congressional Pugilists*
[three states; plates with "17" were restrikes by John McAllister Jr. in the nineteenth century]; artist unknown, Philadelphia, February 1798.
Medium: Etching.

Collections: AAS, CHS, CLM, Collections of the United States House of Representatives (Washington, DC), FLP, HEH (two impressions), HU, Independence National Historical Park Collection (Philadelphia), JCB, LOC, MdHS*, MMA, NYHS, OSU, PEM.
References: *Porcupine's Gazette* (Philadelphia), February 23, 1798; Murrell, fig. 37, p. 42; Weitenkampf, 12.

* *Cudgeling, as by Act in Congress*; artist unknown, place of production unknown, n.d. [1798].
Inscription: [verse under image]
"My sword tho' good, and made of wood, Behind the desk has idle wood; But to redress my grievances wrongs, Behind the desk I sought the tongs, When Griswold with a suit of brass, Laid my nose level with my face."
Collection: Unknown.
Reference: *Rising Sun* (Keene, NH), March 17, 1798.

Figure 25. *Cudgeling as by late Act in Congress, USA*; C. [illegible initial and name], place of production unknown, 1798.
Medium: Line engraving.
Collection: PEM.
References: Murrell, fig. 36, p. 43; Weitenkampf, 12.

Figure 26. *Cudgeling. as by late Act in Congress, U.S.A.*; J.A. [James Akin?], place of production unknown [Philadelphia?], n.d. [1798].

Medium: Engraving.
Collection: CHS.
Reference: Connecticut Historical Society, "Battle of the Wooden Sword."

Figure 24. *Ve—t Politeness*; artist unknown, place of production unknown, n.d. [1798].
Medium: Engraving with hand coloring.
Collections: BPL, PEM*.
References: Murrell, fig. 35, p. 42; Weitenkampf, 12.

Figure 21. *Cinque-tetes, or the Paris Monster*; artist unknown, Philadelphia, n.d. [May 1798].
Medium: Line engraving with hand coloring.
Collections: CLM, HEH.
References: *Porcupine's Gazette* (Philadelphia), May 14, 1798; Murrell, fig. 41, p. 47; Weitenkampf, 12.

Figure 14. *The Times; a Political Portrait*; artist unknown, Philadelphia, n.d. [July 1798].
Medium: Engraving with hand coloring.
Collections: NYHS, private collection.
References: *Porcupine's Gazette* (Philadelphia), July 24, 1798; Murrell, fig. 30, p. 38; Weitenkampf, 11.

1800

The Providential Detection; artist unknown, Philadelphia (?), n.d. [September 1800].
Medium: Line engraving.

Collections: AAS, LCP.
References: *Gazette of the United States* (Philadelphia), September 30, 1800; Murrell, fig. 43, p. 49; Weitenkampf, 13.

1801

Mad Tom in a Rage; artist unknown, place of production unknown, n.d. [1801].
Medium: Etching.
Collections: APS, HEH, HU*, LOC*, MMA, NYPL.
Reference: Weitenkampf, 13.

1802

Figure 29. *A genuine View of the parties in an Affair of Honor, after the fifth shot, at Hobuken* [*sic*], *31st July 1802*; artist unknown, place of production unknown [New York?], 1802.
Medium: Line engraving.
Collection: NYHS.
References: Murrell, fig. 59, p. 68; Weitenkampf, 13.

* [caricature of *Morning Chronicle* editor]; artist unknown, New York, 1802.
Collection: Unknown.
Reference: *Morning Chronicle* (New York), November 13, 1802.

* ["two gentlemen of high official station"]; artist unknown, New York, December 1802.
Collection: Unknown.

Reference: *New-York Evening Post*,
December 28, 1802.

1803

* [Thomas Jefferson with a razor "in the
act of performing the operation of shaving upon one seated in a barber's armchair"]; artist unknown, New Haven,
Connecticut, January 1803.
Collection: Unknown.
Reference: *Salem (MA) Gazette*, January 25, 1803.

1804

* [a crowded scene, consisting of several
figures and notably a horse with three
men in the saddle]; artist unknown,
Albany, New York, 1804.
Collection: Unknown.
Reference: *Albany (NY) Centinel*, April 3,
1804.

Figure 48. *A Philosophic Cock*;
[James Akin]; place of production
unknown [Newburyport, MA], n.d.
[1804–7].
Medium: Line engraving and aquatint.
Collection: AAS.

Figure 30. *Family-Ambition*; artist
unknown, New York, n.d. [April 1804].
Medium: Line engraving.
Collection: BHS.
Reference: *Albany (NY) Centinel*, April 3,
1804.

1805

**Figure 58. *The most Noble Lord Timo-
thy Dexter*;** James Akin, Newburyport,
Massachusetts, June 1, 1805.
Medium: Etching.
Collections: AAS (four impressions),
BA, HSP*, WAM.
Reference: *Newburyport (MA) Herald*,
January 31, 1806; Murrell, fig. 46, p. 52;
Quimby, cat. 45.

* *Presidential Bull-Bait. Feb. 4th, 1805*
[Spain is represented as a bull; Thomas
Jefferson stands to the right of the
image]; artist unknown, place of produc-
tion unknown; February 4, 1805.
Collections: Unknown; NYPL
(photostat).
References: Murrell, 70 ("Presidential
Bull Baiting"); Weitenkampf, 13.

Figure 43. *Infuriated Despondency!*;
James Akin, Newburyport, Massachu-
setts, June 1, 1805.
Medium: Engraving.
Collections: AAS, PEM*, WAM.
References: *Newburyport (MA) Her-
ald*, June 25, 1805; Murrell, fig. 45, p. 52;
Quimby, cat. 44A.

Figure 47. *A Confidential Intrigue!!!*;
James Akin, Newburyport, Massachu-
setts, June 1, 1085 [1805].
Medium: Engraving.
Collection: AAS.
Reference: *Repertory* (Boston), Febru-
ary 14, 1806.

Figure 46. *An Edict from Saint Peter*;
James Akin, Newburyport, Massachu-
setts, June 1, 1805.
Medium: Line and aquatint.
Collection: AAS.
Reference: *Repertory* (Boston), Febru-
ary 14, 1806.

1806

Figure 57. *All in my eye!*; James Akin,
Newburyport, Massachusetts, n.d.
[March or April 1806].
Medium: Hand-colored engraving.
Collection: AAS.

Figure 54. *"The Bloody Arena" / Inde-
pendentiam Vestram Veneramini, vel
omnis Natio vos Concacabit ad libi-
tum Submitted to the opinions of every
descendant of 1776 by their friend and
Countryman James Akin*; James Akin,
Newburyport, May 15, 1806.
Medium: Line engraving and aquatint.
Collection: AAS.

Modern Spectacles Easily Seen Through;
William Charles, New York, December
1806 (reprinted from plate published in
May 1806 in Edinburgh).
Medium: Etching; coloring (YAG).
Collections: HU, LCP, NYPL, PU, YAG
References: Weitenkampf, 13; Lanmon,
cat. 17, fig. 8.

Figures 52 and 53. *A Bug-a-boo to
frighten John Bull, or the Wright mode*

*for kicking up a Bubbery for 200 Dol-
lars Bounty, and 60 Dollars a month,
with other <u>important</u> Perquisites*; James
Akin, n.d. [1806].
Medium: Line engraving and aquatint.
Collections: AAS; BM (cropped).
References: *Newburyport (MA) Herald*,
November 14, 1806; Quimby, cat. 42.

Figure 51. *The Prairie Dog sickened
at the sting of the <u>Hornet</u>—or a Diplomatic Puppet exhibiting his Deceptions!*; James Akin, Newburyport,
Massachusetts, n.d. [1806].
Medium: Line engraving.
Collections: AAS, LOC.
References: *Newburyport (MA) Herald*, November 14, 1806; Quimby, cat. 41,
fig. 3.

** Revolutionary Tumble-Bugs, or Perpetual
Rotation in Office*; artist unknown, Octo-
ber 1806.
Collection: Unknown.
Reference: *The Repertory* (Boston),
October 10, 1806.

1807

Modern Dandy's; William Charles, place
of production unknown [New York?],
n.d. [1806–8].
Medium: Etching.
Collection: HU.
References: Murrell, 81; Lanmon, cat. 21,
fig. 14.

Figure 56. * *The Mandate* ["**Whisker-andos**"]; James Akin, Newburyport, Massachusetts, March 1807.
Medium: Etching.
Collections: Unknown; copperplate has survived at the Historical Society of Newbury (Newburyport, MA).
References: *United States Gazette* (Philadelphia), March 14, 1807; Quimby, cat. 43.

Figure 67. *Apologies for Tippling*; William Charles, after George Woodward, New York, n.d. [1806–8].
Medium: Colored etching.
Collections: HU, LCP.
Reference: Lanmon, cat. 14, p. 42.

Figure 69. *Family Electioneering ___ or Candidate Bob in his Glory*; William Charles, New York, n.d. [March 1807].
Medium: Etching.
Collection: WM.
References: *American Citizen* (New York), April 6, 1807; Murrell, 81; Weitenkampf, 14; Lanmon, cat. 18, p. 44.

Look On This Picture, and On This; artist unknown, New York, June 1807.
Medium: Engraving and etching.
Collections: AAS, APS, NYHS, NYPL, Pennsylvania Academy of the Fine Arts (Philadelphia)
References: *Newburyport (MA) Herald,* July 7, 1807; Weitenkampf, 14.

Jacky Frost and the Old man; William Charles, New York, 1807.

Medium: Colored etching.
Collection: AAS.
Reference: Lanmon, cat. 19, fig. 9. *Le Bon Genre*; William Charles, New York, 1807.
Medium: Etching and stipple engraving.
Collections: AAS, WM*.
References: Murrell, 81; Lanmon, cat. 20, fig. 11.

185

1808

This plate is respectfully dedicated to all the BUTCHERS *in the United States by their obt. Sert. Chrr. Wispart. in honour of our republican Governor Simon Snyder*; Simon Folwell, Philadelphia, December 1808.
Medium: Etching.
Collection: LOC.

Figure 13. *A Trip to Philadelphia; or a hard strain upon the reins of Goverment* [*sic*]; designed and drawn by "Timothy Quiz," printed by "Toby Accurate," and engraved by Anthony "Nettletop," Philadelphia, n.d. [January or February 1808].
Medium: Engraving, later pasted on wood board.
Collection: Collection of Alexandria-Washington Lodge No. 22, George Washington Masonic Memorial (Alexandria, VA).

* [Sloan moving the capitol, seated on a mare]; artist unknown, February 1808.
Collection: Unknown.
Reference: *New-York Commercial Advertiser*, February 10, 1808.

Figure 70. *The Cat Let Out of The Bag*; William Charles, New York, n.d. [January 1808].
Medium: Engraving.
Collections: AAS*, HU, LCP, NYHS, NYPL.
References: *New Hampshire Gazette* (Portsmouth), January 12, 1808; Murrell, fig. 77, p. 86; Weitenkampf, 14; Lanmon, cat. 24, fig. 15.

Ograbme, or, the American Snapping Turtle; Alexander Anderson, New York, n.d. [1807].
Medium: Wood engraving.
Collection: NYHS.
References: Murrell, fig. 63, p. 74; Weitenkampf, 14, 18.

["The State of the Nation": John Bull holding the head of a cow, Bonaparte at the tail, and Jefferson "in a situation to milk her"]; artist unknown, place of production unknown, July 1808.
Medium: Line engraving.
Collection: JCB.
Reference: *North American and Mercantile Daily Advertiser* (Baltimore), July 26, 1808.

* ["Another queer caricature": with Thomas Jefferson and John Randolph on the subject of the Embargo Act]; artist unknown ["the most worthless part of society"], unknown location, September 1808.
Collection: Unknown.

Reference: *New-York Evening Post*, September 23, 1808.

* *King Quilldriver's Experiments on National Defence*; "Peter Pencill," place of production unknown, n.d. [1808?].
Collection: Unknown; AAS and HSP (photostats).
References: Murrell, fig. 55, p. 56; Weitenkampf, 14.

Figure 72. *Between Two Stools my B____ comes to the Ground*; William Charles, place of production unknown [New York?], n.d. [ca. 1808].
Medium: Hand-colored engraving.
Collection: AAS, HU.
References: Murrell, fig. 73, p. 78; Weitenkampf, 15; Lanmon, cat. 26, fig. 17.

Figure 61. *Economical Projects, or an old Philosopher teaching his mad son*; [James Akin], n.d. [December 1808].
Medium: Line engraving.
Collection: FLP.
References: *Washington Federalist* (Georgetown, DC), December 15, 1808; Weitenkampf, 15.

1809

Non Intercourse or Dignified Retirement; "Peter Pencil," place of production unknown, n.d. [1809].
Medium: Etching and stipple with sepia ink.

Collections: HU*, HSP, NYHS, NYPL.
References: Murrell, fig. 56, pp. 63–64;
Weitenkampf, 15.

Intercourse or Impartial Dealings; "Peter
Pencil," 1809.
Medium: Etching and stipple with sepia
ink.
Collections: HU*, HSP, NYHS, NYPL.
References: Murrell, fig. 57, pp. 63–64;
Weitenkampf, 15.

* *Symptoms of Oppugnation*; artist
unknown, Philadelphia, May 1809.
Collection: Unknown.
Reference: *The Tickler* (Philadelphia),
May 10, 1809.

* *The Woeful Plight; or Election of 1809*
[caricature of politicians, including Tim-
othy Pickering, Rufus King, and Thomas
Jefferson]; artist unknown, October 1809.
Collection: Unknown.
References: *Essex Register* (Salem, MA),
October 28, 1809; *American Watchman*
(Wilmington, DE), November 4, 1809.

Copenhagen Monster Muzzled; artist
unknown, New York, December 1809.
Medium: Line engraving.
Collections: HU, NYHS.
References: Murrell, fig. 61, p. 72;
Weitenkampf, 15.

1810

**Figure 62. *Brazen Projectiles, or,
an enforcement of the solid arguments***

of the Old Sceool [*sic*]; Toby Scratch'em
[James Akin], Philadelphia, n.d. [August
1810].
Medium: Engraving.
Collection: BPL.
References: *The Tickler* (Philadel-
phia), August 29, 1810; Murrell, fig. 58,
pp. 67–68; Weitenkampf, 16.

*The Ghost of a Dollar or the Banker's Sur-
prize*; William Charles, Philadelphia, n.d.
[after 1810].
Medium: Line engraving.
Collections: AAS, ChHS*, CW, HSP,
HU, LCP, LOC, Northern Illinois Uni-
versity (DeKalb), NYHS, NYPL.
References: Murrell, fig. 74, p. 80;
Weitenkampf, 13; Lanmon, cat. 38,
fig. 23.

1811

Figure 63. *"Dicky Folwell"*; James Akin,
Philadelphia, n.d. [September 1811].
Medium: Etching with watercolor.
Collection: HSP.
References: *Spirit of the Press* (Philadel-
phia), October 1, 1811; Murrell, fig. 47,
p. 50; Weitenkampf, 14; Quimby, cat. 47.

1812

**Figure 74. *The Present State of our
Country***; William Charles, Philadelphia,
n.d. [1812?].
Medium: Line engraving.
Collections: Lilly Library (Bloomington,
IN), NYPL.

References: Weitenkampf, 16; Lanmon, cat. 28, fig. 22.

The Conspiracy against Baltimore or The War Dance at Montgomery Court House; artist unknown, n.d. [1812].
Collection: MdHS.

1813

Figure 71. *The Tory Editor and his Apes Giveing* [sic] *their pitiful advice to the American Sailors*; William Charles, Philadelphia, n.d. [ca. 1813].
Medium: Engraving.
Collections: AAS*, CHS, CW, HU, Lilly Library (Bloomington, IN) (colored), MdHS*, Northern Illinois University (DeKalb), NYHS, NYPL.
References: Murrell, 88; Weitenkampf, 14; Lanmon, cat. 25, p. 45.

Admiral Cockburn burning and plundering Havre de Grace on the 1st of June 1813. Done from a sketch taken at the spot at the time.; [William Charles], Philadelphia, August 1813.
Medium: Engraving.
Collections: JCB, MdHS, YAG (uncolored).
References: *Democratic Press* (Philadelphia), August 14, 1813; Lanmon, cat. 31, fig. 40.

Figure 77. *The Cock Fight __ or another sting for the Pride of Iohn* [John] *Bull*; William Charles, Philadelphia, n.d. [September 1813].

Medium: Etching with watercolor.
Collections: HSP, HU, LCP.
References: *Democratic Press*, September 16, 1813; Weitenkampf, 17; Lamon, cat. 33, fig. 32.

Figure 75. *A Wasp taking a Frolick Or a Sting for Johnny Bull*; William Charles, Philadelphia, n.d. [1812].
Medium: Etching with watercolor.
Collections: AAS, NYHS, University of Virginia Library (Charlottesville) (uncolored).
References: Weitenkampf, 17; Lanmon, cat. 30, p. 46, fig. 31.

Figure 105. *Josiah the First*; William Charles, Philadelphia, n.d. [1813–14?].
Medium: Etching with watercolor.
Collections: LCP, LOC, WAM.
References: Murrell, fig. 84, p. 94; Weitenkampf, 16; Lanmon, cat. 27, p. 45, fig. 21.

Figure 89. *Columbia Teaching John Bull his new Lesson*; [William Charles and Samuel Kennedy], Philadelphia, n.d. [1813].
Medium: Etching with watercolor.
Collections: HSP, LOC.
References: Weitenkampf, 18; Lanmon, cat. 37, p. 48, fig. 34.

Figure 84. *Johnny Bull in a Fret*; artist unknown [William Charles or S.D.F.?], Philadelphia, n.d. [1813].
Medium: Etching.
Collections: AAS, HSP, NYHS.

References: Murrell, fig. 75, p. 85;
Weitenkampf, 17; Lanmon, fig. 35,
pp. 23–24.

Figure 79. *Iohn* [John] *Bull stung to agony by Insects*; S.D.F., Philadelphia, March 1, 1813.
Medium: Etching.
Collections: AAS, HSP, HU.
References: Murrell, 85; Weitenkampf, 17, Lanmon, fig. 36, pp. 23–24.

Figure 80. *John Bull stung to agony by the Wasp and Hornet / Huzza for "Free Trade and Sailor's Rights"*; artist unknown, place of production unknown [Boston?], n.d. [1813].
Medium: Hand-colored relief cut with gold leaf.
Collections: AAS, NYHS.
Reference: Weitenkampf, 17.

Figure 81. *John Bull stung to agony by the Wasp and the Hornet / Huzza for the American Navy!*; artist unknown, likely Philadelphia, n.d. [1813].
Medium: Engraving.
Collections: BHS, CHS, MHS.
Reference: Weitenkampf, 17.

Figure 76. *The Hornet and Peacock, Or, John Bull in Distress*; Amos Doolittle, New Haven, Connecticut, March 27, 1813.
Medium: Engraving.
Collections: AAS, BHS, HEH, NYHS, YAG.

References: *Boston Patriot*, April 3, 1813; Murrell, fig. 52, pp. 60–61; Weitenkampf, 17.

Figure 90. *Bruin become Mediator or Negociation* [*sic*] *for Peace*; William Charles, Philadelphia, n.d. [1813].
Medium: Etching.
Collections: AAS, CLM, HEH, HSP, HU, Lilly Library (Bloomington, IN), LCP, MdHS*, NYHS, NYPL, WM*, YAG.
References: Weitenkampf, 20; Lanmon, cat. 36, fig. 38.

Figure 85. *A Boxing Match, or, Another Bloody Nose for Iohn* [John] *Bull*; William Charles, Philadelphia, n.d. [September 1813].
Medium: Etching with watercolor.
Collections: AAS, HSP, HU, LCP, Lilly Library (Bloomington, IN), LOC, NYHS*.
References: *Democratic Press* (Philadelphia), September 16, 1813; Weitenkampf, 18; Lanmon, cat. 34, p. 47, fig. 33.

Figure 86. *Queen Charlotte and Johnny Bull got their dose of Perry*; William Charles, Philadelphia, n.d. [September 1813].
Medium: Colored engraving.
Collections: HSP, PMM.
References: *Aurora General Advertiser* (Philadelphia), September 29, 1813; Murrell, fig. 88; Weitenkampf, 17; Lanmon cat. 35, fig. 27.

Figure 97. *Soldiers on a march to Buffalo*; William Charles, Philadelphia, n.d. [1813].
Medium: Etching.
Collections: AAS (two impressions, one colored), ChHS*, CLM (colored), CW, HSP, HU, LCP, Lilly Library (Bloomington, IN), LOC, NYHS, WM*.
References: Murrell, fig. 79, p. 88; Weitenkampf, 18; Lanmon, cat. 39, fig. 41.

Figure 101. *Brother Jonathan <u>Administering</u> a Salutary Cordial to John Bull*; Yankee Doodle Scratcht [Amos Doolittle]; New Haven, Connecticut, n.d. [October 1813?].
Medium: Hand-colored engraving.
Collections: AAS, BHS, CHS, YAG.
References: *National Advocate* (New York), November 15, 1813; Murrell, fig. 53, pp. 61–62; Weitenkampf, 17.

* ["A Caricature" representing "Gov. Strong" as receiving "the Declaration of War from Gen Dearborn" while surrounded by citizens]; artist unknown, December 1813.
Medium: Unknown.
Collection: Unknown.
Reference: *Democratic Press* (Philadelphia), December 29, 1813.

1814

"To the Grave go Sham Protectors of Free Trade and Sailor's Rights"—and all the people say Amen!; Alexander Anderson, New York, 1814.
Medium: Wood engraving.
Collections: NYHS, NYPL.
References: Weitenkampf, 18; Murrell, fig. 64, p. 74.

* ["Senatorial Caricature" depicting "an American senator, and the would-be-king, Josiah the First" in the "Senate Chamber"]; artist unknown, Boston, February 1814.
Collection: Unknown.
Reference: *The Yankee* (Boston), February 4, 1814.

Congress at Vienna in great Consternation; William Charles, Philadelphia, n.d. [1814–18?].
Medium: Etching with aquatint.
Collections: AAS, Bodleian Library at Oxford University, HU, LCP, NYPL*, OSU, WM*.
References: Murrell, fig. 86, p. 94; Lanmon, cat. 46, fig. 52.

Figure 93. *Johnny Bull and the Alexandrians*; William Charles, Philadelphia, n.d. [October 1814].
Medium: Etching with aquatint.
Collections: AAS (two impressions), Alexandria History Museum at the Lyceum (VA), ChHS*, CW, Gilder Lehrman Institute of American History (New York), HEH, HU, LCP, Lilly Library (Bloomington, IN), LOC, LWL, MdHS*, NYHS*, NYPL*, OSU, Philadelphia Museum of Art, PU, Visual

Studies Collection at the Library of Virginia (Richmond).
References: *Aurora General Advertiser* (Philadelphia), October 3, 1814; Murrell, fig. 81, p. 90; Weitenkampf, 19; Lanmon, cat. 41, fig. 49.

Figure 92. *John Bull and the Baltimoreans*; William Charles, Philadelphia, n.d. [October 1814].
Medium: Etching.
Collections: AAS, ChHS*, CLM, Gilder Lehrman Institute for American History (New York), HEH, HSP, HU, The Reverend John J. Albert (Wynnewood, PA), Lilly Library (Bloomington, IN), LCP, LOC, LWL, MdHS, NYHS, NYPL, PU, Visual Studies Collection at the Library of Virginia (Richmond), WAM, WM*, YAG.
References: *Aurora General Advertiser* (Philadelphia), October 3, 1814; Murrell, fig. 82, p. 90; Weitenkampf, 19; Lanmon, cat. 42, fig. 50.

Figure 91. *Iohn* [John] *Bull making a new Batch of Ships to send to the Lakes*; William Charles, Philadelphia, n.d. [October 1814].
Medium: Etching with aquatint and watercolor.
Collections: AAS, ChHS*, CLM, CW, FLP, Gilder Lehrman Institute for American History (New York), HEH, HSP*, HU, LCP, Lilly Library (Bloomington, IN), LOC, Northern Illinois University (DeKalb), NYHS, NYPL, PMM,

Smithsonian American Art Museum (Washington, DC), WM*, YAG.
References: Deposited for copyright October 24, 1814 (LOC); Murrell, fig. 78, p. 88; Weitenkampf, 19; Lanmon, cat. 49, fig. 43.

Figure 109. *The Hartford Convention or Leap No Leap*; William Charles, Philadelphia, n.d. [December 1814].
Medium: Etching with aquatint.
Collections: AAS, CHS, CW*, HEH, HU, LCP, LOC, MdHS*, NYHS (two impressions), NYPL (two impressions), WM*, YAG.
References: Democratic Press (Philadelphia), December 14, 1814; Murrell, fig. 83, p. 91; Weitenkampf, 19; Lanmon, cat. 43, p. 50, fig. 46.

Figure 110. *The Hartford Convention or Leap No Leap* [see above, with the addition of two figures on the right]; artist unknown, place of production unknown [Windsor, VT?], n.d. [1815?].
Medium: Hand-colored engraving with stipple.
Collections: CHS, CW*, Lilly Library (Bloomington, IN), NYHS*.
References: Weitenkampf, 19; Lanmon, cat. 44, p. 50, fig. 48.

Figure 106. *A Scene on the Frontiers as Practiced by the <u>Humane</u> British and their <u>Worthy</u> Allies*; William Charles, Philadelphia, n.d. [1813–14].
Medium: Line engraving, colored.

Collections: AAS, BPL*, HEH, HSP,
HU, LCP, LOC.
References: Lanmon, cat. 49, fig. 26,
p. 46.

192

Figure 108. *A Scene on the Frontiers as Practiced by the Humane British and Their Worthy Allies!*; L.G., place of production unknown, n.d. [1813–14?].
Medium: Line engraving, colored.
Collections: AAS, CLM, CW, LWL.

A scene on the Frontiers as practiced by the Humane British and their Worthy Allies!; artist unknown, place of production unknown unknown, n.d. [1813–14?].
Medium: Etching with watercolor.
Collections: LOC, Lilly Library (Bloomington, IN).

Figure 103. *Bonaparte in Trouble*; Amos Doolittle, Connecticut, n.d. [1814–15?].
Medium: Hand-colored engraving.
Collections: AAS, BPL, CHS, CLM, CW, WAM, YAG.
Reference: Murrell, fig. 54, p. 62.

1815

* ["Madison's Night Cap. A Caricature print of this true Sailor's joke has just made an appearance at Kennedy's Print Shop." Inscribed, "conclusion of the Glorious struggle for 'Free Trade and Sailor's Rights'"]; artist unknown, place of production unknown [Philadelphia?], March 1815.

Reference: *Poulson's American Daily Advertiser* (Philadelphia), March 7, 1815.

Figure 113. *!Tis' Shouldering Lathrop & the Hartford Convention on to Massachusetts*; artist unknown, place of production unknown, n.d. [1815?].
Medium: Etching.
Collection: CHS.

Figure 83. *Iohn* [John] *Bull before New Orleans*; William Charles, Philadelphia, January 8, 1815.
Medium: Etching.
Collections: AAS, ChHS*, CW, HEH, HU, LCP, Louisiana Digital Library (https://louisianadigitallibrary.org), NYPL.
References: Murrell, fig. 85, p. 91; Weitenkampf, 19; Lanmon, cat. 45, fig. 51.

John Bull making what he calls a demonstration on N Orleans and Kentucky volunteer meeting him; artist unknown, place of production unknown, n.d. [dated 1815 by AAS].
Medium: Hand-colored etching.
Collection: AAS.

Figure 100. *Louis XVIII climbing the Mât de Cocagne*; William Charles, Philadelphia, n.d. [December 1815].
Collections: AAS, CW, HU.
References: *The Columbian* (New York), December 14, 1815; Murrell, fig. 87, p. 94; Lanmon, cat. 50, fig. 55.

1816

* [Congressional caricature]; artist unknown, place of production unknown, 1816.
Collection: Unknown.
Reference: *New-York Courier*, February 23, 1816.

Figure 112. *The N. England Convention or the Prophecy of J. Henry Fulfilled!!!!*; artist unknown, place of production unknown [Hartford, CT?], n.d. [after May 1815; 1816–17?].
Medium: Engraving with hand-coloring.
Collection: CHS (two impressions), Lilly Library (Bloomington, IN)*.
Reference: *American Mercury* (Hartford, CT), March 17, 1818.

1817

Figure 115. *Democracy ___ against the ___ Unnatural Union. Trial Oct. 14th 1817*; "Designed and Executed by one who has neither place nor pension" [William Charles], Philadelphia, n.d. [1817].
Medium: Engraving.
Collections: AAS, ChHS, CLM, HEH, HSP, HU, LCP (two impressions), LOC, Newtown Historical Society (PA), Northern Illinois University (DeKalb), NYHS, NYPL, OSU, PU, WM*.
References: Murrell, fig. 88, p. 95; Weitenkampf, 20; Lanmon, cat. 49, fig. 54.

The Soaped Pole. Dishonest Candidates apt to slip down faster than they ascend;

"Democritus the Younger" [George Helmbold, according to William Murrell], n.d. [1817].
Medium: Wood engraving.
Collection: HSP.
References: Murrell, fig. 65, p. 76; Weitenkampf, 20.

1820

* ["A Rider!": a caricature of the Maine and Missouri Bill; Maine is represented as a "young dandy of 21"]; artist unknown, place of production unknown, 1820.
Collection: Unknown.
Reference: *Portsmouth (NH) Oracle*, February 5, 1820.

* ["A Caricature" of the "Vice President in military costume, his sword on the wrong side, approaching the treasury, (a large chest) and demanding '600,000 for extra services. . . . We have never seen a caricature better conceived or more appropriate.'"], artist unknown, place of production unknown, 1820.
Collection: Unknown.
Reference: *New Hampshire Sentinel* (Keene), March 11, 1820.

Figure 114. *Joseph Hiester's claims to the votes of a Christian People, or the Reformer of 1820 exhibiting his love of Liberty and Country / Instruere el servare populum*; unsigned [James Akin], Philadelphia, n.d. [1820].
Medium: Etching.

Collections: HSP, NYHS. Third impression sold at auction at Cowan's, December 6, 2012, lot 2291.
References: Murrell, fig. 66, p. 76; Weitenkampf, 20.

A Case of Infectious Fever before the New York Board of Health; artist unknown, Philadelphia, n.d. [October 1820].
Medium: Etching.
Collections: BPL, HSP, HU, LCP.
References: *The Columbian* (New York), October 9, 1820; Murrell, fig. 92, p. 100; Weitenkampf, 20.

1823

Figure 116. *The five aspirants*; artist unknown, place of production unknown [New York?], n.d. [1823].
Medium: Engraving.
Collection: HU.
References: *Portsmouth (NH) Journal of Literature and Politics*, November 15, 1823; Weitenkampf, 21.

Political Jockies in trouble, or the Race as good as Lost; artist unknown, place of production unknown, n.d. [1823?].
Medium: Engraving.
Collections: AAS, HSP.

1824

If the coat fits Let them wear it; artist unknown, place of production unknown [Connecticut?], n.d. [after 1824?].
Collections: AAS, HEH

Figure 118. *A Caucus held at Albany on Sunday evening April 11th 1824 by the N.Y. city members*; artist unknown, New York, April 1824.
Medium: Etching.
Collections: HEH, HU, LOC.
References: Murrell, fig. 91, p. 98; Weitenkampf, 21.

Figure 120. *A Foot-Race*; "Crackfardi" [David Claypoole Johnston], Boston, n.d. [October 1824].
Medium: Etching.
Collections: AAS, BA, HU*, LCP, LOC, NYHS (two impressions, one without a copyright line), NYPL.
References: *Baltimore Patriot*, October 21, 1824; Murrell, fig. 102, p. 106; Weitenkampf, 21.

Figure 119. *Caucus Curs in full Yell, or a War-Whoop to Saddle on the People, a Pappoose President*; James Akin, n.d. [1824].
Medium: Aquatint and etching.
Collections: HSP, LOC, NYHS.
References: Letter from James Akin to Ralph Earl, November 9, 1824 (Murrell, 135); *Baltimore Patriot*, November 11, 1824; Weitenkampf, 20; Quimby, cat. 50.

An Unexpected Meeting of Old Friends; James Akin, Philadelphia, n.d. [1824].
Medium: Etching and aquatint.
Collection: HU.
References: Murrell, fig. 129, p. 141; Weitenkampf, 23 [dates to 183–?]; Quimby, cat. 49.

1826

Symptoms of Indigestion; artist unknown,
Philadelphia?, n.d. [1826].
Medium: Etching with watercolor.
Collection: LCP.

1827

Figure 124. *Symptoms of a Locked Jaw,
Plain Sewing Done Here*; David Claypoole Johnston, Boston, n.d. [August
1827].
Medium: Lithograph.
Collections: AAS, LOC.
References: *Baltimore Patriot*, August 12,
1827; Murrell, fig. 112, p. 120; Weitenkampf, 34.

1828

Figure 122. *The Pedlar and his Pack or
the Desperate Effort, an Over Balance*;
artist unknown, n.d. [1828?].
Medium: Etching with watercolor.
Collections: AAS (two impressions),
Beinecke Rare Book and Manuscript
Library at Yale University (New Haven,
CT), BPL, CLM, FLP, HU, LCP, Lilly
Library (Bloomington, IN), LOC,
Northern Illinois University (DeKalb);
NYHS, NYPL, PU.
References: Murrell, 90; Weitenkampf,
21; Lanmon, cat. 48.

Figure 117. ["Eagle Chair"]; artist
unknown, place of production unknown,
n.d. [1828?].

Medium: Engraving with watercolor.
Collection: AAS.
References: Murrell, fig. 103, p. 106;
Weitenkampf, 26.

Figure 123. *Philadelphia Taste Dis-
played. Or, Bon-Ton Below Stairs*;
James Akin, Philadelphia, n.d. [1828?].
Medium: Lithograph with watercolor.
Collection: HSP.
Reference: Quimby, cat. 52.

Caricatures with unclear date of
production

*He who fights or runs away May fight
to run another day. Wasbash*]; artist
unknown, place of publication unknown,
n.d. [dated 1791 by Weitenkampf].
Medium: Etching on blue paper.
Collection: NYHS.
Reference: Weitenkampf, 11.

[Untitled caricature consisting of two
male figures holding the newspaper *New-
York Evening Post*]; artist unknown, place
of production unknown [New York?],
n.d. [1806?].
Medium: Line engraving.
Collection: NYHS.
Reference: Weitenkampf, 171.

Brother Jonathan's Soliloquy on the Times;
Thomas Kensett, place of production
unknown [New York? Cheshire, CT?],
n.d. [1812–19? 1832?].
Medium: Engraving with hand-coloring.

Collection: AAS, HU, NYHS, YAG.
References: Weitenkampf, 16.

A Seamans Wifes Reckoning.; William
Charles, after Woodward, Philadelphia,
n.d. [1813–20].
Medium: Etching.
Collection: HU.

Proof Positive; or, No Deceiving a Sailor;
William Charles, Philadelphia, n.d.
[1817–20].
Medium: Etching.
Collection: HU.
Reference: Lanmon, cat. 51, p. 51.

A Cobbler's Cure for a scolding wife; art-
ist unknown [William Charles? S.D.F.?],
Philadelphia, n.d.
Medium: Hand-colored engraving.
Collections: AAS, HU.

A Splendid Procession of Masons; "Gebol-
ibus Crackfardi" [David Claypoole John-
ston]; n.d. [1819? 1832?].
Collection: BPL.
Reference: Weitenkampf, 27

*The March of Death. This March of Death
is respectfully dedicated to the Temperance
Societies throughout the United States;* artist, unknown [Philadelphia]; n.d. [Sep-
tember 1831; previously dated 1820 by
Murrell and Weitenkampf].
Medium: Engraving.
Collection: HSP.
References: *Daily Chronicle* (Philadelphia), September 24, 1831; *Boston Christian Herald,* October 12, 1831; Murrell,
fig. 89, p. 97; Weitenkampf, 20.

Notes

In citing works in the notes, short titles have generally been used. Archives frequently cited have been identified by the abbreviations given in the appendix.

INTRODUCTION

1. McCullough, *John Adams.*

2. Donald, *Age of Caricature*; Hallett, *Spectacle of Difference*; Rauser, *Caricature Unmasked*; Gatrell, *City of Laughter.*

3. Murrell, *History of American Graphic Humor.* Volume 2 is not in the scope of this book; it was published in 1938 and covers caricatures made between 1865 and 1938. Murrell is also the author of "Rise and Fall of Cartoon Symbols."

4. Weitenkampf, "Some American Caricaturists"; Weitenkampf, *American Graphic Art.* Between these two publications, Weitenkampf also turned to British caricature when he focused his attention on the British artist and caricaturist William Hogarth. See Weitenkampf, *Bibliography of William Hogarth.*

5. Stagg, "After the New York Public Library."

6. *New Republic*, April 10, 1944.

7. Clarence Brigham to Frank Weitenkampf, April 7, 1944, Frank Weitenkampf Papers, NYPL.

8. Ibid., December 3, 1953.

9. Brigham, *Fifty Years of Collecting Americana*, 37.

10. Upon her retirement, the AAS digital archive was named GIGI, the acronym for Graphical Interface of Gathered Images—and the name Georgia Barnhill goes by—in recognition of her contributions to the field of American print and ephemeral history.

11. Barnhill, "Catalogue of American Engravings," 114.

12. Masur, "'Pictures Have Now Become a Necessity,'" 1409–10.

CHAPTER 1

1. For a summary of engravings from this period, consult Larson, "Separately Published Engravings."

2. See appendix for catalogue listing of caricatures. The three prints referenced are *What think ye of C_o_n_ss now* (n.d. [1790], "Y.Z. sculp.") and two separate impressions of the caricature titled *Cudgeling as by late Act in Congress, USA* (1798, "C. [illegible initial and last name]") and *Cudgeling. as by late Act in Congress, U.S.A.* (n.d. [1798]. "J.A."). The identities of "Y.Z." and "C." are not known, while the initials "J.A." could potentially belong to James Akin, although Akin did not primarily sign his prints with his initials.

3. *New-York Daily Gazette*, August 29, 1791. Similar notices can also be found in newspapers published in London and in Paris; these notices were often reprinted in American newspapers.

4. *Daily Advertiser* (New York), July 6, 1792.

5. *Vermont Journal and Universal Advertiser*, August 26, 1793 (Windsor); *Hough's Concord (NH) Herald*, August 29, 1793.

6. *Federal Gazette, and Philadelphia Evening Post*, August 19, 1793.

7. Larson in "Separately Published Engravings" (8) identifies Philadelphia, New York, and Boston as the geographic centers for print publishing. Boston did not become a center for the production of caricature until the late 1820s, and therefore is not considered in this chapter.

8. For scholarship on North American and British caricatures published before and during the American Revolution, see Cresswell, *American Revolution in Drawings and Prints*; Thomas, *American Revolution*; and Latham, "Body Politic and the Family Quarrel."

9. There was an established history in the colonies for calling these collections "curious." One example from before the revolution can be observed in the advertisement by Joseph McAdam, "TO BE SOLD, . . . A CURIOUS collection of Prints and PAMPHLETS . . . &c in the hieroglyphick or caricatura manner, with the most severe and entertaining satires on some," *Virginia Gazette* (Williamsburg), October 17, 1766.

10. *Daily Advertiser* (New York), May 27, 1796; *Commercial Advertiser* (New York), July 10, 1798.

11. Like so many other shopkeepers of the period, Paff did not limit his stock to prints or paintings. An advertisement noted that a shipment of "prints, caricatures, and elegant frames" also included "Violins, German and English Flutes, bassoons; Penknives, razors, and other cutlery ware; English ivory and tortoise shell combs; Silver watches, warranted to go well; An elegant clock, marking the hour and seconds, the day of the week, that of the month, the month of the year, high and low water, and the age of moon, whether full or not." *New-York Gazette and General Advertiser*, May 24, 1799.

12. *New-York Gazette and General Advertiser*, April 29, 1799.

13. *Charleston (SC) Courier*, June 18, 1805.

14. Dolmetsch in "Prints in Colonial America" describes imported British art objects during the revolutionary period and the appeal of William Hogarth prints. While his name does not feature in newspaper advertisements from the 1790s to 1810, it does appear in the decades preceding, especially in the 1750s. Nathanial Warner of Boston advertised goods imported from England, including two works by Hogarth: *The Rake's Progress* and *The Harlot's Progress* (*Boston Gazette*, February 7, 1757). A personal letter from Thomas Jones of Williamsburg, Virginia, to his brother living in London included a request for William Hogarth prints, specifying that he already owned *A Midnight Modern Conversation*. See also Hardy, "Idea of Hogarth."

15. Bills, *Art of Satire*, 32.

16. Riely, *Henry William Bunbury*, 5.

17. Ibid., 3.

18. *Royal Gazette* (New York), December 28, 1782.

19. *Independent Gazetteer* (Philadelphia), June 17, 1788.

20. *Aurora General Advertiser* (Philadelphia), June 29, 1795.

21. *Philadelphia Gazette & Universal Daily Advertiser*, July 5, 1796.

22. *City Gazette and Daily Advertiser* (Charleston, SC), December 31, 1800.

23. *Independent Gazetteer* (Philadelphia), June 17, 1788.

24. Recent scholarship on imported caricatures from London to Europe can be found in the exhibition catalogue chapter "The London Print Trade: Commerce, Patriotism and Propaganda" in Clayton and O'Connell, *Bonaparte and the British*, 18–37.

25. *Newport (RI) Mercury*, November 25, 1789 (originally published in London, September 28, 1789).

26. *Daily Advertiser* (New York), January 25, 1791 (originally published in London, November 30, 1790).

27. "Caricature Print" appeared in the *Massachusetts Mercury* (Boston), October 31–November 4, 1794; *General Advertiser and Political, Commercial, Agricultural and Literary Journal* (Philadelphia), November 4, 1794; *American Minerva* (New York), November 6, 1794; *Albany (NY) Gazette*, November 10, 1794; *Hartford (CT) Courant*, November 10, 1794; *Western Star* (Stockbridge, MA), November 18, 1794; *Weekly Register* (Norwich, CT), November 18, 1794;

Virginia Chronicle (Norfolk), November 18, 1794; *Greenfield (MA) Gazette*, November 19, 1794; and *United States Chronicle* (Providence, RI), November 20, 1794.

28. Cuno, *French Caricature*, 58. *Le Bourreau se guillotine lui-même* is in the collection of the Musée de la Ville de Paris.

29. *General Advertiser and Political, Commercial, Agricultural and Literary Journal* (Philadelphia), June 22, 1791. I have not been able to locate a caricature that matches this description.

30. Bindman, *Shadow of the Guillotine*, esp. 106–8.

31. *Federal Gazette and Philadelphia Daily Advertiser*, January 1, 1791 (originally published in London, November 24, 1790). I have been unable to locate a French caricature that matches this description. If the caricature was published in London, a possible candidate for attribution is *The Knight of the woeful countenance going to extirpate the National Assembly* (BM, 1868,0808.5972), published several days before the newspaper notice, on November 15, 1790. On Burke and representations of him in caricature, see Robinson, *Edmund Burke*.

32. *Federal Gazette and Philadelphia Daily Advertiser*, June 18, 1791 (originally published in Paris, March 20, 1791). A possible attribution for the referenced caricature is *Marche du dom quichotte moderne pour la defense du moulin des abus* (uncolored state, BM, 2010,7081.7421; colored version, LOC, 2005685864).

33. *New-Hampshire Sentinel* (Keene), September 29,1804 (originally published in Paris, July 14, 1804). I have been unable to locate a caricature that matches this description.

34. *Chronicle Express* (New York), June 9, 1803.

35. *Commercial Advertiser* (New York), February 11, 1805.

36. *New-Hampshire Spy* (Portsmouth), August 21, 1787. I have been unable to locate a caricature that matches this description.

37. *Pennsylvania Packet and Daily Advertiser* (Philadelphia), July 5, 1790. I have been unable to locate a caricature that matches this description.

38. Theodore Sedgwick to Pamela Dwight Sedgwick, July 4, 1790, Sedgwick Family Papers, Massachusetts Historical Society, Boston. Sedgwick (1746–1813) was a Massachusetts Federalist, served as a delegate to the Second Continental Congress, and was subsequently elected to the United States Congress.

39. *New-Hampshire Gazette, and General Advertiser* (Portsmouth), July 15, 1790.

40. Theodore Sedgwick to Pamela Dwight Sedgwick, July 4, 1790, Sedgwick Family Papers, Massachusetts Historical Society, Boston.

41. Vail suggested that the designer of the caricature was the Boston engraver Henry Jenks. I have not located conclusive evidence for this and I am hesitant to assign the attribution. Vail, "Notes and Documents."

42. *New-Hampshire Gazette, and General Advertiser* (Portsmouth), July 15, 1790; *New-Hampshire Recorder, and the Weekly Advertiser* (Keene), August 26, 1790.

43. DeWitt Clinton to Dr. [Charles?] Clinton, July 20, 1790, in Odgen Goelet, John W. Frances, and Henry T. Tuckerman, *Old New York, or Reminiscences of the Past Sixty Years* [ca. 1660–1897?], NYHS, MS 1347 (New York: Francis Olds), vol. 11, 1458.

44. Theodore Sedgwick to Pamela Dwight Sedgwick, July 4, 1790, Sedgwick Family Papers, Massachusetts Historical Society, Boston. Also reprinted in Welch, *Theodore Sedgwick, Federalist*, 97. Pamela Sedgwick replied to her husband's letter on July 14, 1790, writing that the caricature was, "Truly Laughable but grieved I am that the General Government should at this Early Period be made a Subject of Buffoonery—I really Tremble for the week [*sic*] State of our Government—and Think Such Ill Judged Ridecule [*sic*] may be Big with fatal Consequences." *The Documentary History of the First Federal Congress of the United States, March 4, 1789–March 3, 1791: Digital Edition*, ed. Charlene Bangs Bickford, Kenneth R. Bowling, William C. diGiacomantonio, and Helen E. Veit. Charlottesville: University of Virginia Press, 2019. https://rotunda.upress.virginia.edu/founders/FFCP-01-20-02-0001-0150.

45. Beatty, "Letters of Judge Henry Wynkoop," 204.

200

46. "Paid for caracature [*sic*]," April 22, 1790, Thomas Jefferson Account Book, Massachusetts Historical Society, Boston. See also "Memorandum Books, 1790," *Founders Online*, National Archives, Washington, DC, https://founders.archives.gov/documents/Jefferson/02-01-02-0024 (original source: Jefferson, *Jefferson's Memorandum Books*, 749–807).

47. Thomas Jefferson to Mary Jefferson, May 2, 1790, Thomas Jefferson Account Book, Massachusetts Historical Society, Boston. See also "From Thomas Jefferson to Mary Jefferson, 2 May 1790." *Founders Online*, National Archives, Washington, DC, https://founders.archives.gov/documents/Jefferson/01-16-02-0231 (original source: Jefferson, *November 1789 to July 1790*, 405).

48. Cunningham in *Image of Thomas Jefferson* (111–12) discusses caricatures of Thomas Jefferson but dismisses the idea that they circulated widely. He states incorrectly that "[although] newspaper advertisements and publishers' records show that engraved portraits had a wide market throughout the United States, hardly a reference can be found to caricatures. It would be a mistake to assume that many of Jefferson's contemporaries saw a caricature of him. Had such prints enjoyed a wide circulation, it might be expected that mention of them would be found in contemporary letters or diaries; but if such references exist none have been located."

49. *Gazette of the United States* (Philadelphia), April 5, 1804; it was also believed that Senator Wright did not necessarily want the capital moved to Baltimore but rather wished that the inhabitants of Washington would better accommodate members of Congress and that by introducing a bill he was alarming them into action.

50. *Gazette of the United States* (Philadelphia), April 6, 1804.

51. *Poulson's American Daily Advertiser* (Philadelphia), February 6, 1808.

52. *New-York Commercial Advertiser*, February 10, 1808; *Connecticut Herald* (New Haven), February 16, 1808. These advertisements refer to caricatures of Sloan possibly being published in Washington, DC, noting that in "a letter from Washington. . . . It is said that Mr. Sloan is to be mounted on the old franken mare, with the capitol behind him."

53. For a comprehensive overview of eighteenth- and nineteenth-century portraits of Washington, see Reaves, *George Washington*.

54. It is possible that Washington was the subject of a caricature before his presidency. The only known description of it is Murrell's; he did not see the print but stated "that we have record, in a letter from an old Tory to a friend, of a cartoon depicting Washington on a throne and George III on bended knees before him. This was about 1778 or 1780. There seems to be no copy of this print anywhere." Murrell did not cite the name of the "old Tory"; I have researched the sources given in Murrell's "A Partial List of Works Consulted or Referred to" (241–42) and have been unable to track down the author of this letter. Murrell, *History of American Graphic Humor*, 34. Weitenkampf included Murrell's description in *Political Caricature* without further information.

55. John Armstrong Jr. (1758–1843) was an aide to General Horatio Gates (ca. 1727–1806) during the Revolutionary War.

56. John Armstrong Jr. to Horatio Gates, April 7, 1789, Horatio Gates Papers, NYHS. Also referenced in Skeen, *John Armstrong, Jr.*, 31; and Parton, *Caricature and Other Comic Art*, 309. Parton also alludes to other caricatures that are described in contemporary correspondence without citation of authorship or bibliographical information indicating where he may have seen them (307–10).

57. Lossing, *Our Country*, 2:1123.

58. Murrell does not include the devil in his description of *The Entry*, stating that there seems to be no copy "representing Washington riding upon an ass, supported by his man-servant, and led by Col. David Humphreys, singing doggerel verses. A fair sample of the derisive nature of the whole may be gathered from the couplet of which has been persevered." The couplet is included. Murrell, *History of American Graphic Humor*, 34. Without citing the letter from Armstrong to Gates, Weitenkampf quotes Lossing,

who "speaks of this caricature as 'full of disloyal and profane allusions,' and that it appeared 'on the day after Washington's arrival in New York, as president-elect.'" Humphrey says he is "chanting hosannahs and birthday odes," and the devil remarks, "The glorious time has come to pass when David shall conduct an ass." Murrell is also cited. Weitenkampf, *Political Caricature*, 11.

59. "Notes of Cabinet Meeting on Edmond Charles Genet, 2 August 1793," *Founders Online*, National Archives, Washington, DC, https://founders.archives.gov/documents/Jefferson/01-26-02-0545 (original source: Jefferson, *11 May–31 August 1793*, 601–3).

60. For recent examples, see Chervinksy, *The Cabinet*, 230; and Chernow, *Alexander Hamilton*, 445. Chernow incorrectly writes that Washington was shown a broadside, titled "The Funeral Dirge of George Washington," and not the caricature print. In the quote Chernow reprints, he omits the line that contains the title of the caricature, which Jefferson provides. "The Funeral Dirge of George Washington" was a ballad published after Washington's death and sold in 1800; see advertisement, *Columbian Centinel* (Boston), January 4, 1800, which provides the title, "A Funeral Dirge, on the Death of General Washington." The title of the caricature, as in Jefferson's account from the August 2, 1793, cabinet meeting and contemporary newspaper notices, is *The Funeral of George Washington & James Wilson, king and judge &c.*

61. "Extract of a letter from a gentleman in New-York," *Middlesex Gazette* (Middletown, CT), August 17, 1793; *Daily Advertiser* (New York), August 21, 1793; *Vermont Journal and Universal Advertiser* (Windsor), August 26, 1793; *New-Hampshire Gazette* (Portsmouth), August 27, 1793; *Western Star* (Stockbridge, MA), August 27, 1793; *Essex Journal* (Newburyport, MA), August 28, 1793; *Hough's Concord (NH) Herald*, August 29, 1793; *North Carolina Journal* (Halifax), September 11, 1793.

62. "Thomas Boylston Adams to Abigail Adams, 10 August 1793," *Founders Online*, National Archives, Washington, DC, https://founders.archives.gov/documents/Adams/04-09-02-0254 (original source: Adams Family, *January 1790–December 1793*, 443–44).

63. Thomas Jefferson to Martha Jefferson, August 4, 1793, Thomas Jefferson Account Book, Massachusetts Historical Society, Boston. See also "From Thomas Jefferson to Martha Jefferson Randolph, 4 August 1793," *Founders Online*, National Archives, Washington, DC, https://founders.archives.gov/documents/Jefferson/01-26-02-0558 (original source: Jefferson, *11 May–31 August 1793*, 617).

64. See note 61, above, for the list of newspapers that reprinted the account of the caricature print.

65. *Columbian Centinel* (Boston), December 4, 1793; *American Minerva* (New York), December 16, 1793; *Daily Advertiser* (New York), December 30, 1793; *Columbian Herald* (Charleston, SC), January 10, 1794.

66. *Porcupine's Gazette* (Philadelphia), July 13, 1798. See Stagg, "American Market for Visual Satire."

67. "Circa 1790," in Murrell, *History of American Graphic Humor*, xviii; "1795?," in Weitenkampf, *Political Caricature*, 11; "Chariot of Government Driven by Washington," in Dupuy, "French Revolution," 376. Butterfield is the first historian I have located to theorize that it is Adams who is depicted (*American Past*, 180).

68. See *Look on this picture, and on this* (1807, NYPL); and William Charles, *The Present State of our Country* (1812, NYPL), fig. 74, below.

69. *Reporter* (Brattleboro, VT), February 6, 1809. The caricature appears in the *Baltimore Federal Republican*, January 13, 1809.

70. Cunningham, *Image of Thomas Jefferson*, 113. Cunningham makes no reference to this print in his other publication, *Popular Images*.

71. A more recent account of the events surrounding the election of 1800 covers the era's visual imagery, including *A Peep into the Antifederal Club*: "This 1793 etching is the earliest known anti-Jefferson cartoon." Ferling, *Adams vs. Jefferson*, 55. Other scholarship contends this is a representation of Jefferson; see Dupuy, "French Revolution," 371–84.

72. Murrell, *History of American Graphic Humor*, 38–39.

73. Kelly and Lovell in "Jefferson" (145) asserted that the seated figure with a doll is "Governor DeWitt Clinton." Clinton was a divisive New York politician and the subject of several caricatures when he was mayor of New York in the early 1800s, but he was not the governor of New York in 1793. If this figure is of a member in the Clinton family, then it is most likely DeWitt Clinton's uncle, George Clinton, governor of New York from 1777 until 1795, and chosen by the Jefferson Republicans as their (unsuccessful) vice presidential candidate in the 1793 election. DeWitt Clinton was a member of the Democratic-Republican Party, but he was not active in New York politics until after he became a member of the New York State Assembly in 1798. Kelly and Lovell may have taken this attribution from Munsing, *Made in America* (11), in which she wrote of the figure, "Governor DeWitt Clinton sits on the floor playing with a doll strongly resembling one of the Livingston brothers."

74. Cobbett, *History of the American Jacobins*, 26–27.

75. Fäy, *Two Franklins*, 186–87. According to Fäy, the immediate object of the democratic society was to eliminate Alexander Hamilton, to break down the Federalist Party, and to intimidate President Washington.

76. *Federal Gazette and Philadelphia Daily Advertiser* (Philadelphia), August 19, 1793; *Philadelphia Evening Post*, August 20, 1793; *General Advertiser* (Philadelphia), August 22, 1793.

77. *The Diary; or, Loudon's Register* (New York), September 21, 1793.

78. *Columbian Centinel* (Boston), November 2, 1793.

79. This caricature is referred to in the advertisement as "A well designed and well executed Carricature." *Washington Federalist* (DC), December 13, 1808.

80. William Cobbett Account Book, 1796–1800, AAS, MSS folio vols. C; Gaines, "William Cobbett's Account Book." For a thorough reading of the caricatures sold by Cobbett, see Stagg, "American Market for Visual Satire."

81. The caricature has most commonly been referred to with the title *See Porcupine in Colours Just Portray'd* and was previously believed to have been published between 1796 and 1799. Advertisements published in newspapers referenced here and Cobbett's description of the caricature in 1796 establish a definite date of publication to August 1796 as well as a title.

82. *Porcupine's Gazette* (Philadelphia), December 22, 1798.

83. Médéric Louis Élie Moreau de Saint-Méry was a prominent publisher and bookseller in Philadelphia, where he owned a bookstore and his own printing press, located on the corner of First and Walnut Streets after 1793.

84. Originally published in *Political Censor*, September 1796, and reprinted in *Porcupine's Works* 4 (May 1801): 116–19. Cobbett refers to the artist on page 55 and Moreau on page 57 of *Political Censor*. One of the names represented in the caricature that Cobbett mentions is John Swanwick (1740–1798), a United States representative from Pennsylvania and a Philadelphia merchant who traded outside the British Empire and argued for a democratic American mercantilist empire.

85. *Gazette of the United States* (Philadelphia), September 5, 1796.

86. The advertisement states that the caricature was "taken from an original Painting, in the possession of C. G. Minister of the Home Department." The initials might refer to Charles Greville (1749–1809), a British politician and collector of art. *Porcupine's Gazette* (Philadelphia), May 14, 16, 21, 1798.

87. *Western Star* (Stockbridge, MA), June 4, 1798.

88. *Columbian Mirror and Alexandria (VA) Gazette*, August 9, 1798.

89. Benjamin Davies opened his first bookstore in New York in the 1770s, but according to newspaper advertisements he moved to Philadelphia sometime in the 1790s. Many of his advertisements appear in Cobbett's *Political Censor* in 1796. His business was located at 63 High Street, Philadelphia. Cobbett's first publisher was Thomas Bradford, but their partnership was dissolved in March 1796. After that, Cobbett employed Benjamin Davies on an interim basis. See Gaines, "William Cobbett's Account Book."

90. *Porcupine's Gazette* (Philadelphia), July 23, 24, August 1, 4, 1798.

91. *Porcupine's Gazette* (Philadelphia) March 28, 1799; *J. Russell's Gazette Commercial and Political* (Boston), April 8, 1799.

92. Cobbett Account Book, 1796–1800, AAS, MSS folio vols. C, 96, 98, 113.

93. Fordham, "Hogarth's Act."

94. A Bill for the Encouragement of Learning [...], H.R. 75, 10th Cong. (1808).

95. *Essex Gazette* (Haverhill, MA), May 28, 1831.

96. See Connecticut Historical Society, "Battle of the Wooden Sword." "J.A." could possibly refer to James Akin, but I am hesitant to assign attribution. The Peabody Essex Museum impression was known to both Murrell and Weitenkampf. According to a newspaper source, it is possible a third copy was published, which contained a verse under the scene. *Rising Sun* (Keene, NH), March 17, 1798.

97. *Attic Miscellany*, printed for Bentley and Co., February 1790. I am grateful to Michael Kahn for showing me his copy of this publication.

98. Impression of *Congressional Pugilists*, CHS.

99. Lambert, *Travels Through Canada & the United States*, 49.

100. Freeman, *Affairs of Honor*, 182.

101. Colonel Smith was married to Abigail (Nabby) Adams and was the son-in-law of former president John Adams.

102. For a thorough account of this caricature, and of the caricature *Family-Ambition* (fig. 30), see Stagg, "'Family-Ambition.'"

103. Fowble, "William Charles FAMILY ELECTIONEERING," 16–18.

104. Isenberg, *Fallen Founder*, 252.

105. See Stagg, "Family-Ambition."

106. *Albany (NY) Centinel*, April 3, 1804.

107. For examples of caricatures done in a similar style, see William Humphreys, *The Modern Paradise, or Adam and Eve regenerated*, 1786 (LWL); and James Gillray, *The Tree of LIBERTY . . . with the devil Tempting John Bull*, 1796 (BM 1868,0808.6739).

108. *New-York Evening Post*, December 28, 1802.

109. *Boston Daily Advertiser*, April 6, 1813.

110. *Daily Advertiser* (New York), December 20, 1792.

111. Abigail Adams to Elizabeth Cranch, July 18, 1786, in Adams Family, January 1786–February 1787, 256–60. The caricature *The Bosom Friends* was published by S. W. Fores in London on May 28, 1786 (BM 1851,0901.303).

112. Wilson, *Paine and Cobbett*, 112; Cobbett's Philadelphia shop was located at 25 North Second Street, a strategic location that allowed for passing trade.

113. Original reference quoted in Clark, *Peter Porcupine*, 64.

114. *Aurora General Advertiser* (Philadelphia), August 9, 1798.

115. See Stagg, "American 'Dressing Academy.'"

116. Wright, *American Wags*, 73.

117. See two English prints: Robert Dighton, *Intelligence on the Change of the Ministry*, 1782–84 (BM 2010,7081.1165); and Thomas Rowlandson, *A Barbers Shop*, December 13, 1780 (BM Satires, 5765).

118. *Centinel of Freedom* (Newark, NJ), July 3, 1798.

119. *Alexandria (VA) Daily Gazette, Commercial and Political*, August 1, 1810. The caricature could be the British caricature print by Isaac Cruikshank, *The Devil won't take him; what a pity!!!*, July 1803? (BM, 1868,0808.7232).

120. *Salem (MA) Gazette*, January 25, 1803. Impressions of this caricature have not been located.

121. *Morning Chronicle* (New York), June 15, 1803.

122. *New-York Evening Post*, July 1, 1805. Murrell included this advertisement in *History of American Graphic Humor* (56) and expressed his personal frustration at not knowing the specific caricatures: "Would that we could see them now!"

123. *People's Friend and Daily Advertiser* (New York), November 17, 1806.

124. For more on the print market in late eighteenth-century London, see Bills, *Art of Satire*, esp. chapter 1, "Satirizing London," 10–39.

125. As quoted in Alexander, *Richard Newton and English Caricature*, 19.

126. *Portsmouth (NH) Oracle*, June 6, 1807.

CHAPTER 2

1. Birth and baptism records have not been discovered for Akin; however, a newspaper obituary stated that Akin's age at death on July 18, 1846, was "73 years." *Public Ledger* (Philadelphia), July 20, 1846. Akin's parents Thomas Akin (1744/47–1781) and Ann Christie (1752–1831) were married in 1768 in Charleston and had three children: in addition to James, a daughter Elizabeth (April 26, 1772–April 5, 1842) and a second son Thomas (August 1776–June 4, 1841). Akin outlived both of his siblings. I am indebted to Nic Butler, historian at the Charleston County Public Library, for his assistance in locating information on the history of the Akin family in Charleston and for his insightful knowledge of the city's eighteenth- and nineteenth-century culture and society.

2. Nic Butler, "The Forgotten Akin Family of Charleston," Charleston County Public Library, October 12, 2018, https://www.ccpl.org/charleston-time-machine/forgotten-akin-family-charleston. Thomas Akin's 1778 will assigned three guardians to watch over his three children: his brother James Akin (d. 1780), his brother-in-law Jacob Deveaux (1740–1803), and the Reverend Dr. Robert Smith of St. Philips Parish in Charleston. Smith and the Akin family shared a close relationship. It is believed that he married Thomas and Ann Christie in 1768 and baptized James. James Akin was in receipt of at least two inheritances: one from his father and one from his uncle James, who was childless.

3. Smith founded the academy on July 3, 1785; records do not survive for the first class of students, so it is not possible to determine for certain if Akin and his brother were registered students. For an advertisement for Smith's academy, see *Columbian Herald or the Patriotic Courier* (Charleston, SC), June 10, 1785; "Parents of all ranks and conditions" sent their children to Smith's academy. Easterby, *History of the College of Charleston*, 27–28. I am grateful to Dorothy Glover of the South Carolina History Room at the Charleston County Public Library for assistance and for directing my attention to this source.

4. I am indebted to Danielle Spittle, Centre for Research Collections, University of Edinburgh, for confirming Thomas Akin's registration as a medical student and recipient of a doctorate in medicine.

5. Timothy Pickering to Theophilus Parsons, November 5, 1805, Timothy Pickering Papers, Massachusetts Historical Society, Boston, microfilm, reel 43, letter 134; Akin was serving as a clerk in 1798, but it is unclear when he started and stopped.

6. Weekley, *Painters and Paintings*, esp. 328.

7. Rather, *American School*, 53–54, 79.

8. Weekley, *Painters and Paintings*, 298; *South Carolina State Gazette, and General Advertiser* (Charleston), November 25, 1784. This advertisement appeared in Charleston newspapers for several months, at least until January 1785.

9. *South-Carolina Weekly Gazette* (Charleston), November 20, 1784.

10. David Oliphant advertised in Charleston newspapers in 1786, adding that "the terms will be made as low and convenient as possible." *Charleston (SC) Morning Post and Daily Advertiser*, November 17, 1786.

11. *Columbian Herald* (Charleston), November 23, 1786.

12. Stewart, "Portraits of Henry Benbridge."

13. The artist James Earl (1761–1796) can also be linked with Akin during this time. Earl, a native of Massachusetts, settled in Charleston in 1794. Although little is known of Earl's early training, he did follow his older brother Ralph Earl, also an artist, to England. While there, James Earl exhibited at the Royal Academy in London in 1787 and later enrolled as student in 1789. Earl moved to Charleston because it was known to be a bustling city, brimming with wealthy and prominent patrons eager to have their likenesses painted by artists with credentials from London and the Royal Academy. Akin might have first received advice on how best to succeed as an artist from these practitioners, especially the benefit of going abroad to

study in London. Earl is directly connected to Akin's guardian and to the Rutledge family, having received painting commissions from them. For Earl's biography, see "James Earl (1761–1796)," Early American Paintings, Worcester Art Museum, https://www.worcesterart.org/collection/Early_American/Artists/earl_j/biography/index.html.

In 1799, Akin advertised an engraving after Earl's 1795 portrait of General Charles Cotesworth Pinckney of South Carolina (Gibbes Museum of Art, Charleston, SC, 1957.029.0001). *Porcupine's Gazette* (Philadelphia), April 11, 1799. Correspondence from 1818 indicates that Akin befriended Earl's nephew Ralph E. W. Earl. Stephens, *Selling Andrew Jackson*.

14. Sizer, *Autobiography of John Trumbull*, 167–68.

15. *City Gazette and Daily Advertiser* (Charleston, SC), December 7, 1795.

16. Mathew Carey Account Books, AAS, vol. 3, acct. 1054. The "Map of Scotland" was first published in 1796. I am grateful to Ashley Cataldo, curator of manuscripts at the American Antiquarian Society, for deciphering the writing and numbers on this invoice and other assistance with the Carey materials.

17. James Akin to Thomas Bewick, January 28, 1803, Thomas Bewick Papers, Tyne and Wear Archives, Newcastle, UK, box 2, 4388. Bewick made a notation on the reverse of the letter that he responded to Akin on April 19, 1803. The whereabouts of Bewick's letter to Akin are not known.

18. Special Collections, Edinburgh University Library, matriculation album 1796, EUA IN1/ADS/STA/2. There is also a remote possibility that Akin went to London while serving as a clerk for the United States government. Evidence from the period directly before and after his trip suggests, however, that politics was not the primary reason for his visit.

19. *Jenks' Portland (ME) Gazette*, May 12, 1804.

20. *The Repertory* (Boston), February 26, 1805.

21. "Benjamin West Lecture Pass Signed as President of the Royal Academy in London 'Benj. West,'" Heritage Auctions, sold October 18, 2013, https://historical.ha.com/itm/autographs/artists/benjamin-west-lecture-pass-signed-as-president-of-the-royal-academy-in-london-benj-west-/a/6102-34863.s. Now in a private collection. I am grateful to Martin Myrone for conversations and insight on this object.

22. Myrone, *Making the Modern Artist*, 72–74, as well as chart 6, "Social Origins or Status of Students, Compared to the General Population" (79).

23. Kamensky, *Revolution in Color*, 91–92.

24. Ward, *Charles Willson Peale*, 29.

25. Weber, "Temple of History Painting."

26. Peale, "Notes and Queries," 308.

27. Myrone, *Making the Modern Artist*, 63.

28. Clayton and O'Connell, *Bonaparte and the British*, 18.

29. Bills, *Samuel William Fores*, 18; Griffiths, *Print Before Photography*, 362.

30. Thomas Rowlandson's 1793 caricature *A Tit Bit for the Buggs* (BM, 8392); Bills, *Samuel William Fores*, 22–23.

31. The first date for this advertisement that I have located is *Claypoole's American Daily Advertiser* (Philadelphia), June 20, 1797. It was also published in New York and South Carolina through August. In September, I have only located this advertisement in South Carolina newspapers. The wording remained consistent throughout these months, except that for the Charleston advertisements Akin chose to name only local agents in the subscription list: "Thomas Coram," "Frenau and Paine," and "Major Shubrick." Coram and Shubrick are named in advertisements found in New York and Philadelphia.

32. Benjamin West wanted to produce a series of paintings on the American Revolution, but his strong connection to the king, the Royal Academy, and his distance from the physical geography of the United States made it impossible to do so, which is one of the reasons Trumbull started a similar series, completed in the mid-1820s.

33. *Gazette of the United States* (New York), April 21, 1790.

34. Sizer, "Tentative 'Short-Title' Check-List," 218.

35. *Time Piece, and Literary Companion* (New York), May 17, 1797.

36. Impressions of this engraving are in the collections of the Library of Congress in Washington, DC, the Pennsylvania Academy of the Fine Arts in Philadelphia, and the Metropolitan Museum of Art in New York. I have not been able to locate the painting by Elkanah Tisdale.

37. The only monograph on Stothard does not list these paintings; see Coxhead, *Thomas Stothard, R.A.* The capture of Major John André, a British spy found guilty and sentenced to hang for his treason, was popular in England. However, the subject of *The Battle at Eutaw Springs,* which was one of the bloodiest conflicts of the revolution, would lead one to believe that it would not have been of interest to a British artist, who would not have had the perspective of the audience in South Carolina, where this was a significant event. I have only found one account mentioned in a British newspaper; see *London Chronicle,* January 3, 1782.

38. *Philadelphia Gazette & Universal Daily Advertiser,* April 7, 1795.

39. Tiebout was active in New York between 1796 and 1799, at which point his name no longer appears in city directories, after which he was active in Philadelphia until 1825. Little is known about his time in London. Dunlap in *History of the Rise and Progress* (1:30) states that "Mr. Tiebout was the first American who went to London for instruction in engraving." O'Brien in *Amos Doolittle* (27) indicates that Tiebout was in London between 1793 and 1796, having left New York because of the yellow fever epidemic.

40. Richardson, "Charles Willson Peale's 'Engravings,'" 169.

41. Presses were available to purchase but were probably too expensive for Akin and Edwin when they were starting out. For example, in Philadelphia, John Innes, "Printers' Joiner" sold printers presses for cash (*Philadelphia Gazette,* October 27, 1797), while Henry Ouram made and sold "printers and bookbinders presses" in 1797 in Philadelphia (*Porcupine's Gazette,* April 5, 1797). Ouram sold a press to Mathew Carey in 1804 for $115. Silver, "Costs of Mathew Carey's Printing Equipment," 88. Silver provides information on the amount of repair and attention these presses needed by exploring invoices between Carey, Ramage and Ouram. A young engraver starting out might not want to take on such expenses, and likely Akin paid for the use of a printing press. Not until 1802 does Adam Ramage advertise the availability of a copperplate press: that he "continues to make Printing, Bookbinders, Copperplate, and Cutting PRESSES for papermakers and stationers." *Philadelphia Gazette,* January 22, 1802.

42. These reminiscences are republished in Fielding, "David Edwin, Engraver." Edwin does not identify the principal printer in Philadelphia at the time, although Tristam Bampyfylde Freeman was active in Philadelphia and advertised during this period. Likewise, in 1797, William Cobbett used the firm "Budd & Bartram" in Philadelphia; Gaines, "William Cobbett's Account Book," 305.

43. Richardson, "Charles Willson Peale's 'Engravings.'"

44. The marriage between James Akin and Eliza Cox took place on November 30, 1797, at Christ Church, Philadelphia. Christ Church Marriage Records, Christ Church, Philadelphia, Book 1709–1800, 4560. Eliza died in Philadelphia in 1834, and it is not known if they had any children. Akin married for a second time, because in his will he names his wife as Ophelia Akin and an infant daughter Caroline Christie Akin. He had other children who are not named in the will but for whom guardians are named. James Akin, will no. 174 (1846), Philadelphia City Archives, Will Book No. 18, 434. One daughter from his marriage to Ophelia, Ann Caroline Akin, born in 1838, died of dysentery at the age of two in 1840.

45. Timothy Pickering to Theophilus Parsons, November 5, 1805, Timothy Pickering Papers, Massachusetts Historical Society, Boston, microfilm, reel 14, letter 134.

46. "Removal of the Office," Timothy Pickering Papers, Massachusetts Historical Society, Boston, microfilm, reel 10, letter 16.

47. Harrison worked primarily in bank notes, and it is possible that he introduced Akin to Jacob Perkins. Cole in "James Akin" (217–19) gives the date for this commission as "circa 1798," but I believe it might have been designed and printed in 1799. (Cole as Maureen O'Brien Quimby, is also the author of "Political Art of James Akin.")

48. *Porcupine's Gazette* (Philadelphia), April 13, 1799; this advertisement merely stated that the print could be purchased at Akin's address, "James Akin, no. 14, Carter's alley." The print also includes the names of "C. & A. Tiebout, New York." It is not clear if Akin and the Tiebout brothers worked together, or if the print was also sold in New York.

49. *Aurora General Advertiser* (Philadelphia), January 11, 1800. Charles Willson Peale's painting *Thomas Jefferson* (1791) is in the collection of Independence National Historical Park in Philadelphia.

50. Reaves, *George Washington*, 70–71, 138–41.

51. Reaves in *George Washington* provides examples of the three states, including inspiration for the profile images of Washington, which were altered in states 2 and 3, and prints after Akin and Harrison's image. For more on the market for Liverpool pottery in late eighteenth- and nineteenth-century North America, see Nelson, "Transfer-Printed Creamware and Pearlware." The Akin and Harrison memorial image on a Liverpool jug is illustrated in Halfpenny et al., *Success to America*, 76, 211.

52. "Illustrious General Washington," broadside, January 24, 1800, printed by Henry Tuckniss, Philadelphia, LCP. Reproduced in Cunningham, *Popular Images*, 8.

53. James Akin and William Harrison Jr. to John Adams, January 28,1800, Adams Family Papers, Massachusetts Historical Society, Boston. While the letter has survived in the Adams Papers, the memorial print sent by Akin and Harrison has not been saved with the correspondence, and its whereabouts are unknown.

54. The location of the Benjamin Rush painting by Jeremiah Paul Jr. is not known. Paul and Akin enjoyed a professional relationship that may have lasted several years; in fact, Paul

exhibited his painting *Venus and Cupid* at the office of "James Akin, engraver," in 1811. Quimby, "Political Art of James Akin," 62. Paul was an art teacher and portrait painter in Philadelphia during the late 1790s, cofounded the Columbianum Artists Association, and had been a pupil of Charles Willson Peale. Dunlap's impression of Paul was not favorable: "This is one of the unfortunate individuals who, showing what is called genius in early life . . . are induced to devote themselves to the fine arts, without means of improvement or the education necessary to fit them for a liberal profession. . . . He was a man of vulgar appearance and awkward manners." Dunlap, *History of the Rise and Progress*, 1:102–3.

55. This inscription can be found on the engraving located at the Pennsylvania Academy of Fine Arts in Philadelphia. A second impression omits the lengthy inscription to reveal a name, "J. Wiggins." This name does not appear on any engraving from this period and may have been a pseudonym used by Akin or copied by another individual.

56. James Akin to Benjamin Rush, May 8, 1805, Rush Family Papers, LCP. The name of the mutual friend was Peter A. Browne, a Philadelphia lawyer.

57. *Philadelphia Gazette*, May 4, 1802.

58. Benjamin West to Charles Willson Peale, as quoted in Dunlap, *History of the Rise and Progress*, 1:93.

59. *Philadelphia Gazette*, May 7, 1802.

60. *Philadelphia Gazette*, June 23, 1802. Interestingly the advertisement that appears directly above Akin's is for an "American Gallery of Distinguished Public Characters" organized by George Helmbold, featuring paintings by Gilbert Stuart and engravings by David Edwin.

61. Gillingham, "Old Business Cards of Philadelphia," esp. 216; Quimby, "Political Art of James Akin," 62.

62. The impression of this book at the Sinclair Hamilton Collection of American Illustrated Books at the Princeton University Library includes an engraving signed by Eliza Akin. Other impressions lack signatures; however, the title page states that the book is "adorned with

cuts by James Akin." It is not possible to attribute any of the other engravings to Eliza in this book, and no other engravings from their time in Philadelphia have yet been attributed to her.

63. The engraving after drawings by Titian Peale were published in Wister, "Description of the Bones." See also Stagg, *"Nature."*

64. Kneass went on to have a successful career and was named engraver of the United States Mint in 1824.

65. "Kneass, William, engraver v. James Akin," McAllister Miscellaneous Manuscripts, McAllister Collection, LCP, MSS 025. According to the invoice, Kneass had previously worked as an apprentice for the Philadelphia engraver James Thackara, but this arrangement expired on September 25, 1802. Kneass likely worked out of Akin's address, "37 Pewter Platter Alley," the same address provided by Akin in newspaper advertisements for his bleeding services.

66. Weekley, *Painters and Paintings,* 298.

67. *Gazette of the United States* (Philadelphia), March 23, 1799, through May 1799; *Newburyport (MA) Herald,* May 14, 1799, to June 1799. I have been unable to locate information on Robert Scot.

68. For the limited scholarship on Perkins, see Bathe and Bathe, *Jacob Perkins;* and Harris, "Jacob Perkins, William Congreve." James Heath also had an established relationship with Thomas Stothard, whose paintings Akin proposed to engrave in 1797. Smith, *James Heath,* 3.

CHAPTER 3

1. Benes, *Old-Town and the Waterside,* 19.

2. *Newburyport (MA) Herald,* November 14, 1804, September 3, 1799, April 4, 1801, May 17, 1804.

3. *Newburyport (MA) Herald,* January 9, 1801, January 14, 1805.

4. Benes, *Old-Town and the Waterside,* 92–93.

5. *Newburyport (MA) Herald,* July 6, June 15, 1802.

6. *Newburyport (MA) Herald,* May 21, 1802.

7. *Newburyport (MA) Herald,* November 6, 1804.

8. *Newburyport (MA) Herald,* through most of 1804, until October 5, when the newspaper provides the address of 8 State Street, Edmund Blunt's former premises.

9. *Newburyport (MA) Herald,* April 24, 1804.

10. *Newburyport (MA) Herald,* June 7, 1803.

11. Hill and Hill, *Yankee City,* 35–36. Jacob Perkins may have lived and worked in a family home and shop on Merrimack Street until 1805, when he purchased a grand house at 16–18 Fruit Street. In the back garden he built a brick building out of which he printed bank notes. This building is now owned and operated by the Museum of Old Newbury. Deposition by Jonathon Titcomb on the boundary of Jacob Perkins and Edmund Titcomb, June 1, 1804, Essex County Deeds, 1804, 141–42; Charlotte Hamilton to Jacob Perkins, Newburyport, September 28, 1805, Essex County Deeds, 1805. I am grateful to Becky Geller, staff librarian, and Sharon Spieldenner, senior librarian/archivist, at the Newburyport Public Library Archival Center for their assistance in locating these documents.

12. The exact date of James and Eliza Akin's arrival in Newburyport is not clear, although a number of surviving membership certificates issued by the Female Charitable Society of Newburyport, engraved by Eliza, bear the date of June 3, 1803. An impression can be found in the Smithsonian American Art Museum, Washington, DC (1984.5).

13. Baron, *Exhibition of the Genuine Principles;* Rubenstein, "James Akin in Newburyport," 285. *The New American Practical Navigator* is the first publication advertised by Blunt to include information about "copperplate" illustrations. *Newburyport (MA) Herald,* May 18, 1804.

14. *Newburyport (MA) Herald,* April 8, 1803, and throughout the month of April and May.

15. *Newburyport (MA) Herald,* June 21, 1803, and in July.

16. *Newburyport (MA) Herald,* June 21, 1803. George Franklin Williams countered with his own notice against Blunt. *New-England Repertory* (Newburyport), October 1, 1803.

17. *Blunt v. Aken* [*sic*] *and Stedman,* case 107, Supreme Judicial Court, Essex County Records,

1806 November, SJC.ES / series 002, Massachusetts Supreme Judicial Court Archives, Boston, SJC.ES / series 002 (hereafter cited as Essex County Records).

18. James Akin is listed in the Philadelphia directories for 1803, 1804, and 1805, with his address located at "143 Walnut"; Akin's friend Peter A. Browne, attorney, evidently lived or worked out of this location until March 1804. Browne, whom Rush had cared for during the yellow fever epidemic, commissioned Akin to engrave bookplates. James Akin to Benjamin Rush, May 8, 1805, Rush Family Papers, LCP. See chapter 2, note 000, above.

19. *Newburyport (MA) Herald*, April 27, 1804. The same advertisement was also published in other Massachusetts cities, such as Boston, New Bedford, and Salem, as well as Portsmouth, New Hampshire, and Portland, Maine, during the end of April and into the month of May.

20. *Blunt v. Aken* [*sic*] *and Stedman*, case 107, 1806 November, Essex County Records.

21. *Boston Gazette*, March 29, 1804.

22. *Newburyport (MA) Herald*, May 4, 1804; Bishop Edward Bass (1726–1803) resided in Newburyport, where he died at age seventy-seven.

23. *Newburyport (MA) Herald*, May 22, 1804; further descriptions of the designs or subject matter were not included in this advertisement.

24. *Blunt v. Aken* [*sic*] *and Stedman*, case 107, 1806 November, Essex County Records.

25. *Commonwealth v. Akin*, 1805 November, Essex County Records.

26. *Blunt v. Aken* [*sic*] *and Stedman*, case 107, 1806 November, Essex County Records; *Newburyport (MA) Herald*, January, 1, 1805.

27. *Akin v. Blunt*, case 72, *Akin v. Blunt*, case 80, *Blunt v. Aken* [*sic*], case 107, *Blunt v. Aken* [*sic*], case 108, 1806 November, Essex County Records.

28. *Newburyport (MA) Herald*, January 8, 1805. Thomas and Whipple advertised "a FRONT CHAMBER, which is large and commodious, pleasantly situated in Market-Square, over the Bookstore of Thomas & Whipple. The above would make a very pleasant Office, or well

accommodate some Mechanic." *Newburyport (MA) Herald*, May 22, 1804, and published until the end of August. Akin's space was next to the tailor Joseph Hervey, a tenant of Thomas and Whipple until his departure in November 1806. *Newburyport (MA) Herald*, January 10, 1804, November 7, 1806.

29. *Newburyport (MA) Herald*, February 1, 11, 1805. King was a cabinetmaker and itinerant silhouette artist. See Benes, *Old-Town and the Waterside*, 97.

30. For more on the physiognotrace, see Miles, *Saint-Mémin*; and Rather, *American School*, 193.

31. *Newburyport (MA) Herald*, February 9, 1805.

32. *Political Calendar and Essex Advertiser* (Newburyport, MA), March 4, 1805; despite these two advertisements, silhouettes attributed to Akin have yet to be discovered. Akin ceased advertising his use of this device after 1805.

33. *Newburyport (MA) Herald*, March 8, 1805.

34. These profiles that Sanborn in "Thomas Leavitt" (229) states were completed in 1808 are now lost. However, Akin was in Philadelphia in 1808, and it is possible he traveled while in Newburyport at this time. In 1806, Akin completed the engraving of the town of Hampton, after a drawing by Thomas Leavitt. The profiles may have been produced earlier than the engraved map.

35. *Newburyport (MA) Herald*, May 3, 1805.

36. John McKown to James Akin, June 3, 1805, James Akin Collection, CLM; *James Akin v. John McKown*, no. 141, March Term 1806, vol. 9, p. 115, November 1805–March 1807, Record Volumes, 1764–1839, Cumberland Court of Common Pleas, 1764–1839, Judicial Branch, Record Group 40, Maine State Archives, Augusta.

37. Both Quimby and Rubenstein give the date of the "skillet incident" as October 27, 1804, referencing court documents for this date. Although the event is alluded to, no date is provided in the cases they both cite. October 27, 1804, is the date Akin ceased working for Blunt, but November 3, 1804, is the stated date when Akin challenged Blunt to a duel. Based on the

court documents, I conclude that if the incident took place, it must have occurred on November 3, 1804. The earliest reference I have found is in Sanborn, "Thomas Leavitt," 226–27.

38. Although Sanborn named Josiah Foster as the proprietor of the hardware store, I have been unable to locate a listing for this business in Newburyport.

39. *Newburyport (MA) Herald*, November 9, 1804. Akin sought an apprentice in copperplate printing. *Salem (MA) Gazette*, November 29, 1804. Although it is not known where Akin acquired this press, it may have come from Adam Ramage. In 1805, the Boston book and job printing firm of Joshua Belcher and Samuel T. Armstrong purchased two presses "of Adam Ramage" for $136 each. The reference is in Armstrong's manuscript journal, Edes Papers, Massachusetts Historical Society, Boston, cited in Silver, "Belcher and Armstrong Set Up Shop," 202; I am grateful to the author for reprinting the complete invoice that appears in Armstrong's manuscript journal. Also in 1805, Mathew Carey purchased from Ramage a mahogany printing press for $130 and a standing press for $61. Silver, "Costs of Mathew Carey's Printing."

40. *Newburyport (MA) Herald*, July 5, 1805. Akin advertised two other prints, titled "Turkeys" and "Sailor's Glee."

41. Sanborn, "Thomas Leavitt," 227–29; Quimby, "Political Art of James Akin," 62–64; Rubenstein, "James Akin in Newburyport," 287.

42. Little, "Cartoons of James Akin." For more general references, see Smith, *Illustrated Guide to Liverpool*, esp. 59 for Akin; and Hyland, *Herculaneum Pottery*. Christina Nelson in "Transfer-Printed Creamware and Pearlware" (95–97) has suggested that maps of Newburyport published by Blunt are also found on Liverpool pottery. Perhaps Blunt and Akin used the same source, or Akin used Blunt's source.

43. The only known pitcher featuring the full-size Blunt caricature is in a private collection. It has been reproduced in Little, *Little by Little*, 34.

44. *Blunt v. Aken [sic]*, case 108, 1806 November, Essex County Records.

45. *Merrimack Magazine and Ladies Literary Cabinet* (Newburyport, MA), November 2, 1805; *The Repertory* (Boston), November 8, 1805.

46. Timothy Pickering to James Akin, November 5, 1805, Timothy Pickering Papers, Massachusetts Historical Society, Boston, microfilm, reel 14, letter 135. Between October 1805 and January 1806, the two main topics discussed in their correspondence were Akin's situation with Blunt and his career as an artist. *Merrimack Magazine and Ladies Literary Cabinet* (Newburyport, MA), November 2, 1805; *The Repertory* (Boston), November 8, 1805.

47. James Akin to Timothy Pickering, October 31, 1805, and undated letter, 1805, Timothy Pickering Papers, Massachusetts Historical Society, Boston, microfilm, reel 14, letters 68, 69.

48. James Akin to Timothy Pickering, undated letter (likely November or December 1805). Akin's last known letter to Pickering is dated January 2, 1806. Timothy Pickering Papers, Massachusetts Historical Society, Boston, microfilm, reel 43, letters 69, 72.

49. See Gordon-Reed, *Hemingses of Monticello*, esp. 540–61. Gordon-Reed notes that in the September 14, 1801, issue of the *Virginia Federalist*, published by William Rind in Richmond, there is an allusion to Jefferson and Hemings, although neither is referred to by name (551).

50. *Richmond (VA) Recorder*, August 25, 1802.

51. James Akin to Thomas Bewick, January 28, 1803, Tyne and Wear Archives, Newcastle, UK, box 2, 4388.

52. Bewick, *History and Description of Land Birds*, 276. *The Pheasant* is the other image printed in the prospectus.

53. Akin purchased volume 1 in the United States, while he was a subscriber to the 1804 volume, *History and Description of Water Birds*. See Gardner-Medwin, "Bicentenary of Thomas Bewick's History." Gardner-Medwin includes a reproduction of the page from the "Subscribers to 2nd Volume of Birds" that names Akin: "Akin, Engraver Newbury Port American" and "July 12" [1804], the date the volume was sent to him (fig. 14, 249). The original is in the collection of Tyne and Wear Archives, Newcastle, UK, 1269/135.

54. *New-York Gazette*, May 12, 1806. For more on Huggins and his dressing academy, see Stagg, "American 'Dressing Academy.'"

55. This caricature was not known to either Murrell or Weitenkampf. The hornet might be a reference to a caricature by Robert Dighton, *Intelligence on the Change of the Ministry*. See Dupuy, "French Revolution," 383–84.

56. George, *Catalogue of Personal and Political Satires*; and George, "America in English Satirical Prints," 535. George offered her hypothesis as to the subject: "seemingly an attack either on Non-Intercourse or on the ensuing war, which an American student could probably interpret more precisely." As the work was published in 1806, it is not accurate to date it to the period around the Non-Intercourse Act or the War of 1812. *A Bug-A-Boo to frighten John Bull, or the Wright mode for kicking up the Bubbery* (BM, 10260).

57. Quimby, "Political Art of James Akin," 96.

58. *New-York Herald*, March 18, 1807.

59. The advertisement for the hotel can be found in the *Newburyport (MA) Herald*, May 5, 1807; a modern impression of the handbill taken from the plate is in the collection of the Museum of Old Newbury.

60. *Newburyport (MA) Herald*, January 30, 1807.

61. See Stagg, "All in My Eye!"

62. *The Repertory* (Boston), February 21, 1806.

63. *Newburyport (MA) Herald*, November 14, 1806; *The Repertory* (Boston), November 21, 1806.

64. *Commercial Advertiser* (New York), August 5, 1806; *Morning Chronicle* (New York), August 7, 1806.

65. The Charles Peirce Collection of Social and Political Caricatures and Ballads was the gift of the heirs of Harold Peirce to the American Antiquarian Society in February 1991. For the illustrated inventory, see https://www.americanantiquarian.org/peirce.htm.

66. Email correspondence with Babette Gehnrich, chief conservator at the American Antiquarian Society, April 12, 2021.

67. *Newburyport (MA) Herald*, May 7, 1805.

68. *Newburyport (MA) Herald*, June 28, 1805.

69. *Newburyport (MA) Herald*, February 7, 1807.

70. *Newburyport (MA) Herald*, October 30, 1807.

71. "List of the Members of the Newburyport Female Charitable Society." Account Book, 1803–1810, Newburyport Public Library Archival Center, Newburyport, MA.

72. Unclaimed letters addressed to James Akin are included in the February 29, 1808, list published by the New York City Post Office. *American Citizen* (New York), March 3, 1808.

73. *Aurora General Advertiser* (Philadelphia), February 7, 1808.

74. *Washington Federalist* (Georgetown, DC), December 15, 1808, March 11, 1809.

75. *The Tickler* (Philadelphia), August 29, September 12, 1810.

76. *The Tickler* (Philadelphia), July 3, 1811, and again in August and September of that year.

77. *Spirit of the Press* (Philadelphia), October 1, 1811.

78. *The Tickler* (Philadelphia), October 16, 1811.

79. *The Tickler* (Philadelphia), August 21, 1811.

80. *Political and Commercial Advertiser* (Philadelphia), May 14, 1811.

81. Akin's address for 1813 was 39 North Sixth Street. *Geographical and Military Museum* (Albany, NY), May 16, 1814; "E. Tisdale, Lebanon" is also listed as an agent. Elkanah Tisdale (1771–1835) was responsible for *The Gerrymander*, a caricature engraving published in 1812.

82. *Democratic Press* (Philadelphia), December 29, 1813.

CHAPTER 4

1. *New-York Gazette and General Advertiser*, December 6, 1806; *People's Friend and Daily Advertiser* (New York), December 6, 1806; *New-York Gazette and General Advertiser*, December 8, 1806.

2. Physical description of "William Charles . . . reported himself an engraver," *Aurora General Advertiser* (Philadelphia), October 21, 1814.

3. See, for example, H. Charles, "A Falsehood detected!," *American Citizen* (New York), January 31, 1807; and the same advertisement by W. Charles in *People's Friend and Daily Advertiser* (New York), February 2, 1807.

4. *Virginia Patriot* (Richmond), August 2, 1815 (reprinted from a "N.Y. Paper," with no date given).

5. *Democratic Press* (Philadelphia), April 3, 1813.

6. The date and place of his birth are recorded in the Charles family bible. In 1976, the Bible was still owned by a descendant, the Reverend John J. Albert in Wynnewood, Pennsylvania, "a great-great-great-grandson" of Charles. Lanmon, "American Caricature."

7. Marriage of William Charles, Bachelor, and Mary Graham, Spinster, St. Mary's Church, Lambeth, February 26, 1803, no. 1671, England, Surrey Parish Registers, 1536–1992, https://www.familysearch.org/ark:/61903/3:1:3QS7-89X7-XCL8.

8. *Gulliver and His Guide; or, A Check String to the Corsican*, August 1803 (BM, 1868,0808.7187), *Thoughts on Invasion, Both Sides the Water*, October 11, 1803 (BM, 1868,0808.7203), *Iohnny's Old Tune on his new fiddle*, October 28, 1803 (not found in the BM; private collection of Andrew Edmunds, London; also in the collection of the John Carter Brown Library, Brown University, Providence, RI; and William B. Osgood Collection, Houghton Library, Harvard University, Cambridge, MA, MS Am 2818 [27]), and *Boney's Last Supper or the Night Before Invasion* (not found in the BM; William B. Osgood Collection, MS Am 2818 [25]), all provide his London address. The first two caricatures listed here are reproduced in Lanmon, "American Caricature," 11; on Charles in London, see also Stagg, "Scottish Caricaturist in Philadelphia"; for a map locating print sellers in London, although Charles is not included, see Bills, *Art of Satire*, 222–23.

9. *John Bull's Reply to the Watchman over the Cellar*, July 1804 (William B. Osgood Collection, MS Am 2818 [6]); Murrell, *History of American Graphic Humor*, 80; see also Lanmon, "American Caricature," 11.

10. *Rewards for Past Favors or Intrusive Visitors*, May 21, 1806, "by W. & H. Charles 7 North Bridge Edinburgh" (the only known impression is in the print collection of Andrew Edmunds, London); and *Modern Spectacles Easily Seen Through*, published by "W. & H. Charles, May 12, 1806" (LCP). There is a hand-colored impression of *Modern Spectacles* (YAG) in which some of the text, including the date, has been wiped, a possible indication that Charles brought the plate with him to New York and printed additional copies.

11. *New-York Herald*, May 2, 1807.

12. Lossing, *Lossing's Pictorial Field Book*, 289. The incorrect date and circumstances of Charles's arrival in New York have been cited by Weitenkampf, Murrell, and Fielding, among others.

13. Henry Charles naturalization, June 28, 1811, Pennsylvania, Eastern District Petitions for Naturalization, 1795–1931, https://www.familysearch.org/ark:/61903/3:1:33S7-9PTZ-SLKR?i=32.

14. *Aurora General Advertiser* (Philadelphia), October 21, 1814.

15. Bills, *Art of Satire*, 32–33.

16. *American Citizen* (New York), April 6, 1807; for a discussion of this caricature, see Fowble, "William Charles FAMILY ELECTIONEERING," 16–18.

17. *People's Friend and Daily Advertiser* (New York), April 27, 1807.

18. *New-York Herald*, May 2, 1807; I am indebted to Thomas Baker, professor of history at State University of New York at Potsdam, for discussions related to this newspaper notice.

19. *New-Hampshire Gazette* (Portsmouth), January 12, 1808.

20. Murrell dates the caricature to 1808 (*History of American Graphic Humor*, 84). Lanmon agreed with this date; Weitenkampf dates it to 1809. There is no reason given for the date variations. All three agreed this is a caricature depicting Thomas Paine. It is possible that the plate for this caricature was reused, as lines and scratches seen beneath the design may indicate that it had previously been used for a map.

21. Charles also published at least three caricatures that were not political, copying directly

from British sources. *Jacky Frost and the Old Man* was copied from a George Woodward caricature of the same name, while *La walse / Le bon genre* was copied from a James Gillray caricature. A third caricature, *Modern Dandy's*, may have been published in New York. All are reproduced in Lanmon, "American Caricature," 7–10.

22. Newspaper notices in October offered the Liberty Street address, a two-story house, as available for let from November 1. *Commercial Advertiser* (New York), October 7, 1807.

23. For two illustrations by Charles for the *American Magazine of Wit*, including *The Court of Dover in Full Session* and an untitled image of a "newly employed waiter," see Murrell, *History of American Graphic Humor*, 79, 82. I am grateful to Laura Wasowicz, curator of children's literature at the American Antiquarian Society, for sharing her unpublished research on the children's books by William Charles.

24. "M. Carey Bot [Bought] of Wm. Charles," March 28, 1808, Mathew Carey Account Books, AAS, vol. 22, acct. 1101; for a brief overview of invoices between Carey and Charles, see Weiss, *William Charles.*

25. The profession for Henry Charles as noted in *Philadelphia Directory for 1809: Containing the Names, Trades, and Residence of the Inhabitants of the City, Southwark, and Northern Liberties* (mainly authored by James Robinson) (British Library, London). Henry worked consistently for Carey as a printer, engraver, and "colour[er] of caricatures." October 13, 1808, Mathew Carey Account Books, AAS, vol. 22, acct. 1104.

26. Invoice, September 26, 1808, Mathew Carey Account Book, AAS, vol. 22, acct. 1102. Advertisements placed by Mrs. Todd at the 195 Broadway address, where "Specimens of her cutting, shading the hair, and frames could be seen," is further evidence that Charles had left. *Mercantile Advertiser* (New York), June 9, 1808.

27. Mathew Carey Account Books, AAS, vol. 23, acct. 1425.

28. Invoice, July 11, 1810, Mathew Carey Account Books, AAS, vol. 24, acct. 1959. No address is provided here for Charles's store in Philadelphia.

29. For communications from two generations of the McAllister family with information about Charles, see Lossing, *Lossing's Pictorial Field Book*, 228. This reference is to a letter from the John A. McAllister Collection, LCP, McA MSS 001, box 2, folder 12.

30. "Engraving plate for Washington's Life," n.d., but a bill for his brother Henry is on the same page and dated 1811; see Mathew Carey Account Books, AAS, vol. 24, acct. 2248; regarding the coloring of maps, see Mathew Carey Account Books, AAS, vol. 27, accts. 3153–57.

31. Mathew Carey Account Books, AAS, vol. 24, acct. 2248, and vol. 25, acct. 2536. William McCulloch had a store in November 1812 at "no. 306 Market-Square" and was a "Printer, Bookseller, and Stationer." *Star of Liberty* (Philadelphia), November 7, 1812.

32. Some aspects, such as the clouds and portraits in profile in the corner of the print, are similar to a London caricature Charles completed in 1805, *Innocence the best Defence against False Accusations* (BM, 1948,0214.695).

33. Lanmon included this caricature in her broad survey, "American Caricature," but not in the more focused discussion, "William Charles."

34. The signature was spelled Pencil or Pencill. The titles are *King Quilldriver's Experiments on National Defence* (1808?), *Non Intercourse or Dignified Retirement* (1809), and *Intercourse or Impartial Dealings* (1809). The pseudonym can be associated with the *Boston Patriot* editor Alexander Hill Everitt, but there is not enough evidence to attribute these prints to Everitt or anyone else. See the catalogue entries in the appendix.

35. For more on Alexander Anderson, see the foundational work by Pomeroy, *Alexander Anderson*; see also Gardner, "Doctor Alexander Anderson."

36. *New-York Herald*, April 27, 1814.

37. Doolittle might have been responsible for an earlier caricature print, *The Looking Glass for 1787, A House divided against itself cannot stand*. A 1998 auction catalogue is the first publication to link Doolittle with this caricature, and this

attribution was largely based on the fact that the print addresses Connecticut issues, and Doolittle was already an active and successful engraver in New Haven. See Sotheby's, *Fine Printed and Manuscript Americana.* Murrell does not include the print in *History of American Graphic Humor,* perhaps because it was not known to him in the early 1930s. Weitenkampf included the caricature in his 1954 catalogue, but without an artist attribution, writing, "This roughly done and somewhat scattered design has to do with taxes affecting Connecticut" (*Political Caricature,* 11). This caricature may have been by St. John Honeywood (1763–1798), who was also active in Connecticut and remembered as a great wit. Reportedly, he excelled at a number of mediums, including caricature, although none have yet been attributed to him. See Baldwin, "St. John Honeywood," 308.

38. I am indebted to Georgia Barnhill for directing me to the probable dating of this caricature print to 1812.

39. On Doolittle's engravings in the late 1790s and early 1800s, see O'Brien, *Amos Doolittle,* esp. 64–73. O'Brien considers a theory that this print was not engraved by Doolittle but rather by one of his apprentices.

40. *American Mercury* (Hartford, CT), March 26, 1813.

41. *The Yankee* (Boston), April 2, 1813.

42. *Boston Patriot,* April 3, 1813; for similar advertisements also listing the sale of the caricature at Paul Mondelly's shop, at 63 Cornhill, see *The Yankee,* April 9, 1813; and *Independent Chronicle* (Boston), April 12, 1813.

43. *Mercantile Advertiser* (New York), April 21, 1813.

44. *American Mercury* (Hartford, CT), April 14, 1813; *Rutland (VT) Herald,* April 21, 1813; *Green-Mountain Farmer* (Bennington, VT), April 27, 1813.

45. *The Enquirer* (Richmond, VA), April 16, 1813; *City Gazette and Commercial Daily Advertiser* (Charleston, SC), April 22, 1813; *Albany (NY) Argus,* April 30, 1813.

46. See especially *Gulliver and his Guide, or a Check String to the Corsican,* 1803 (BM, 1868,0808.7187).

47. The attribution to Samuel Folwell can be found in Murrell, *History of American Graphic Humor,* 86.

48. His manufactory and store were listed in Philadelphia city directories between 1813 and 1820 (British Library); in 1819, the directory also notes his exhibition of the Society of American Artists.

49. *Aurora General Advertiser* (Philadelphia), October 21, 1812.

50. *Poulson's American Daily Advertiser* (Philadelphia), May 11, 12, 13, 14, 15, 17, 1813; *Democratic Press* (Philadelphia), May 10, 12, 13, 14, 1813; *Aurora General Advertiser* (Philadelphia), May 12, 14, 17, 1813.

51. Lanmon, "American Caricature," 21.

52. Ibid.; Charles's depiction, and indeed others from this period, may have found inspiration from a caricature published by George Woodward and Charles Williams, *John Bull Threatened by Insects from All Quarters* (London, 1807). A cross-eyed John Bull is surrounded by flying insects with identifying names such as "French the Dragon Fly," "Italian Butterfly," and "American Hornet." Although the insects do not bear any resemblance to the large hornet attacking the peacock in Charles's print, the London caricature depicts naval scenes, with three large ships on either side of Bull, a feature that was copied by most American-based caricaturists. Lanmon notes this connection on page 24.

53. Evidence that this caricature was also designed by Folwell can be found in an advertisement that announced copperplates available at auction. The plates for these specific two caricatures evidently survived through the 1810s and 1820s and were auctioned off in 1827. "T. B. Freeman and Son," *National Gazette and Literary Register* (Philadelphia), March 28, 1827.

54. *Baltimore Patriot,* May 16, 1814.

55. *Democratic Press* (Philadelphia), May 27, 1813.

56. *Aurora General Advertiser* (Philadelphia), July 7, 1813.

57. The final caricature connecting Charles and Kennedy was published in December of 1814, *The Hartford Convention or Leap No Leap.*

58. *Democratic Press* (Philadelphia), October 21, 1814. Charles was initially included in a list of "Alien Enemies," but a correction in the same newspaper from the Marshall's Office stated that "William Charles having been naturalized on the 27th of November last, and not having been reported at this office, his name has been published with the others."

59. *Democratic Press* (Philadelphia), March 7, 1814.

60. The address can be found on the advertisements for *Johnny Bull and the Alexandrians* and *John Bull and the Baltimoreans*; see *Aurora General Advertiser* (Philadelphia), October 5, 1814.

61. *The Repertory* (Boston), June 27, 1814.

62. *Democratic Press* (Philadelphia), September 16, 1813.

63. *Aurora General Advertiser* (Philadelphia), September 29, 1813; *Democratic Press* (Philadelphia), September 29, 1813.

64. Invoices from 1813, Mathew Carey Account Books, AAS, vol. 26, accts. 2842 and 2843.

65. Weitenkampf, *American Graphic Art*, 17, 20; Lanmon, "American Caricature," 47–48.

66. *Aurora General Advertiser* (Philadelphia), October 5, 1814. This is the same address given for Charles in the 1816 Philadelphia directory (British Library).

67. *American Watchman* (Wilmington, DE), October 19, 1814, October 22, November 23, December 14, 21, 24, 28, 1814, March 8, July 22, 1815.

68. Hackwood, *William Hone*, 106–7.

69. *Middlesex Gazette* (Middletown, CT), December 14, 1815; *Poulson's American Daily Advertiser* (Philadelphia), December 15, 1815 (repr. from *Boston Evening Gazette*, December 9, 1815).

70. Address: Philadelphia directories, 1817–19. Bookstore: advertisements in *Poulson's American Daily Advertiser* (Philadelphia), February 9, March 30, 1818.

71. Lossing, "Spectre from Elbe," 266.

72. *Brother Jonathan Administering a Salutary Cordial to John Bull* and letter to John Binns, AAS.

73. *The Columbian* (New York), November 1, 1813; reprinted verbatim in the *City Gazette and Commercial Daily Advertiser* (Charleston, SC), November 13, 1813.

74. *Baltimore Patriot*, November 3, 1813. This advertisement was first published in the *National Advocate* (New York), November 1, 1813, and included the address where the caricature could be purchased (90 Broadway); see also *Farmer's Repository* (Charles Town, WV), November 11, 1813, with no address.

75. Invoices, 1806–14 and 1815, Mathew Carey Account Books, AAS, vol. 27, acct. 4018, vol. 28, acct. 4018. Carey's 1815 advertisement, two years after the Doolittle caricature was published, states that "M.C. has still on hand a few copies of John Bull and Brother Jonathan, with Caricature Engravings.—Price 75 cents in boards." The phrasing of this notice suggests that this might have been a pamphlet or a book. *Political and Commercial Register* (Philadelphia), September 25, 1815.

76. Shadwell, *American Printmaking*, 120.

77. "We made a number of additions to our collection of 'American graphics,' as the 'in' phrase goes. The oldest of these was a cartoon 'Bonaparte in Trouble,' by Amos Doolittle, the well-known New Haven engraver. Facts must be faced; Doolittle was not a very talented artist. The print is rare; Doolittle's name has a certain cachet; we are pleased to have one of his three known cartoons." *Annual Report of the Library Company of Philadelphia*, 52.

78. Thomas Kensett was an engraver who had arrived in United States from London in 1812, where he had previously been employed at Hampton Court.

79. Elezebeth Edgar (McCreery) was born in 1796 and died in 1842; if Edgar completed this watercolor in 1815, she would have been less than twenty years old.

80. Sanborn, "Thomas Leavitt," 230.

81. Two caricatures published in the early 1800s also included Napoleon, *Intercourse or Impartial Dealings* and *Non Intercourse or Dignified Retirement* (New-York Historical Society). Signed by Peter Pencil, they are the only two caricatures

to have been located by this artist. Neither is similar in either style or skill to Akin, Charles, or Doolittle; as yet, no attribution can be made.

82. *The Yankee* (Boston), July 1, 1814.

83. *The Yankee* (Boston), February 4, 1814. The identity of the second individual is unclear, although the most likely candidates are the two Massachusetts senators at the time: Christopher Gore (Federalist, in office from May 5, 1813, to May 30, 1816) and Joseph Bradley Varnum (Democratic-Republican, in office from June 29, 1811, to March 3, 1817).

84. *The Yankee* (Boston), July 1, 1814.

85. Murrell, Weitenkampf, and Quimby all assign a publication date of 1812.

86. *The Yankee* (Boston), November 19, 1813.

87. *Boston Patriot*, November 13, 1813.

88. *Rutland (VT) Herald*, November 3, 1813.

89. *The Yankee* (Boston), December 10, 1813.

90. *The Yankee* (Boston), December 17, 1813.

91. Written on the reverse of the colored impression of this caricature at the Library of Congress: "Deposited 10th Decm. 1814 by Samuel Kennedy as Proprietor." *Democratic Press* (Philadelphia), December 14, 1814.

92. Barnhill, "Political Cartoons of New England," 86n4. Barnhill cites the Eddy attribution to the Vermont Historical Society publication *Windsor County Engravers*, 4.

93. Taylor, *Origin and Growth*, 324.

94. *American Mercury* (Hartford, CT), March 24, 1818.

95. Lanmon, "William Charles," 106; see also notice of the circumstances surrounding his death in the *Democratic Press* (Philadelphia), August 11, 1820.

96. Charles was listed as a "bookseller, stationer, copperplate engraver and printer." Edward Whitely, *Philadelphia Directory and Register for 1820* (British Library).

97. Dunlap, *History of the Rise and Progress*, 3:393.

98. *National Advocate* (New York), August 12, 1820; *Free Press* (Lancaster, PA), August 17, 1820; *Weekly Recorder* (Chillicothe, OH), August 24, 1820. The reprinted obituary outside of Philadelphia stated that the news of his death "was communicated to the distressed widow and seven children of the late Wm. Charles." Another obituary stated that Charles had eight children; either this was an error, or Mary Charles was pregnant at the time of his death. *City of Washington Gazette*, August 14, 1820.

CHAPTER 5

1. Many of the contemporary documents from the 1820s spell Johnston's name "Johnson." For consistency and in keeping with the modern scholarship on him, I refer to him in this chapter as "Johnston"; however, I have kept the spelling of "Johnson" in the quoted passages from contemporary newspapers.

2. On the introduction of lithography in the United States, see Weimerskirch, "Lithographic Stone in America." David Tatham in the introduction to *Prints and Printmakers* provides 1825 as the crucial moment for the change to lithography; for a summary of the process and history, see Pierce, *Early American Lithography*, 9–23, esp. 9–11.

3. Senefelder's invention, termed, "Poly Autography," was reported as in American newspapers as early as 1803; he came to be described as "the inventor of Lithography." *Chronicle Express* (New York), September 12, 1803.

4. *Farmer's Repository* (Charles Town, WV), April 21, 1819.

5. Davis, "Bass Otis," 11–23; Weimerskirch, "Lithographic Stone in America," 2–16.

6. Tatham, *Prints and Printmakers*, 8n1. In 1825, Anthony Imbert opened his shop in New York and the Pendleton firm opened in Boston; see Carbonell, "Anthony Imbert."

7. Murrell, *History of American Graphic Humor*, 115–16.

8. Temi Odumosa focuses on the representations of people of color in British caricature in *Africans in English Caricature*. See pp. 79–80 for a short description of *A Peep into the Antifederal Club* (fig. 15), which includes at far right a person of color identified as "Citizen Mungo."

9. *Commercial Advertiser* (New York), March 14, 1809.

10. *Portsmouth (NH) Oracle*, February 5, 1820; *Hallowell (ME) Gazette*, February 9, 1820; *Daily Advertiser* (New York), February 9, 1820; *Boston Intelligencer*, February 12, 1820; *Poulson's American Daily Advertiser* (Philadelphia), February 12, 1820; *Baltimore Patriot*, February 14, 1820; *Northern Whig* (Hartford, CT), February 15, 1820; *American Beacon and Norfolk (VA) and Portsmouth (VA) Daily Advertiser*, February 18, 1820; *Providence (RI) Gazette*, February 18, 1820; *New-Hampshire Sentinel* (Keene), February 19, 1820; *Vermont Intelligencer* (Bellows Falls), February 28, 1820; *National Standard* (Middlebury, VT), February 29, 1820; *Hampden Federalist* (Springfield, MA), March 1, 1820; *Kentucky Reporter* (Lexington), March 8, 1820; *Brookville (IN) Gazette*, March 30, 1820; *Edwardsville (IN) Spectator*, April 18, 1820.

11. *Franklin Gazette* (Philadelphia), September 28, 1820.

12. *Franklin Gazette* (Philadelphia), July 20, 1820; *Free Press* (Lancaster, PA), July 13, 1820; "Hiester and Slavery from the Pennsylvania Gazette," *Free Press* (Lancaster, PA), July 6, 1820; *Franklin Gazette* (Philadelphia), August 11, 28, 1820.

13. Murrell, *History of American Graphic Humor*, 76.

14. I am grateful for discussions on this topic with historian Nic Butler of the Charleston County Public Library; see also "Street Auctions and Slave Marts in Antebellum Charleston," Charleston County Public Library, n.d., https://www.ccpl.org/charleston-time-machine/street-auctions-and-slave-marts-antebellum-charleston.

15. "Pennsylvania 1820 Governor," A New Nation Votes: American Election Returns, 1787–1825, https://elections.lib.tufts.edu/catalog/kd17cto5q. Hiester received 68,242 votes to Findlay's 66,766, narrowly winning the election. Unsurprisingly, the Federalist-leaning Locust Ward voted overwhelmingly for Hiester in the election (337 votes to Findlay's 129).

16. "Pennsylvania 1820, Philadelphia City, Locust Ward," A New Nation Votes: American Election Returns, 1787–1825, https://elections

.lib.tufts.edu/catalog/3t945q89v. Akin lost to the Federalist candidate, Isaac Deaves. Akin's name has not been found associated with any other elections. The results were published on September 30, 1820, in *Poulson's American Daily Advertiser* (Philadelphia).

17. Murrell, *History of American Graphic Humor*, 76; Weitenkampf, *Political Caricature*, 20. Weitenkampf questioned the dating of 1817 by Murrell, who included a question mark after the date; Murrell only provided the first half of the title, *Joseph Hiester's claims to the votes of the Christian People*, while Weitenkampf included the full title with the date. It is possible that Murrell did not see the original caricature but only a reproduction, and either he was unable to decipher the second half of the title or the full title was not included in the reprint.

18. *New-Hampshire Sentinel* (Keene), March 11, 1810; *The Columbian* (New York), April 3, 1820; *Freeman's Journal* (Cooperstown, NY), April 10, 1820 (originally published in *Lansingburgh [NY] Gazette*, date unknown). Impressions of this caricature have not been located. Daniel Tompkins was Monroe's vice president for both presidential terms, serving between 1817 and 1825.

19. Lorant, *Glorious Burden*, 105–7.

20. Weitenkampf, *Political Caricature*, 21; Tyler, *Image of America in Caricature and Cartoon*, 62. Murrell did not include this caricature. The only known impression is at Harvard University's Houghton Library. Weitenkampf states that the American Antiquarian Society holds an impression of the print; if it does, there is not a record of it, nor can it be found in the present caricature collection.

21. *Portsmouth (NH) Journal of Literature and Politics*, November 15, 1823; *Salem (MA) Gazette*, November 20, 1823.

22. Cornag, *Birth of an Empire*, 147.

23. *Portsmouth (NH) Journal of Literature and Politics*, November 15, 1823; *Salem (MA) Gazette*, November 20, 1823.

24. Weitenkampf dates this caricature to 1832 (26–27); titled "Eagle Chair" in Murrell, *History of American Graphic Humor*, 102, 106. The print is

218

pasted on a separate sheet of paper, on which has been written by a modern hand, "Presidential Campaign 1832, Andrew Jackson Candidate for President / Martin van Buren Vice President."

25. Cornag, "Empires Fall," 304.

26. *Boston Commercial Gazette*, April 19, 1824.

27. Caricature description: *Baltimore Patriot*, October 21, 1824. For references to Johnston in Baltimore, see *Baltimore Patriot*, October 10, 1823.

28. *Columbian Centinel* (Boston), October 6, 16, 23, 1824. The caricature was sold by "S. H. Parker, 12, Cornhill."

29. *New-York Evening Post*, October 23, 1824; Hutchens with incorrect statement: *Providence (RI) Gazette*, November 6, 1824.

30. McInnis, "Little of Artistic Merit?," esp. 11.

31. Brigham, "David Claypoole Johnston."

32. Ibid., 99.

33. *Baltimore Patriot*, November 11, 1824.

34. For more on newspapers and their role in elections, see Nagel, "Election of 1824."

35. *Salem (MA) Gazette*, November 19, 1824.

36. *Baltimore Patriot*, November 13, 1824.

37. For a survey of portraits of Jackson, see Barber, *Andrew Jackson* (esp. 43–45, on Earl's Nashville Museum). Rachel Stephens has written the most thorough account of the relationship between Earl and Jackson; see *Selling Andrew Jackson*.

38. Earl received this title upon his death from the printer Francis P. Blair. See Barber, *Andrew Jackson*, 146.

39. Barber, *Andrew Jackson*, 135–49, esp. 135.

40. Stephens, *Selling Andrew Jackson*, 34.

41. Ibid., 110. Earle supplied Ralph Earl with frames; see also Ralph Earl to James Akin, November 15, 1819, John Spencer Bass Papers, LOC, box 31, folder 3.

42. *Poulson's American Daily Advertiser* (Philadelphia), April 24, 1811.

43. Barber, *Andrew Jackson*, 43.

44. *American Justice!! or The Ferocious Yankee Genl. Jack's Reward for Butchering Two British Subjects* (BM 13218); an impression is also housed in the collection at the Tennessee State Museum, Nashville.

45. Barber, *Andrew Jackson*, 54.

46. James Akin to Ralph E. W. Earl, February 17, 1819, Earl Family Papers, AAS.

47. This painting was most likely the 1818 full portrait of Jackson now in the Tennessee State Museum. Barber, *Andrew Jackson*, 152.

48. Godfrey and Hallett, *James Gillray*, 158, esp. fig. 141.

49. Ralph Earl to James Akin, November 15, 1819, John Spencer Bass Papers, LOC, box 31, folder 3.

50. James Akin to Ralph E. W. Earl. Murrell wrote that Harry McNeill Bland "kindly allowed me to copy this letter." Now lost, the brief letter is reprinted in Murrell, *History of American Graphic Humor*, 135. Unlike Murrell's copy, the surviving letters between Akin and Earl from 1818 and 1819 are wordier.

51. James Akin to Andrew Jackson, March 13, 1829, Letters of Application and Recommendation During the Administration of Andrew Jackson, 1829–1837, National Archives, Washington, DC (hereafter cited as Jackson Letters of Application).

52. Petition, April 8, 1829, Jackson Letters of Application. Letters of support for Akin in 1828 have not yet been located, although two petitions from December 1828 have survived. The Adams administration had named Dr. Thomas Jones as superintendent, but he was removed from office in June 1829.

53. *Daily Chronicle* (Philadelphia), February 4, 1829, and throughout the rest of February, March, and April.

54. James Akin to Andrew Jackson, March 13, 1829, Jackson Letters of Application; Akin also claimed to have exhibited three painted transparencies in support of Jackson, depicting him as a "general, President, and Farmer."

55. Letters of support for Akin's application were sent starting in February 1829, with petitions arriving as early as the prior December. The Rev. Ezra Stiles Ely to Andrew Jackson, February 2, 1829; William Shaw to William Ramsey, February 10, 1829; William Shaw to Samuel D. Ingham, February 16, 1829; petition addressed to Martin Van Buren, March 12, 1829; petition, December 10, 1828; petition, December 20, 1828;

William Ramsey to Martin Van Buren, March 5, 1829; petition addressed to Martin Van Buren, April 8, 1829; all in Jackson Letters of Application.

56. Andrew Jackson to Ralph E. W. Earl, March 16, 1829, Jackson Letters of Application.

57. *Baltimore Patriot*, June 13, 1829.

58. James Akin to Martin Van Buren, April 16, 1829, Jackson Letters of Application.

59. The coffin handbill was published by John Binns, editor of the *Democratic Press* (Philadelphia). Several versions have survived. For a brief summary, see Barber, *Andrew Jackson*, 153–54.

60. James Akin to Martin Van Buren, May 15, 1829, Jackson Letters of Application.

61. *Richmond (VA) Enquirer*, April 18, 1828.

62. One potential caricature printed during this period was *An Unexpected Meeting of Old Friends*, but it does not appear to depict Jackson. I agree with Murrell's assumption that "the exact meaning of this cartoon is obscure" (*History of American Graphic Humor*, 140–41). See also Quimby, "Political Art of James Akin," 98–99; and Weitenkampf, *Political Caricature*, 23.

63. Reilly, *American Political Prints*, 89.

64. *New-Hampshire Sentinel* (Keene), January 11, 1828.

65. "The Rural Lodge Hotel" on Francis Lane "opposite the New State Penitentiary," *Poulson's American Daily Advertiser* (Philadelphia), May 1, 1824; "Traveler's Lodging House," 17 Chestnut Street between Front and Second Streets, Philadelphia, *New York Inquirer*, June 26, 1828; "Taken a convenient house and cellar" at No. 63 Dock Street, *Philadelphia Inquirer*, January 16, 1830.

66. Quimby notes that "Joseph Jackson, in his Philadelphia Encyclopaedia, identifies the oyster cellar as one owned by James Prossler [*sic*], a 'fine looking mulatto,' who operated an oyster cellar at 806 Market Street [the 1890 street address] from about 1830. . . . Jackson credits Akin with having made the lithograph in 1829" ("Political Art of James Akin," 75–76; see also 76n43). The Library Company of Philadelphia website and entry for the caricature also cites James Prosser (incorrectly listed as Prossler); see LCP, HSP Bb 38 O 97, https://digital.librarycompany.org/islandora/object/digitool%3A64146. According to

Philadelphia newspapers, James Prosser was selling turtle soup as early as 1816 and operating an "Oyster Cellar" in 1818. *Poulson's American Daily Advertiser*, July 24, 1816, December 7, 1818. In the 1822 Philadelphia directory, he is listed as "oysterman" (British Library, London). In 1825, Prosser moved his premises to 244 Market Street, where he advertised that he had an Oyster Cellar with "Oysters and Terrapins" of a superior quality. *Poulson's American Daily Advertiser*, November 3, 1825. He is listed in the Philadelphia directory as "Prosser, James, oyster cellar High n 8th d h 15. Elizabeth" (British Library). For a brief summary of Prosser and his competition in Philadelphia, see Shields, *Culinarians*, 39–43.

67. "Lithography No. 90 South Third-street, Kennedy & Lucas inform the Public that they have opened their Establishment for Lithographic Printing," *Poulson's American Daily Advertiser*, October 30, 1828. See also Piola, *Philadelphia on Stone*.

68. *Eastern Argus* (Portland, ME), April 27, 1827.

69. The publication date for this caricature is 1827, although 1834 has routinely (and erroneously) been given. Sullivan located the caricature *Plain Sewing* in *Kentucky Reporter* (Lexington), August 29, 1827. Sullivan, "Jackson Caricatured."

70. David Claypoole Johnston Collection, AAS, box 8.

71. *Baltimore Patriot*, August 12, 1827.

72. *National Journal* (Washington, DC), August 16, 1827.

73. *Rhode-Island American and Providence Gazette*, August 17, 1827.

74. *Rhode-Island Republican* (Newport), August 23, 1827 (originally published in the *Boston Advertiser*, date unknown).

75. *Eastern Argus* (Portland, ME), February 19, 1828.

76. Murrell, *History of American Graphic Humor*, 120; Weitenkampf, *Political Caricature*, 34; Nevins and Weitenkampf, *Century of Political Cartoons*, 44; Reilly, *American Political Prints*, 68–69.

77. Nevins and Weitenkampf, *Century of Political Cartoons*, 44.

CONCLUSION

1. "To Thomas Jefferson from Robert Smith, 2 September 1825," *Founders Online*, National Archives, Washington, DC, https://founders.archives.gov/documents/Jefferson/98-01-02-5508.

2. John Armstrong Jr. to Horatio Gates, April 7, 1789, Horatio Gates Papers, NYHS.

3. *Orange County Patriot* (Goshen, NY), February 9, 1813.

Bibliography

PRIMARY SOURCES

Archives and Museums

UNITED STATES

American Antiquarian Society, Worcester,
Massachusetts
Charles Peirce Collection of Social and
Political Caricatures and Ballads
David Claypoole Johnston Collection
Earl Family Papers
Graphic Arts Collection
Mathew Carey Account Books
William Cobbett Account Book, 1796–1800
American Philosophical Society, Philadelphia,
Pennsylvania
Billy Ireland Cartoon Library and Museum,
Ohio State University, Columbus, Ohio
Boston Athenaeum, Boston, Massachusetts
Boston Public Library, Boston, Massachusetts
Arts Collection
Center for Brooklyn History, Brooklyn, New
York (formerly Brooklyn Historical
Society)
Charleston County Public Library, Charleston,
South Carolina
South Carolina History Room
Chicago Historical Society, Chicago, Illinois
Christ Church, Philadelphia, Pennsylvania
Christ Church Marriage Records
Clements Library, University of Michigan, Ann
Arbor, Michigan
James Akin Collection

Colonial Williamsburg, Williamsburg, Virginia
Graphic Arts Collection
Connecticut Historical Society, Hartford,
Connecticut
Graphic Arts Collection
Free Library of Philadelphia, Philadelphia,
Pennsylvania
Print and Picture Department
George Washington Masonic Memorial, Alexan-
dria, Virginia
Collection of Alexandria-Washington Lodge
No. 22
Henry E. Huntington Library, San Marino,
California
Historical Society of Newbury, Newburyport,
Massachusetts
Historical Society of Pennsylvania, Philadelphia,
Pennsylvania
Houghton Library, Harvard University, Cam-
bridge, Massachusetts
American Prints
William B. Osgood Collection
Independence National Historical Park, Phila-
delphia, Pennsylvania
Independence Seaport Museum, Philadelphia,
Pennsylvania (formerly Philadelphia
Maritime Museum)
John Carter Brown Library, Brown University,
Providence, Rhode Island
Graphic Arts Collection
Lewis Walpole Library, Yale University, Farm-
ington, Connecticut

222

Library Company of Philadelphia, Philadelphia, Pennsylvania
Graphic Arts Collection
John A. McAllister Collection
Rush Family Papers
Library of Congress, Washington, DC
John Spencer Bass Papers
Manuscript Division
Prints and Photographs Division
Maine State Archives, Augusta, Maine
Maryland Center for History and Culture (formerly Maryland Historical Society), Baltimore, Maryland
Massachusetts Historical Society, Boston, Massachusetts
Adams Papers
Edes Papers
Sedgwick Family Papers
Thomas Jefferson Account Book
Timothy Pickering Papers
Massachusetts Supreme Judicial Court Archives, Boston, Massachusetts
Essex County Records
Metropolitan Museum of Art, New York, New York
Department of Drawings and Prints
Museum of Old Newbury, Newburyport, Massachusetts
National Archives, Washington, DC
Founders Online
Letters of Application and Recommendation During the Administration of Andrew Jackson, 1829–1837
Newburyport Public Library Archival Center, Newburyport, Massachusetts
Essex County Deeds
New-York Historical Society, New York, New York
Clinton Family Papers
Horatio Gates Papers
Graphic Arts Collection
King Family Papers
New York Public Library, New York, New York
Graphic Arts Collection
Frank Weitenkampf Papers
Peabody Essex Museum, Salem, Massachusetts (formerly Essex Institute)

Pennsylvania Academy of Fine Arts, Philadelphia, Pennsylvania
Philadelphia City Archives, Philadelphia, Pennsylvania
Phillips Library, Peabody Essex Museum, Salem, Massachusetts
Stillman Papers
Ichabod Tucker Papers
Princeton University Art Museum, Princeton, New Jersey
Princeton University Library, Princeton, New Jersey
Sinclair Hamilton Collection of American Illustrated Books
Smithsonian American Art Museum, Washington, DC
Tennessee State Museum, Nashville
Winterthur Museum, Garden, and Library, Delaware
Graphic Arts Collection
Worcester Art Museum, Worcester, Massachusetts
Yale University Library, New Haven, Connecticut
John Trumbull Papers

UNITED KINGDOM
British Library, London
Rare Books Collection
British Museum, London
Department of Prints and Drawings
Edinburgh University Library, Edinburgh
Centre for Research Collections
Special Collections
Tyne and Wear Archives, Newcastle
Thomas Bewick Papers

US Periodicals

CONNECTICUT
American Mercury (Hartford)
American Telegraphe (Newfield)
Connecticut Herald (New Haven)
Hartford Courant
Middlesex Gazette (Middletown)
Northern Whig (Hartford)
Weekly Register (Norwich)

DELAWARE
American Watchman (Wilmington)

DISTRICT OF COLUMBIA
City of Washington Gazette
National Journal
Washington Federalist (Georgetown)

INDIANA
Brookville Gazette
Edwardsville Spectator

KENTUCKY
Kentucky Reporter (Lexington)

MAINE
Eastern Argus (Portland)
Hallowell Gazette
Jenks' Portland Gazette

MARYLAND
Baltimore Federal Republican
Baltimore Patriot
North American and Mercantile Daily Advertiser
(Baltimore)

MASSACHUSETTS
Boston Christian Herald
Boston Commercial Gazette
Boston Daily Advertiser
Boston Evening Gazette
Boston Intelligencer
Boston Patriot
Columbian Centinel (Boston)
Essex Gazette (Haverhill)
Essex Journal (Newburyport)
Essex Register (Salem)
Greenfield Gazette
Hampden Federalist (Springfield)
Independent Chronicle (Boston)
Massachusetts Mercury (Boston)
Merrimack Magazine and Ladies Literary Cabinet
(Newburyport)
Newburyport Herald

New-England Repertory (Newburyport)
Political Calendar and Essex Advertiser
(Newburyport)
J. Russell's Gazette Commercial and Political
(Boston)
The Repertory (Boston)
Salem Gazette
Western Star (Stockbridge)
The Yankee (Boston)

NEW HAMPSHIRE
Hough's Concord Herald
New-Hampshire Gazette (Portsmouth)
New-Hampshire Gazette, and General Advertiser
(Portsmouth)
*New-Hampshire Recorder, and the Weekly Adver-
tiser* (Keene)
New-Hampshire Sentinel (Keene)
New-Hampshire Spy (Portsmouth)
Portsmouth Journal of Literature and Politics
Portsmouth Oracle
Rising Sun (Keene)

NEW JERSEY
Centinel of Freedom (Newark)

NEW YORK
Albany Argus
Albany Centinel
Albany Gazette
American Citizen (New York)
American Minerva (New York)
Chronicle Express (New York)
The Columbian (New York)
Commercial Advertiser (New York)
Daily Advertiser (New York)
The Diary; or, Loudon's Register (New York)
Freeman's Journal (Cooperstown)
Gazette of the United States (New York)
Geographical and Military Museum (Albany)
Lansingburgh Gazette
Mercantile Advertiser (New York)
Minerva & Mercantile Evening Advertiser (New
York)
Morning Chronicle (New York)

National Advocate
New-York Commercial Advertiser
New-York Daily Gazette
New-York Evening Post
New-York Gazette
New-York Gazette and General Advertiser
New-York Herald
New York Inquirer
Orange County Patriot (Goshen)
People's Friend and Daily Advertiser (New York)
Royal Gazette (New York)
Time Piece, and Literary Companion (New York)

NORTH CAROLINA
North Carolina Journal (Halifax)

OHIO
Weekly Recorder (Chillicothe)

PENNSYLVANIA
Aurora General Advertiser (Philadelphia)
Carey's Daily Advertiser (Philadelphia)
Claypoole's American Daily Advertiser
    (Philadelphia)
Daily Chronicle (Philadelphia)
Democratic Press (Philadelphia)
Federal Gazette, and Philadelphia Evening Post
Federal Gazette and Philadelphia Daily Advertiser
Franklin Gazette (Philadelphia)
Free Press (Lancaster)
Gazette of the United States (Philadelphia)
General Advertiser (Philadelphia)
*General Advertiser and Political, Commer-
    cial, Agricultural and Literary Journal*
    (Philadelphia)
Independent Gazetteer (Philadelphia)
National Gazette and Literary Register
    (Philadelphia)
Pennsylvania Journal or Weekly Advertiser
    (Philadelphia)
Pennsylvania Packet and Daily Advertiser
    (Philadelphia)
Philadelphia Evening Post
Philadelphia Gazette
Philadelphia Gazette and Daily Advertiser

Philadelphia Inquirer
Political and Commercial Register (Philadelphia)
Porcupine's Gazette (Philadelphia)
Poulson's American Daily Advertiser
    (Philadelphia)
Public Ledger (Philadelphia)
Spirit of the Press (Philadelphia)
Star of Liberty (Philadelphia)
The Tickler (Philadelphia)
United States Gazette (Philadelphia)

RHODE ISLAND
Newport Mercury
Providence Gazette
Rhode-Island American and Providence Gazette
Rhode-Island Republican (Newport)
United States Chronicle (Providence)

SOUTH CAROLINA
Charleston Courier
Charleston Morning Post and Daily Advertiser
City Gazette and Daily Advertiser (Charleston)
City Gazette and Commercial Daily Advertiser
    (Charleston)
Columbian Herald (Charleston)
Columbian Herald or the Patriotic Courier
    (Charleston)
*South Carolina State Gazette, and General Adver-
    tiser* (Charleston)
South-Carolina Weekly Gazette (Charleston)

VERMONT
Green-Mountain Farmer (Bennington)
National Standard (Middlebury)
Rutland Herald
Vermont Intelligencer (Bellows Falls)
Vermont Journal and Universal Advertiser
    (Windsor)

VIRGINIA
*Alexandria Daily Gazette, Commercial and
    Political*
American Beacon (Norfolk)
*American Beacon and Norfolk and Portsmouth
    Daily Advertiser*

Columbian Mirror and Alexandria Gazette
The Enquirer (Richmond)
Richmond Enquirer
Richmond Recorder
Virginia Chronicle (Norfolk)
Virginia Gazette (Williamsburg)
Virginia Patriot (Richmond)

WEST VIRGINIA
Farmer's Repository (Charles Town)

Contemporary Letters, Documents, and Publications

Adams Family. *January 1786–February 1787.*
Edited by Margaret A. Hogan, C. James
Taylor, Celeste Walker, Anne Decker
Cecere, Gregg L. Lint, Hobson Wood-
ward, and Mary T. Claffey. Vol. 7 of
The Adams Papers, ser. 2, *Adams Family
Correspondence.* Cambridge, MA: Har-
vard University Press, 2005.
———. *January 1790–December 1793.* Edited by
C. James Taylor, Margaret A. Hogan,
Karen N. Barzilay, Gregg L. Lint, Hobson Woodward, Mary T. Claffey, Robert F. Karachuk, and Sara B. Sikes. Vol. 9
of *The Adams Papers*, ser. 2, *Adams Family Correspondence.* Cambridge, MA:
Harvard University Press, 2009.
*Attic Miscellany; or, characteristic mirror of men
and things, including the correspondent's
museum* 1, no. 3 (February 1790).
Baron, George. *Exhibition of the Genuine Principles of Common Navigation, with complete refutation of the false and spurious
principles ignorantly imposed on the public in the "New American practical navigator."* New York, 1803.
Bewick, Thomas. *History and Description of Land
Birds.* Vol. 1 of *A History of British Birds.*
Newcastle, UK, 1797.
Cobbett, William. *History of the American Jacobins.* Philadelphia, 1796.
Dunlap, William. *A History of the Rise and Progress of the Arts of Design in the United
States.* 3 vols. Philadelphia, 1834.

Huggins, John Richard Desborus. *Hugginiana;
or Huggins' Fantasy.* New York, 1808.
Jefferson, Thomas. *Jefferson's Memorandum
Books.* Edited by James A. Bear Jr. and
Lucia C. Stanton. Vol. 1 of *The Papers of
Thomas Jefferson*, 2nd ser. Princeton, NJ:
Princeton University Press, 1997.
———. *30 November 1789–4 July 1790.* Edited by
Julian P. Boyd. Vol. 16 of *The Papers of
Thomas Jefferson.* Princeton, NJ: Prince-
ton University Press, 1961.
———. *11 May–31 August 1793.* Edited by John
Catanzariti. Vol. 26 of *The Papers of
Thomas Jefferson.* Princeton, NJ: Prince-
ton University Press, 1995.
Lambert, John. *Travels Through Canada & the
United States of North America, in the
years 1806, 1807, & 1808.* Vol. 2. London,
1816.
Wister, C. "A Description of the Bones Deposited, by the President, in the Museum of
the Society, and Represented in Annexed
Plates." *Transactions of the American Philosophical Society* 4 (1799): 526–31.

SECONDARY SOURCES

Alberts, Robert C. *Benjamin West: A Biography.*
Boston: Houghton Mifflin, 1978.
Alexander, David. *Richard Newton and English
Caricature in the 1790s.* Manchester:
Manchester University Press, 1998.
*Annual Report of the Library Company of Phila-
delphia.* Philadelphia: Library Company
of Philadelphia, 1968.
Baldwin, Christopher Columbus. "St. John Hon-
eywood." *Worcester Magazine and His-
torical Journal* 1 (1826): 305–8.
Barber, James C. *Andrew Jackson: A Portrait
Study.* Washington, DC: National Por-
trait Gallery, 1991.
Barnhill, Georgia. *Bibliography on American
Prints of the Seventeenth Through the
Nineteenth Centuries.* New Castle, DE:
Oak Knoll Press, 2006.
———. "The Catalogue of American Engrav-
ings: A Manual for Users." *Proceedings*

226

of the American Antiquarian Society 108 (April 1999): 113–247.

———. "Political Cartoons of New England." In *Prints of New England*, edited by Georgia Brady Barnhill, 83–104. Worcester, MA: American Antiquarian Society, 1991.

Bathe, Greville, and Dorothy Bathe. *Jacob Perkins: His Inventions, His Times, and His Contemporaries.* Philadelphia: Historical Society of Pennsylvania, 1943.

Beatty, Joseph M., Jr. "The Letters of Judge Henry Wynkoop." *Pennsylvania Magazine of History and Biography* 38, no. 1 (1914): 183–205.

Benes, Peter. *Old-Town and the Waterside: Two Hundred Years of Tradition and Change in Newbury, Newburyport, and West Newbury.* Newburyport, MA: Cushing House Museum, 1985.

Bills, Mark, *The Art of Satire: London in Caricature.* London: Philip Wilson, 2006.

———. *Samuel William Fores, Satirist: Caricatures from the Reform Club.* Sudbury, UK: Gainsborough's House Society, 2014.

Bindman, David. *The Shadow of the Guillotine: Britain and the French Revolution.* London: British Museum Press, 1989.

Blaisdell, T. C. *The American Presidency in Political Cartoons.* Berkeley: University Art Museum, 1976.

Brigham, Clarence S. "David Claypoole Johnston, 'The American Cruikshank.'" *Proceedings of the American Antiquarian Society* 50 (April 1940): 98–110.

———. *Fifty Years of Collecting Americana for the Library of the American Antiquarian Society, 1908–1958.* Worcester, MA: American Antiquarian Society, 1958.

Butterfield, Roger. *The American Past.* New York: Simon and Schuster, 1947.

Carbonell, John. "Anthony Imbert: New York's Pioneer Lithographer." In *Prints and Printmakers of New York State, 1825–1940*, edited by David Tatham, 11–42.

Ithaca, NY: Cornell University Press, 1986.

Chernow, Ron. *Alexander Hamilton.* New York: Penguin, 2004.

Chervinksy, Lindsay. *The Cabinet: George Washington and the Creation of an American Institution.* Cambridge, MA: Harvard University Press, 2020.

Clark, Mary E. *Peter Porcupine in America: The Career of William Cobbett.* New York: Beekman, 1974.

Clayton, Tim, and Sheila O'Connell. *Bonaparte and the British: Prints and Propaganda in the Age of Napoleon.* London: British Museum, 2015.

Cole, Maureen O'Brien. "James Akin, Engraver and Social Critic." MA thesis, University of Delaware, 1967.

Connecticut Historical Society. "Battle of the Wooden Sword." *Bulletin of the Connecticut Historical Society* 27, no.1 (January 1962): 28–32.

Cornag, Evan. *The Birth of an Empire: DeWitt Clinton and the American Experience, 1769–1828.* Oxford: Oxford University Press, 2000.

———. "Empires Fall." *New York History* 84, no. 3 (Summer 2003): 301–13.

Coxhead, A. C. *Thomas Stothard, R.A.: An Illustrated Monograph.* London: A. H. Bullen, 1906.

Cresswell, Donald, ed. *The American Revolution in Drawings and Prints: A Checklist of the 1765–1790 Graphics in the Library of Congress.* Mansfield Center, CT: Martino Publishing, 1975.

Cunningham, Noble, Jr. *The Image of Thomas Jefferson in the Public Eye: Portraits for the People, 1800–1809.* Charlottesville: University of Virginia Press, 1981.

———. *Popular Images of the Presidency: From Washington to Lincoln.* Columbia: University of Missouri Press, 1991.

Cuno, James. *French Caricature and the French Revolution, 1789–1799.* Chicago: University of Chicago Press, 1988.

Currier, John J. *History of Newburyport, 1764–1909*. Newburyport, MA, 1909.

Davis, Gainor B. "Bass Otis: Painter, Portraitist, and Engraver." In *Bass Otis: Painter, Portraitist and Engraver*, by Gainor B. Davis and Wayne Craven, 1–23. Wilmington: Historical Society of Delaware, 1976.

Dickson, H. E. "Day vs. Jarvis: With Notes of the Early Years of John Wesley Jarvis." *Pennsylvania Magazine of History and Biography* 63, no. 2 (April 1939): 169–88.

Dolmetsch, Joan. "Prints in Colonial America: Supply and Demand in the Mid-Eighteenth Century." In *Prints in and of America to 1850*, edited by J. D. Morse, 53–74. Charlottesville: University of Virginia Press, 1970.

Donald, Diana. *The Age of Caricature: Satirical Prints in the Reign of George III*. New Haven, CT: Yale University Press, 1996.

Dupuy, Pascal. "The French Revolution in American Satirical Prints." *Print Quarterly* 15, no. 4 (1998): 371–88.

Easterby, J. H. *History of the College of Charleston*. New York: Scribner Press, 1935.

Evans, Dorinda. *Benjamin West and His American Students*. Washington, DC: Smithsonian Institution Press, 1980.

Fäy, Bernard. *The Two Franklins: Fathers of American Democracy*. Boston: Little, Brown, 1933.

Ferling, John E. *Adams vs. Jefferson: The Tumultuous Election of 1800*. Oxford: Oxford University Press, 2004.

Fielding, Mantle. *American Engravers upon Copper and Steel*. Philadelphia, 1917.

———. "David Edwin, Engraver." *Pennsylvania Magazine of History and Biography* 29, no. 1 (1905): 8.

Fordham, Douglas. "Hogarth's Act and the Professional Caricaturist." In *Hogarth's Legacy*, edited by Cynthia Ellen Roman, 23–50. New Haven, CT: Yale University Press, 2016.

Fowble, E. McSherry. "The Movement Toward Acceptance of the Nude as an Art Form in America, 1800–1825." *Winterthur Portfolio* 9 (1974): 103–21.

———. *Two Centuries of Prints in America, 1680–1880*. Charlottesville: University of Virginia Press, 1987.

———. "William Charles FAMILY ELECTIONEERING—or Candidate Bob in His GLORY." *Imprint* 3, no. 1 (1978): 16–18, 20.

Freeman, Joanne B. *Affairs of Honor: National Politics in the Early Republic*. New Haven, CT: Yale University Press, 2001.

Gaines, Pierce W. "William Cobbett's Account Book." *Proceedings of the American Antiquarian Society* 77 (October 1969): 299–312.

Gardner, Albert Ten Eyck. "Doctor Alexander Anderson, the Pirates' Friend." *Metropolitan Museum of Art Bulletin* 9, no. 8 (1951): 218–24.

Gardner-Medwin, David. "The Bicentenary of Thomas Bewick's History of British Birds." *Transactions of the Natural History Society of Northumbria* 65, pt. 3 (March 2007): 223–52.

Gatrell, Vic. *City of Laughter: Sex and Satire in Eighteenth-Century England*. London: Atlantic Books, 2007.

George, M. Dorothy. "America in English Satirical Prints." *William and Mary Quarterly*, 3rd ser., 10, no. 4 (October 1953): 511–37.

———. *Catalogue of Personal and Political Satires Preserved in the Department of Prints and Drawings in the British Museum*. Vol. 7. London: British Museum, 1947.

———. *English Political Caricature: A Study of Opinion and Propaganda*. Oxford: Clarendon Press, 1959.

Gillingham, Harold E. "Old Business Cards of Philadelphia." *Pennsylvania Magazine of History and Biography* 53 (July 1929): 203–29.

Godfrey, Richard. *English Caricature, 1620 to the Present: Caricaturists and Satirists, Their Purpose and Influence*. London: Victoria and Albert Museum, 1984.

Godfrey, Richard, and Mark Hallett. *James Gillray: The Art of Caricature*. London: Tate, 2001.

Goodspeed, Charles. *A History of the Rise and Progress of the Arts of Design in the United States*. Boston: Charles E. Goodspeed, 1912.

Gordon-Reed, Annette. *The Hemingses of Monticello: An American Family*. New York: W. W. Norton, 2008.

Griffiths, Antony. *The Print Before Photography: An Introduction to European Printmaking 1550–1820*. London: British Museum, 2016.

Hackwood, Frederick W. *William Hone: His Life and Times*. London: T. F. Unwin, 1912.

Halfpenny, Patricia A., Robert S. Teitelman, Ronald W. Fuchs, Wendell D. Garrett, and Robin Emmerson. *Success to America: Creamware for the American Market Featuring the S. Robert Teitelman Collection at Winterthur*. London: Antique Collectors Club, 2010.

Hallett, Mark. *The Spectacle of Difference: Graphic Satire in the Age of Hogarth*. New Haven, CT: Yale University Press, 1999.

Hardy, Dominic. "The Idea of Hogarth in American Print Culture from the Revolutionary Era to the 1830s." In *Hogarth's Legacy*, edited by Cynthia Ellen Roman, 196–227. New Haven, CT: Yale University Press, 2016.

Harris, Elizabeth. "Jacob Perkins, William Congreve, and Counterfeit Printing in 1820." In *Prints in and of America to 1850*, edited by J. D. Morse, 197–214. Charlottesville: University of Virginia Press, 1970.

Hill, Sarah, and Harry B. Hill Jr. *Yankee City: Faces from Our Past*. Newburyport, MA: Newburyport Five Cents Savings Bank, 1982.

Hunter, Edith Fisher. "All I Wanted to Do Was Put the Vacuum Cleaner in the Closet." Unpublished manuscript, American Antiquarian Society.

Hyland, Peter. *The Herculaneum Pottery: Liverpool's Forgotten Glory*. Liverpool: Liverpool University Press, 2005.

Isenberg, Nancy. *Fallen Founder: The Life of Aaron Burr*. New York: Viking Press, 2007.

Kamensky, Jane. *A Revolution in Color: The World of John Singleton Copley*. New York: W. W. Norton, 2016.

Kelly, James, and B. S. Lovell. "Jefferson: His Friends and Foes." *Virginia Magazine of History and Biography* 101, no. 1 (January 1993): 133–57.

Lanmon, Lorraine Welling. "American Caricature in the English Tradition: The Personal and Political Satires of William Charles." *Winterthur Portfolio* 11, no. 1 (1976): 1–51.

———. "William Charles and His War of 1812 Caricatures." In *Philadelphia Printmaking: American Prints Before 1860*, edited by Robert F. Looney, 91–109. West Chester, PA: Tinicum Press, 1976.

Larson, Judy L. "Separately Published Engravings in the Early Republic: An Introduction to Copperplate Engravings and Printmaking in America Through 1820." *Printing History* 6, no. 1 (1984): 3–24.

Latham, Thomas Edward Mere. "The Body Politic and the Family Quarrel: The War of American Independence, Metaphor and Visual Imagery in Britain." PhD diss., University College London, 2005.

Lawrence, Vera Brodsky. *Music for Patriots, Politicians, and Presidents: Harmonies and Discords of the First Hundred Years*. New York: Macmillan, 1975.

Little, Nina Fletcher. "The Cartoons of James Akin upon Liverpool Ware." *Old-Time New England* 28, no. 3 (January 1938): 103–8.

———. *Little by Little: Six Decades of Collecting American Decorative Arts*. Boston: Historic New England, 1998.

Looney, Robert F., ed. *Philadelphia Printmaking: American Prints Before 1860*. West Chester, PA: Tinicum Press, 1976.

Lorant, Stefan. *The Glorious Burden*. New York: Harper and Row, 1968.

Lossing, Benson. *Lossing's Pictorial Field Book of the War of 1812*. New York, 1869.

———. *Our Country: A Household History of the United States for All Readers, from the Discovery of America to the Present Time*. Philadelphia, 1878.

———. "The Spectre from Elbe." *Harper's New Monthly Magazine* 43 (July 1871).

Masur, Louis. "'Pictures Have Now Become a Necessity': The Use of Images in American History Textbooks." *Journal of American History* 84, no. 4 (March 1998): 1409–24.

May, Stephen. "An Enduring Legacy: The Pennsylvania Academy of the Fine Arts, 1805–2005." In *Pennsylvania Academy of the Fine Arts: 200 Years of Excellence*, edited by Jane Watkins, 10–27. Philadelphia: Pennsylvania Academy of the Fine Arts, 2005.

McCullough, David. *John Adams*. New York: Simon and Schuster, 2001.

McInnis, Maurie. "Little of Artistic Merit? The Problem and Promise of Southern Art History." *American Art* 19, no. 2 (Summer 2005): 11–18.

———. *Slaves Waiting for Sale: Abolitionist Art and the American Slave Trade*. Chicago: University of Chicago Press, 2011.

Miles, Ellen G. *Saint-Mémin and the Neoclassical Profile Portrait in America*. Washington, DC: National Portrait Gallery, 1994.

Miller, Richard G. "The Federal City 1783–1800." In *Philadelphia: A 300-Year History*, edited by Russell F. Weigley, 155–207. Philadelphia: Barra Foundation, 1982.

Minnigerode, Meade. *Jefferson, Friend of France: The Career of Edmund Charles Genet, Minister Plenipotentiary from the French Republic to the United States, as Revealed by his Private Papers, 1734–1834*. New York: G. P. Putnam's Sons, 1928.

Morse, J. D. *Prints in and of America to 1850*. Charlottesville: University of Virginia Press, 1970.

Munsing, Stephanie. *Made in America: Printmaking, 1760–1860*. Philadelphia: Library Company of Philadelphia, 1973.

Murrell, William. *A History of American Graphic Humor*. Vol. 1, *1747–1865*. New York: Whitney Museum of American Art, 1933.

———. "Rise and Fall of Cartoon Symbols." *American Scholar* 4, no. 3 (Summer 1935): 306–15.

Myrone, Martin. *Making the Modern Artist: Culture, Class, and Art-Educational Opportunity in Romantic Britain*. New Haven, CT: Yale University Press, 2020.

Nagel, Paul C. "The Election of 1824: A Reconsideration Based on Newspaper Opinion." *Journal of Southern History* 26, no. 3 (August 1960): 315–29.

Neff, Emily Bellew, and Kaylin H. Weber. *American Adversaries: West and Copley in a Transatlantic World*. New Haven, CT: Yale University Press, 2013.

Nelson, Christina. "Transfer-Printed Creamware and Pearlware for the American Market." *Winterthur Portfolio* 15, no. 2 (Summer 1980): 93–115.

Nevins, Allan, and Frank Weitenkampf. *A Century of Political Cartoons: Caricature in the United States from 1800 to 1900*. New York: Charles Scribner's Sons, 1944.

O'Brien, Donald C. *Amos Doolittle: Engraver of the New Republic*. New Castle, DE: Oak Knoll Press, 2008.

Odumosa, Temi. *Africans in English Caricature 1769–1819: Black Jokes, White Humor*. London: Harvey Miller, 2017.

Parton, James. *Caricature and Other Comic Art*. New York, 1877.

Peale, Rembrandt. "Notes and Queries." *The Crayon* 4 (October 1857).

Pierce, Sally. *Early American Lithography: Images to 1830*. Boston: Boston Athenaeum, 1997.

Piola, Erika, ed. *Philadelphia on Stone: Commercial Lithography in Philadelphia, 1828–1878*. University Park: Penn State University Press, 2012.

Pomeroy, Jane. *Alexander Anderson, 1775–1870, Wood Engraver and Illustrator, an Annotated Bibliography*. New Castle, DE: Oak

Knoll Press; Worcester, MA: American Antiquarian Society, 2005.

Quimby, Ian M. G. "The Doolittle of the Battle of Lexington and Concord." *Winterthur Portfolio* 4 (1968): 83–108.

Quimby, Maureen O'Brien. "The Political Art of James Akin." *Winterthur Portfolio* 7 (1972): 59–112.

———. See also Cole, Maureen O'Brien.

Rather, Susan. *The American School: Artists and Status in the Late Colonial and Early National Era*. New Haven, CT: Yale University Press, 2016.

Rauser, Amelia. *Caricature Unmasked: Irony, Authenticity and Individualism in Eighteenth-Century Prints*. Newark: University of Delaware Press, 2008.

Reaves, Wendy Wick. *George Washington, an American Icon: The Eighteenth-Century Graphic Portraits*. Washington, DC: Smithsonian Institution Traveling Service, 1982.

Reilly, Bernard, Jr. *American Political Prints, 1766–1876: Catalogue of the Collection in the Library of Congress*. Boston: G. K. Hall, 1991.

Reitzel, William. "The Purchasing of English Books in Philadelphia, 1790–1800." *Modern Philology* 35, no. 2 (November 1937): 159–71.

Richardson, Edgar P. *Charles Willson Peale and His World*. New York: Harry N. Abrams, 1982.

———. "Charles Willson Peale's 'Engravings in the Year of National Crisis, 1787.'" *Winterthur Portfolio* 1 (1964): 166–81.

Riely, John. *Henry William Bunbury*. Suffolk, UK: Gainsborough House, 1983.

Robinson, Nicholas K. *Edmund Burke: A Life in Caricature*. New Haven, CT: Yale University Press, 1996.

Roman, Cynthia Ellen, ed. *Hogarth's Legacy*. New Haven, CT: Yale University Press, 2016.

Rubenstein, Lewis. "James Akin in Newburyport." *Essex Institute Historical Collections* 102, no. 4 (October 1966): 285–98.

Sanborn, F. B. "Thomas Leavitt and His Artist Friend, James Akin." *Granite Monthly* 25 (October 1898): 225–34.

Shadwell, Wendy J. *American Printmaking: The First 150 Years*. Washington, DC: Museum of Graphic Art, 1969.

———. *Catalogue of American Portraits in the New-York Historical Society*. 2 vols. New Haven, CT: Published for the New-York Historical Society by Yale University Press, 1974.

Shields, David. *The Culinarians: Lives and Careers from the First Age of American Fine Dining*. Chicago: University of Chicago Press, 2017.

Silver, Rollo G. "Belcher and Armstrong Set Up Shop: 1805." *Studies in Bibliography* 4 (1951/52): 201–4.

———. "The Costs of Mathew Carey's Printing Equipment." *Studies in Bibliography* 19 (1966): 85–122.

Sizer, Theodore. *Autobiography of John Trumbull, Patriot-Artist, 1756–1843*. New Haven, CT: Yale University Press, 1953.

———. "A Tentative 'Short-Title' Check-List of the Works of Col. John Trumbull." *Art Bulletin* 30, no. 3 (September 1948): 214–23.

Skeen, C. Edward. *John Armstrong, Jr., 1758–1843: A Biography*. Syracuse, NY: Syracuse University Press, 1981.

Smith, Alan. *The Illustrated Guide to Liverpool Herculaneum Pottery: 1790–1840*. London: Barrie and Jacobs, 1970.

Smith, D. E. Huger, and A. S. Salley Jr., eds. *Register of St. Philip's Parish, Charles Town, or Charleston, S.C., 1754–1810*. Columbia: University of South Carolina Press, 1971.

Smith, George W. *James Heath: Engraver to Kings and Tutor to Many*. Chelmsford, UK: G. W. Smith, 1989.

Snyder, Martin. *City of Independence: Views of Philadelphia Before 1800*. New York: Praeger Press, 1975.

Sotheby's. *Fine Printed and Manuscript Americana*. Catalogue no. 44 for the April 16, 1988, auction sale. New York: Sotheby's, 1988.

Spalding, James Alfred. *Dr. Lyman Spalding: Originator of the United States Pharmacopeia*. Boston: W. M. Leonard, 1916.

Stagg, Allison M. "After the New York Public Library: Frank Weitenkampf and His Scholarship on American Political Caricatures." *Imprint* 37, no. 1 (Spring 2012): 14–24.

———. "'All in My Eye!': James Akin and His Newburyport Social Caricatures." *Common-Place* 10, no. 2 (January 2010). http://commonplace.online/article/all-in-my-eye-james-akin.

———. "The American 'Dressing Academy': Venues for Political Caricature and Prints in the Early Republic." *Journal for Art Market Studies* 2, no. 1 (2018). https://doi.org/10.23690/jams.v2i1.24.

———. "An American Market for Visual Satire: William Cobbett, James Gillray, and American Caricature in 1790s Philadelphia." *Print Quarterly* 36, no. 3 (September 2019): 263–74.

———. "The Art of Wit: American Political Caricature, 1780–1830" unpublished PhD diss., University College London, 2011.

———. "'Family-Ambition': A Political Caricature of the 1804 New York Gubernatorial Election." *Imprint* 35, no. 1 (2010): 2–9.

———. "*Nature*: A Nineteenth-Century Engraving Linking Charles Willson Peale, James Akin, and Peale's Mastodon." *Panorama: Journal of the Association of Historians of American Art* 7, no. 1 (Spring 2021). https://doi.org/10.24926/24716839.11722.

———. "A Scottish Caricaturist in Philadelphia: William Charles, the War of 1812, and the Market for Caricature in America." *Visual Culture in Britain* 20, no. 1 (July 2019): 1–15.

Stephens, Rachel. *Selling Andrew Jackson: Ralph E. W. Earl and the Politics of Portraiture*. Columbia: University of South Carolina Press, 2018.

Stewart, Robert C. "The Portraits of Henry Benbridge." *American Art Journal* 2, no. 2 (Autumn 1970): 58–71.

Strachan, John. *Advertising and Satirical Culture in the Romantic Period*. Cambridge: Cambridge University Press, 2007.

———. "'Trimming the Muse of Satire': J. R. D. Huggins and the Poetry of Hair Cutting." In *The Satiric Eye: Forms of Satire in the Romantic Period*, edited by Steven Jones, 188–206. New York: Palgrave Macmillan, 2003.

Strazdes, Diana. "The Amateur Aesthetic and the Draughtsman in Early America." *Archives of American Art Journal* 19, no. 1 (1979): 15–23.

Sullivan, John. "Case of 'A Late Student': Pictorial Satire in Jacksonian America." *Proceedings of the American Antiquarian Society* 83 (October 1973): 277–86.

———. "Jackson Caricatured: Two Historical Errors." *Tennessee Historical Quarterly* 31, no. 1 (Spring 1972): 39–43.

Tatham, David, ed. *Prints and Printmakers of New York State, 1825–1940*. Ithaca, NY: Cornell University Press, 1986.

Taylor, Hannis. *The Origin and Growth of the American Constitution*. Boston: Houghton Mifflin, 1911.

Thomas, Peter David Garner. *The American Revolution*. Cambridge: Chadwyck-Healey, 1986.

Tyler, Ron. *The Image of America in Caricature and Cartoon*. Fort Worth, TX: Amon Carter Museum of Western Art, 1976.

Vail, Robert. "Notes and Documents: A Rare Robert Morris Caricature." *Pennsylvania Magazine of History and Biography* 60, no. 2 (April 1936): 184–88.

Ward, David A. *Charles Willson Peale: Art and Selfhood in the Early Republic*. Berkeley: University of California Press, 2004.

Watkins, Jane, ed. *Pennsylvania Academy of the Fine Arts: 200 Years of Excellence*. Philadelphia: Pennsylvania Academy of the Fine Arts, 2005.

Weber, Kaylin H. "A Temple of History Painting: West's Newman Street Studio and Art

Collection." In *American Adversaries: West and Copley in a Transatlantic World*, edited by Emily Bellew Neff and Kaylin H. Weber, 14–49. New Haven, CT: Yale University Press, 2013.

Weekley, Carolyn J. *Painters and Paintings in the Early American South*. New Haven, CT: Yale University Press, 2013.

———. "1735–1790: Painters, Paintings, and the American South." *Magazine Antiques*, January/February 2013. https://www.themagazineantiques.com/article/painters-and-paintings.

Weimerskirch, Philip. "Lithographic Stone in America." *Printing History* 11, no. 1 (1989): 2–16.

Weiss, Harry B. *William Charles: Early Caricaturist, Engraver and Publisher of Children's Books, with a List of Works by Him in the New York Public Library Collections*. 1931. Reprint, New York: New York Public Library, 1932.

Weitenkampf, Frank. *American Graphic Art*. New York: Macmillan, 1924.

———. *A Bibliography of William Hogarth*. Cambridge, MA: Library of Harvard University Press, 1890.

———. *Political Caricature in the United States in Separately Published Cartoons*. New York: New York Public Library, 1953.

———. "Some American Caricaturists." *The Journalist*, November 19, 1887.

Welch, Richard E., Jr. *Theodore Sedgwick, Federalist: A Political Portrait*. Middletown, CT: Wesleyan University Press, 1965.

Wilson, David A. *Paine and Cobbett: The Transatlantic Connection*. Kingston: McGill-Queen's University Press, 1988.

Windsor County Engravers, 1809–1860. Montpelier: Vermont Historical Society, 1982.

Wright, Richardson. *American Wags and Eccentrics: From Colonial Times to the Civil War*. New York: Frederick Ungar, 1965.

244

246